W9-BWR-416

The Communicative Act of Oral Interpretation

Keith Brooks
Director of Communications
The Ohio State University

Eugene Bahn
Professor of Speech
Wayne State University

L. LaMont Okey
Professor of Speech
The University of Michigan

Allyn and Bacon, Inc. · Boston

Library of Congress Catalog Card Number: 67–23464

Printed in the United States of America

Third Printing . . . . May, 1970

To our influential triumvirate—

Anne E. Okey

Margaret E. Bahn

Laquata S. Brooks

Preface

The Communicative Act of Oral Interpretation places emphasis on the dynamics involved in the oral approach to the study of literature. It recognizes that literature is action-oriented and that the function of the oral interpreter is to *discover* and *share* this action. This process—the communicative act of oral interpretation—is accomplished only as there is a union among the component parts; the literature, the reader, and the listener. Without this union, the teaching of literature and your understanding and appreciation of literature are incomplete.

It is important to keep in mind that as an oral interpreter of literature you are an uncommon literary critic. You are unique. You are the only literary critic whose analysis is but a means to an end—that end being a synthesis through vocal and physical suggestion. Furthermore, your uniqueness as a literary critic includes a social responsibility—an obligation to involve your listener in your judgments of the intent of the literature.

The first section—*The Past and the Present*—begins with an overview of the history of oral interpretation and proceeds to a discussion of oral interpretation today. It is intended that Chapter I will provide you with an historical perspective and an improved basis for understanding modern trends. Chapter II, through its definitions and communication models (the first ever published in oral interpretation), provides a frame of reference for the entire book. This chapter is particularly significant and should be studied with care. Section Two—*Your Literature and You*—and Section Three—*Discovering Meanings and Emotions*—contain five chapters devoted to preliminary considerations in preparing for the communicative act: four prerequisites; vocal and physical responsiveness; imagery in literature; emphasis, sense units, and the pause; and structure in literature. These chapters provide the foundation for an effective oral synthesis. They present areas of concentration which, when mastered, prepare you for *Sharing Prose, Poetry, and Drama:* Section Four. This section provides an in-depth discussion of each of the dominant literary forms and concludes with a unique chapter on humor which is applicable wherever humor is found, regardless of form. Section Five—*Specialized Formats*—focuses on the oral book review and readers' theatre. Although these formats frequently comprise the co-curricular activity in oral interpretation, the increasingly substantive nature of each has resulted in specialized courses in the modern curriculum. The book concludes with a section devoted to *Evaluation and Research.* You may find, and many teachers will insist, that Chapter XIV (Evaluating the Communicative Act) is of particular value early in your term of study because it provides criteria for literary evaluation, self-evaluation, peer-evaluation, and teacher evaluation. Judgments must be made. Standards must be evolved. This chapter encourages you to discipline your thinking in both of those directions. Systematic creativity is a challenge, not a contradiction. Finally, you are exposed to a chapter on research in oral interpretation. In actuality, the entire book and every course in oral interpretation is research-oriented. The process starts with your selection of a piece of literature, continues through your analysis of the literature, approaches fruition through a series of literary and communication judgments, comes to life in your oral synthesis, and can be made permanent through the oral and written record of the process. This classroom orientation provides a point of departure for more advanced scholarly research. The chapter introduces you to the variety of interests pursued by graduate students during a five year period, discusses briefly the three predominant research methodologies in oral interpretation, and suggests areas for future research. The chapter invites you to continue your interest in the field of oral interpretation.

This book was written as a guide for your progress. Your instructor will undoubtedly introduce many significant ideas not treated in these pages. This is as it should be for no book can, or should, usurp that privilege. Some may feel that all, or most, of the content of this book can profitably be handled in a single course, others may prefer to use it for more than one course. Regardless of the potential variety of uses, the authors have strived to achieve a balance between literary analysis and interpretative technique: a balance essential to an effective communicative act of oral interpretation. This balanced approach should be carefully weighed in any discussion on separating the parts.

ACKNOWLEDGEMENTS

18 — Karl R. Wallace, ed., *History of Speech Education in America* (New York: Appleton-Century-Crofts, Inc., 1954), p. 500. Reprinted by permission of the publisher.

57 — J. Clark Weaver, "Rain In The Wheat." Reprinted by permission of the author.

72 — Louis Ginsberg, "Morning In Spring" (Boston: The Atlantic Monthly Company, 1955). Reprinted by permission of the author.

73 — Anton P. Chekhov, *Uncle Vanya,* trans. Marian Fell, from *Contemporary Drama — Fifteen Plays,* sel. and ed. by E. Bradlee Watson and Benfield Pressey (New York: Charles Scribner's Sons, 1959), p. 91.

82 — From John Dos Passos, *1919,* 2nd vol. of *USA* trilogy. Copyright 1932 by John Dos Passos (renewed 1960). Published by Houghton Mifflin Company, Boston. Reprinted by permission of John Dos Passos.

87 — Dylan Thomas, *Under Milk Wood.* All Rights Reserved. Copyright 1954 by New Directions. Reprinted by permission of New Directions Publishing Corporation.

93 — Katherine F. Wells, *Kinesiology,* 4th Ed. (Philadelphia: W. B. Saunders Company), 1966.

97 — Peter Bowman, *Red Beach,* p. 47. Copyright 1945 by Peter Bowman, reprinted by permission of Random House, Inc., New York.

104 — Walter de la Mare, "Silver." Reprinted by permission of The Literary Trustees of Walter de la Mare and the Society of Authors as their representative.

107-108 — Federico Garcia Lorca, "Walking Asleep," in *The Gypsy Ballads of Federico Garcia Lorca,* trans. Rolfe Humphries. Copyright 1953 by Rolfe Humphries. Reprinted by permission of Indiana University Press, Bloomington.

108 — Lloyd Douglas, *The Robe* (Boston: Houghton Mifflin Company, 1942), p. 508.

109 — Robert Tristram Coffin, "Crystal Moment," in *Collected Poems* (New York: The Macmillan Company, 1932). Copyright renewed 1960 by Margaret Halvosa. Reprinted by permission of The Macmillan Company.

109-110 — Christopher Morley, "Smells," *Poems.* Copyright 1919, 1947 by Christopher Morley. Published by J. B. Lippincott Company, Philadelphia.

110 — Jessamyn West, *Cress Delahanty,* p. 67. Reprinted by permission of Harcourt, Brace & World, Inc., New York.

110 — From Margaret Mitchell, *Gone With the Wind* (New York: The Macmillan Company, 1936). Copyright renewed 1964. Reprinted by permission of the publisher and owner.

113 — From Edna St. Vincent Millay, *Collected Poems* (New York: Harper & Row). Copyright 1923, 1951 by Edna St. Vincent Millay and Norma Millay Ellis. Reprinted by permission of Norma Millay Ellis.

114, 129-130, 268-270 — E. A. Robinson, "Mr. Flood's Party," *Collected Poems.* Reprinted by permission of The Macmillan Company, New York. Copyright 1921 by E. A. Robinson, renewed 1949 by Ruth Nivison.

115 — Robinson Jeffers, "Hurt Hawks," *The Selected Poetry of Robinson Jeffers* (New York: Random House, Inc., 1928). Copyright renewed 1956 by Robinson Jeffers.

115-116 — James Hearst, "After Chores," *Country Men.* Copyright 1937 by James Hearst. Published by The Prairie Press, Muscatine, Iowa, 1943, p. 67. Reprinted by permission of James Hearst.

116 — Karl Shapiro, "Auto Wreck." Reprinted by permission of Random House, Inc., New York.

116 — Carl Sandburg, "Prayers of Steel," in *Cornhuskers* (New York: Holt, Rinehart and Winston, Inc., 1918). Copyright 1946 by Carl Sandburg. Reprinted by permission of Holt, Rinehart and Winston, Inc.

117 — Vachel Lindsay, "Abraham Lincoln Walks at Midnight," in *Collected Poems* (New York: The Macmillan Company, 1914). Copyright renewed 1942 by Elizabeth C. Lindsay. Reprinted by permission of The Macmillan Company.

130 — Carl Sandburg, "A Couple," in *Good Morning, America.* Copyright 1928, © 1956 by Carl Sandburg. Reprinted by permission of Harcourt, Brace & World, Inc., New York.

131 — Harper Lee, *To Kill a Mockingbird.* Published by J. B. Lippincott Company, Philadelphia. Copyright 1960 by Harper Lee. Reprinted by permission of the publisher, p. 71.

131 — Peter Bowman, *Red Beach.* Copyright 1945 by Peter Bowman. Reprinted by permission of Random House, Inc., New York, p. 64.

133-135 — Archibald MacLeish, "Wildwest," *Poems 1924-1933* (Boston: Houghton Mifflin Company), pp. 171-175.

136 — Rupert Brook, "The Great Lover," *The Collected Poems of Rupert Brook* (New York: Dodd, Mead & Company, 1915). Copyright 1943 by Edward Marsh.

141 — From "Catiline's Speech To His Troops," in *A Treasury of the World's Great Speeches,* sel. and ed. by Houston Peterson (New York: Simon and Schuster, Inc., 1954). Reprinted by permission of the publisher.

146 — Rudyard Kipling, "The Ballad of East and West," in *Rudyard Kipling's Verse: Definitive Edition.* Reprinted by permission of Mrs. George Bambridge and Doubleday & Company, Inc., New York.

146-147 — Stephen Vincent Benét, "John Brown's Body," in *Selected Works of Stephen Vincent Benét.* Published by Holt, Rinehart & Winston, New York. Copyright 1927, 1928 by Stephen Vincent Benét. Copyright renewed 1955 by Rosemary Carr Benét. Reprinted by permission of Brandt & Brandt, New York.

147, 176-177 — Thomas Wolfe, *You Can't Go Home Again,* pp. 435, 508. Copyright 1940 by Maxwell Perkins, as executor. Reprinted with permission of Harper & Row, Publishers, Inc., New York.

148 — D. H. Lawrence, "The Rocking Horse Winner," in *The Complete Short Stories of D. H. Lawrence.* Copyright 1933 by the estate of D. H. Lawrence; copyright 1961 by Angelo Ravagli and C. Montague Weekley, Executors of the estate of Frieda Lawrence Ravagli. Reprinted by permission of The Viking Press, Inc., New York.

148 — Richard M. Rothman, "The Tree." Reprinted by permission of the author.

149 — John Masefield, "The Downland," in *Lollingdon Downs and Other Poems* by John Masefield (New York: The Macmillan Company, 1917). Copyright renewed 1945 by John Masefield.

150-151 — Mary Lavin, "The Will," in *Selected Stories* by Mary Lavin. Copyright 1959 by Mary Lavin. Reprinted by permission of The Macmillan Company, New York.

158 — Robert Frost, "Mending Wall," in *Complete Poems of Robert Frost* (New York: Holt, Rinehart and Winston, Inc., 1930, 1939). Copyright 1958 by Robert Frost. Reprinted by permission of Holt, Rinehart and Winston, Inc.

173 — Edith Rickert, *New Methods for the Study of Literature* (Chicago: University of Chicago Press, 1937), pp. 192, 208. Reprinted with the permission of the publisher.

177 — Marcus Tullius Cicero, "The Second Speech Against Gaius Verres," from *The Verrine Orations,* vol. II, trans. by L. H. G. Greenwood (Cambridge: Harvard University Press). Reprinted by permission of the publisher and The Loeb Classical Library.

178 — From Demosthenes, "On the Crown," in *Attic Orators From Antiphon to Isaeos* by R. C. Jebb (New York: Russell and Russell, Inc., 1962), p. 411. Reprinted by permission of the publisher.

179 — John Fox, Jr., *The Little Shepherd of Kingdom Come* (New York: Charles Scribner's Sons, 1903, 1931), pp. 173-174. Copyright 1931 by Minnie C. Fox. Reprinted by permission of the publishers.

181 — William Butler Yeats, "A Deep-Sworn Vow," in *Collected Poems* by William Butler Yeats (New York: The Macmillan Company, 1919). Copyright renewed 1946 by Bertha Georgie Yeats. Reprinted by permission of The Macmillan Company.

182-183 — William March, "The Little Wife," in *A William March Omnibus,* pp. 155-156 (New York: Holt, Rinehart and Winston, Inc.). Copyright 1930 by W. E. M. Campbell. Reprinted by permission of Harold Ober Associates, New York.

190, 191-193 — From Gustave Flaubert, *Madame Bovary.* Reprinted by permission of Random House, Inc., New York.

191 — Anton Chekhov, "A Father," from the Russian by Constance Garnett, in *The Chorus Girl and Other Stories* by Anton Chekhov (New York: The Macmillan Company, Inc., 1920). Copyright renewed 1948 by David Garnett.

216-231 — Arthur Cavanaugh, "What I Wish I Had Said," *McCall's Magazine,* August 1963. Copyright 1963 by Arthur Cavanaugh. Reprinted by permission of Ashley Famous Agency, Inc., New York.

235 — From T. S. Eliot, "The Hollow Men," in *The Complete Poems and Plays 1909-1950 of T. S. Eliot* (New York: Harcourt, Brace & World, Inc.). Reprinted by permission of the publisher.

238 — From T. S. Eliot, "The Waste Land," in *Collected Poems 1909-1962 of T. S. Eliot* (New York: Harcourt, Brace & World, Inc., 1936). Copyright 1963, 1964 by T. S. Eliot. Reprinted by permission of the publisher.

239-240 — Hillaire Belloc, "Tarantella." Reprinted by permission of A. D. Peters & Company, London.

240 — Lew Sarett, "The Squaw Dance," in *Covenant with Earth* by Lew Sarett. Edited and copyrighted 1956 by Alma Johnson Sarett and published by the University of Florida Press. Reprinted by permission of Mrs. Sarett.

248 — Helen Hoyt, "Rain At Night." Reprinted by permission of the author.
248 — Ogden Nash, "The Panther," in *The Face Is Familiar* by Ogden Nash. Copyright 1940 by The Curtis Publishing Company. Reprinted by permission of Little, Brown and Company, Publishers.
249 — Richard Armour, "Money," in *Yours For the Asking* (Boston: Bruce Humphries, Inc.). Reprinted by permission of the publisher.
255 — William Butler Yeats, "For Anne Gregory," in *Collected Poems* by William Butlers Yeats (New York: The Macmillan Company, 1933). Renewed 1961 by Bertha Georgie Yeats.
255-256 — John Crowe Ransom, "Piazza Piece," in *Selected Poems* by John Crowe Ransom (New York: Alfred A. Knopf, Inc., 1927). Renewed 1955 by John Crowe Ransom.
256-257 — Walter de la Mare, "The Ghost." Reprinted by permission of The Literary Trustees of Walter de la Mare and the Society of Authors as their representative.
257 — W. H. Auden, "O Where Are You Going?" in *The Collected Poetry of W. H. Auden* (New York: Random House, Inc., 1934). Renewed 1961 by W. H. Auden.
258 — Carl Sandburg, "Foolish About Windows," in *Good Morning, America* by Carl Sandburg (New York: Harcourt, Brace & World, Inc., 1928). Renewed 1956 by Carl Sandburg.
259-260 — A. E. Housman, "Into My Heart An Air That Kills," in "A Shropshire Lad" — Authorized Edition — from *The Collected Poems of A. E. Housman.* Copyright 1939, 1940, © 1959 by Holt, Rinehart and Winston, Inc., New York.
260 — Conrad Aiken, "Music I Heard With You," from *Collected Poems* by Conrad Aiken. Copyright 1953 by Conrad Aiken. Reprinted by permission of Oxford University Press, Inc., New York.
262-263 — Sonnet XVIII from "Epitaph for the Race of Man," from *Collected Poems,* Harper & Row. Copyright 1921, 1934, 1948, 1962 by Edna St. Vincent Millay and Norma Millay Ellis. Reprinted with permission of Norma Millay Ellis.
263-264 — C. Day Lewis, "Maple and Sumach" (New York: Oxford University Press, Inc., 1940, 1943). Reprinted by permission of the Harold Matson Company, Inc.
270-271 — Walter de la Mare, "Goliath." Reprinted by permission of The Literary Trustees of Walter de la Mare and the Society of Authors as their representative.
274 — Stephen Spender, "The Express," from *Collected Poems 1928-1953* by Stephen Spender. (New York: Random House, Inc., 1934). Renewed 1961 by Stephen Spender.
279 — Gerald Manley Hopkins, "The Leaden Echo," in *The Hopkins Reader,* sel. by John Pick (New York and London: Oxford University Press, 1953).
280-281 — Gerald Manley Hopkins, "The Golden Echo," in *The Hopkins Reader,* sel. by John Pick (New York and London: Oxford University Press, 1953).
284-285 — John Crowe Ransom, "Parting Without a Sequel," in *Selected Poems* by John Crowe Ransom (New York: Alfred A. Knopf, Inc., 1927). Renewed 1955 by John Crowe Ransom.
293-294 — James M. Barrie, The Introduction to "The Twelve-Pound Look," in *The Plays of J. M. Barrie* (New York: Charles Scribner's Sons, 1928). Renewed 1956 by Cynthia Asquith, Peter Llewlyn Davies and Barclay's Bank, Ltd.
304-305 — Eugene O'Neill, from "Ah, Wilderness!" in *Ah, Wilderness! And Two Other Plays,* by Eugene O'Neill (New York: Random House, Inc., 1933). Renewed 1960 by Carlotta Monterey O'Neill. Reprinted by permission of Random House, Inc.
311 — J. M. Synge, "Riders To The Sea," in *J. M. Synge's Plays, Poems and Prose,* Everyman's Library (New York: E. P. Dutton & Company, 1954). Reprinted by permission of E. P. Dutton & Company.
316-317 — Robert E. Sherwood, *Abe Lincoln In Illinois,* p. 5. Copyright 1937, 1939 Robert E. Sherwood. Renewed © 1965 Madeline H. Sherwood. Reprinted by permission of Charles Scribner's Sons, New York.
335 — Kay Nelson, "My Mother," in *Look Magazine,* May 22, 1962. Reprinted by permission of the author and *Look Magazine.*
338-340 — Kenneth Grahame, *The Wind in the Willows* (New York: Charles Scribner's Sons, 1908), pp. 238-242.
340-341 — Robert Benchley, "Family Life in America," in *Inside Benchley,* by Robert Benchley (New York: Harper & Brothers, 1922), p. 114. Reprinted by permission of Harper & Row, Publishers, Inc.
341-343 — Terry Siegel, "Fun With Hamlet and His Friends." Reprinted by permission of the author.
343-345 — Art Buchwald, "New Math Doesn't Add Up." Reprinted by permission of Art Buchwald and Publishers Newspaper Syndicate.

345-347 — Frank Sullivan, "An Innocent in Texas," in *The Night the Old Nostalgia Burned Down,* by Frank Sullivan (Philadelphia: The Curtis Publishing Company, 1948), pp. 54-57. Copyright 1948 by The Curtis Publishing Company, Philadelphia. Originally appeared in *Holiday.* Reprinted by permission of Little, Brown and Company.

347-349 — "Colonel Crockett Delivering His Celebrated Speech To Congress On The State of Finances, State Officers and State Affairs in General," in *Davy Crockett, American Comic Legend,* sel. and ed. by Richard M. Dorson. Printed at Spiral Press for Rockland Editions, N.Y., 1939, pp. 150-151. Reprinted by permission of Richard M. Dorson.

349-350 — Will Rogers, from "Ether and Me or 'Just Relax'" (Philadelphia: The Curtis Publishing Company, 1927). Copyright 1929 by Will Rogers. Published by G. P. Putnam's Sons, New York, pp. 23-24. Reprinted by permission of the publisher.

352-353 — Leonard Q. Ross, from *The Education of Hyman Kaplan* (New York: Harcourt, Brace & World, Inc., 1937). Renewed © 1965 by Leo Rosten. Reprinted by permission of the publishers.

354-358 — Corey Ford, "Your Wife Is Like That," published in *The Saturday Evening Post,* January 12, 1952. Copyright 1952 by Corey Ford. Reprinted by permission of Harold Ober Associates, Inc., New York.

358-359 — Wende Devlin, "Transfixed." Reprinted by permission from *Good Housekeeping Magazine,* July, 1961, p. 38. Copyright 1961 by the Hearst Corporation.

359-363 — "The Culprit" by Anton Checkov. From *The Portable Checkov* edited by Avrahm Yarmolinsky. Copyright 1947 by The Viking Press, Inc. Reprinted by permission of The Viking Press, Inc.

375-376 — Catherine Marshall, *Beyond Our Selves* (New York: McGraw-Hill Book Company, Inc., 1961), p. xiv.

376-377 — Jack Fishman, *My Darling Clementine* (London: W. H. Allen & Company, 1963), p. xi. Reprinted by permission of the publisher and David McKay Company, Inc., New York.

378 — F. O. Matthiessen, "The Winter Critic," *The Atlantic Monthly,* October, 1952, p. 88 (Boston: The Atlantic Monthly Company, 1952). Reprinted by permission of the publisher.

378 — From a review of *The Adventures of Davy Crockett, illustrated* by John W. Thomason, Jr., reviewed by William Rose Benét, *Saturday Review,* February 24, 1934. Reprinted by permission of *Saturday Review.*

379 — From "Magic and Mystery in the Sky," by Quentin Reynolds, a review of Ernest Gann's *Fate Is The Hunter, Saturday Review,* February 18, 1961. Reprinted by permission of *Saturday Review.*

380 — From "Hunt Without Quarry," by William Peden, a review of M. B. Longman's *The Power of Black, Saturday Review,* March 25, 1961. Reprinted by permission of *Saturday Review.*

380 — From a review of *In Retrospect: The History of a Historian* by Arthur M. Schlesinger and reviewed by Edward Weeks, *Atlantic Monthly,* April, 1964. Reprinted by permission of *Atlantic Monthly.*

380 — From a review of *The Letters of David Garrick,* ed. by David M. Little and George M. Kahrl, *The Spectator,* February 28, 1964. Reprinted by permission of The Spectator, Ltd., London.

381 — From a review of *The Norse Atlantic Saga* by Gwyn Jones, and reviewed by Dom Moraes in *The Spectator,* March 6, 1964. Reprinted by permission of The Spectator, Ltd., London.

381-382 — From a review of *The Remainderman* by Terrance de Vere White and reviewed by David Lodge in *The Spectator,* August 16, 1963. Reprinted by permission of The Spectator, Ltd., London.

382 — From "Counterpoint to the Tune of Love," by Otis Fellows, a review of Elaine Marks' *Colette, Saturday Review,* September 3, 1960. Reprinted by permission of *Saturday Review.*

382 — From a review of *All But My Life* by Stirling Moss and Ken W. Purdy, reviewed by Robert Daley in *The New York Times,* November 17, 1963. Reprinted by permission of *The New York Times* and Robert Daley.

An asterisk in the index refers to an excerpt from the work listed.

Contents

Part One

The Past and the Present: A Frame of Reference

Chapter I

Our Heritage: An Overview

The art of reading aloud, frequently referred to today as the oral interpretation of literature, is the oldest of the speech arts—predating even the formal study of rhetoric. So rich an oral heritage is eminently worthy of study and review. In this chapter we shall briefly trace its history from ancient days through the current emphasis of the twentieth century. The perspective suggested by this overview will provide you with a frame of reference for continued study.

I. ANCIENT GREECE

In a land where for a long time even the laws were unwritten, one can understand why the oral arts were at least as important as the written word. Such was the case in ancient Greece.

Before the days of recorded history, men turned to reciting and storytelling for many purposes. The first person to tell us of the use of oral recitation was the blind poet, Homer, who is traditionally regarded as the author of the *Iliad* and the *Odyssey*. The events of which he tells took place about 1200 B.C. Some authorities think that these verses were passed down by oral recitation, from one generation to another, until they were finally put into writing about 700 B.C. or earlier, very possibly by Homer.

In twentieth-century Greece there are still evidences of the continuation of this ancient, centuries-old tradition. On the Isle of Crete verses are still recited, chanted and sung perhaps in the same manner they were when Troy was sacked. Verses are still handed down orally from age to age in Crete, while others are spontaneously composed at the time they are recited, for the Cretans can compose verses almost as easily as other people speak in limping prose.

In the *Odyssey,* Homer describes how the minstrel, a favored member of the royal court, told tales of valor to inspire, entertain and move his audience. With his lyre in hand, he extolled the deeds of the great and he passed on from generation to generation the history of the people, which gave them pride in their ancestors and faith in themselves. Sometimes he moved them to tears. In the ancient royal court the minstrel was highly respected, and when he appeared before the royal household he was given, according to Homer, a silver-encrusted chair, food and wine.[1]

Later, Plato described another kind of minstrel, the rhapsode, who for a long time restricted himself to reciting Homer's *Iliad* and *Odyssey.*[2] Richly attired, with myrtle or laurel staff, or lyre in hand, he travelled from place to place reciting to gathering crowds, particularly at the many festivals in Epidaurus, Olympia, Delos, Athens, Sicyon and other places. Reciting from the *Iliad* and *Odyssey,* he inspired and moved the people with religious and historical tales. So important did the rhapsodes become that Cleisthenes had to pass a law forbidding verse-speaking contests in Sicyon because the traditional enemies, Argos and the Argives, were constantly glorified in Homer's verses.[3]

Poets and historians also recited aloud. Poets published their poems not by writing, but by reciting them. The poet, Hesiod (ca. 800 B.C.) who said he received his laurel staff from the gods, recited at festivals. Solon, lawmaker and poet, roused the citizens to war when, acting as if mad, with a garland on his head, he rushed into the agora and either he, or a herald, recited his poem "Elegy on Salamis." So deeply did he move the people that war was declared and Salamis conquered.[4] Herodotus, the father of history, also recited his prose histories, going from

[1] Homer, *The Odyssey,* trans. by William Cullen Bryant (Boston: Houghton Mifflin and Co., 1871), Book VIII, lines 78–84, pp. 153–154.

[2] The Dialogues of Plato, trans. by B. Jowett (Oxford University Press, 1892), 3rd ed., Vol. I, "Ion," p. 497.

[3] Herodotus, *The Histories,* trans. by Aubrey de Selincourt (Baltimore, Md.: Penguin Books, 1954), pp. 334–335.

[4] Diogenes Laertius, *Lives of Eminent Philosophers,* trans. by R. D. Hicks (Cambridge: Harvard University Press, 1959), Vol. I, Book I, Chapter 2, pp. 47–49.

Also Plutarch's *Lives,* trans. by Bernadotte Perrin (London, Wm. Heinemann, 1928), Vol. I, "Solon," VIII, pp. 421–423.

one country to another to collect his facts. Thucydides, who rose to great stature as an historian, probably heard Herodotus recite, for he rather proudly indicated that his own histories followed exact knowledge rather than a desire to please "the ear."[5]

Recitation and reading were also used for criticism and teaching. Plato and Aristotle indicate this, and Theophrastus, another philosopher, who read his lectures to 2,000 pupils, reported that he dared not ignore the critical comments of his students nor avoid the revisions which they deemed necessary.[6] Even the ordinary citizens enjoyed reciting. When the Athenians were captured in Sicily their ability to recite from Euripides brought them not only food but even their freedom.[7]

II. CLASSICAL ROME

As civilization moved westward to Rome, so did Greek customs of reciting. In 272 B.C., a Greek slave, Livius Andronicus, was brought to Rome where he recited his verses and, after he lost his voice, he acted out his poems while someone else repeated the words.[8] He brought to Rome a major heritage when he translated the *Odyssey* into Latin.

It was not too long before Roman poets appeared and recited. Quintus Ennius, the father of Latin literature, read from his own poetry.[9] In the Augustan age (42 B.C.–17 A.D.), Virgil, noted for his beautiful voice and warmth of expression, followed this tradition and, with Maecenas, recited his *Georgics* to the Emperor Augustus for four days after the Battle of Actium.[10] He also read parts of his *Aeneid* to the Emperor and Octavia.[11]

[5] Thucydides, *History of the Peloponnesian War,* trans. by C. Forster Smith (London: William Heinemann, MCMLVI), Volume I, Book I, 22, pp. 39, 41.

[6] Diogenes Laertius, op. cit., 1959, Vol. I, Book V, Chapter 2, pp. 483–485.

[7] *Plutarch's Lives,* trans. by Bernadotte Perrin (London: William Heinemann, 1915), Vol. III, "Nicias," XXIX, 2–3, p. 309.

[8] Livy, trans. by B. O. Foster (London: William Heinemann, 1924), Vol. III, Book VII, 2, lines 8–13, p. 363.

[9] Suetonius, "De Grammaticis," trans. by J. C. Rolfe (London: William Heinemann, 1924), Vol. II, p. 397.

[10] Suetonius, "De Poetis," The Life of Virgil, trans. by J. C. Rolfe (London: William Heinemann, 1924), Vol. II, p. 473.

[11] *Ibid.,* p. 475.

Asinius Pollio, Virgil's patron, started the tradition of having poets recite their verses before a public audience. Virgil avoided reading before large groups,[12] and Horace (65 B.C.–8 B.C.) recited only to friends.[13] But Ovid (43 B.C.–18 A.D.) admitted that he started to recite in public before he had scarcely begun to shave.[14]

In the Silver Age of Latin Literature (14–130 A.D.), public recitations by poets were very popular. Lucan joined a plot to kill Nero, and he was apprehended and executed, passionately reciting one of his poems before his execution.[15]

The poet Statius (45–96 A.D.) drew Rome's society to hear him when, with his beautiful voice, he recited his *Thebais*.[16] But the life of a poet was often difficult; when a rich man lent him a neglected mansion for a recital, he had to arrange for programs as well as benches and platforms, which he had to return after the event.[17]

Despite such difficulties, recitals became so popular that Pliny the Younger (61–113 A.D.) says that in one month there was a recital nearly every day.[18] Some of these poet-reciters who were not sufficiently gifted to recite publicly, nevertheless did thrust themselves on the public; others drew crowds because of the unsavory nature of their verses, and still others were so vain they enjoyed appearing in gorgeous array even if they had nothing to say.[19] Such mediocrity could not hold the interest of intelligent or sophisticated people, and many stood in the lobby visiting during the recital and entered the hall only when they were sure the recital was nearly finished.[20] Slaves, freedmen, lovers, plagiarists (who

[12] *Ibid.*, p. 475.

[13] The Works of Horace, trans. by Sir Theodore Martin (Edinburgh and London: William Blackwood and Sons, 1888), Vol. II, Bk. I, Satire 4, p. 127.

[14] Ovid, *Tristia and Ex Ponto,* trans. by Arthur Leslie Wheeler (London: William Heinemann, 1924), "Tristia," IV, 10, lines 57–58, p. 201.

[15] Tacitus, *The Annals,* XV, 70, p. 175 in *The Annals and The Histories* by P. Cornelius Tacitus (Vol. 15) in *Great Books of the Western World,* Robert Maynard Hutchins, Ed. (Chicago: Encyclopaedia Britannica, 1952).

[16] *Juvenal and Persius,* trans. by G. G. Ramsay (Revised) (Cambridge: Harvard University Press, 1950), Juvenal, Satire VII, lines 82–87, p. 145.

[17] Juvenal, Satire VII, lines 36–53, p. 141.

[18] Pliny, *Letters,* trans. by William Melmoth (London: William Heinemann, 1923), Vol. I, Book I, XIII, p. 45.

[19] *Juvenal and Persius,* trans. by G. G. Ramsay (Revised) (Cambridge: Harvard University Press, 1950), Persius, Satire I, lines 13–20, p. 319.

[20] Pliny, *Letters,* trans. by William Melmoth (London: William Heinemann, 1923), Vol. I, Book I, XIII, p. 47.

pretended to write what they had purloined), and even emperors recited. None was so vain as Nero, who is supposed to have recited verses while Rome burned.[21]

Like the Greeks, many poets read to hear the critical comments of their friends. Cicero, Virgil, Ovid, Terence and Pliny approved of this practice; and Virgil often altered his lines following the reading of his poems to respected critics. Horace, who was aware of the problems related to sound criticism, warned against accepting as truth the words of a sycophant who would praise falsely to please a patron.[22] Pliny saw the dangers of a voice so beautiful that it could make even mediocre verses sound impressive.[23]

In the schools, too, pupils read and recited. Quintilian, the educator, regarded understanding as the foundation of good reading. Both Cicero and Quintilian refer to aspects of reading and delivery, such as proper breathing, pitch, pausing, thought units, emotion, volume, and tempo. Quintilian even recommended that the reader change his voice to distinguish the voice of the poet from that of the characters. He thought poetry should be read with a certain manliness, combined with "dignity and charm."[24]

III. MIDDLE AGES

As the Roman Empire in the west declined and finally collapsed in 476 A.D., the rising poets and scholars were churchmen whose lives were centered around the Bible and other religious literature. They were deeply inspired when they listened to their companions read the Bible.

Reading aloud had become a major means for spreading the Chris-

[21] Suetonius, *The Lives of the Caesars,* trans. by J. C. Rolfe (London, William Heinemann, 1924), "Nero," Book VI, XXXVIII. Vol. II, p. 157.

[22] Horace, "The Art of Poetry," in *The Works of Horace,* trans. by Sir Theodore Martin (Edinburgh and London: William Blackwood and Sons, 1888), Vol. II, pp. 398–399.

[23] Pliny, *Letters,* trans. by William Melmoth (London: William Heinemann, 1923), Vol. I, III, XV, p. 245.

[24] *Quintilian, The Institutio Oratoria of,* trans. by H. E. Butler (London: William Heinemann, 1920), Vol. I, Book I, VIII, 2, p. 147.

tian religion and it helped give a sense of comfort and unity to the Christians. In the monasteries, each meal was accompanied by a member of the group reading to the assembled monks.[25] St. Benedict's Rule, which established oral reading in the monasteries, served as an example for future rules. When St. Augustine went from Rome to England in 597, he took the Benedictine Rule, so the tradition of reading aloud was carried on there as well.

In Anglo-Saxon England the reciter was well known. *Beowulf,* "Widsith," and "Deor's Lament" all depict the minstrel of that age. But when William the Conqueror and the Normans conquered England in 1066, Taillefer, a colorful minstrel, was at the head of the conquering army, chanting the stirring songs of Roland and Charlemagne, and juggling his sword.

This minstrel entertained in the great hall of the castle after the sometimes boisterous crowd had eaten, the tables had been removed, and a degree of peace had been established. He told stories of adventure, romance, wonder, war and the supernatural. These romances were classified as "Matters of Britain," "Matters of France," and "Matters of Rome." Some were short enough to be told in a single evening, while others took several evenings. Frequently, the minstrel used words such as "Listen," "Hear," "Herkeneth to me," and "Lordys" to establish a close contact between the reciter and the hearer. Repetition was common and frequently repeated phrases were used such as those found in *Havelok the Dane:*

> He broken armes, he broken knes,
> He broken shankes, he broken thes.[26]

Transitions from one scene to another were abrupt. Theories differ as to how these romances were delivered; some contend they were given in recitative, while others think they were chanted with a monotonous beat.

As literacy increased and ways of life changed, the minstrel sank

[25] The Rule of St. Benet, Ch. XXXVIII, p. 130, in Three Middle-English Versions of The Rule of St. Benet, Ed. by Ernst A. Kock (London: Early English Text Society, Kegan Paul, Trench, Trübner and Co., Ltd., 1902).

[26] *Havelok the Dane,* Ed. by Walter W. Skeat (London: Early English Text Society, Kegan Paul, Trench, Trubner and Co., 1868), p. 52, lines 1902–1903.

in social status, and story telling and reading were taken over by the people. Such was the case in Chaucer's *Canterbury Tales,* where the pilgrims themselves took turns telling stories. One of the very early descriptions in English secular literature of the art of effective delivery is found in Chaucer's "Squire's Tale" when the stranger-Knight stood before the King and gave his "tale"

> . . . with a manly voys. . . .
> After the forme uséd in his langage,
> Withouten vice of silable, or of lettre;
> And for his tale sholde seme the bettre,
> Accordant to his wordés was his cheere,
> As techeth art of speche hem that it leere.[27]

IV. RENAISSANCE ENGLAND

In Renaissance England, reading aloud and story telling continued. Books addressed to "readers and hearers" were often read aloud in the family circle and stories of love, adventure, and the marvelous were very popular. In the royal court stately and ceremonious recitations were a part of the pompous processions at the time of a ruler's coronation. When James I was crowned, a "poetical oration" was delivered. When his queen was on her way to London, an entertainment, under the direction of Ben Jonson, was given at Althorp where a satyr leaped out, spoke his verses, and disappeared into the woods.[28] When the Danish King and James I were entertained at the Earl of Salisbury's, verses of congratulation, again composed by Ben Jonson, were recited.[29]

Interest in speech went beyond such formal uses. The Renaissance gentleman as a cultured person was expected to learn how to use lan-

[27] "Squire's Tale," *The Works of Chaucer,* Ed. by Alfred W. Pollard, H. Frank Heath, Mark H. Liddell and W. S. McCormick (London: Macmillan and Co., Ltd., 1925), p. 220, lines 99, 100–104.

[28] G. B. Harrison, *A Jacobean Journal—1603–1606* (New York: The Macmillan Co., 1941), p. 41.

[29] *Ibid.,* p. 324.

guage effectively in terms of word choice and construction; moreover, he was expected to convey nuances of meaning with his voice, facial expression, and gesture in delivering his own ideas, in reading, and in reciting. He was expected to be able to tell a story "without peine not onlie in woordes but in gestures, the thynge a man pourposeth to expresse, that unto the hearers he may appeere to do before their eyes the thinges he speaketh of."[30] He was taught how to do this in school, for such training was encouraged by leading educators of the day. Pupils learned to read and recite passages from literature. School statutes required that students be able to speak distinctly and accurately, "keeping due decorum both with their body and their mouth." At Winchester College the pupils were to learn to read the Bible "distinctly and apertly." In other schools Virgil, Sallust, Ovid, and other poets were to be recited with correct vocal intonations.

A number of principles of effective reading were well known at this time. One of the earliest English theories of reading aloud was presented in *The Pastime of Pleasure* (1509) by Stephen Hawes, who said that one must not tell a story in a barbarous way but discreetly, intelligently, without impediment, in pleasing manner and countenance, using voice and manner "moderatly." Moreover, he should respond to the emotions of his story. James Cleland said that poetry should not be read like prose. His advice was to begin reading leisurely, pause, take a breath "at the broken points," and lower or raise the voice as the subject demands.

The Bible was one of the significant factors in increasing literacy and in encouraging oral reading. When the Great Bible was printed in English in 1539, Henry VIII ordered that a copy be placed in every parish church for the people to read. At St. Paul's Cathedral, London, six of these copies were chained to the wall. Those who were literate read the Bible themselves, and those unable to read listened to others read it. One man, John Porter, was so famous for his skillful reading that large crowds gathered to hear him. Schools, too, required the oral reading of the Bible. In the seventeenth century reading the Bible aloud was a daily practice in almost every English home.

[30] *The Courtyer of Count Baldessar Castilio,* Divided into Foure Bookes. Done into Englyshe by Thomas Hoby, 1561. Ed. by Janet E. Ashbee (London: E. Arnold, The Essex House Press, 1900), p. 155.

V. EIGHTEENTH-CENTURY ENGLAND

In the eighteenth century, England was faced with problems of oral delivery in the church service. The clergy were severely criticized for their poor preaching and their inadequate reading of the liturgy. *The Tatler* reported that "if our preachers would learn to speak and our readers to read, within six months time we should not have a dissenter within a mile of a church in Great Britain." All through the 18th century elocutionists tried to find the best methods of improving the delivery of the clergy both in reading and speaking. The most prominent elocutionists in this century were Thomas Sheridan, often considered the leader of the "natural" approach, and John Walker, the leader of the "mechanical" approach to reading. This classification is somewhat arbitrary, for even those who, like Walker and Joshua Steele, perpetrated many rules and notational systems did not outlaw the importance of thought. Walker himself said that getting the *sense* was the first objective in reading aloud.

Actually, the theme, "follow nature," was the keynote of this age. People turned to nature for their philosophy. They saw in it the elements of reason and order which they admired and by which they wanted to direct their lives. The writers on elocution echoed this philosophy. John Mason emphasized the study of nature. Thomas Sheridan admired the Greeks because they founded their concept of art on reason, and reason, he said, showed that nature's laws must be obeyed. In the latter half of the century feeling was emphasized rather than reason. There were various ideas as to what "follow nature" meant. The predominant view was that nature needed to be modified in order to produce a work of art. William Cockin, an authority in the 18th century, said that reading and speaking are arts which can be classified as those which *improve* nature.[31]

The methods of achieving a natural style of reading varied. Some, such as John Rice, were opposed to any "mechanical system or arbitrary

[31] William Cockin, *The Art of Delivering Written Language* (London: H. Hughs for J. Dodsley, 1775), p. 112.

mode of pause and cadence, . . . in prose, or in any kind of poetry"[32] that might interfere with natural expression. Cockin disapproved of any *system* of vocal or bodily expression. Thomas Sheridan had some "mechanical" ideas even though he is often regarded as a leader of the "natural" approach.

The supporters of the mechanical concept of reading believed in the efficacy of rules to produce good reading. John Walker set forth many rules for reading which, from our standpoint today, hinder rather than help one read well. Joshua Steele, in *An Essay Towards Establishing the Melody and Measure of Speech,* used a notational system resembling that of music. Both of these methods were followed for many years. Another approach to reading was the imitative method which was used in the 18th century just as it had been used long before, and after as well. John Mason thought that imitation was the best way to learn elocution. John Walker wanted the pupil to reproduce the identical inflections his teacher used. But there were others who saw, quite rightly, the dangers of imitation.

Since reading received so much attention at this time the question arose as to what it actually was. Sheridan clearly believed that the reader must convey the sentiments of the author to the hearer. Walker said that reading is "that system of rules, which teaches us to pronounce written composition with justness, energy, variety, and ease."[33] Some explained the nature of reading by comparing it to conversation, speaking, and reflective thinking. Walker believed that the rules learned in the art of reading could be applied in teaching speaking.

Understanding what one reads was regarded as very important. Emotional response was advocated. Sheridan believed that if a reader understood and entered "into the spirit of the Author's sentiments"[34] as well as into the meaning of his words, good vocal expression would follow. If the reader had trouble in grasping the emotion, Walker advised him to imitate the emotion in order to arouse it. In *The Art of Speaking* (1761), James Burgh described each emotion and how it could be portrayed by the body. In 1806, another book, Gilbert Austin's

[32] John Rice, *An Introduction to the Art of Reading,* 1765 (London: Tonson), pp. 152–53.

[33] John Walker, *Elements of Elocution,* 3rd Edition, 1806 (London: J. Johnson), p. 1.

[34] Thomas Sheridan, *A Complete Dictionary of the English Language,* 4th edition (London: Charles Dilly), 1797, Vol. I, pp. LXVI–LXVII.

Chironomia, analyzed gesture and delivery and related action to feeling.

In this period, both poetry and prose were used for reading. Because it presented less of a problem than poetry, prose was often recommended for beginners. Reading and reciting were by no means only classroom activities, for there were programs given by such outstanding persons as Thomas Sheridan, John Walker, and the actor, David Garrick. Sheridan read the liturgy and from poets, such as Dryden and Gray, with great success, and Walker was noted for his interpretation of Milton. When Garrick read an ode at the Shakespeare Jubilee, Boswell, Johnson's biographer, enthusiastically reported that it was like an exhibition in Athens or Rome. Besides such public demonstrations writers continued to read their work aloud for purposes of criticism; and throughout the land versions of the age-old tales and legends were repeated, along with the reading of the Bible and other religious books, at the table and by the fireside.

VI. EIGHTEENTH- AND NINETEENTH-CENTURY AMERICA

In the early American colonies, the English elocutionists continued to hold sway. In American colleges reciting, reading, and other speech activities were popular, and in the late eighteenth century books on elocution written by American authors began to appear.

In nineteenth-century America, speech training developed in the curriculum of the colleges and the private schools. Some of the best known schools were in Boston, such as Murdoch and Russell's School of Practical Oratory, The School of Oratory of Boston University, The Curry School of Expression, and the Emerson College of Oratory. Other schools were established in New York, Pittsburgh, Cincinnati, Chicago, Kansas City and elsewhere.

In this century both reading from the page and reciting from memory were practiced. Some favored memorization because they thought it helped the student to express himself with greater freedom and without having the encumbrance of a book in his hand. Others preferred reading from book or manuscript because it permitted the reader to "saunter and pause," it helped keep reading from becoming acting, and from being affected or unnatural.

The influence of the eighteenth-century elocutionists continued to a considerable extent throughout much of the nineteenth century. But there were some important influences which came out of the nineteenth century itself. The first of these came from an American physician, Dr. James Rush, who published *The Philosophy of the Human Voice* in 1827. Rush described the numerous aspects of voice at length as they were related to quality, force, time, abruptness, and pitch. He was convinced that his method was founded upon nature. He described the elements of sound as tonics, subtonics, and atonics. His interest in the orotund vocal quality led him to recommend it as the only quality appropriate to epic and dramatic reading, the church service, and Shakespeare and Milton. Rush wished to give a physiological history of the vocal means for representing the various states of thought and emotion; to indicate their modes, forms, and varieties, and to give them a definite nomenclature. He used the term "elocution" to indicate the use of the voice to express thought and feeling, and held that it included all forms of correct reading and public and colloquial speech. With many devout followers, he was a leading influence throughout the nineteenth century even though all aspects of his work were not always accepted.

A second important influence came from France through François Delsarte. Delsarte himself never came to America, yet he was to have a tremendous influence here through Steele Mackaye, his ardent disciple, who studied with him in France. Mackaye returned to America filled with enthusiasm for Delsarte's philosophy in which the concept of the trinity was the keynote. Man, for example, consisted of life, soul, and mind; beauty and tones likewise had three parts. Some have called Delsarte's approach a philosophy, while others have labelled it a system. As it was generally followed in America it became a system although it apparently had some philosophical elements as Delsarte himself conceived of it. Some of the mechanical aspects of his approach made it easy to grasp certain fundamental principles and to apply them.

Another influence, which has lasted up through the twentieth century, was the growing interest in psychology. Gradually psychological terminology began to creep into the field of reading and speaking. After

William James published *The Principles of Psychology* in 1890 and *Psychology* in 1892, the influence of psychology in the speech arts gained momentum.

The interest in reading and reciting extended in this century, as in the 18th century, beyond the walls of schools and colleges. In villages, towns, and cities, the reader or reciter could draw large crowds. Many leading teachers of elocution and many prominent actors gave programs throughout the country to audiences who flocked to hear them. Writers, too, such as Harriet Beecher Stowe, Charles Dickens, and Mark Twain were among the many to entertain the public. All in all, it was an exciting century, for America had grown from a small nation to one of significance, and her artistic interests endeavored to equal her general growth and expansion. Many of the principles set forth then in the art of reading aloud are respected today.

VII. TWENTIETH-CENTURY AMERICA

Some of the schools of speech arts which flourished abundantly in the nineteenth century continued to attract and train many students in the twentieth century. In addition to these schools, speech came increasingly into the realm of the college and university. There had already been, in the 19th century, those in the universities who supported the speech arts, such as Thomas C. Trueblood of the University of Michigan, Hiram Corson of Cornell University and J. H. McIlvaine of Princeton. Now schools of speech like the Emerson College of Oratory, the Curry School of Expression, and The Leland Powers School began to send many more of their graduates as instructors in oral interpretation and other speech arts into universities and colleges. As late as 1922 these schools supplied most of the teachers of oral interpretation.

Charles Wesley Emerson, S. S. Curry, Leland Powers, Robert I. Fulton, Thomas C. Trueblood, and A. E. Phillips were among the prominent who were active in both centuries.

Before the turn of the century the term "elocution" began to lose favor because it suggested an exaggerated and melodramatic style of reading and reciting, and the name "expression" was favored instead. Emphasis began to shift away from memorized recitation to reading aloud from manuscripts. Gradually the term "interpretative reading" was used. Books began to appear using the terms "expressive reading," "oral reading," the "oral interpretation of literature," and "interpretative reading."

There was, however, considerable opposition to reading aloud. One group that opposed reading contended that it interfered with bodily action and reduced expression to mere reading without interpretation. These divergent views continued for a long time in the twentieth century. As late as 1914 it was reported that many still favored reciting, but that reading aloud was gaining favor because of its literary values. When S. H. Clark published *Interpretation of the Printed Page* (1915) it was clear that reading instead of memorized recitation was winning out.

Public reading and recitation continued to be popular in the twentieth century and drew large audiences. One of the most important media for these presentations was the Chautauqua program which sent readers throughout the country and also presented many reading programs at its headquarters in Chautauqua, New York. S. H. Clark was head of the Chautauqua School of Expression for many years.

Well-known readers in the first third of the century included S. H. Clark, Anna Baright Curry, H. L. Southwick, Leland Powers, Rollo Anson Tallcott, Phidelah Rice, Mary Agnes Doyle, Ralph Dennis, Gertrude Johnson, Davis Edwards and others. Poets and novelists, too, gave programs.

The phonograph, radio and television opened new outlets for reading aloud. Many turned to the phonograph to hear the verses of James Whitcomb Riley, readings from the Bible and selections from drama, poetry and classical literature. When radio became popular, reading aloud was actually the medium for all radio presentations. Specific programs devoted to reading literature aloud were given by a number of people at local radio stations and on national chains. David Ross, Tony Wons, Ted Malone, Anne Campbell and others were popular. The fear that the reader's effect would be diminished because he could not be seen was dispelled, for readers created the situation in the minds of the listeners so effectively that the intellectual and emotional contact between the material, the reader and the listener was successful. With the advent of television, a form of reading aloud continued in the use of large print to supply television performers with their lines, and occasional readings from literature were also presented.

Because of the increasing emphasis on science, the oral interpretation of literature needed to be re-evaluated. As has been noted, interest in the relation of psychology to reading aloud was recognized in the nineteenth century, especially through William James. Just before the turn of the century, in 1898, S. H. Clark recommended a knowledge of psychology for the reader because "vocal expression is the outcome of complicated mental processes." He was among those who saw in psychology a "mental technique" rather than a physical or pseudo-philosophical method. Psychology and new educational theories were influential in gradually shifting the concept of oral interpretation from showmanship and performance to that of individual growth through the development and sharing of literary appreciation. These influences upon oral interpretation have been significant throughout the twentieth century.

Oral interpretation has been related to several other disciplines in this century. It is allied to literary criticism and analysis just as it had been in antiquity. It has also been regarded as an art form subject to the principles of aesthetics. New or revived forms of reading aloud such as choral reading and readers theatre have been, and are, enjoying increased popularity.

The formal study of oral interpretation, along with many other disciplines in the field of speech, gained improved perspective following the founding in 1914 of the National Association of Academic Teachers of Public Speaking, known today as the Speech Association of America. The seventeen charter members of this Association provided the impetus which led ultimately to the academic acceptance of speech education in America. "The founders offered a new focus for the relatively random efforts of teachers and associations that had for twenty-five years or more striven, with occasional success, to unify, to place on a solid foundation, and to give academic stature to training in speech which was something more than 'elocution.' They were aiming at a balanced, well-developed program of speech education in both the high school and college. Deploring the abuses of elocution, they saw delivery, not as vocal and gestural display, but as voice and action tied to the meaning of ideas and giving effectiveness to thought. The principles of delivery, indeed, were equally valid for the actor, the reader and declaimer, and the public speaker."[35]

The first annual convention of the Association was held at Chicago in 1915. Oral interpretation was a part of that convention. On the third day(Saturday, November 27), Maud May Babcock, of The University of Utah, presented a paper entitled "Interpretative Presentation versus Impersonative Presentation." S. H. Clark of The University of Chicago led the discussion. Miss Babcock's paper, which precipitated a long-lasting controversy over presentational techniques, was published the following year in *The Quarterly Journal of Speech,* Vol. II, January, 1916, pp. 18–25. Papers on a variety of topics in oral interpretation have been presented at all conventions of the Association since that auspicious start.

The convention program of 1925 lists, for the first time, an *Interpretation Group Meeting,* Gertrude E. Johnson presiding. Although it would be another thirty years (1955) before the Association officially established seventeen interest groups, the oral interpretation people were already meeting as a group. Their interests were substantially polarized at the 1926 convention when Miss Johnson, of The University of Wisconsin, responded to a suggestion from the convention floor that interpretative reading had about faded from the scene. She rose and called a meeting of all interested in interpretation; it was reportedly the largest and most enthusiastic group at the convention. At that time a committee was formed. Reading programs were initiated the following year (1927) and have to this day remained the most popular, best attended programs of the annual convention.

The most frequent participants in oral interpretation meetings, as listed in the programs of the Association conventions from 1915 through the 1940's, included most of the significant names in that period of our history: Maud May Babcock (University of Utah), Frank Rarig (University of Minnesota), Wayland M. Parrish (University of Pittsburgh), Davis Edwards (University of Chicago), Gertrude E. Johnson (University of Wisconsin), Severina Nelson (University of Illinois), J. T. Marshman (Ohio Wesleyan University), C. C. Cunningham (Northwestern University), Louis M. Eich (University of Michigan), William J. Farma (New York University), Magdalene Kramer (Columbia Uni-

[35] Karl R. Wallace, ed., *History of Speech Education in America* (New York: Appleton-Century-Crofts, Inc.), 500.

versity), Charles P. Greene (University of Oklahoma), Sara Lowrey (Furman University), Harriett E. Grim (University of Wisconsin), and E. Ray Skinner (Wayne State University). The active participation of several of these people continued into the 1950's and the influence of all is still very much a part of our thinking today.

During the 1950's a number of new names came into prominence. These people gained recognition in the field through their published articles, textbooks, and Association activities. A bibliography of textbooks and articles can be found at the end of this chapter. In 1955 the Association formally established seventeen interest groups, one of which was the Oral Interpretation of Literature Interest Group. From the beginning and to this day the Interpretation Interest Group has been one of the largest, and frequently *the* largest, of all Interest Groups. National leadership since 1955 in oral interpretation is reflected in the following roster of Interest Group officers:

Officers of Interpretation Interest Group

1955

Committee on Interpretation
Chairman: Garff Wilson (University of California, Berkeley)
Vice-Chairman: Charlotte Lee (Northwestern University)
Secretary: Ray Irwin (Syracuse University)

1956

Chairman: Charlotte Lee (Northwestern University)
Vice-Chairman: Ray Irwin (Syracuse University)
Secretary: LaMont Okey (University of Michigan)

1957

Chairman: Ray Irwin (Syracuse University)
Vice-Chairman: LaMont Okey (University of Michigan)
Secretary: Melvin White (Brooklyn College)

1958

Chairman: LaMont Okey (University of Michigan)
Vice-Chairman: Melvin R. White (Brooklyn College)
Secretary: Keith Brooks (Ohio State University)

1959

Chairman: Melvin R. White (Brooklyn College)
Vice-Chairman: Keith Brooks (Ohio State University)
Secretary: Chloe Armstrong (Baylor University)

1960

Chairman: Keith Brooks (Ohio State University)
Vice-Chairman: Chloe Armstrong (Baylor University)
Secretary: Francine Merritt (Louisiana State University)

1961

Chairman: Chloe Armstrong (Baylor University)
Vice-Chairman: Wilma Grimes (University of Washington)
Secretary: Francine Merritt (Louisiana State University)

1962

Chairman: Wilma Grimes (University of Washington)
Vice-Chairman: Robert Breen (Northwestern University)
Secretary: Reverend John Boyle, S. J. (Bellarmine College)

1963

Chairman: Robert Breen (Northwestern University)
Vice-Chairman: Janet Bolton (University of Southern California)
Secretary-Treasurer: Reverend John Boyle, S. J. (Loyola Seminary)

1964

Chairman: Janet Bolton (University of Southern California)
Vice-Chairman: Johnnye Akin (University of Denver)
Vice-Chairman Elect: Don Geiger (University of California)
Secretary-Treasurer: Leslie Irene Coger (Southwest Missouri State)

1965

Chairman: Johnnye Akin (University of Denver)
Vice-Chairman: Don Geiger (University of California, Berkeley)
Vice-Chairman Elect: Elbert Bowen (Central Michigan University)
Secretary-Treasurer: Leslie Irene Coger (Southwest Missouri State)

1966

Chairman: Don Geiger (University of California, Berkeley)
Vice-Chairman: Elbert Bowen (Central Michigan University)
Vice-Chairman Elect: Eugene Bahn (Wayne State University)
Secretary-Treasurer: Lilla Heston (Northwestern University)

1967

Chairman: Elbert Bowen (Central Michigan University)
Vice-Chairman: Eugene Bahn (Wayne State University)
Vice-Chairman Elect: Lea Park (Memphis State University)
Secretary: Lilla Heston (Northwestern University)

STUDY QUESTIONS

1. Do you know of any oral interpretation festivals held today? How do they compare to those held in Greece in terms of reading or reciting, literature, the readers themselves and the occasion?

2. What do you think the basic underlying causes of the decline of good oral reading were in Rome? Can you relate this to social history?

3. In which historical periods was the oral reading of literature related to religion?

4. What "*internal*" evidence can you find in the *Canterbury Tales* to indicate their relation to oral style?

5. Why was there a great surge of interest in learning to read in 16th and 17th century England?

6. What did Cockin mean when he said that reading and speaking are among those arts which improve nature?

7. What do you mean when you tell someone to read "naturally"?

8. Why do you think so few books on the speech arts were written in 18th century America?

9. What arguments can one present in favor of, and in opposition to, memorized recitation? Why?

ORAL INTERPRETATION BIBLIOGRAPHY

Textbooks

Aggert, Otis J. and Elbert R. Bowen	*Communicative Reading* (2nd ed.)	New York: The Macmillan Company	1963
Armstrong, Chloe and Paul Brandes	*The Oral Interpretation of Literature*	New York: McGraw-Hill Book Company	1963
Bacon, Wallace A. and Robert S. Breen	*Literature as Experience*	New York: McGraw-Hill Book Company	1959
Beloof, Robert	*The Performing Voice in Literature*	Boston, Mass.: Little, Brown and Company	1966
Campbell, Paul N.	*Oral Interpretation*	New York: The Macmillan Company	1966
Cobin, Martin	*Theory and Technique of Interpretation*	New Jersey: Prentice-Hall, Inc.	1959
Crocker, Lionel G. and Louis Eich	*Oral Reading* (2nd ed.)	New Jersey: Prentice-Hall, Inc.	1955
Dolman, John Jr.	*The Art of Reading Aloud*	New York: Harper and Bros.	1956
Geiger, Don	*The Sound, Sense, and Performance of Literature*	Chicago, Ill., Scott, Foresman and Company	1963

Grimes, Wilma H. and Alethea Smith Mattingly	*Interpretation: Writer-Reader-Audience*	Belmont, Calif.: Wadsworth Publishing Co., Inc.	1961
Lee, Charlotte	*Oral Interpretation* (3rd ed.)	Boston, Mass.: Houghton-Mifflin Company	1965
Lowrey, Sara and Gertrude E. Johnson	*Interpretative Reading* (Rev. Ed.)	New York: Appleton-Century-Crofts	1953
Lynch, Gladys and Harold C. Crain	*Projects in Oral Interpretation*	New York: Henry Holt and Company	1959
Mouat, Lawrence	*Reading Literature Aloud*	New York: Oxford University Press	1962
Parrish, Wayland M.	*Reading Aloud* (3rd ed.)	New York: The Ronald Press Company	1953
Smith, Joseph and James Linn	*Skill in Reading Aloud*	New York: Harper and Row Publishers	1960
Thompson, David W. and Virginia Fredricks	*Oral Interpretation of Fiction*	Minneapolis, Minn.: Burgess Publishing Company	1964
Woolbert, Charles H. and Severina E. Nelson	*The Art of Interpretative Speech* (4th ed.)	New York: Appleton-Century-Crofts	1956

Articles in The Quarterly Journal of Speech

1915 Babcock, Maude May—"Teaching Interpretation," Vol. I, 2, 173–176

1916 Babcock, Maude May—"Interpretative Presentation Versus Impersonative Presentation," Vol. II, 1, 18–25

Tallcott, R. A.—"The Place for Personation," Vol. II, 2, 116–122

Pearson, T. M.—"Artistic Interpretation," Vol. II, 3, 286–292

Babcock, Maude May—"Impersonation vs. Interpretation," Vol. II, 4, 340–343

1918 Newcomb, Charles M.—"How to Stimulate Imagination in Interpretative Reading," Vol. IV, 1, 135–149

1920 Herring, Bertha Forbes—"Vocal Interpretation of Literature in High Schools," Vol. VI, 4, 52–58

1922 Dennis, Ralph B.—"One Imperative Plus," Vol. VIII, 3, 218–223

1923 Tallcott, Rollo Anson—"Teaching Public Reading," Vol. IX, 1, 53–66

Lane, A. H.—"Literary Study as a Preparation for Oral Presentation," Vol. IX, 2, 181–187

1925 Cheeseman, Grace—"The Concept of Naturalness as a Basis for Criticism," Vol. XI, 1, 37–45

Fry, Dorothea—"Learning Material for Oral Interpretation," Vol. XI, 3, 253–258

Tassin, Algernon—"Oral Reading as an Intelligence Test," Vol. XI, 3, 258–266

1926 Crocker, Lionel—"The Voice Element in Prose," Vol. XII, 2, 168–175

Barnes, John—"Vital Capacity and Ability in Oral Reading," Vol. XII, 3, 176–182

Wilson, Helene—"Some Statistics Concerning Interpretation Courses," Vol. XII, 4, 342–352

1927 Hannah, Robert—"The Interpretation of the Prologue and Epilogue," Vol. XIII, 2, 123–132

Parrish, W. M.—"Interpretative Reading," Vol. XIII, 2, 160–168

Jacob, Cary—"Rhythm in Prose and Poetry," Vol. XIII, 4, 357–375

1929 Crocker, Lionel—"The Refrain in Oratorical Prose," Vol. XV, 1, 25–29

Spaeth, J. Duncan—"On Standardizing Pronunciation," Vol. XV, 3, 323–330

Hannah, Robert—"The Oral Interpretation of Lyric Poetry," Vol. XV, 3, 374–380

1930 Latham, Azubah J.—"Abandon: A Characteristic of Perfected Speech," XVI, 2, 171–175

Simon, Clarence T.—"Appreciation in Reading," Vol. XVI, 2, 185–193

Kaucher, Dorothy J.—"O Wad Some Power," Vol. XVI, 4, 445–453

Wichelns, H. A.—"The Undergraduate Reads from the Poets," Vol. XVI, 4, 454–458

1931 Kaucher. Dorothy—"The Verse-Speaking Choir," Vol. XVII, 1, 64–73

Runchey, Geraldine—"The Oral Approach to the Study of Literature," Vol. XVII, 1, 89–95

Saunders, Mary Evans—"The Oxford Verse Speaking Contest," Vol. XVII, 3, 395–400

Eubank, Henry Lee—"Four Approaches to the Study of Speech Style," Vol. XVII, 4, 458–465

Mandell, Sybil—"The Relation of Language to Thought," Vol. XVII, 4, 522–531

1932 Bassett, Lee Emerson—"Adapting Courses in Interpretation to the Academic Mind," Vol. XVIII, 1, 175–187

Flemming, Edwin G.—"Expression and Personality," Vol. XVIII, 2, 270–276

Bahn, Eugene—"Interpretative Reading in Ancient Greece," Vol. XVIII, 3, 432–440

Gray, Giles Wilkeson—"Sidelights on the Pronunciation of English," Vol. XVIII, 4, 546–560

1933 Rasmussen, Carrie—"Choral Speaking in the Grades," Vol. XIX, 1, 43–51

McLane, Lucy Neely—"Sound-Values in 'The Cloud'," Vol. XIX, 2, 224–227

Dennis, Ralph—"The Progressive Teacher," Vol. XIX, 2, 242–247

Little, Theodore—"A Unit in Interpretation," Vol. XIX, 4, 540–544

1934 Morris, A. R.—"A Note on the Inflection of Julia Marlowe," Vol. XX, 2, 200–202

Rasmussen, Carrie—"Verse Speaking and Bodily Activity," Vol. XX, 2, 282–286

Henderson, Ellen C.—"Some Principles of Oral Reading," Vol. XX, 2, 287–299

Paul, Vera Alice—"Suggestions for Teaching Oral Reading," Vol. XX, 2, 299–306

Heaps, Willard A.—"Choosing Literature for Reading Contests," Vol. XX, 3, 410–414

1935 Gray, J. Stanley—"A Behavioristic Interpretation of Language," Vol. XXI, 1, 36–53

Ketcham, V. A.—"The Probability of a Word-Atom Hypothesis," Vol. XXI, 2, 157–168

Gray, J. Stanley—"A Behavioristic Interpretation of Language—II," Vol. XXI, 2, 168–177

Wilke, Walter H.—"An Efficient Text of Diction," Vol. XXI, 2, 192–194

Walsh, Rose—"Whither the Verse-Speaking Choir," Vol. XXI, 4, 461–466

Jones, Jean Brady—"Oral Reading in the Miry Pit," Vol. XXI, 4, 524–534

1936 Borchers, Gladys—"An Approach to the Problem of Oral Style," Vol. XXII, 1, 114–117

Meader, Emma Grant—"Choral Speaking and Its Values," Vol. XXII, 2, 235–245

Booth, Miriam B.—"Interpretative Reading in the Secondary Schools," Vol. XXII, 2, 270–277

Henning, J. H.—"The Development of Literary Appreciation Through Speech," Vol. XXII, 2, 278–283

Parrish, W. M.—"Objective Literary Standards in Interpretation," Vol. XXII, 2, 368–379

Galbraith, Esther A.—"A Note on Three Choral Readings," Vol. XXII, 4, 648–651

Downs, Sophie W.—"Speech-Chorus Work in the Elementary Schools of Germany," Vol. XXII, 4, 669–670

1937 Lewis, Richard and Holland Roberts—"Director's Part in Verse Choir," Vol. XXIII, 1, 63–66

Bahn, Eugene—"Interpretative Reading in Classical Rome," Vol. XXIII, 2, 202–213

Marsh, Thomas H.—"Some Problems of Oral Bible Reading," Vol. XXIII, 3, 396–402

Crawford, Mary Major—"Speech Choirs in Europe," Vol. XXIII, 3, 444–449

Pellegrini, Angelo M.—"The Aim and Educational Content of Oral Reading," Vol. XXIII, 4, 643–647

1938 Armstrong, Mary Halderman—"Certain Aspects of Choral Speech," Vol. XXIV, 1, 117–119

Marsh, Thomas H.—"The Bible as Source Material for Public Speaking and Oral Reading," Vol. XXIV, 2, 199–204

Rodigan, Mary Virginia—"New Approaches to Aims in Interpretative Reading in Teachers Colleges," Vol. XXIV, 2, 205–208

Adam, Harlen M.—"Listening," Vol. XXIV, 2, 209–211

Dusenbury, Delwin and Franklin H. Knower—"Experimental Studies of the Symbolism of Action and Voice," Vol. XXIV, 3, 424–436

Robbins, R. H.—"A Further Justification of Choral Speaking," Vol. XXIV, 3, 437–442

Bradford, Arthur L.—"When Oral Interpretation Comes of Age," Vol. XXIV, 3, 444–452

Baird, A. Craig—"The Educational Philosophy of the Teacher of Speech," Vol. XXIV, 4, 546–553

Bryngelson, Bryng—"The Interpretative Symbol," Vol. XXIV 4, 569–573

Marshman, J. T.—"The Mystery of Oral Interpretation," Vol. XXIV, 4, 596–603

1939 Brees, Paul R.—"The Teacher of Interpretation as a Reader," Vol. XXV, 1, 62–66

Dusenbury, Delwin and Franklin H. Knower—"Experimental Studies of the Symbolism of Action and Voice: II," Vol. XXV, 1, 67–75

Weaver, Andrew Thomas—"The Case for Speech," Vol. XXV, 2, 181–188

Hamm, Agnes Curren—"Choral Speaking—A Word of Warning," Vol. XXV, 2, 225–227

Robbins, R. H.—"Choral Speaking at the Oxford Festivals," Vol. XXV, 2, 227–235

Eich, Louis M.—"The Relation of Content, Form and Style to Interpretative Reading," Vol. XXV, 2, 281–285

Dow, Clyde W.—"A Literary Interpretation Analysis Blank," Vol. XXV, 2, 285–288

1940 Braden, Waldo W.—"The Interpretative Reading Festival," Vol. XXVI, 1, 101–104

Rarig, Frank M.—"Some Elementary Contributions of Aesthetics to Interpretative Speech," Vol. XXVI, 4, 527–539

Norvelle, Lee and Raymond Smith—"Testing for Improvement in Oral Interpretation," Vol. XXVI, 4, 540–545

Lea, Charlotte I.—"Choric Reading and Kinetic Projection," Vol. XXVI, 4, 545–550

1941 Allen, Willadel—"Teaching Interpretative Reading in the High School," Vol. XXVII, 1, 115–119

Hollister, R. D. T.—"The Application of Aesthetic Criteria to the Oral Presentation of Literature," Vol. XXVII, 2, 281–289

Irwin, R. L.—"Declamation—A Cultural Lag," Vol. XXVII, 2, 289–291

1942 Marshman, J. T.—"The Paradox of Oral Interpretation," XXVIII, 1, 31–36

Cunningham, Cornelius C.—"The Sepia School of Interpretative Reading," Vol. XXVIII, 1, 37–41

Williams, Helen D.—"You Might Like the Verse Speaking Choir," Vol. XXVIII, 1, 41–45

Black, John—"A Study of Voice Merit," Vol. XXVIII, 1, 67–74

Flaccus, Kimball—"An Adventure in Poetry," Vol. XXVIII, 3, 315–323

Wilson, Willard—"Breath Control, A Common Sense Summary," Vol. XXVIII, 3, 338–343

1943 Wells, Henry W.—"Literature and the Phonograph," Vol. XXIX, 1, 68–73

Paul, Vera Alice—"The Relation of Oral Reading to Remedial Reading in Elementary and Secondary Schools," Vol. XXIX, 2, 217–222

Gray, G. W.—"The 'Voice Qualities' in the History of Elocution," Vol. XXIX, 4, 475–480

1945 Kaucher, Dorothy—"Try It Again," Vol. XXXI, 1, 47–54

Cunningham, Cornelius C.—"Stress Variations in Oral Interpretation," Vol. XXXI, 1, 55–62

Price, Helen and J. B. Stroud—"A Note on Oral Reading," Vol. XXXI, 3, 340–343

Burklund, Carl E.—"On the Oral Reading of Poetry," Vol. XXXI, 3, 344–350

Lowrey, Sara—"Interpretative Reading as an Aid to Speech Correction, Acting and Radio," Vol. XXXI, 4, 459–464

1946 Duncan, Melba Hurd—"Localizing Individual Problems in Oral Interpretation," Vol. XXXII, 2, 213–216

Cunningham, Cornelius C.—"The Rhythm of Robinson Jeffers' Poetry as Revealed by Oral Reading," Vol. XXXII, 3, 351–357

Wiksell, Wesley—"The Problem of Listening," Vol. XXXII, 4, 505–508

1947 Nichols, Ralph G.—"Listening: Questions and Problems," Vol. XXXIII, 1, 83–86

Edwards, Davis—"The Real Source of Vachel Lindsay's Poetic Technique," Vol. XXXIII, 2, 182–195

Murphy, Theresa and Richard Murphy—"Charles Dickens as Professional Reader," Vol. XXXIII, 3, 299–303

Donner, Stanley T.—"Mark Twain as a Reader," Vol. XXXIII, 3, 308–311

Nauss, Lorraine—"Reading the Language of Literature," Vol. XXXIII, 4, 474–479

1948 McCoard, William B.—"Report on the Reading of Hiroshima," Vol. XXXIV, 2, 174–176

1949 Kernodle, George R.—"Basic Problems in Reading Shakespeare," Vol. XXXV, 1, 36–42

Bacon, Wallace A.—"Graduate Studies in Interpretation," Vol. XXXV, 3, 316–319

Fleischman, Earl E.—"Let's Take Another Look at Interpretation," Vol. XXXV, 4, 477–484

Mouat, L. H.—"The Question Method for Teaching Emphasis in Oral Reading," Vol. XXXV, 4, 485–488

1950 Smith, Herbert L.—"Objective Meaning and Dramatic Interpretation," Vol. XXXVI, 1, 39–43

Geiger, Don—"Oral Interpretation and the 'New Criticism'," Vol. XXXVI, 4, 508–513

1951 Marshman, John T.—"Art Approach to Reading Aloud," Vol. XXXVII, 1, 35–40

Burklund, Carl E.—"Poetry: A Symphonic Structure," Vol. XXXVII, 2, 179–184

1952 Neihardt, John G.—"The Interpretation of Poetry," Vol. XXXVIII, 1, 74–78

Geiger, Don—"A 'Dramatic' Approach to Interpretative Analysis," XXXVIII, 2, 189–194

Martin, Albert—"The Oral Interpreter and the Phonograph," Vol. XXXVIII, 2, 195–198

Kaucher, Dorothy—"Interpretation and the Etymon," Vol. XXXVIII, 3, 300–304

1953 Burklund, Carl E.—"Melody in Verse," Vol. XXXIX, 1, 57–60

Bacon, Wallace A.—"Scholarship and the Interpreter," Vol. XXXIX, 2, 187–192

1954 Geiger, Don—"Oral Interpretation in the Liberal Arts Context," Vol. XL, 2, 137–144

Marsh, Gerald E.—"An Interpretative Approach to Speech," Vol. XL, 3, 269–271

1955 Geiger, Don—"Pluralism in the Interpreter's Search for Sanctions," Vol. XLI, 1, 43–56

Herrick, Marvin T.—"The Teacher as Reader and Interpreter of Literature," Vol. XLI, 2, 110–113

Murphy, Theresa—"Interpretation in the Dickens Period," Vol. XLI, 3, 243–249

1956 Bennett, Daphne N.—"Auden's 'September 1, 1939': An Interpreter's Analysis," Vol. XLII, 1, 1–13

Grimes, Wilma H.—"Choosing Literature for Oral Reading: A Psychological Basis," Vol. XLII, 2, 133–138

Thompson, David W.—"Interpretative Reading as Symbolic Action," Vol. XLII, 4, 389–397

1957 Parrish, W. M.—"Elocution—a Definition and a Challenge," Vol. XLIII, 1, 1–11

Chatman, Seymour—"Linguistics, Poetics, and Interpretation: The Phonemic Dimension," Vol. XLIII, 3, 248–256

Hollis, C. Carroll—"Whitman and the American Idiom," Vol. XLIII, 4, 408–420

1958 Cobin, Martin—"An Oral Interpreter's Index to Quintilian," Vol. XLIV, 1, 61–66

Ostroff, Anthony—"Notes Toward A Theory of Diction," Vol. XLIV, 2, 166–174

1959 Howell, Wilbur Samuel—"Sources of the Elocutionary Movement in England: 1700–1748," Vol. XLV, 1, 1–18

Dickinson, Hugh—"Readers or Rhapsodes?" Vol. XLV, 3, 258–263

1960 Gray, Giles Wilkeson—"What Was Elocution?" XLVI, 1, 1–7

Bacon, Wallace A.—"The Dangerous Shores: From Elocution to Interpretation," Vol. XLVI, 2, 148–152

1961 Black, John W.—"Aural Reception of Sentences of Different Lengths," Vol. XLVII, 1, 51–53

Bessinger, J. B.—"The Aural Text of Ezra Pound's 'The Seafarer'," Vol. XLVII, 2, 173–177

Reynolds, Nydia Jones—"It Wasn't Elocution': Five Professional Oral Interpreters, 1900–1925," Vol. XLVII, 3, 244–252

Rasmus, Ward—"Voice and Diction: Historical Perspective," Vol. XLVII, 3, 253–261

1962 Bahn, Eugene—"Interpretative Reading in Contemporary Greece," Vol. XLVIII, 3, 271–276

Brown, Charles T. and Paul W. Keller—"A Modest Proposal for Listening Training," Vol. XLVIII, 4, 395–399

Cobin, Martin—"Response to Eye-Contact," Vol. XLVIII, 4, 415–418

Blankenship, Jane—"A Linguistic Analysis of Oral and Written Style," Vol. XLVIII, 4, 419–422

1963 Coger, Leslie Irene—"Interpreter's Theatre: Theatre of the Mind," Vol. XLIX, 2, 157–164

Krempel, Daniel—" 'Imaginary Forces'—A Minority Report," Vol. XLIX, 4, 383–388

1965 Sloan, Thomas O.—"The Persona as Rhetor: An Interpretation of Donne's Satyre III," Vol. LI, 1, 14–27

Loesch, Katharine T.—"Literary Ambiguity and Oral Performance," Vol. LI, 3, 258–267

1966 Mohrman, G. P.—"The Language of Nature and Elocutionary Theory," Vol. LII, 2, 116–124

Articles in The Speech Teacher

1952 Wilson, Garff—"The Growth of Oral Interpretation at the University of California," Vol. I, 3, 187–192

1953 Hile, Frederick W. and Sholie R. Brown—"The 49ers and Three Experiments in Oral Interpretation," Vol. II, 2, 105–108

1956 Robb, Mary Margaret—"Oral Interpretation and the Book Review," Vol. V, 4, 285–289

1957 Schmidt, Ralph N.—"Co-operation between High School and College in the Teaching of Oral Interpretation," Vol. VI, 1, 48–54

Seedorf, Evelyn H.—"The Phonetic Approach to Choral Reading," Vol. VI, 2, 117–122

Smiley, Anne—"Hints for the Student Reader," Vol. VI, 3, 233–236

1958 Hunsinger, Paul—"Festivals and Changing Patterns," Vol. VII, 2, 93–98

Bowen, Elbert R.—"Promoting Dynamic Interpretative Reading," Vol. VII, 2, 118–120

Grimes, Wilma H.—"Oral Reading Activities in Colleges and Universities," Vol. VII, 4, 332–335

Hillbruner, Anthony—"Interpretation, Aesthetics, and the Speech Curriculum," Vol. VIII, 1, 22–26

Cobin, Martin—"Utilizing Television in the Interpretation Program," Vol. VIII, 1, 31–40

1959 Mattingly, Alethea Smith—"The Teacher as Critic in Interpretation Performance," Vol. VIII, 4, 321–324

1960 Abernathy, Rose L.—"The Role of Storytelling—A Preliminary Report of an Investigation in the United States," Vol. IX, 4, 283–286

1961 Crocker, Lionel G.—"How to Multiply the Side Values of Oral Interpretation," Vol. X, 1, 63–64

Hoopes, Ned E.—"What Literature Should Be Used in Oral Interpretation?" Vol. X, 3, 206–210

1962 Bronstein, Arthur J. and Dorothy E. Rambo—"Language Analysis and the Speech Teacher," Vol. XI, 2, 130–135

Geiger, Don—"Oral Interpretation and the Teaching of Literature," Vol. XI, 3, 202–207

Reclam, Herta—"Choric Speaking in Greek Tragedies, Performed by Students," Vol. XI, 4, 283–289
Kershner, Jr., A. G.—"John Dolman, Jr.," Vol. XI, 4, 290–292
Thompson, David W.—"Frank M. Rarig," Vol. XI, 4, 292–294
Gilbert, Edna—"Ralph Dennis," Vol. XI, 4, 294–297
Lee, Charlotte I.—"Cornelius Carman Cunningham," Vol. XI, 4, 297–299
Mouat, Lawrence H.—"Lee Emerson Bassett," Vol. XI, 4, 299–302
Nelson, Severina E.—"Charles Henry Woolbert," Vol. XI, 4, 302–304
Okey, L. LaMont—"Thomas Clarkson Trueblood, Pioneer, 1856–1951," Vol. XI, 1, 10–14.
Smith, Joseph F.—"Maude May Babcock," Vol. XI, 4, 304–307
Murphy, Richard—"Wayland Maxfield Parrish," Vol. XI, 4, 307–310

1963 Brooks, Keith, Robert C. Henderhan, and Alan Billings—"A Philosophy on Reader's Theatre," Vol. XII, 3, 229–232
Kramer, Magdalene—"Azubah J. Latham: Creative Teacher," Vol. XII, 3, 187–190
Robb, Mary Margaret—"Growing a Taste for Poetry," Vol. XII, 4, 317–321
Coger, Leslie Irene—"Theatre for Oral Interpreters," Vol. XII, 4, 322–330

1964 MacArthur, David E.—"Reader's Theatre: Variations on A Theme," Vol. XIII, 1, 47–51
Mohrmann, G. P.—"Children's Literature and the Beginning Class in Oral Interpretation," Vol. XIII, 2, 128–132
Wamboldt, Helen Jane—"Haiku as a Tool in Teaching Oral Interpretation," Vol. XIII, 3, 171–175

1965 Stevens, Phillip Boyd—"Acting and Interpretation: The Reader Faces the Contest," Vol. XIV, 2, 116–122
Kleinau, Marion L. and Marvin D. Kleinau—"Scene Location in Reader's Theatre: Static or Dynamic?" Vol. XIV, 3, 193–199
Skinner, E. Ray—"Gertrude Johnson: Pioneer in the Oral Interpretation of Literature," Vol. XIV, 3, 226–229

1966 McCurdy, Frances Lea—"Reading Symbols of Poetry," Vol. XV, 1, 42–48
Reitz, F. Mathias—"Application of Selected Dramatic Theories to Disunity in Readers' Theatre," Vol. XV, 3, 191–196.

Articles in Speech Monographs

1937 Ortleb, Ruth and Joseph Tiffin—"An Objective Study of Emphasis in Oral Reading of Emotional and Unemotional Material," Vol. IV, 56–68

1944 Snidecar, John C.—"An Objective Study of Phrasing in Impromptu Speaking and Oral Reading," Vol. XI, 97–104

1948 Barnett, Wynett—"An Experimental Study in the Teaching of Voice and Diction Through the Ear Training, Phonetic, and Oral Reading Approaches," Vol. XV, 2, 142–153

1951 Guthrie, Warren—"The Elocution Movement—England," Vol. XVIII, 1, 17–30

McCoard, W. B. and S. N. LeCount—"An Oral Evaluation of Good and Poor Silent Readers," Vol. XVIII, 4, 288–291

1953 Geiger, Don—"Modern Literary Thought: The Consciousness of Abstracting," Vol. XX, 1, 1–22

Vandraegen, Daniel A.—"Thomas Sheridan and the Natural School," Vol. XX, 1, 58–64

Young, James D.—"Vocabulary Growth Through Oral Reading, Silent Reading and Listening," Vol. XX, 4, 273–276

1956 Shepherd, John R. and T. M. Scheidel—"Personality of Oral Readers," Vol. XXIII, 3, 298–304

1959 Clevenger, Theodore Jr. and Martin T. Cobin—"An Experiment in Open Circuit Television Instruction in the Basic Course in Oral Interpretation," Vol. XXVI, 2, 149–154

1961 Cobin, Martin T. and Theodore Clevenger, Jr.—"Television Instruction Course Content, and Teaching Experience Level: An Experimental Study in the Basic Course in Oral Interpretation," Vol. XXVIII, 1, 16–20

Diehl, Charles F., Richard C. White and Paul H. Satz—"Pitch Change and Comprehension," Vol. XXVIII, 1, 65–68

1963 Lee, Charlotte I.—"The Line As A Rhythmic Unit in the Poetry of Theodore Roethke," Vol. XXX, 1, 15–22

1964 Bacon, Wallace A.—"The Elocutionary Career of Thomas Sheridan (1719–1788)," Vol. XXXI, 1, 1–53

Brooks, Keith and Sister I. Marie Wulftange—"Listener Response to Oral Interpretation," Vol. XXXI, 1, 73–79

Mattingly, Alethea Smith—"Follow Nature: A Synthesis of Eighteenth Century Views," Vol. XXXI, 1, 80–84

1965 Frandsen, Kenneth D., James R. Rockey, and Marion Kleinau—"Semantic Differential for Reader's Theatre," Vol. XXXII, 2, 112–118

Lamb, Jack Hall—"John Walker and Joshua Steele," Vol. XXXII, 4, 411–419

Chapter II

Oral Interpretation Today*

The serious student of oral interpretation will find the *oral* approach to the study and communication of literature a dynamic experience, for not only must you come to understand and appreciate selected literature, you must *share* that understanding and appreciation with your listeners. You, of course, will always be your own most sensitive listener. This combination of analyzing *and* communicating the printed page provides an unparalleled cultural experience in literature, for not only are you held responsible for researching the literature and the writer, but you are obligated to involve your listeners in the experience you believe to be the intent of the literature. It is this combination that provides you with a unique and dynamic experience in literature: a cultural experience in the finest tradition of the humanities.

Today's academic area of oral interpretation places *equal* emphasis on literature, reader, and listener, with a clear recognition that each is *dependent* on the other. A review of our oral heritage reveals that this was not always true. The pendulum of emphasis has swung in various directions. For example, consideration was entirely on the reader and his delivery during several periods of history. When the stress has been placed on literary analysis and synthesis, with the interpreter and the listener in subordinate positions, the bias of the individual trained in the traditional non-oral approach has been dominant. The importance of the listener has never been the predominant emphasis, and this lack of attention has been a serious error. Its inclusion, given impetus by the

* The models and major portions of the discussion in this chapter are reprinted from *The Communicative Arts and Sciences of Speech* (Chapter 19), Keith Brooks, ed., with the permission of Charles E. Merrill Books, Inc., Columbus, Ohio, 1967.

significant increase in listening research, has added stature and totality to the academic study of oral interpretation. Academicians have come to realize that there can be no weak link in this triangular emphasis if the *oral* approach to the study and communication of literature is to be thoughtfully pursued.

The validity of the *equality* and the *interdependence* of the divisions is probably felt most keenly during the communicative act of oral interpretation—that time of actual reading aloud to a listener or to a group of listeners. It is at this time of sharing that a union of literature, reader, and listener becomes the immediate goal; any weakness in the triangular emphasis minimizes the effectiveness of the communicative act. Among the specific reasons leading to minimal effectiveness are the following: unworthy literature, literature inappropriate for oral interpretation, questionable judgments as revealed by the reader through his vocal and physical suggestions of the intent of the literature, lack of skill in oral and physical suggestion, lack of reader sensitivity to listener response, and lack of listener sensitivity to cues communicated by the oral interpreter.

Preparation leading to the communicative act must be *thorough, thoughtful,* and *time consuming:* thorough, to insure attention to all parts; thoughtful, to gain insight and understanding; and time consuming, to allow for adjustments of behavioral responses and personal enrichment.

Responsibilities involved in preparing for the communicative act include the selection of literature appropriate to oral interpretation, to a specified listener or group of listeners, and to the interpreter; the analysis and synthesis of the intent of the literature; the analysis, synthesis and practice of the behavioral responses of the oral interpreter most appropriate to communicating the intent of the literature; and an analysis and synthesis of desired listener responses. Although each of these prerequisites will be given consideration in isolation, each must eventually be considered in relation to the other. A synthesis of all prerequisites to the communicative act is imperative.

The particular consideration of this chapter is contemporary theories of the communicative act of oral interpretation. It is hoped that this emphasis will be clarified through the definition of the communicative *act,* the communication *models,* and a discussion of *creativity and style.*

I. THE COMMUNICATIVE ACT DEFINED

The communicative act of oral interpretation is the process of stimulating a listener response which is favorable to the intent of the literature in terms of the reader's judgments, as communicated from the manuscript through vocal and physical suggestions.

The minimal implications of this definition are: (1) oral interpretation is primarily concerned with communication; (2) the communicative act of oral interpretation involves a listener, an oral interpreter, and a piece of literature—each dependent on the other; (3) the listener is stimulated by the vocal and physical suggestions of the oral interpreter; (4) the listener response is favorable when it reflects and fulfills the suggestions (judgments) of the oral interpreter; (5) the oral interpreter's judgments are dependent on a study of the intent of the literature.

The first two implications speak for themselves. The others deserve additional comment, since they represent three of the most important concepts in oral interpretation.

The listener is stimulated by the vocal and physical suggestions of the oral interpreter. You have only two ways of communicating with a listener: vocally and physically. It follows, therefore, that your vocal and physical cues must be both vivid and accurate, in terms of your judgments of the intent of the literature. If the listener lacks sufficient direction from the reader's cues, he cannot be expected to become involved, as intended, in the literary experience being communicated. If the reader's cues are confused, it follows that the listener's response will be confused. The function of the reader is to *assist* the listener. The better the assistance (the more vivid and accurate the vocal and physical suggestions), the better the response.

The word *suggestion* is considered by many to be the all-important qualifying term in the communicative act of oral interpretation. Many authorities would say that oral interpretation is the *art of suggestion.* This is another way of saying that the oral interpreter, in sharing a literary experience with a listener, has the function of *leading* the listener in the desired direction to the extent that the listener is then capable of completing the literary journey himself. The oral interpreter works *with* the listener rather than *for* the listener. The oral interpreter *suggests,* and as his suggestions are vivid and accurate, the listener will be able to *fulfill* those suggestions in his own mind. The oral interpreter would be leaving the realm of suggestion if his vocal and physical cues became so literal that the listener could witness the literary experience as though it were in front of him—on-stage. If, then, we are to talk in terms of reader function and listener function, we could summarize by saying that the function of the reader is to *suggest the potential* of the literary experience in such a way that the listener is better able to *fulfill the potential* of the literary experience in his own mind.

The question "How does one know when the oral interpreter has left the realm of suggestion?" cannot be answered easily in terms of specifics. An arbitrary line should not be drawn beyond which the interpreter cannot go, for too many differences exist between listeners' abilities to perceive and appreciate, and between readers' abilities to communicate. We need to remain flexible to allow for adjustments to reader and listener effectiveness. One listener, or one group of listeners, may require less assistance than another. One reader may be more responsive than another. Because of these individual differences, and because of justifiable differences in judgments of the intent of the literature, there is no single right way of communicating any single piece of literature. Even if these differences did not exist, we would still recognize the merit of difference due to the personality differences of readers. Nevertheless, we can answer the original question by means of an important, and significant, generalization. *When the vocal and physical responsiveness of the oral interpreter usurps the function of the listener (to fulfill the potential of the literary experience in his own mind), the oral interpreter has gone beyond the realm of suggestion.*

The listener response is favorable when it reflects and fulfills the suggestions (judgments) of the interpreter. Effectiveness of the communicative act is evaluated on the basis of listener response. When a listener becomes involved in a literary experience as the reader intended him to become involved, the communicative act has been effective. When a listener fails to respond in this way, the fault rests with one or more of the following: ineffective listening, ineffective and/or insufficient cues from the reader, and literature inappropriate to either the listener, the reader, or to oral interpretation. Methods of evaluating listener response are discussed in another chapter of this book.

The interpreter's judgments are dependent on a study of the intent of the literature. Your first obligation is to discover the intent of the literature through a close examination of the *text of the work*. The *writer's* intent, insofar as it can be determined, is a supplementary aid to the examination of the text. Sometimes you cannot be sure of the writer's intent, but you must be confident, during the communicative act, of your judgments of the intent based on a close examination of the work. Discussion following the communicative act may reveal meanings not previously grasped and, as a result, your post-discussion reading may be improved. However, as previously stated, if you are confused during the communicative act you will communicate this uncertainty to a sensitive listener. Also, it is to be recognized that different readers' judgments of the intent of the literature will frequently vary in terms of shades of emphasis. This is to be expected. The individuality of the reader should not be denied. *The personality of the reader should be a unique and important part of each reading.* Nevertheless, you should *always* be able to justify your judgments in terms of your research on the literature, the writer, and, when possible, the critical reviews of the literature and the writer.

II. THE LINEAR STIMULUS-RESPONSE PATTERN

Effective imaginative listening is the first obligation of the listener. This responsibility is dependent on listening skill and, in large part, on the ability of the oral interpreter to stimulate the listener. In turn, the ability of the interpreter to stimulate is dependent, in large part, on his understanding and appreciation of the literature *and* on his skill in suggesting this understanding and appreciation. The literature, therefore, remains the stimulus *source* for both oral interpreter and listener. In the case of the interpreter, the literature is the *direct* stimulus source. In the case of the listener, the literature is the *indirect* stimulus source because it is channeled through the oral interpreter. This stimulus-response pattern may be clarified by a diagram.

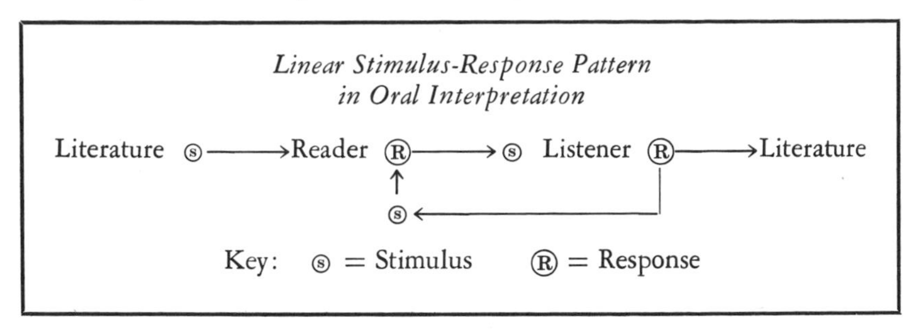

It is important to remember that the immediate goal of the communicative act is a union of literature, reader and listener. You, the reader, are the middleman in this process, bringing the listener and the literature together.

The pattern diagrammed in the model above suggests the following. The literature (S) is the stimulus source. In turn you, the interpreter, respond. Your response (R) is in the form of vocal and physical cues. These responses become the stimuli (S) for the listener who, in turn, responds (R) (emotionally, intellectually, esthetically) to the literature. The listener response to the literature also serves as an additional stimulus to the reader. It is the basis for on-the-spot adjustments (feedback) by the reader. The linear process is complete as the goal acquisition—the union of literature, reader, and listener—has been achieved.

It is particularly important that the listener become primarily involved with the literature rather than with the reader. The reader, as a dynamic means to an end, is secondary to the literature. The spotlight is on the literature, as a result of the reader's suggestions. If the reader becomes more attractive than the literature (and the listener response goes to the reader as a performer rather than to the literature), the linear response has been interrupted and the communicative act of *oral interpretation* has failed.

III. COMMUNICATIVE ACT MODELS

Although the linear stimulus-response pattern provides a frame of reference for understanding the communicative act of oral interpretation, there are additional parts and relationships which need to be considered. The following graphic model further defines and refines these parts and relationships. Study it carefully to locate notions already expressed and, more importantly, to discover ideas not yet mentioned. Having studied the diagram in detail, compare your findings with those in the discussion which follows.

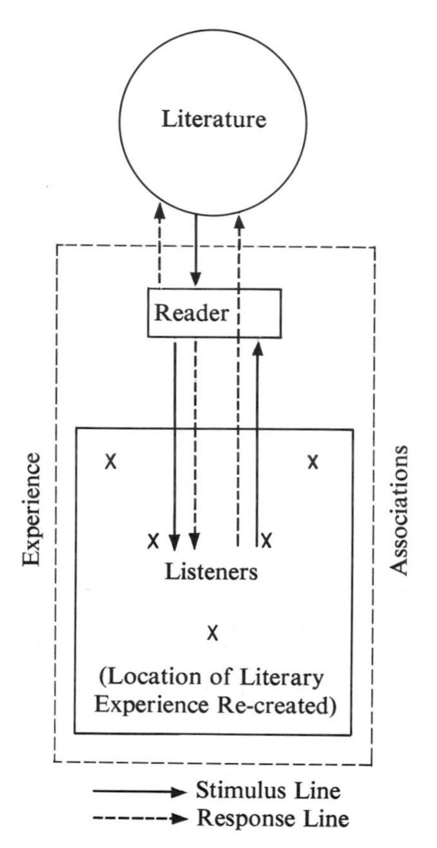

Graphic Model of
The Communicative Act of Oral Interpretation

In looking at the graphic model, it can be seen at a glance that oral interpretation includes three separate entities, each dependent on the other. The circle represents the particular piece of literature being read, the rectangle represents the communicator (reader), and the Xs represent the communicatees (listeners).

It is also obvious that the communicative act can be diagrammed in terms of stimulus-response lines representing the processes (dynamics) of the communicative act and their relationships. These lines indicate that the literature stimulates the reader and that the reader responds to the literature. This relationship should be regarded (1) as prerequisite to the reader's communicating with the listener *and* (2) as a *continuing* process while reading to the listener.

In following the lines going from the reader to the listeners, it can be seen that the reader stimulates the listener and that the reader responds to the listener. This response, on the part of the reader, is called *feedback* and is recognized as an important adjustment factor in the behavior of all communicators.

In following the lines leading from the listener we note that the listener stimulates the interpreter and, most important, that the listener responds to the literature *through the interpreter.* Note that this response line does not end with the reader nor does it circumvent the reader. It goes through the reader to the literature. We have stressed that listener involvement must be with the literature and, at the same time, we recognize that this involvement is aided and directed by the vocal and physical suggestions of the interpreter.

The Xs in the diagram represent the realm of the audience. This area is boxed and identified as the location of the literary experience re-created. This represents the notion previously discussed that the function of the listener in oral interpretation is to *fulfill* the potential of the literary experience in his own mind. A listener cannot sit back and witness a literary experience in front of him, as if he were in the theatre responding to actors. He must listen *imaginatively,* catching cues from the reader, so that he can re-create the experience by fulfilling it in his own mind.

A final concept is suggested by the broken-line box surrounding the reader and the listeners. This area is identified by the words *experiences* and *associations.* Human behavior is dependent, in large part, on past experiences and associations. Readers and listeners will differ in degree because of their individual and varying experiences and associations. It should therefore be noted that the reader's response to the literature and his communication of that response is governed, in part, by his own experiences and associations. Likewise, it should be noted that the listener's response to the literature through the reader's suggestions is also governed, in part, by his own experiences and associations.

Particular attention needs to be given to the location of the reader in the graphic model. This location is significant for at least four reasons. (1) The location identifies the reader as the middle man (the expressive agent, the dynamic means to an end) between literature and listener. (2) The location, apart from the literature and the listeners, implies

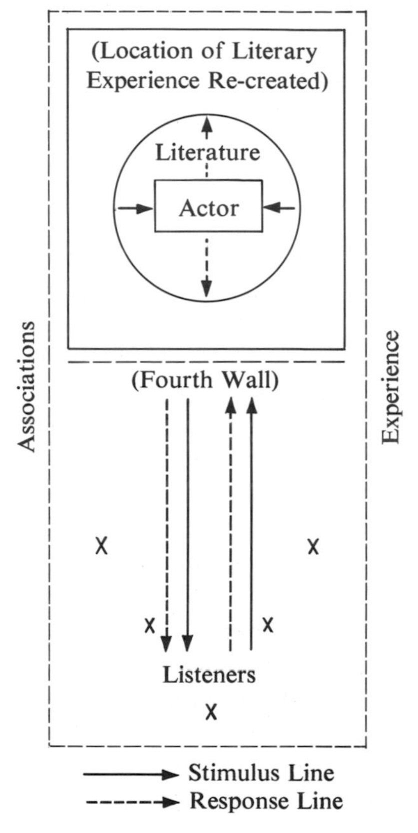

Graphic Model of
The Communicative Act of Acting

that the reader in oral interpretation retains his own identity. (3) The reader location also suggests a degree of "artistic detachment" from the literature. Although the stimulus-response lines reveal the ongoing process of empathy, the reader functions as a controlled observer. (4) The reader's communicated suggestions, represented by a stimulus line, are focused directly into the realm of the audience. The pertinence of these reasons may be more apparent when the location of the communicator in oral interpretation is contrasted with the location of the communicator in the communicative act of acting.

Many students understand the role of the public speaker and the role of the actor better than that of the oral interpreter. This is probably true because they have played these roles and have seen these roles played more frequently. The role of the public speaker is rarely confused with the role of the oral interpreter—although there are some similarities. The role of the actor, however, is frequently confused with that of the oral interpreter. Although there are some similarities, there are also some basic differences which have been discussed many times by many writers. Nevertheless, the beginning student needs to have these similarities and differences clarified.

The graphic model of the communicative act of acting represents the traditional proscenium arch type of production. Study it carefully. Compare and contrast it with the graphic model for oral interpretation. Perhaps the following statements and questions will assist you.

(1) Each model includes literature, listener, and communicator. In one model the communicator is called an actor and in the other he is called a reader.

(2) Each model includes stimulus-response patterns between the communicator and the literature.

(3) Each model identifies the location of the literary experience re-created. In one model the location is in the realm of the audience and in the other the location is on-stage. Why?

(4) Does this difference of location of the literary experience re-created suggest a difference in listener function? If so, which listener has the primary function of *witnessing* and which listener has the primary function of actively participating in *re-creating* (fulfilling) the literary experience?

(5) Why does one model locate the communicator within the circle representing literature while the other locates the communicator outside the circle? Does this suggest a difference between the roles being played by these two communicators?

(6) Which communicator says that he is *not* the source of the literary experience and which communicator wants the listener to believe in him as the source? Is this another reason for the different locations of the oral interpreter and the actor?

(7) What principle is contrasted by the suggestion of a fourth wall in one graphic model and the absence of this suggestion in the other graphic model? Does this refer to a difference in focus between the oral interpreter and the actor? What are the implications in this difference? Does this suggest a difference in the environment of the two communicators, in terms of communicator-audience relationship?

(8) Which communicator is primarily concerned with *fulfilling* the potential of the literary experience and which with *suggesting* the potential? What aspects of the diagram suggest this difference?

(9) Why does the broken-line box suggesting *experiences* and *associations* completely surround one model and only partially surround the other? Is it because literature is static until activated by an individual? Is this true because meanings reside in people rather than in words?

If the graphic models of the communicative acts of oral interpretation and acting have helped to clarify and contrast the processes and relationships involved, you are now in a position to arrive at several more ideas. It should be realized, for example, that the oral interpreter *never* assumes the source—as does the actor. The interpreter retains his own identity. He says to his listeners, "I am *not* the source of this literary experience. The literature is the source. I am myself—suggesting what *I* believe to be the intent of the literature. As a matter of fact, the manuscript which I hold is not only a stimulus aid, it is *symbolic* of the source." The actor says, "Believe in me as the source (the character). I will lose my identity in my attempt to 'become' somebody else. Identify me not as myself but as the character involved." Consequently, the actor locates himself *within* the literary experience (*assuming* the source) while the oral interpreter stands apart from it. The actor locates the literary experience in front of the listener (on-stage) for the listener to witness. The reader projects the literary experience into the realm of the audience for each listener to fulfill in his own mind imaginatively. The interpreter's focus, therefore, is always into the realm of the audience. There is no "fourth wall" to separate the oral interpreter from the listener.

In summary, it should be recognized that among the differences between the oral interpreter and the actor are matters of *function* (to suggest the potential versus fulfill), *attitude* (to communicate with versus for), *focus* (into the realm of the audience versus on-stage), *identity* (self versus "becoming" another), and *environment* (close association with listener versus apart from listener). Listeners differ in terms of function, with the listener in the oral interpretation situation primarily concerned with re-creating the suggested literary experience in his own mind, while the listener in the acting situation is primarily concerned with witnessing the literary experience re-created for him on-stage.

Likewise, it should be recognized that among the similarities between the oral interpreter and the actor are matters of making judgments concerning the intent of the literature, being obligated to stimulate the listener appropriately, and being motivated to make literature come alive and, thereby, contributing to a cultural impact.

IV. THE DYNAMICS OF THE STRUCTURE

The stimulus-response patterns suggest the dynamics of the communicative act. Without these ongoing interactions we have only a structure: a construct without dynamics.

The life blood of the communicative act of oral interpretation is dependent, in large part, on the ability of the reader and the listener to respond to the assumed intent of the stimulus *and* in the ability of the reader to be a controlled observer. These processes, these dynamics, will be identified and discussed as *empathy* and *aesthetic distance.*

Empathy

Empathy has been a useful term in the arts for many years. More recently it has been a concept of interest to the behavioral sciences—particularly psychology and psychiatry. The use of the term has become almost casual and, as a result, it has come to mean different things to different people. Among the "synonyms" which have become attached to it are identification, prediction, imitation, projection, sympathy and role playing. Some scholars have been predominantly concerned with the empathic process while others have concentrated on the empathic effect. Most have been concerned with empathy as an emotional process and effect (usually observable) but some have concentrated on the intellectual process and effect (primarily where an individual's ability to *predict* was the effect tested). Although these differences exist, there remains a common denominator. That common denominator, which is implicit in the Greek root of the word empathy, is *to feel into.* It is this "feeling into" which has been the focal point for theorists and researchers. It is this "feeling into" which has been an attractive concept to artists and social scientists alike. Its application to art creativity, to social interaction, to behavioral understanding, to personal growth, is apparent. Its importance to the communicative act of oral interpretation is obvious. Nevertheless, its implementation is not automatic. H. A. Overstreet stated it this way: "Our everyday experience, in brief, testifies to the fact that empathy is one of our human potentials and it can go far toward saving man from psychic isolation. Also, however, our everyday experience and the desperate plight of our world, testify to the fact that empathic potential remains chiefly a potential. Those whom it has genuinely released from immature egocentricity into mature sociocentricity are rare among us. The arrested development of the imagination is, perhaps, the most common tragedy of our human existence."[1]

To "feel into" involves a causal stimulus-response relationship. We respond because we have been stimulated. We feel into (a response) because we have *allowed* rapport with something or somebody (a stimulus). It should be understood that in this discussion we are talking about empathy as a response which is favorable to the assumed intent of the stimulus. If we substitute the word empathy, in this context, in our definition of the communicative act of oral interpretation, we could say, "The communicative act of oral interpretation is the process of encouraging empathy between listener and literature by means of the vocal and physical suggestions of a reader."

Responses may be categorized as predominantly *intellectual* or predominantly *emotional.* The intellectual response is concerned with the receiving of information at an objective level. The emotional response

[1] H. A. Overstreet, *The Mature Mind* (New York: W. W. Norton and Co., Inc., 1949), pp. 65–66.

is concerned with the receiving of feelings and sensations at a subjective level. This dichotomy is obviously oversimplified and may even be misleading if we conclude that a response must be categorized as one or the other. One type of response is not necessarily devoid of the other type. Certainly it is possible to respond emotionally with some degree of objectivity. Likewise, it is possible for an intellectual response to be heightened through a degree of emotional involvement. Actually, the chances for effectiveness in communication are heightened by both possibilities. The reporting of information without conviction is, in some instances, as serious a fault as communicating feelings without some intellectual frame of reference.

In the communicative act of oral interpretation, literature is the stimulus source. As such it provides potential for intellectual power and emotional power. The effects of this power can be measured in terms of the understanding of the literature (the intellectual response) and in terms of the appreciation of the literature (the emotional response). It can be argued that one reinforces the other and, of course, there is such a thing as emotional understanding and intellectual appreciation. As we come to understand the literature, we may come to appreciate it. As we gain a sense of appreciation for a piece of literature, we may gain insight into its content or, at least, we may gain motivation for the study of its parts. On the other hand it needs to be recognized that it is possible to understand without appreciating, just as it is possible to appreciate without understanding. Nevertheless, the combined response (when favorable to the assumed intent of the stimulus) should prove more rewarding to the oral interpreter and to the listener.

It is well known that mere knowledge of an event differs from experiencing that event. It is one thing to know *about* the horrors of war. It is quite another thing to be a member of a fighting unit. In other words, experiencing an event means personal involvement. One of the functions of literature is to bridge the gap so that we know *about* something *through experiencing* it. The writer of prose, poetry, or drama selects events, ideas, emotions, people, etc., and selects and arranges his language so that the reader (and the listener) can become involved in the experience. It is this involvement, this feeling into, this experiencing (intellectually *and* emotionally) that we refer to as empathy.

Many authorities have indicated that an empathic response is an observable response. An individual can be observed crying in a movie. If it can be assumed that the tears were in response to the stimulus of the moment on the screen, the witness has observed an empathic effect of the process of empathy. The process was dependent on an intellectual and emotional response. Some degree of ordering (cortical control) gave way to personal involvement at the emotional level. The individual was thinking and feeling *into* the situation. The observable effect was tears. Another individual may be observed making a sudden move. He is witnessing a boxing match. The fighter has thrown a vicious left hook. The individual has moved with, or away from, the blow. His thinking and feeling into the situation have been observable. The muscular response (the empathic effect) has been evidence of his having empathized. It is probable that there is always a muscular effect in empathy, but it is not always as easy to observe as in the cases just cited.

Some psychologists have interpreted feeling into as thinking into. In these instances they have been concerned with the ability of one person to *predict* the thinking of another person. The situation might be structured in this way. Person A is given the opportunity to visit with a stranger, Person B, for a short period of time—perhaps twenty minutes. At the conclusion of the visit, Person B leaves. Person A is then asked to predict certain attitudes of Person B which were not discussed during their visit. The predictions of Person A are then checked with the actual attitudes of Person B. The extent to which A has been able to predict B is felt to be a measure of empathic response. A high level of accuracy would suggest that A was able to feel into (think into) B—to empathize with B. It is possible to argue, in this instance, that a low score does not necessarily mean an absence of empathy. It may be that one can *feel into* while in the presence of the stimulus without being able to project this state by means of prediction. Nevertheless, this technique for measuring empathic response, or ability to empathize, is an interesting one and worthy of consideration.

In oral interpretation, you must empathize with the literature. You need to feel into the literary experience you believe intended by the literature. As you are able to feel into, so should you be better motivated to communicate the literary experience. The effect of this process should be observable in your vocal and physical response. Reader responsiveness which lacks the motivation of empathizing may be mechanical. The mechanical response provides a less effective stimulus as a basis for listener empathy. It is important for you to remember that empathy must be an ongoing process—immediately prior to *and* continuing through the duration of the communicative act.

Aesthetic Distance

It was indicated at the beginning of this section that the ability of the oral interpreter to be a controlled observer would be identified and discussed as aesthetic distance. A number of references to the oral interpreter have already been made which, if recalled, will assist in understanding this point of view. The diagram of the communicative act of oral interpretation is one of these references. That diagram located the oral interpreter in an area between the literature and the listener. This location provided the point of departure for a number of implications and relationships. Among these were (1) the oral interpreter is the dynamic means to an end, (2) the oral interpreter maintains his own identity, and (3) the oral interpreter is the middleman. They, in total, indicate that the interpreter is an *observer* of the literary experience rather than a *representative* of the literary experience (as the actor is). Although the interpreter must empathize with the experience, he must also stand apart from it. This degree of "artistic detachment" is required of most artists. However, among the justifications for this detachment, some of the following are unique to the oral interpreter.

The oral interpreter must stand apart because he is required to comment (to editorialize) on the literary experience. He is expected to comment by revealing his rapport with the intent of the literature. As the interpreter reveals *his* rapport through his smiles, his frowns, his inflections, not only is he suggesting the intent of the literary experience—he is revealing his personal reaction to that intent. He is providing an additional aid to the listener: his personal reaction.

The oral interpreter must stand apart because he must keep *all* of the parts of the literary experience in proper perspective. Although the actor must keep his particular character in proper perspective, he is able to devote most of his energy to the single character he is portraying. The interpreter has the added obligation of keeping all characters, or all segments, in proper balance. He would do an injustice to the literature if he empathized with one segment to the extent that he lost sight of another segment.

The oral interpreter, as well as all other artists, must stand apart in order to maintain the *ability* to communicate the contrasts among ideas and emotions. When the interpreter empathizes to the point that he loses control of himself (and, consequently, loses the literary perspective), he has minimized control of his voice and body.

The oral interpreter must stand apart because he must not usurp the function of the listener. The interpreter communicates the empathic *effect* of the process of empathy. This communicated effect needs to stay in the realm of suggestion. The interpreter, therefore, needs to exercise control so that the effect does not become literal.

Perhaps an illustration will serve to clarify. Let us assume that the oral interpreter has arrived at an emotional peak in the literary experience he is interpreting. Let us also assume that empathic effects have been observable in his vocal and physical suggestions and that the listener response to the literary experience has been favorable. Suddenly the interpreter breaks into tears. He loses control. In so doing he has probably lost his ability to comment on the literature as an observer, he has probably lost his perspective of the parts of the literature, he has probably lost his ability (for the moment at least) to continue to communicate, and he has probably usurped the function of the listeners by doing for them what they should have *imagined* for themselves. Most significant, however, he has focused attention on himself rather than on the literature. It is quite possible that the listener has now become concerned with the interpreter's tears and the interpreter's loss of control rather than with the emotional impact of the literary experience itself. *The interpreter had empathized, but his degree of empathizing lacked aesthetic distance.* He had lost his ability to be a controlled observer.

V. CREATIVITY AND STYLE

Obviously, the effective oral interpreter is a creative person, with his own individual style, who gives life to the printed pages of literature by means of his imaginative power and his sensitive nature. He is at all times a lively and alert creator who takes a mass of printed symbols and gives them meaning.

Whether or not you give them more meaning and more significant relationships than the silent reader who reads to himself, depends upon your interpretative power as well as upon the personal preferences and reading skills and habits of the silent reader. If the oral interpreter is incapable of bringing out a fullness of meaning, then the good silent reader can probably do more on his own. Perhaps the silent reader has read so extensively and with such insight and depth that he can build into his reading all of those nuances, shadings of tone, and significance of relationships. If this is the case he may get more meaning by reading silently just as the rare reader of music can experience silently what most people can only get by hearing it.

Such ability on the part of the silent reader does not minimize the creative role of the oral reader. He is a creator whether all people require him or not; his status is permanent despite the variance in the needs or interests of an audience.

When you plan to read a literary selection aloud, you go through a number of stages before you arrive at the finished product or art form. First, of course, you read the material and decide whether or not it has certain values. Then you study and analyze it to discover the relationship of its ideas and emotions which are strengthened through imagery and other devices. Your imagination takes an active part in this process which will require patience, an awareness of the total idea, and the variations within it. This total process is not only intellectual, but emotional as well, for the rational mind alone is not enough. The rate at which this process is accomplished depends upon the individual, upon the complexity of the literature, and upon the background reading and study which the material demands. As these intellectual and emotional discoveries develop there will be an ever-increasing relationship between the literature and yourself. Gradually there is a fusion of these elements to such an extent that a oneness is achieved. The whole unifying process involves the study and analysis of the literature, rational and emotional insight, imagination, and the effective use of voice and body.

Your individual style as an interpreter emerges from this process, for style is the way a man expresses his thoughts and reveals his feelings. P. Emmons called it "the frame to hold our thoughts," while Amos

Bronson Alcott said that "a good style fits like a good costume." Your style, as a reader, will grow out of your basic philosophy, out of the way you think, and out of the kind of person you are. As Goethe said, the style of an author is usually a good copy of his mind. This is equally true of a reader. Your style will be unique because you yourself are a distinctive personality.

If, however, you are too conscious of creating an individual style you may easily become affected and this affectation will stand in the way of effective interpretation. Your style in reading will develop as you enrich your knowledge and deepen your insight. It will evolve as you become more adept in the use of your voice with its ranges in quality, pitch, inflection, tempo and intensity. But remember that any conscious use of these skills merely to call attention to your versatility or to you will, instead of developing or strengthening your style, actually destroy it and mark you as an exhibitionist instead of an artist. You must focus upon revealing the thought and feelings in the literature you are reading. When you step into the background and place the interpretation of the literature in the foreground, you are making a major step toward developing style.

There is another sense in which the word "style" may be used: namely, in relation to a specific writer. An author has his own style just as a reader has. Hugh Blair said that "Style has always some reference to an author's manner of thinking. It is a picture of the ideas which rise in his mind, and of the manner in which they rise there. . . ." For example, Tennyson, the Victorian poet, likes to moralize, is picturesque, uses imagery, and is clear and musical. His writing displays an ordered mind. Whitman, on the other hand, breaks tradition, expresses himself impulsively, uses vernacular speech, is optimistic and adventuresome, and has certain mystical qualities. Dorothy Parker, whether talking as herself or as one of her characters, has the terseness of twentieth century sophistication in her urbane character studies. Emily Dickinson was compact, selective, precise, and highly imaginative. Her strong images and metaphors are striking. James M. Barrie was interested in the world of make-believe and created characters as delicate as a silhoutte; Eugene O'Neill was interested in probing into the psychological depths of his characters in a realistic manner.

So you can see that each author has some distinctive quality or qualities that set him apart from other writers. The author's style as it is reflected in the manuscript is your guide in reading, and your reading should reflect this style, an achievement which will grow only out of your complete understanding and assimilation of the manuscript. You must grasp and convey the meaning of the literature to your audience and when you do this effectively you will maintain the necessary unity between yourself and the literary experience. Your reading will then reflect the "intended" style.

STUDY QUESTIONS

1. John Dolman, Jr., in his book *The Art of Reading Aloud* (New York: Harper and Brothers, 1956) includes two diagrams and a discussion contrasting oral interpretation and acting on pages 28 and 29. Relate these diagrams to the graphic models in this book. What is the additional idea represented in Dolman's diagrams?

2. A. Craig Baird and Franklin H. Knower include a model and a discussion of speech behavior on pages 9 and 10 of their book *General Speech* (New York: McGraw-Hill, 3rd ed., 1963). What additional ideas are suggested in this model? How might these ideas be applicable to the models in this chapter?

3. If you were to make a list of similarities and differences between the communicative acts of oral interpretation and acting (on the basis of the two models in this chapter), what would be included?

4. List the differences between the communicative acts of oral interpretation and public speaking. In what instances is the oral interpreter more like the public speaker than the actor?

5. What are the major differences between oral interpretation today and oral interpretation during various periods in the past as discussed in Chapter I?

BIBLIOGRAPHY

Barnlund, Dean C., "Toward a Meaning Centered Philosophy of Communication." *Journal of Communications,* 1962, 12, p. 211.

Berlo, David K., *The Process of Communication.* New York: Holt, Rinehart and Winston, 1960.

Fearing, Franklin, "Toward a Psychological Theory of Human Communication." *Journal of Person.*, 1952, 22, pp. 71–88.

Ghiselin, Brewster, Ed., *The Creative Process.* New York: Mentor Books, 1955.

Schramm, Wilbur, *The Science of Human Communication.* New York: Basic Books, Inc., 1963.

Whitehead, Alfred North, *The Aims of Education and Other Essays.* New York: Mentor Book, 1949.

Part Two

Your Literature and You

Chapter III

Four Prerequisites

In the art of oral interpretation there are certain indispensable elements which will help you in the preparation and presentation of your material. First, you must learn to focus your attention on what you are doing. This focusing of attention will assist you in becoming involved in the experience of the literature. Second, your involvement will lead to understanding: intellectual as well as emotional. Third, your imagination, stimulated through involvement, will empower you to see beyond the words on the page and to go into the realm of the literary experience. Fourth, transference or recall will enable you to bring past experiences and emotions to bear upon the literature you are interpreting, and will help you give added depth of understanding and feeling to the material. In this chapter you will find a discussion of these four prerequisites and how they apply to the art of oral interpretation.

I. FOCUSING ATTENTION

Focusing attention is essential to any creative activity. It is the bringing of one's whole intellectual and emotional process to bear upon an idea or an object. The oral interpreter, when he focuses his attention on an idea, takes the first step in the creative process.

When you are interested in something, you usually give it your attention with relative ease. You find that you can concentrate on it because it demands your attention in some way; either because it is repugnant or because it is pleasant to you. If it is a picture you might like its colors, composition, figures, landscape, mood, or the story it tells.

Any one, or all, of these factors may be strong enough to interest you and thereby hold your attention. You may find yourself responding to sensory activity, such as strong movement, sounds, colors, sights, tastes, and odors, which in themselves are pleasant or unique enough to hold your attention. You must, however, remember that your attention span is neither constant nor consistent. Actually it is not a long and continued process, for one tends to concentrate only for short periods at a time. As space learning is preferable to mass learning (several periods versus one long period), so is space involvement to be preferred during preparation.

This renewal of interest in a piece of literature depends upon the possibilities of development and growth inherent within it. As it grows and presents new facets, you will find that you are intrigued and want to look for other possibilities in it. You will be drawn back to it repeatedly in a succession of adventures to see where the path will lead you. Each new meaning you discover will give you a sense of pleasure and accomplishment, which will serve as a stimulus for further adventure. Each time that you come back to the material you will find that you have a greater understanding of it. This process ultimately leads to your control over the literary experience and to improved confidence in reading it aloud.

Also, you will find that your desire to *share* the literary experience with a listener serves as an aid to sharpen your attention as well as the attention of your listener. Your desire to share carries with it several cautions. Do not rush *into* a reading or rush *while* you are reading. After you have the material in your hands or on the reading stand, do not feel that you must start at once. Take time to bring your mind to your material, to the ideas you wish to share. In other words, do not start to read until your mind is focused upon your material with clarity and assurance. Then you are ready to share with your listeners an experience that you are having while you read. While you are reading take as much time as you need to convey the material as a living experience. You will not be able to grasp certain reflective or contemplative literature, or to convey its meaning, if you do not let time come to your aid.

When you read the following selections focus on two things: first, the intellectual and emotional content of the literature, and secondly, allow sufficient time for the involvement of yourself and your listener.

"Rain In The Wheat"*

by J. Clark Weaver

The shower had come suddenly voice with thunder,
And we had fled triumphant to the barn.
I remember how we sat,
Sprawled wet upon the hay,
Comparing luck and talk of work in wheat.
We cursed the man who paid our fare
And told us toil like this with bed and board was good.
We cursed. Our words of labor in the wheat
Beat loud against the roof that echoed harvest rain.

Then quietly we sat
With hands upon the silences
That creep down after rain on roof
And smell of sudden wetness in the wheat.
We breathed in deep the reckless pungency
That made us glad for rest,
Until within our sight
The distances came forward in the sun,
And we went forth
With strength for harvest wheat again.

"The Cottager To Her Infant"†

by Dorothy Wordsworth

The days are cold, the nights are long,
The North wind sings a doleful song;
Then hush again upon my breast;
All merry things are now at rest,
Save thee, my pretty love!

* Published by permission of the author.

† Chosen and classified by Kate Douglas Wiggin and Nora Archibald Smith, *The Posy Ring* (New York: McClure, Phillips & Co., 1903), p. 230.

The kitten sleeps upon the hearth;
The crickets long have ceased their mirth;
There's nothing stirring in the house
Save one *wee,* hungry, nibbling mouse,
Then why so busy thou?

Nay! start not at that sparkling light;
'Tis but the moon that shines so bright
On the window-pane bedropped with rain:
There, little darling! sleep again,
And wake when it is day.

Our revels now are ended. These our actors,
As I foretold you, were all spirits, and
Are melted into air, into thin air.
And, like the baseless fabric of this vision,
The cloud-capped towers, the gorgeous palaces,
The solemn temples, the great globe itself—
Yea, all which it inherit—shall dissolve
And, like this insubstantial pageant faded,
Leave not a rack behind. We are such stuff
As dreams are made on, and our little life
Is rounded with a sleep.

(*The Tempest,* Act IV, Sc i)

II. UNDERSTANDING

The relation of understanding to reading aloud has been stressed for centuries. The ancient Roman educator, Quintilian, regarded understanding as the foundation of good reading. The Old Testament relates understanding to wisdom: "a man of understanding hath wisdom" (Prov. 10:23). It was recommended as a great help to man, even to being "a well-spring of life to him that hath it." (Prov. 16:22). Centuries later Sir Thomas Elyot related understanding to perception and said that it is ". . . the principall parte of the soule. . . . ,"[1] and Robert Burton spelled it out as "a power of the soule, by which we perceive, know, remember, and judge . . ."[2] Perhaps one of the definitions which describes it most clearly is that which likens understanding to the fingers of the mind by which a number of ideas are held in one grasp and drawn together more tightly into a "common idea or denomination."

A. *Thought*

Charles Wesley Emerson, founder of Emerson College, used as one of his guiding principles "trust in the power of thought." You will find this essential for two stages in working with literature. You must *think* as you study and analyze your material and you must think *while* you are reading the material aloud to your listeners.

John Ruskin, in his lecture, "Of Kings' Treasuries"[3] said, . . .

> When you come to a good book, you must ask yourself, "Am I inclined to work as an Australian miner would? Are my pickaxes and shovels in good order, and am I in good trim myself, my sleeves well up to the elbow, and my breath good, and my temper?" And, keeping the figure a little longer, even at the cost of tiresomeness, for it is a thoroughly useful one, the metal you are in search of being the author's mind or meaning, his words are as the rock which you have to crush and smelt in order to get at it. And your pickaxes are your own care, wit, and learning; your smelting-furnace is your thoughtful soul. Do not hope to get any good author's meaning without those tools and that fire; often you will need sharpest, finest chiselling and patientest fusing, before you can gather one grain of metal.

[1] *The Boke Named The Governour,* devised by Sir Thomas Elyot Knight (London: Paul, Trench, and Co., 1883), II, 369.

[2] Robert Burton, Democritus Junior (pseudo), *The Anatomy of Melancholy* (New York: A. C. Armstrong & Son, 1880), Section I, Member II, Subsection X, p. 219.

[3] John Ruskin, *Sesame and Lilies* (New York: John Wiley & Sons, 1883), pp. 19–21.

> And, therefore, first of all, I tell you earnestly, and authoritatively, (I *know* I am right in this), you must get in the habit of looking intensely at words, and assuring yourself of their meaning, syllable by syllable—nay, letter by letter . . . if you read ten pages of a good book letter by letter,—that is to say, with real accuracy,—you are for evermore in some measure an educated person. The entire difference between education and non-education (as regards the merely intellectual part of it), consists in this accuracy.

Alexander Melville Bell said that a reader should proceed "thought by thought" as he reads aloud. If he reads mechanically, without thought, he could only be "likened to the chatter of a parrot." So, as an oral interpreter, cultivate your ability *to think* both in your preparation *and* while you are in the process of reading, for it will give rich dividends to both you and your listener.

B. *Emotion*

Just as thought is essential to understanding in oral interpretation, so is emotion. The emotional response which you have to your material brings life, spirit and feeling to the literary experience. DeQuincey said that literature is of two kinds, literature of knowledge and literature of power. He indicated that the purpose of the former was "to teach" and that of the latter was "to move." This is a useful distinction in many instances, but very often the literature that teaches may have the power to move as well. The distinguishing feature of literature of power is its emotional strength. The oral interpreter must curb the tendency to add dimensions not intended. Let the literature dictate the emotion! A study of the manuscript itself will tell you, directly or indirectly, what feelings or emotions are involved. The literature may reveal itself directly, as is the case in the following excerpt from Longfellow's "The Day is Done,"[4] which reveals the emotion of sadness:

> The day is done, and the darkness
> Falls from the wings of Night,

[4] *The Best Loved Poems of the American People,* selected by Hazel Felleman (Garden City: Garden City Pub. Co., Inc., 1936), p. 115.

As a feather is wafted downward
From an eagle in his flight.

I see the lights of the village
Gleam through the rain and the mist:
And a feeling of sadness comes o'er me
That my soul cannot resist:

A feeling of sadness and longing,
That is not akin to pain,
And resembles sorrow only
As the mist resembles the rain.

Or, the poem may reveal happiness, as in Walt Whitman's short poem "Joy, Shipmate, Joy!"[5]

Joy, shipmate, joy!
(Pleas'd to my soul at death I cry)
Our life is closed, our life begins,
The long, long anchorage we leave,
The ship is clear at last, she leaps!
She swiftly courses from the shore,
Joy, shipmate, joy.

If the literature presents the emotion indirectly it may describe the feelings of a character in such a way that you know how the character feels, although the literature does not actually name the emotions involved, as in the ballad of "The Wife of Usher's Well."[6]

There lived a wife at Usher's Well,
And a wealthy wife was she;
She had three stout and stalwart sons,
And sent them oer the sea.

They hadna been a week from her,
A week but barely ane,

[5] *The Poetry and Prose of Walt Whitman,* edited by Louis Untermeyer (New York: Simon and Schuster, 1949), p. 444.

[6] *Reading Poems,* An Introduction to Critical Study, by Wright Thomas and Stuart Gerry Brown (New York: Oxford University Press, Inc., 1941), pp. 196–197.

Whan word came to the carlin wife
That her three sons were gane.

They hadna been a week from her,
A week but barely three,
Whan word came to the carlin wife
That her sons she'd never see.

'I wish the wind may never cease,
Nor fashes in the flood,
Till my three sons come hame to me,
In earthly flesh and blood.'

It fell about the Martinmass,
When nights are lang and mirk,
The carlin wife's three sons came hame,
And their hats were o the birk.

It neither grew in syke nor ditch,
Nor yet in ony sheugh;
But at the gates o Paradise,
That birk grew fair eneugh.

* * *

'Blow up the fire, my maidens,
Bring water from the well;
For a' my house shall feast this night,
Since my three sons are well.'

And she has made to them a bed,
She's made it large and wide,
And she's taen her mantle her about,
Sat down at the bed-side.

* * *

Up then crew the red, red cock,
And up and crew the gray;
The eldest to the youngest said,
'Tis time we were away.

The cock he hadna crawd but once,
And clappd his wings at a',

When the youngest to the eldest said,
    Brother, we must awa.

The cock doth craw, the day doth daw;
    The channerin worm doth chide;
Gin we be mist out o our place,
    A sair pain we maun bide.

'Fare ye weel, my mother dear!
    Fareweel to barn and byre!
And fare ye weel, the bonny lass
    That kindles my mother's fire!'

Anonymous

But whether direct or indirect, the emotional power is there for you to find. Naturally, where it is indirectly indicated it may take longer to discover but the search for it will be worth your time.

At this point, you may wonder whether or not you have emotional sensitivity to literature, and if not, what you can do about it. Alexander Melville Bell said you must "learn to feel; and to keep . . . [your] fine-strung organs of expressiveness in a state of delicate susceptibility."[7] This statement tells you what the result must be but it does not tell you how to arrive at it. In order for an emotion to be valid it must grow out of something and into something. It comes out of the idea in the literature and it must have its foundation in that idea. The emotion shared by the oral interpreter represents his judgment of the intent of the literature: his thoughtful response to the literary experience.

One of the most important means of getting the corresponding emotional response is through careful literary analysis. Careless analysis can set up tensions which will destroy subtlety and thereby impede communication. You, the reader, in order to conceal your lack of understanding will become tense and uncommunicative or you may tend to exaggerate. Tenseness and exaggeration destroy perspective so that reading becomes a gruelling reality instead of a sensitive suggestion. Sometimes when you are told to give a selection more emotional response, more "feeling," you give a very strong pseudo-response which

[7] Alexander M. Bell, *The Principles of Elocution* (Salem: James P. Burbank, 1878), p. 113.

you think is what is desired. Excessive emotion, beyond the demands of the literature, is merely an outward display without any relation to the experience and, instead of helping to interpret a piece of literature, actually destroys its meaning.

Emotions have been classified in a number of ways. Wundt, the psychologist, favored three sets of feelings consisting of the pleasant and the unpleasant; tension and relaxation, or relief; and excitement and subdued feelings. Aaron Hill, in "An Essay on the Art of Acting," said there were ten emotions or "dramatic passions—Joy, Grief, Fear, Anger, Pity, Scorn, Hatred, Jealousy, Wonder, and Love"—and that all other emotions were related to or were merely degrees of these. In the literary material which follows in this chapter decide to which categories of emotion each of the selections belongs.

The James-Lange theory relates emotion to bodily action. Instead of regarding the bodily change as the result of the emotion the order was reversed so that the emotion was the result of the bodily change. James said,[8] "My theory . . . is that the bodily changes follow directly the perception of the exciting fact, and that our feeling of the same changes as they occur IS the emotion."

He then made an observation that is of particular significance to the oral interpreter. He said that if all of the bodily symptoms of an emotion were removed the emotion itself would disappear. Let us consider the relation of this in reading the following selection:

God's bread! It makes me mad.
Day, night, hour, tide, time, work, play,
Alone, in company, still my care hath been
To have her matched. And having now provided
A gentleman of noble parentage,
Of fair demesnes, youthful, and nobly trained,
Stuffed, as they say, with honourable parts,
Proportioned as one's thought would wish a man—
And then to have a wretched puling fool,
A whining mammet, in her fortune's tender,
To answer, "I'll not wed, I cannot love,
I am too young, I pray you, pardon me."

[8] William James, *The Principles of Psychology* (New York: Henry Holt and Company, 1890), II, 449.

But, an you will not wed, I'll pardon you.
Graze where you will, you shall not house with me.
Look to 't, think on 't, I do not use to jest.
Thursday is near. Lay hand on heart, advise.
An you be mine, I'll give you to my friend.
An you be not, hang, beg, starve, die in the streets,
For, by my soul, I'll ne'er acknowledge thee,
Nor what is mine shall never do thee good—
Trust to 't, bethink you, I'll not be forsworn.

(*Romeo and Juliet,* Act III, Sc v)

If you read the lines of the noble Capulet, quick-tempered, excited and angry father of Juliet, with poor posture and relaxed arms and body, you may find it difficult to express his rage. Instead, you may find your mind dull, your voice monotonous, and your tempo slow. You may have scarcely any emotional feeling at all. Now, try it again. This time, clench your fists, plant your feet firmly, have a good supply of breath and use abrupt movements. This bodily action may help evoke the rage of Capulet. If the James-Lange theory is applicable to your responsive nature, you may find that your second reading was better than your first. Even though your bodily response may be overdone at this stage you can gradually "tone it down."

Now read "A Lament" by Shelley,[9] the title of which gives the clue to the emotion involved.

O world! O life! O time!
On whose last steps I climb,
Trembling at that where I had stood before;
When will return the glory of your prime?
No more—Oh, never more!

Out of the day and night
A joy has taken flight;
Fresh spring, and summer, and winter hoar,
Move my faint heart with grief, but with delight
No more—Oh, never more!

[9] *The Atlantic Book of British and American Poetry,* edited by Dame Edith Sitwell (Boston: Little, Brown and Company: Toronto, 1958), p. 616.

If on your first reading you stood in a formal, sedate manner, with your shoulders back and head up, the result may have been far from the intent of the literature. Now read it again, but instead of a militaristic stance, allow yourself to relax, droop your shoulders slightly, and you may find it much easier to sink into the dejection suggested within the poem.

Thus you will see that if the "bodily symptoms," as James calls them, are removed, the emotion which you wish to experience and convey will develop much more slowly, if at all. If you allow your body to respond freely to the emotions the literature suggests, it will help encourage emotional response.

Your emotional response must be guided by the best available judgments (yours included) concerning the intent of the literary experience. Again—let the literature dictate the response. Test yourself with the following excerpt. Is it an overwhelming, violent jealousy, such as Othello felt when he murdered Desdemona, or is it a "feline" jealousy which grows out of rivalry in love, such as Hermia experiences when she turns on her erstwhile friend and now rival?

Hermia: O me! you juggler! you canker blossom!
You thief of love! What, have you come by night
And stolen my love's heart from him?
Helena: Fine, i' faith!
Have you no modesty, no maiden shame,
No touch of bashfulness? What, will you tear
Impatient answers from my gentle tongue?
Fie, fie! You counterfeit, you puppet you!
Hermia: Puppet? Why so! Ay, that way goes the game.
Now I perceive that she hath made compare
Between our statures; she hath urged her height,
And with her personage, her tall personage,
Her height, forsooth, she hath prevail'd with him.
And are you grown so high in his esteem
Because I am so dwarfish and so low?
How low am I, thou painted maypole? Speak!
How low am I? I am not yet so low
But that my nails can reach unto thine eyes.

(*A Midsummer Night's Dream,* Act III, Sc ii)

In attempting to get an emotional response, avoid giving a "powerful exhibition of precocious hot-house passion." Hiram Corson sums it up when he says that reading must lose all "strain of expression."[10] But, on the other hand, you must remember too that "a man whose blood/ Is very snow-broth; one who never feels/The wanton stings and motions of the sense,"[11] will not make a good reader. You, the reader, must indeed avoid the strain of expression. You must also avoid trying to be a literal representation of reality. Oral interpretation is the art of suggestion. In this way, it can be more real in its abstraction than the visual object we are accustomed to call reality.

III. IMAGINATION

Imagination in the arts, as in living, is indispensable. John Keats said, "I am certain of nothing but of the holiness of the Heart's affections and the truth of Imagination. . . ."[12] Great creative minds have very fertile imaginations; they can be carried into realms of a rich and fanciful world with ease, as is Mercutio in his famous speech, which begins,

> O then, I see Queen Mab hath been with you.
> She is the fairies' midwife, and she comes
> In shape no bigger than an agate stone
> On the forefinger of an alderman,
> Drawn with a team of little atomies
> Athwart men's noses as they lie asleep—
>
> (*Romeo and Juliet,* Act I, Sc iv)

Theseus, in *A Midsummer Night's Dream,* observed that the lunatic, lover, and poet had similar imaginative qualities. Of the poet he said,

[10] Hiram Corson, *The Voice and Spiritual Education* (New York: The Macmillan Co., 1903), p. 96.

[11] William Shakespeare, *Measure for Measure,* Act I, Sc iv.

[12] The Letters of John Keats, ed. by Maurice B. Forman (Great Britain: Oxford University Press, 1935), Letter to Benjamin Bailey, Saturday, 22 Nov. 1817, p. 67.

The poet's eye, in a fine frenzy rolling,
Doth glance from heaven to earth, from earth to heaven,
And as imagination bodies forth
The forms of things unknown, the poet's pen
Turns them to shapes, and gives to airy nothing
A local habitation and a name.
Such tricks hath strong imagination
That if it would but apprehend some joy,
It comprehends some bringer of that joy;
Or in the night, imagining some fear,
How easy is a bush supposed a bear!

(*A Midsummer Night's Dream,* Act V, Sc i)

But not everyone is so richly endowed, as Macaulay observed when he described the imagination of the poet, John Dryden, in these words: "His imagination resembled the ways of an ostrich. It enabled him to run, though not to soar."

While few will attain the imaginative richness of Shakespeare, it is equally true that the imagination can be developed.

In oral interpretation you must enter other worlds: literary-worlds which the oral interpreter shares as listener-worlds. It is the power of imagination that enables one to perceive the impossible and to make it seem possible. This is what Shakespeare did in *A Midsummer Night's Dream,* when he peopled the forest with imaginative creatures; it is what Barrie did in creating the fantastic Peter Pan; and it is what Kenneth Grahame did in *The Wind in the Willows,* where Mr. Toad and his comrades assume remarkably human characteristics. It is this same gift that enables an author to mold one character from many characters he has known and to take an event, or a series of events, and develop a piece of literature of breadth and scope with a universal quality in it.

Just as the writer himself may draw from many sources to form his ideas, his setting, or his characters, you, as the interpreter, will draw upon ideas, characters, settings, and situations within your realm of experience. You fuse the known with the unknown through the activity of your imagination.

IV. RECALL AND TRANSFERENCE

Sometimes when you study the material you plan to read aloud you may be confronted with an emotion that is difficult for you to understand, or you may have trouble recalling an experience with a similar emotion. Therefore when you are faced with it in reading, you may be at a loss as to how to express such an emotion. Try to recall from your own primary experiences events that aroused similar emotions within you. The revival of these memories may help you transfer that past feeling that you once experienced to the present emotional situation. Probably you will recall an incident, a place, and a time when a particular event occurred which brought forth a certain emotional response within you. The memory of this emotion may be strong enough for you to transfer it to the present situation so that you can grasp, in a similar manner, the emotional significance of the present. The great actor, David Garrick, learned to express certain emotions by watching the repeated actions of a demented and grief-stricken father, distraught by the accidental death of his infant child. In the same manner a student who had witnessed a fatal accident recalled that situation and used it as a starting point in reading "The Stone" by W. W. Gibson:[13]

> "And will you cut a stone for him,
> To set above his head?
> And will you cut a stone for him—
> A stone for him?" she said.
>
> Three days before, a splintered rock
> Had struck her lover dead—
> Had struck him in the quarry dead,
> Where, careless of the warning call,
> He loitered, while the shot was fired—
> A lively stripling, brave and tall,
> And sure of all his heart desired . . .

[13] Wilfred Gibson, *Collected Poems 1905–1925* (London: The Macmillan Company, 1926), pp. 154–156.

A flash, a shock,
A rumbling fall . . .
And, broken 'neath the broken rock,
A lifeless heap, with face of clay,
And still as any stone he lay,
With eyes that saw the end of all.

I went to break the news to her:
And I could hear my own heart beat
With dread of what my lips might say;
But some poor fool had sped before;
And, flinging wide her father's door,
Had blurted out the news to her,
Had struck her lover dead for her,
Had struck the girl's heart dead in her,
Had struck life, lifeless, at a word,
And dropped it at her feet:
Then hurried on his witless way,
Scarce knowing she had heard.

And when I came, she stood alone—
A woman, turned to stone:
And, though no word at all she said,
I knew that all was known.

Because her heart was dead,
She did not sigh nor moan.
His mother wept:
She could not weep.
Her lover slept:
She could not sleep.
Three days, three nights,
She did not stir:
Three days, three nights,
Were one to her,
Who never closed her eyes
From sunset to sunrise,
From dawn to evenfall—

Her tearless, staring eyes,
That, seeing naught, saw all.

The fourth night when I came from work,
I found her at my door.
"And will you cut a stone for him?"
She said: and spoke no more:
But followed me, as I went in,
And sank upon a chair;
And fixed her grey eyes on my face,
With still, unseeing stare.
And, as she waited patiently,
I could not bear to feel
Those still, grey eyes that followed me,
Those eyes that plucked the heart from me,
Those eyes that sucked the breath from me
And curdled the warm blood in me,
Those eyes that cut me to the bone,
And pierced my marrow like cold steel.

And so I rose, and sought a stone;
And cut it, smooth and square:
And, as I worked, she sat and watched,
Beside me, in her chair.
Night after night, by candlelight,
I cut her lover's name:
Night after night, so still and white,
And like a ghost she came;
And sat beside me, in her chair,
And watched with eyes aflame.

She eyed each stroke,
And hardly stirred:
She never spoke
A single word:
And not a sound or murmur broke
The quiet, save the mallet-stroke.
With still eyes ever on my hands,

With eyes that seemed to burn my hands,
My wincing, overwearied hands,
She watched, with bloodless lips apart,
And silent, indrawn breath:
Death cut still deeper in her heart:
The two of us were chiselling,
Together, I and death.

And when at length the job was done,
And I had laid the mallet by,
As if, at last, her peace were won,
She breathed his name; and, with a sigh,
Passed slowly through the open door:
And never crossed my threshold more.

Next night I laboured late, alone,
To cut her name upon the stone.

In the following poem, "Morning in Spring," it may not be too difficult for you to recall and transfer to your reading this emotional response because you will probably remember a similar morning in your own life.

"Morning in Spring"

by Louis Ginsberg

One morning when I went downtown,
I felt such sunlight capsize down
That streets were glutted with more gold
Than all my heart could ever hold.
I thought a glory much like this
Must have been poured from Genesis.
I had not noticed until now
Such glittering of leaf and bough.
Not for a moment could I doubt
Telephone poles might start to sprout.
Brilliant gas stations, like bazaars,
Were jubilating with the cars.
The traffic in some triumph went
In pageant of astonishment.

And all the things in all the stores
Were like abundant metaphors.
More than the sun illumined sight;
More than the sun and more than light
Seeped on the avenue a wonder
That everything grew porous under.
Houses and people, trees and I
Replied to each, as earth to sky.
I felt all objects linked and set
As in a vast, transparent net;
I felt that everything was part
Of rapture answering my heart;
Until I knew, until I knew
I was the world I wandered through.

When you recall something that actually happened to you, you are recalling a primary experience. But there are also other ways you can call up an emotional experience. You may remember literature, movies, and plays you have seen, and draw from these certain memories which will be of help to you in understanding and experiencing a present situation in your reading. These *vicarious* experiences can sometimes be as strong as primary experiences. Therefore, when you read a passage which seems to arouse little response within you, recall the people, events, or objects you have encountered in literature and plays, and see if they can help you understand the emotional situation which confronts you. Transfer the memory of this earlier response, be it primary or vicarious, to the new situation and see if it will uncover feelings and attitudes which will help you comprehend the present emotion.

In preparing to read "Soliloquy of the Spanish Cloister," by Robert Browning, you may have difficulty in arousing a feeling of hatred. If this is the case, you might recall an excerpt from an essay, or excerpts from a play, which you have read, such as *Uncle Vanya* by Anton Chekhov where Uncle Vanya (Voitski) expresses his hatred for his brother-in-law, the Professor:

Voitsky: For twenty-five years I have been sitting here with my mother like a mole in a burrow. Our every thought and hope was yours and yours only. By day we talked with pride of you and your work, and spoke your name with veneration; our nights we wasted reading the books and papers which my soul now loathes.

. . .

We used to think of you as almost superhuman, but now the scales have fallen from my eyes and I see you as you are! You write on art without knowing anything about it. Those books of yours which I used to admire are not worth one copper kopeck. You are a hoax!

. . .

. . . You have wrecked my life. I have never lived. My best years have gone for nothing, have been ruined, thanks to you. You are my most bitter enemy!

(Chekhov, *Uncle Vanya,* Act III)

Thus you can go from that experienced in *Uncle Vanya,* to the unknown, in "Soliloquy of the Spanish Cloister" and transfer something of the feeling of one into the other:

Gr-r-r—there go, my heart's abhorrence!
Water your damned flower-pots, do!
If hate killed men, Brother Lawrence,
God's blood, would not mine kill you!
What? your myrtle-bush wants trimming?
Oh, that rose has prior claims—
Needs its leaden vase filled brimming?
Hell dry you up with its flames!

At the meal we sit together:
Salve tibi! I must hear
Wise talk of the kind of weather,
Sort of season, time of year:
Not a plenteous cork-crop; scarcely
Dare we hope oak-galls, I doubt;
What's the Latin name for "parsley"?
What's the Greek name for Swine's Snout?

Whew! We'll have our platter burnished,
Laid with care on our own shelf!

With a fire-new spoon we're furnished,
    And a goblet for ourself,
Rinsed like something sacrificial
    Ere 'tis fit to touch our chaps—
Marked with L for our initial.
    (He-he! There his lily snaps!)

Saint, forsooth! While brown Dolores
    Squats outside the Convent bank
With Sanchicha, telling stories,
    Steeping tresses in the tank,
Blue-black, lustrous, thick like horsehairs
    —Can't I see his dead eye glow,
Bright as 'twere a Barbary corsair's?
    (That is, if he'd let it show!)

When he finishes refection,
    Knife and fork he never lays
Cross-wise, to my recollection,
    As do I, in Jesu's praise.
I the Trinity illustrate,
    Drinking watered orange-pulp—
In three sips the Arian frustrate;
    While he drains his at one gulp.

Oh, those melons! If he's able
    We're to have a feast! so nice!
One goes to the Abbot's table,
    All of us get each a slice.
How go on your flowers? None double?
    Not one fruit-sort can you spy?
Strange!—And I, too, at such trouble
    Keep them close-nipped on the sly!

There's a great text in Galatians,
    Once you trip on it, entails
Twenty-nine distinct damnations,
    One sure, if another fails:
If I trip him just a-dying,
    Sure of heaven as sure can be,

Spin him round and send him flying
Off to hell, a Manichee?

Or, my scrofulous French novel
On gray paper with blunt type!
Simply glance at it, you grovel
Hand and foot in Belial's gripe;
If I double down its pages
At the woeful sixteenth print,
When he gathers his greengages,
Ope a sieve and slip it in 't?

Or, there's Satan!—one might venture
Pledge one's soul to him, yet leave
Such a flaw in the indenture
As he'd miss till, past retrieve,
Blasted lay that rose-acacia
We're so proud of! *Hy, Zy, Hine* . . .
'St., there's Vespers! *Plena grâtia,*
Ave, Virgo! Gr-r-r—you swine!

STUDY QUESTIONS

1. Can you compare your focus of attention in reading literature aloud with, for example, watching a football game?
2. In what activities do you find you have the most consistent and unbroken attention?
3. What is the psychological basis for the desire to "share" something, be it literature, a joke or good news?
4. Can you think of any literature in which "understanding" is not important?
5. Do you agree with Alexander Melville Bell's statement on the reading of poetry? Will it have any mechanical tendencies?
6. Can you think of any great literature which has knowledge alone for its purpose?
7. Do you think it is better to err on the side of too much emotion or too little emotion in reading aloud?
8. What do you think of Hill's classification of the emotions?

9. How do you compare the imaginative elements involved in "A Midsummer Night's Dream" and "As You Like It"?

10. Are recall and transference equally important in reading silently and in reading aloud?

11. Can you relate painting to literature through recall and transference?

BIBLIOGRAPHY

Boring, E. G., *A History of Experimental Psychology,* Second Edition. New York: Appleton-Century-Crofts, 1950.

Clark, S. H., *Interpretation of the Printed Page: Mental Technique of Speech* . . . revised by Maude May Babcock. New York: Prentice-Hall, Inc., 1940.

Cole, Toby, and Helen Krich Chinoy, *Actors on Acting.* New York: Crown Publishers, 1949.

Curry, S. S., *Imagination and Dramatic Instinct.* Boston: School of Expression, 1896.

Hilgard, Ernest R., *Introduction to Psychology.* New York: Harcourt, Brace and Co., 1962, also 2nd ed., 1957.

Hill, John, *Actor: or A Treatise on the Art of Playing.* London: 1755.

James, William, *The Principles of Psychology.* New York: H. Holt and Company, 1918.

Johnson, Gertrude, *Studies in the Art of Interpretation.* Selected, arranged and edited by Gertrude E. Johnson, New York, London: D. Appleton-Century Co., Inc., 1940.

Lange, Carl Georg, and William James, *The Emotions.* Baltimore: Williams and Wilkins Company, 1922.

Lessing, G. E., *Laocoön, An Essay on the Limits of Painting and Poetry.* Introduction and notes by Edward Allen McCormick, Indianapolis: Bobbs-Merrill, 1962.

Locke, John, *Human Understanding.* 1695.

Lowrey, Sara, and Gertrude E. Johnson, *Interpretative Reading.* New York: Appleton-Century-Crofts, Inc., 1953.

Reynolds, Sir Joshua, *Discourses on Art.* Ed. by Robert Wark, San Marino, Cal.: Huntington Library, 1959.

Richards, I. A., *Principles of Literary Criticism.* New York: Harcourt, Brace and Co., 1961.

Robinson, E. S., and F. E. Robinson, *Reading in General Psychology*. Chicago, Ill.: The University of Chicago Press, 1929.

Ruch, Floyd L., *Psychology and Life*. Chicago, New York: Scott, Foresman and Company, 5th Ed., 1941.

Woodworth, Robert Sessions, and Donald G. Marquis, *Psychology*. New York: H. Holt, 1947, 5th Ed.

Chapter IV

Vocal and Physical Responsiveness

Listeners are dependent on your vocal (verbal) and physical (nonverbal) responsiveness as cues for their involvement in the literary experience being read. What you *say* and *do* while reading aloud should serve to assist your listener in understanding and appreciating what you believe to be the intent of the literature. Even if your only listener is yourself, there is every reason to believe that your responsiveness while reading aloud allows for greater personal enrichment than might be gained through a silent reading only.

To devote a single chapter in a book on *oral* interpretation to vocal and physical responsiveness is, indeed, deceiving. In reality, all of oral interpretation is concerned with the *experiencing* of literature through reading aloud and listening. All steps in your preparation—selection of literature, literary analysis, audience analysis, oral analysis, rehearsal periods—are related to the effective communication of the literature. The end product is *oral* interpretation—not *silent* interpretation (although one certainly enhances the other). You will find, therefore, that all of the chapters in this book call attention to your responsiveness to literature and that the content of this chapter, although specific in focus, is related to all of the other chapters.

I. VOCAL RESPONSIVENESS

Communicating aloud, although universally practiced in human societies, is the most complex of all aspects of human behavior. In general, the communicative act is not so perceived. The notion that "anybody can communicate, it just comes naturally" is a gross overstatement and, in part, a falsehood. Oral communication is a *learned* behavior. It does not "just come naturally." It is a learned behavior involving numerous variables, each of which interacts with the other.

This chapter will focus on those variables related to the vocal and physical aspects of oral communication. Although we will deal with these properties in isolation it must be remembered that in practice they are not isolated. They are related—one complementing the other and all dependent on the context of the literature, the interpreter, and the occasion. In oral interpretation the voice and the body are your only means of suggesting the potential of the literary experience. It is therefore imperative that your mastery of each allow a responsiveness which is at all times appropriate to the intent of the literature.

A. *Resonance*

The basic quality or tone of voice that you use should be rich and resonant. There are certain parts of the body which serve to resonate the tone and which are called resonators: the pharynx, nasal cavities, mouth, and probably the trachea.

To achieve good resonance you should avoid undue bodily tension, especially in the throat. Keep the jaw relaxed and the tongue as flat as possible in the mouth. Resonance is also related to articulation and can be developed by the practice of certain sounds. For instance, you can read aloud selections with m, n, and ng sounds and with open vowel sounds, such as ah (father), o (home), and ow (town) to help increase your resonance. You can do this by chanting at first. Try to sustain especially the m, n, ng sounds. Good resonance comes more easily with pleasant emotions than with those which cause tension. Read aloud the following excerpts trying to bring out the resonant values just mentioned, and remember that relaxation and good articulation will help. Put your hand on your chest to feel the vibration. Concentrate upon "feeling" the sound rather than on trying to hear how you sound.

The ocean old,
Centuries old,
Strong as youth, and as uncontrolled,
Paces restless to and fro,

Up and down the sands of gold.
His beating heart is not at rest;
And far and wide,
With ceaseless flow,
His beard of snow
Heaves with the heaving of his breast: . . .

("The Launching of the Ship," by H. W. Longfellow)

Here, where the world is quiet,
Here, where all trouble seems
Dead winds' and spent waves' riot
In doubtful dreams of dreams;
I watch the green field growing
For reaping folk and sowing,
For harvest-time and mowing,
A sleepy world of streams.

("The Garden of Proserpine," by Algernon Charles Swinburne)

B. *Pitch*

An expressive voice is a "musical voice" in that a variety of *appropriate* tones can be heard. The tone heard is referred to as pitch and corresponds to a note on the musical scale. It can be measured through the frequency of sound waves: the greater the frequency, the higher the pitch. In general the pitch of the male voice is lower than that of the female voice. Few of us use our potential pitch range and tend, instead, to limit our pitch variety to only a few notes. This is less true in our everyday animated conversation, where we are less inhibited, than it is in those situations where we are suddenly conscious of the significance of the voice in communicating. As our inhibitions lessen, so does the possibility for variety in pitch increase.

We, of course, are not interested in variety in pitch for its own sake. Vocal gymnastics went out of style with the passing of the emphasis on exhibitionism during the elocutionary movement. We are interested in the *appropriateness* of the pitch to the idea and to the emotion being suggested. This is not to say that a particular pitch can be associated with a particular idea or emotion, but rather that as content varies so may changes in pitch help to clarify and heighten the content. We are interested in the contribution of pitch to the discovery of meaning. It is therefore essential that you become pitch conscious and that you regard variety in pitch as a *means* toward this end.

When we talk about *inflection,* we are talking about changes in pitch during the production of a tone. Voices devoid of inflection (a very rare occurrence) are referred to as monotones—one pitch voices. Although this singularity of pitch is rarely heard and certainly an undesirable characteristic in any voice, there is literature which seems to dictate its use as being appropriate. An example of this is in the following excerpt from "The Body of an American" by John Dos Passos. The opening paragraph reflects the boredom of a ritual too often performed by the speaker.

> Whereasthe Congressoftheunitedstates byaconcurrentresolutionadoptedon the4thdayofmarch lastauthorizedthe Secretaryofwar to cause to be brought to theunitedstatesthe body of an Americanwhowasamemberoftheamericanexpeditionaryforcesineurope wholosthislifeduringtheworldwarandwhoseidentityhasnotbeenestablished for burial inthememorialamphitheatreofthenationalcemeteryatarlingtonvirginia
>
> In the tarpaper morgue at Chalons-sur-Marne in the reek of chloride of lime and the dead, they picked out the pine box that held all that was left of
>
> enie menie minie moe plenty other pine boxes stacked up there containing what they'd scraped up of Richard Roe
>
> and other person or persons unknown. Only one can go. How did they pick John Doe?

For the most part, however, our understanding of literature dictates changes in pitch. These changes occur in a series of *steps* and *glides.* A step occurs when a word or a syllable ends at one pitch and the succeeding word or syllable begins at another. The command "Go Home!" would be spoken with a step if *home* were uttered at a lower and single pitch than *go* and a sudden break separated the two. If, however, a pitch change occurred during the utterance of the vowel in either word, the change would be called a glide: Go Hooome!, Goo Home!, Goo Hoome!. Traditionally, the rising inflection (upward glide) is used on the last syllable of a question and the falling inflection (downward glide) on the last syllable of a factual statement. (The notable exception being the American elementary student who substitutes the rising inflection for the falling in his factual answers. Question: "What is your name?" Answer: "Todd Randall?" Question: "Where were you born?" Answer: "Columbus?")

It is truly amazing to realize the contribution that changes in pitch can make to the clarification of the meaning we assign to a word or to a group of words. Although the step is abrupt and is limited to a single change in pitch, it is an effective vocal device and should be utilized when dictated by the intent of the literature. The inflectional glide allows much more flexibility in its utterance than does the step because within the glide the pitch range is not confined to two notes. Experiment with a word by assigning several meanings to it and then suggesting each meaning by sounding the word with an appropriate pitch change. For example, suggest how the pitch might change with the word *love* for each of the following meanings: a tender experience, a disgusting concept, a frightening relationship.

Demonstrate how many meanings you can suggest for the following words through inflectional glides: hello, goodby, yes, golden.

Demonstrate how many meanings you can suggest for the following groups of words through steps and glides: oh-oh, yes sir, why me, I think so, only tomorrow, if I must.

As previously stated, a change in pitch must be motivated by your understanding of the intent of the literature. The context of the word, or words, is all-important. Read the following excerpts aloud to discover the impact of inflection on communicating what you believe to be the intended meaning.

> But, Mistress, know yourself. Down on your knees
> and thank Heaven, fasting, for a good man's love. For I
> must tell you friendly in your ear,
> Sell when you can. You are not for all markets.
> Cry the man mercy, love him, take his offer.
> Foul is most foul, being foul to be a scoffer.
> So take her to thee, shepherd. Fare you well.
>
> (*As You Like It,* Act III, Sc v)

Ah, did you once see Shelley plain,
And did he stop and speak to you,
And did you speak to him again?
How strange it seems and new!

("Memorabilia," by Robert Browning)

Stand still, true poet that you are!
I know you; let me try and draw you.
Some night you'll fail us: when afar
You rise, remember one man saw you,
Knew you, and named a star!

("Popularity," by Robert Browning)

In the poem, "Up-Hill," by Christina Rossetti, there is a definite range in pitch in the question-and-answer structure the writer uses. Read it aloud, letting the questions motivate your inflections, and listen carefully to the meanings suggested.

"Up-Hill," by Christina Rossetti

Does the road wind uphill all the
way?
Yes to the very end.
Will the day's journey take the whole
long day?
From morn to night, my friend.
But is there for the night a resting
place?
A roof for when the slow dark
hours begin.
May not the darkness hide it from
my face?
You cannot miss that inn.
Shall I meet other wayfarers at
night?
Those who have gone before.

Then must I knock, or call when
just in sight?
They will not keep you standing
at that door.
Shall I find comfort, travel-sore and
weak?
Of labour you shall find the sum.
Will there be beds for me and all
who seek?
Yea, beds for all who come.

C. *Tempo*

Differences in tempo are one of the most subtle means of achieving variety in your reading. In all cases, remember that the meaning of the material is the primary determinant of rate.

Tempo, or rate, is sometimes classified as rapid, medium, and slow. In excitement or in suggesting quick movement the tempo may become more rapid, while in sadness, dignity, deep admiration, or seriousness a slow tempo may be effective. But here again, there may be exceptions. If your material suggests a slow tempo, this may be achieved (1) by pausing at the end of a sense unit, which also gives you a chance to take a breath and gives the impression of a slow tempo; (2) by sustaining the vowel sounds, the m, n, ng sounds and the l, y, w, and r sounds; and (3) by decreasing the number of words uttered within a given time period. Conversely, you may increase your tempo by less sustension of pauses and of the vowel sounds, and by articulating more words within a given time period.

Not only must tempo reflect the content, it must also allow time for you and for your listener to become involved. Light, humorous, easy-to-understand material can usually be read with a quicker tempo than can heavy, serious, thoughtful material. There will, of course, be exceptions. *In general, the more profound the content the slower the tempo.*

Read aloud the excerpts which follow and concentrate on the contrasts in tempo which are suggested by the content. Which excerpt would you read with a quickened tempo? Why? Which excerpt would require a slower tempo to allow adequate time for reader and listener involvement?

We sped like meteors through the sky,
When with its crackling sound the night
Is chequer'd with the northern light.

* * *

No, no! from out the forest prance
A trampling troop; I see them come!
In one vast squadron they advance!
I strove to cry—my lips were dumb.
The steeds rush on in plunging pride;
But where are they the reins to guide?
A thousand horse—and none to ride!
With flowing tail and flying mane,
Wide nostrils—never stretch'd by pain,
Mouths bloodless to the bit or rein,
And feet that iron never shod,
And flanks unscarr'd by spur or rod,
A thousand horse, the wild, the free,
Like waves that follow o'er the sea,
Came thickly thundering on,
As if our faint approach to meet;

(Byron, "Mazeppa," Parts XI and XVII)

Suddenly the waters around them slowly swelled in broad circles; then quickly unheaved, as if sideways sliding from a submerged berg of ice, swiftly rising to the surface. A low rumbling sound was heard; a subterraneous hum; and then all held their breaths; as bedraggled with trailing ropes, and harpoons, and lances, a vast form shot lengthwise, but obliquely from the sea. Shrouded in a thin drooping veil of mist, it hovered for a moment in the rainbowed air; and then fell swamping back into the deep. Crushed thirty feet upwards, the waters flashed for an instant like heaps of fountains, then brokenly sank in a shower of flakes, leaving the circling surface creamed like new milk round the marble trunk of the whale.

(Herman Melville, *Moby Dick,* Chapter CXXXV)

To begin at the beginning:

It is Spring, moonless night in the small town, starless and bible-black, the cobblestreets silent and the hunched, courters'-and-rabbits' wood limping invisible down to the sloeblack, slow, black, crowblack, fishingboat-bobbing sea. The houses are blind as moles (though moles see fine to-night in the snouting, velvet dingles) or blind as Captain Cat there in the muffled middle by the pump and the town clock, the shops in mourning, the Welfare Hall in widows' weeds. And all the people of the lulled and dumbfound town are sleeping now.

Hush, the babies are sleeping, the farmers, the fishers, the tradesmen and pensioners, cobbler, schoolteacher, postman and publican, the undertaker and the fancy woman, drunkard, dress-maker, preacher, policeman, the webfoot cocklewomen and the tidy wives. Young girls lie bedded soft or glide in their dreams, with rings and trousseaux, bridesmaided by glowworms down the aisles of the organplaying wood. The boys are dreaming wicked or of the bucking ranches of the night and the jollyrodgered sea. And the anthracite statues of the horses sleep in the fields, and the cows in the byres, and the dogs in the wetnosed yards; and the cats nap in the slant corners or lope sly, streaking and needling, on the one cloud of the roofs.

You can hear the dew falling, and the hushed town breathing.

Only *your* eyes are unclosed to see the black and folded town fast, and slow, asleep.

(Dylan Thomas, *Under Milk Wood*)

D. *Force, Loudness, Intensity*

Changes in force can be used to achieve highly emotional effects as well as subtle intellectual effects. The continuum of potential effects is enormous. Whether you choose a deliberate, step-by-step increase from a low to a high level of force or the opposite will, of course, depend on which technique is most worthy of the literature being read.

The following selections require varying degrees of force. Listen as you read them aloud. Be conscious of your emotional changes and how they are complemented by appropriate changes in force. If you doubt the function of force changes, read the excerpts with indifference and coldness. What do you hear? What was your level of involvement? Would your listeners have sensed the intent of the literature?

> When, therefore, O my countrymen! When will you exert your vigour? When roused by some event? When forced by some necessity?
> What then are we to think of our present condition? . . .
>
> (Demosthenes to the Athenians Against Philip)

"Sudden Light," by Dante Gabriel Rossetti

I have been here before,
But when or how I cannot tell:
I know the grass beyond the door,
The sweet keen smell,
The sighing sound, the lights around the shore.

You have been mine before,—
How long ago I may not know:
But just when at that swallow's soar
Your neck turned so,
Some veil did fall,—I knew it all of yore.

Has this been thus before?
And shall not thus time's eddying flight
Still with our lives our loves restore
In death's despite,
And day and night yield one delight once more?

> From Berlin, Rome, and Tokyo we have been described as a nation of weaklings—"playboys"—who would hire British soldiers, or Russian soldiers, or Chinese soldiers to do our fighting for us.
> Let them repeat that now!
> Let them tell that to General MacArthur and his men.
> Let them tell that to the sailors who today are hitting hard in the

far waters of the Pacific.
Let them tell that to the boys in the Flying Fortresses.
Let them tell that to the Marines!

(Franklin Delano Roosevelt, Speech, February 23, 1942)

Democracy is based upon the conviction that there are extraordinary possibilities in ordinary people.

(Harry Emerson Fosdick, *Democracy*)

Tybalt: What! drawn, and talk of Peace? I hate the word
As I hate hell, all Montagues, and thee.
Have at thee, coward!

(*Romeo and Juliet,* Act I, Sc i)

E. *Articulation*

For good articulation it is necessary to use the agents which help form sounds with a certain degree of precision. These agents of articulation are the jaw, lips, teeth, tongue, soft palate, and hard palate. As a reader you must keep your jaw relaxed, you must train your lips to help form many of your sounds, and you must develop a flexible tongue.

Here we are going to discuss some of the problems of articulation which students frequently encounter.

1. *The Flat a.* One of the most troublesome sounds in American speech is the so-called "flat a." This is the sound you find in such words as man, can, hat, fat, bat, land, banana, and piano. This sound is often given a nasal twang. To avoid this, this sound should be given with the soft palate lifted, the jaw relaxed, and the lips not drawn tightly to each side. Practice saying the following words and sentences so that you can produce them with good tone, avoiding a flat nasal quality.

band	aunt	cat
hand	Canada	can't
calendar	pan	slack

Ann has a handsome black hat in her hand.
Aunt Hattie can dance in an entrancing manner.

2. *The ĭ* (ɪ) *and ĕ sounds.* Frequently the ĭ sound is substituted for the ĕ, so that words like get, send, pen, men, lend, and many become git, sind, pin, min, lind, and miny. To make the ĕ vowel, as in *get,* the front of the tongue is lower than for the ĭ as in *pit.* When you say the following pairs of words, try to make a distinction between ĭ and ĕ.

sinned	send
pin	pen
ilk	elk
big	beg
bid	bed
rid	red
lid	led
hid	head

Send him a peck of pepper.

3. *The ow* (aʊ) *sound.* Another sound that is frequently misused is the diphthong ow as in "brown cow." Keep the lips somewhat rounded when you make this sound and do not let them be drawn back at the sides. The first part of this sound is not "a" as in "brat," but nearer "a" as in "father." When this flat "a" as in "brat" is used, the sound often becomes nasal.

how	plow
brow	loud
crowd	about
rowdy	round

The rowdy crowd plowed through the town and vowed to show its power.

4. *The oi sound.* In some localities the oi sound as in "boil" and the "er" sound as in "pearl" are exchanged, so that "boil" becomes "berl" and "pearl" becomes "poil." This should be corrected. Practice the following words and sentences.

royal	boil	curl	bird	murder
coil	toil	soil	shirt	burst
loin	void	heard	learn	first

Pearl joined the boys and girls.
First hoist the flag early on Thursday.
The boys work and toil to make olive oil.

5. *The ng sound.* There are two faults connected with the ng sound. Sometimes it is entirely omitted so that the reader says "goin' " instead of "going," "singin' " instead of "singing," and "lookin' " instead of "looking." To correct this one should omit the n and add the ng sound which is produced by lifting the back of the tongue to the soft palate, relaxing the soft palate, and then allowing the air to come out through the nasal passages.

The second fault is that of adding an explosive "g" sound after the "ng." In this case the word "going" becomes "going-g," "singing" becomes "sing-ging-g," and "looking" becomes "looking-g." In correcting this you must realize that the ng sound as in "sing" is a continuant sound which you can hold as long as you have enough breath. But, when you add the g sound to this, you are adding an explosive sound and can then no longer continue the original ng, thus the word erroneously ends as an explosive instead of as a continuant sound.

bring	thing	strong
song	morning	evening
ringer	singer	thinking

I am going singing and dancing this evening.

6. *The r sound.* When the r sound is made with the tongue drawn back and inverted, an unpleasant r sound is made. Therefore, do not allow the tongue to retract. Lift the tongue so that the sides touch the dental ridge and leave the tip open in the front of the mouth.

bird	paper	car
further	arm	girl
purse	river	ran

Robert heard a better lecture on Thursday morning before working on his car.
Brown beavers and large bears wandered at random over the rough ground.
Every word the farmer heard around the tower was bitter that summer.

7. *The th sound.* In some localities the th is changed into a d or a t sound making the word "wid" or "wit" instead of "with." The th sound is made by bringing the tip of the tongue into contact with the upper front teeth.

this	thus	those	breathe
that	lather	feather	thine

Mother soothed those that were bothered by the weather.

8. *The t sound.* Sometimes the medial or final t is omitted. The t is produced by placing the tip of the tongue firmly against the ridge behind the upper teeth.

water	swiftly	lift	east
softly	almost	west	roast

He almost boasts about his first and worst post.

9. *The s sound.* A very common fault in producing the s sound is to change it into a th sound. For example, sister becomes "thithter" and first becomes "firtht." To produce the s sound swing the sides of the tongue against the dental ridge on each side. Keep the tip free and just posterior to the front teeth. Keep a narrow furrow in the middle of the tongue for the escape of air, pressing the tongue tightly against the roof of the mouth to maintain the furrow as narrow as possible.

this	skates	yesterday	smiles
miss	universities	Saturday	stresses

Sister Susie sings sweetly.
Six thick thistles stick through the fence.

F. *Projection*

Some think, erroneously, that one should raise the pitch of his voice to be heard. There are more effective ways for achieving projection than this. First of all, it is necessary to have good abdominal support for the breath in exhalation. Secondly, resonance, as you have seen, gives strength and carrying power to the voice. The third way of achieving projection is distinct articulation.

All of these are very important in enabling one to be heard and understood, but there is one more element which is also indispensable, namely, the desire to convey to others what you are reading. If one does not have this desire, mere techniques may communicate sounds, but they will not necessarily communicate meaning.

Demosthenes to the Athenians

Such, O, men of Athens! were your ancestors: so glorious in the eye of the world; so bountiful and munificent to their country; so sparing, so modest, so self-denying, to themselves. What resemblance can we find, in the present generation, to these great men? At the time when your ancient competitors have left you a clear stage, when the Lacedemonians are disabled, the Thebans employed in troubles of their own, when no other state whatever is in a condition to rival or molest you—in short, when you are at full liberty, when you have the opportunity and the power to become once more the sole arbiters of Greece—you permit, patiently, whole provinces to be wrested from you; you lavish the public money in scandalous and obscure uses; you suffer your allies to perish in time of peace, whom you preserved in time of war; and, to sum up all, you yourselves, by your mercenary court, and servile resignation to the will and pleasure of designing, insidious leaders, abet, encourage, and strengthen, the most dangerous and formidable of your enemies. Yes, Athenians, I repeat it, you yourselves are the contrivers of your own ruin.

II. PHYSICAL RESPONSIVENESS

Katherine F. Wells, in *Kinesiology,* says that the body will continue to be at rest until it is acted upon by some force. In the case of oral interpretation, this force is literature. It may be powerful enough to bring forth physical response of some degree beyond the use of the voice. This physical response may be primarily covert, so that an observer is scarcely aware of it, or it may be overt and more obvious. You may be only vaguely aware of your physical response while reading aloud, or you may be fully conscious of it, especially during the preparation period.

A. *Nature, Degree, and Extent*

Many people believe, quite erroneously, that the oral interpreter should not use *any* bodily action. If he does, they argue, he has gone into the realm of *acting.* This is not the case at all. The physical responsiveness of your body is a natural expressive agent and a required aid for listener involvement. It is not the absence or presence of action that distinguishes an interpreter from an actor, but rather it is the nature, degree, and extent of the action, among other things, that is a determining factor.

How much action is acceptable in oral interpretation? Should you use facial expression? Should you use your arms, legs, and your torso? Indeed, you may use all parts of your body. Only when your physical responsiveness becomes literal should it be avoided. The guideline for the interpreter is *totality of responsiveness within the realm of suggestion.*

Remember that the way you use the parts of your body depends, first of all, upon you as a person. If you are by nature a very "expressive" individual, you may possibly use a greater range of action than a person who is "quiet," "conservative," or "retiring." Also, the nature of your action may be determined by your national background. If you have been exposed to nordic influences, you will probably tend to use much less bodily action than if you have had close contact with southern people such as those of the Mediterranean area. But do not use a geographic location as an excuse for too little or too much action. Secondly, your degree of responsiveness may depend on the needs of your listeners. Obviously, some audiences need more assistance than others. For example, children are highly motivated by action and, as a result, you would undoubtedly choose to enlarge your bodily suggestion while reading to them. Primarily, however, *the nature of your action depends upon the material you are reading.* For example, the subjective grief of

Tennyson's "Break, Break, Break" will require considerably less overt physical response than the volatile Rosa in Tennessee Williams' *The Rose Tattoo.* Likewise, Whitman's "O Captain! My Captain!" or Tennyson's "Ode on the Death of the Duke of Wellington" will require less overt action than the famous duelling speech in Rostand's *Cyrano de Bergerac.* In your period of preparation, experiment with action. Use various degrees of it. But remember to let the nature of your material be your guide. Let the literature dictate the response!

Physical action in oral interpretation should follow certain principles. One should omit all unnecessary movements which do not clearly and specifically suggest the idea, mood, or emotion of the literature. In other words, avoid extraneous movement when you read. Movement must seem to be effortless on the part of the interpreter. It must always call attention to the literary experience, never to the interpreter. This will come about through adequate relaxation, through your involvement in the literary experience, through your desire to involve the listener and, finally, through the confidence that comes from conscientious preparation.

B. *An Approach to Physical Action*

There are two ways to approach your study of physical action. One of these is to assume the bodily position that you think best conveys the purpose and the attitude of the literature, and then to allow the emotions to grow out of that. Another is to allow the idea and feeling to dominate so strongly that your body will follow the suggestions coming from the mind and respond accordingly. Both of these methods are valid and you may find both of them helpful. The second method, however, is perhaps safer, for it may help to avoid artificiality.

Physical action is not the isolated activity of only one part of the body. Rather, it is a matter of the responsiveness of the entire body. Therefore, as an interpreter, do not think of a hand gesture as an act by itself, but as a mere segment of the total bodily response. You, as a human being, respond as a complete unit in which the whole body plays a part even though you, the interpreter, or the listener may not always be aware of it. It is not one part of you, but all of you that suggests an emotion.

Often you will find it helpful, while you are preparing, to use a considerable range of movement. You may want to let your arms fly, to lift your body, or even to walk as you read. In the early stages of oral preparation you will find that this will enable you to free yourself. In fact, the actual movement that you use may reveal new attitudes toward your material that a more inhibited approach has not made possible. This freedom of expression may aid you especially in developing an understanding of characters in plays, narrative poems, and stories. After you have given the characters this kind of exaggerated treatment, you will be able to keep the essence of the character with his subtler elements by eliminating the gross qualities, thus bringing your reading into the realm of oral interpretation.

1. *Your hands and arms.* Like most people learning to read aloud you will probably ask, "Where should I put my hands when I read?" If you are extremely aware of your hands, it is possible that you need to concentrate more on what you are reading, for this will help you to forget them. As you focus your attention more completely on your material than on yourself, your hands will tend to take care of themselves. But since this is not always easy there are several suggestions which might help. First of all, do not put your hands in your pockets. This interferes with your freedom of expression and stands as a barrier between you and your listener. Perhaps the best advice is for you to let your hands drop at your sides or, if you use a reading stand, to let them rest lightly on it. Then, when the impulse is strong enough, let your hands, arms, and body respond to the ideas and feelings of the literature. Whether you use arm or hand gestures depends upon you, upon how you feel about your material, upon the needs of your listeners and, most importantly, upon the material itself. In reading you may generally use as your guide the dictum: *the more thoughtful and philosophical your material, the subtler will be your physical responsiveness.*

When and if you use hand and arm movements, avoid using the same habitual and repeated movements to express every idea regardless of what it may be. This is mere *movement,* not purposeful suggestion. Hamlet's advice, "Do not saw the air thus with your hands," is as applicable to the oral interpreter as to the actor. Your physical responsiveness should suggest the idea visually just as clearly as your vocal responsiveness should suggest the idea aurally. Each must complement the other.

2. *Reader's Stance.* Sometimes interpreters stand rigidly in front of their listeners. This, of course, makes the reader inflexible and prevents him from adjusting easily from one idea to another in both mind and body. A reader needs a flexible foot base to permit freedom of response to the material he reads. To allow for this you should stand so that you can shift your weight easily from one leg to the other, with your weight on the balls of your feet rather than on the heels.

The stance that you use may vary with the material you read. A wide base, with the feet farther apart, which suggests power and strength, may be more effective for certain kinds of material including characters such as the spirited Henry V, the fiery Hotspur, the determined Captain Ahab, the defiant Antigone, or the resolute Goliath. A narrower base may better suggest the delicacy of the French Princess in *Henry the Fifth,* the fanciful petulance of Helena in *A Midsummer Night's Dream,* the weak spirit of Richard the Second, or the fretful, self-centered Zeena in *Ethan Frome.* But it is not only characters in a story, narrative poem, play, or novel that may influence your stance: ideas also have a physical effect upon you as a reader. The following ironic passage from *Beach Red,* by Peter Bowman, may suggest how the reflections of a soldier can influence stance.

> There is a tide in the affairs of man, which,
> taken between a blood test and an induction notice, leads
> on to the Army. It's been a big adventure so
> far. You've traveled and you've been around and you've seen
> things and much has happened to you. But water is
> wet whether it's off the shore of this island or
> in Lake Michigan and mud is still dirty whether it's
> on the banks of a jungle stream or near Claibourne,
> Louisiana, and wherever you go you'll always find a placard
> on a pine box saying, "Servicemen Admitted at No Charge."

In the interpretation of any material your stance should reflect the attitude, the ideas, or the character you are trying to suggest. Experiment and vary your stance so that it reinforces the material.

STUDY QUESTIONS

1. Do you feel that you have developed as much resonance in your voice as you can? What is the basis of your opinion?

2. Can you think of any readers, actors or acquaintances who seem to use too much pitch range? Who talk in a monotone? Do either of these tendencies seem to affect the personality? Which fault do you find less objectionable? Why?

3. Which do you think conveys more subtlety, the single change in pitch or the glide?

4. How would you compare the tempo used in "The Brook," by Tennyson, and that used in "Silver," by Walter de la Mare? How do you arrive at your decision?

5. Can you find various degrees of intensity in Mark Antony's oration? How does it compare with Lincoln's Gettysburg Address or the Sermon on the Mount in terms of intensity?

6. Do you find it easy, or difficult, to separate the various aspects of voice as you listen to someone read? Do you think this is a compliment to the reader?

7. Do most readers whom you have observed use bodily action to help convey the intent of their material?

8. Do you think you use too much or too little bodily action? What causes you to draw this conclusion?

9. Do you think that you would feel comfortable in using extensive and realistic action in reading Dylan Thomas's poetry? Edith Sitwell's? Vachel Lindsay's? Why?

10. How can you compare the action to be used in reading a play and that used in a sonnet? Are the differences or similarities always constant?

BIBLIOGRAPHY

Allport, Gordon, and P. E. Vernon, *Studies in Expressive Movement.* New York: Macmillan, 1933.

Aubert, Charles, *The Art of Pantomime.* Trans. by Edith Sears, New York: Henry Holt, 1927.

Eisenson, Jon, *The Improvement of Voice and Diction.* 2nd Edition. New York: Macmillan Co., 1965.

Fisher, Hilda B., *Improving Voice and Articulation.* Boston: Houghton Mifflin Co., 1966.

Gordon, Morton J., Helene H. Wong, *A Manual for Speech Improvement.* Englewood Cliffs, N.J.: Prentice-Hall, Inc., 1961.

Grasham, John A., Glenn G. Gooder, *Improving Your Speech.* New York: Harcourt, Brace and Co., 1960.

Grim, Harriett Elizabeth, *Practical Voice Training: A Manual for Developing the Voice.* New York: Appleton-Century-Crofts, Inc., 1948.

Hahn, Elise, Charles W. Lomas, Donald E. Hargis, Daniel Vandraegen, *Basic Voice Training for Speech.* New York: McGraw-Hill Book Co., Inc., 1952.

Hanley, Theodore D., Wayne L. Thurman, *Developing Vocal Skills.* New York: Holt, Rinehart and Winston, 1962.

Heinberg, Paul, *Voice Training for Speaking and Reading Aloud.* New York: The Ronald Press Co., 1964.

Hibbitt, George W., Richard A. Norman, *Guide to Speech Training: Voice, Articulation, and Oral Reading.* New York: The Ronald Press Co., 1964.

Judson, Lyman Spicer, Andrew Thomas Weaver, *Voice Science.* New York: F. S. Crofts & Co., 1942.

Kantner, Claude E., Ph.D., Robert West, Ph.D., *Phonetics.* Revised Edition, New York: Harper & Brothers, 1960.

Kaplan, Harold M., *Anatomy and Physiology of Speech.* New York: McGraw-Hill Book Co., Inc., 1960.

Karr, Harrison M., *Developing Your Speaking Voice.* New York: Harper & Row, 1953.

Todd, Mabel Elsworth, *The Thinking Body.* New York, London: P. B. Hoeber, Inc., 1937.

Wells, Katherine F., *Kinesiology.* 4th edition, Philadelphia: W. B. Saunders Co., 1966.

Part Three

Discovering Meanings and Emotions

Chapter V

Imagery in Literature

Ross Stagner, the psychologist, says that an image "is the conscious content of a sensory experience recalled in the absence of the physical stimulus." A layman might say that an image is the recall of an experience which he has at some time received through one or more of the senses. In oral interpretation, the words of the author are the stimuli acting in the absence of reality. The conscious content of the sensory response, the image, may be the result of recall and, *in addition,* it may be the result of involvement in a new literary experience. Whether the image is predominantly the result of past experiences, present associations, or a combination of these, it is imperative that you be sensitive to verbal stimuli for the enrichment of experiences past and present. Without this kind of sensitivity it is impossible to embrace the essence of the literary experience.

A sensory response is an empathic response which is not necessarily an automatic response. You must be willing to become involved, to let go of your inhibitions, to concentrate on the experience suggested by the literature. You must become "sensory receptive" to word association, whether it be through the sense of sight, smell, hearing, touch, taste, pain, temperature, motion, hunger, thirst, or equilibrium. All of your senses are stimulated daily in a variety of ways. You must allow language to be your major stimulus, for to become involved in the language of the literature is to experience the imagery.

I. THE TYPES OF IMAGERY

In your oral preparation feel free to respond physically if impelled to do so. This is particularly true with kinesthetic imagery. If it is auditory, you may want to turn your head or even your body to hear the sound. If it is visual it will help you to look beyond the realm of the audience to focus on the object. In general, try to look up from your book as you experience imagery for this will give you an improved sense of freedom.

Study the following excerpts included in each of the types of imagery below. Read them silently and aloud, and as you read *take the time to become involved.* Remember that *time* is the oral interpreter's ally, as well as the listener's ally, in responding to imagery.

A. *Visual*

Of all the senses, man depends more upon his sight than upon any other. He relies almost constantly upon his eyes to get him through his day's work or play, for they can distinguish color, form, distance, depth and perspective. As man looks at an object he stores an image which he keeps for future use. Because we are so accustomed to using our eyes we can generally recall visual images more easily than other types of imagery. Literature abounds in visual images.

Your sensitivity to color will assist you in your ability to respond to visual imagery. An author, not unlike a stage designer, uses color to convey certain feelings and attitudes in regard to a person, a place or an event. Colors have the power to suggest mood just as does music. Both the poet and the novelist are so aware of the value of color that they often use it as effectively as does an artist in painting a picture. The following excerpts include form, distance, depth and perspective as well as color.

In the poem "Silver," by Walter de la Mare, the color of silver pervades the poem to create a monochromatic picture of repose, quiet, and peace:

> Slowly, silently, now the moon
> Walks the night in her silver shoon;
> This way, and that, she peers, and sees
> Silver fruit upon silver trees;
> One by one the casements catch
> Her beams beneath the silvery thatch;

Couched in his kennel, like a log,
With paws of silver sleeps the dog;
From their shadowy cote the white breasts peep
Of doves in a silver-feathered sleep;
A harvest mouse goes scampering by,
With silver claws, and silver eye;
And moveless fish in the water gleam,
By silver reeds in a silver stream.

Other colors carry different emotional and mental connotations. Orange and red sometimes suggest unrest, intensity and strength. Notice how different this color picture is from silver.

All in a hot and copper sky,
The bloody Sun, at noon,
Right up above the mast did stand,
No bigger than the Moon.

(Coleridge, "The Rime of the
Ancient Mariner," Part II)

Red may suggest horror as it does in Poe's "Masque of the Red Death," or murder and guilt as it does in Shakespeare's *Macbeth:*

Will all great Neptune's ocean wash this blood
Clean from my hand? No. This my hand will rather
The multitudinous seas incarnadine,
Making the green one red.

(Act II, Sc ii)

In a more cheerful tone, Robert Burns uses red as a sign of life, freshness and brightness in "A Red, Red Rose."

O, my luve is like a red, red rose,
That's newly sprung in June.
O, my luve is like the melodie,
That's sweetly play'd in tune.

While white and black are, technically, not colors, they can affect your emotional response to an experience. White often suggests purity, innocence, radiance, clarity or mystical qualities. In "Epithalamion" Spenser writes of the bride:

> Loe! where she comes along with portly pace,
> Lyke Phoebe, from her chamber of the east,
> Arysing forth to run her mighty race,
> Clad all in white, that seems a virgin best.

George Croly admires the white lily of the valley as an object of gentleness in "The Lily of the Valley."

> White bud, that in meek beauty dost lean
> Thy cloister'd cheek as pale as moonlight snow,
> Thou seem'st beneath thy huge, high leaf of green,
> An Eremite beneath his mountain's brow.

> . . . for thou rememberest how
> In those old days, one summer noon, an arm
> Rose up from out the bosom of the lake,
> Clothed in white samite, mystic, wonderful,
> Holding the sword . . .
>
> (Tennyson, "The Passing of Arthur,"
> *Idylls of the King*)

Black, like white, denotes certain feelings. It may suggest richness if we associate it with ebony, or it may suggest gloom, hopelessness, or foreboding. Hamlet says to his mother "Tis not alone my inky cloak, good mother,/Nor customary suits of solemn black, . . ." (Act I, Sc ii)

W. E. Henley, in "Invictus," uses black to suggest despair as he says:

> Out of the night that covers me,
> Black as the Pit from pole to pole,
> I thank whatever gods may be
> For my unconquerable soul.

Sometimes blue suggests celestial qualities as in paintings of the Madonna and Child, or it suggests serenity as in "L'Oiseau Bleu" by Mary Coleridge:

The lake lay blue below the hill.
O'er it, as I looked, there flew
Across the waters, cold and still,
A bird whose wings were palest blue.

The sky above was blue at last,
The sky beneath me blue in blue.
A moment, ere the bird had passed,
It caught his image as he flew.

But blue may also suggest the ominous and sinister as it does in "The Lotus-Eaters" by Tennyson:

Hateful is the dark-blue sky,
Vaulted o'er the dark-blue sea.
Death is the end of life; ah, why
Should life all labour be?

(Choric Song, Part IV)

As you see, the color blue has been used by these authors to help create and intensify the mood and thereby strengthen the experience. Green, too, suggests various emotional responses. In "Walking Asleep," Federico Garcia Lorca, who is well known for his love of color, uses green repeatedly to create a mood.[1]

Green as I would have you be.
Green wind. Green boughs.
The boat on the sea
And the horse on the mountain.
With shadow around her waist
She is dreaming at her railing,
Green flesh, green hair,
Eyes of frozen silver.
Green as I would have you be.

[1] It has been suggested that he used green to emphasize "the imprint of Islamic fatalism" upon Spain. See *Lorca: A Collection of Critical Essays,* ed. by Manuel Duran, Prentice-Hall, Inc., Englewood Cliffs, N.J., p. 59. Essay entitled "A Poet Crazy About Color," by Louis Parrot, trans. by Gloria Bradley.

Under the gypsy moon,
Things are watching her,
Things she cannot see.

As you have seen, color is a powerful factor in stimulating man's emotional responses. At the same time you as a reader must realize the importance of the other functions which your eyes can perform, such as distinguishing form, distance, depth, and perspective, for all of these are also components of visual imagery.

B. *Auditory*

The following excerpts relate to the sense of hearing.

Now, lay thine ear against the golden sand,
And thou shalt hear the music of the sea,
Those hollow tones it plays against the land—
Is't not a rich and wondrous melody?
I have lain hours, and fancied in its tone
I heard the languages of ages gone.

(T. Hood, "The Music of the Sea")

Throughout the daylight hours, the business streets were gorged with milling crowds on foot, into which the more privileged ruthlessly rode their horses or were borne on litters and portable chairs; but when twilight fell, the harsh rasp and clatter of heavy iron wheels grinding the cobblestones set up a nerve-racking cacophony accompanied by the agonized squawk of dry axles, the cracking of whips, and the shrill quarrels of contenders for the right of way; nor did this maddening racket cease until another day had dawned. This was every night, the whole year round.

(Lloyd Douglas, *The Robe,* Chapter 22)

Yell'd on the view the opening pack;
Rock, glen, and cavern, paid them back;

To many a mingled sound at once
The awaken'd mountain gave response.
A hundred dogs bay'd deep and strong,
Clatter'd a hundred steeds along,
Their peal the merry horns rung out,
A hundred voices join'd the shout; . . .

(Scott, "Lady of the Lake," Canto First III)

From my boyhood I remember
A crystal moment of September.

A wooded island rang with sounds
Of church bells in the throats of hounds.

("Crystal Moment," by Robert P. Tristram Coffin)

C. *Olfactory, Gustatory, Hunger and Thirst*

The senses of smell and taste are known as the chemical senses because they respond to chemical stimuli. Nature has made man sensitive to both smell and taste, to keep him from danger and to attract him to food and other odors.

In addition, odors frequently stimulate one to such an extent that certain memories are revived. A certain antiseptic odor may remind one of a childhood experience, the scent of a candle may recall a happy Christmas. While olfactory images are not found as frequently as are visual images there are, nevertheless, many of them in poetry and fiction.

In "Smells" Christopher Morley brings together some olfactory images which apparently intrigue a child:

My Daddy smells like tobacco and books,
Mother, like lavender and listerine;
Uncle John carries a whiff of cigars,
Nannie smells starchy and soapy and clean.

Shandy, my dog, has a smell of his own
(When he's been out in the rain he smells most);
But Katie, the cook is more splendid than all—
She smells exactly like hot buttered toast!

In *Cress Delahanty* you will find images reminiscent of a seaside resort:

> . . . There were all the smells of salt and seaweed, of fish and water and wind. There were all the human smells too of the hundreds of people who filled the boardwalk: ladies in print dresses smelling like passing gardens; swimmers with their scents of suntan oils and skin lotions; there were the smells of the eating places: of mustard and onions, of hamburgers frying; and the sudden sharp smell of stacks of dill pickles, as brisk in the nose as a sudden unintended inhalation of sea water.
>
> (Jessamyn West, *Cress Delahanty,* first edition, Part II Thirteen, Summer II, p. 67.)

In *Gone With the Wind* the author wants the reader to associate the pleasant odor of lemon verbena with one of the characters, Scarlett's mother:[2]

> . . . There entered with her the faint fragrance of lemon verbena sachet, which seemed always to creep from the folds of her dresses, a fragrance that was always linked in Scarlett's mind with her mother.
>
> (Margaret Mitchell, *Gone With the Wind*)

The sense of taste, like that of smell, is very highly developed. Sometimes tastes are classified as sweet, sour, bitter and salt. Often it is easy to confuse taste and smell, probably because the nasal and oral cavities are so near each other; or taste and sight, for you may dislike shrimp or eel because of its appearance rather than its taste. Likewise one may confuse taste and touch, maintaining that he does not like oysters, when he actually dislikes the texture, the "slippery" quality, rather than the taste.

Here are several examples of gustatory (taste) imagery:

[2] Margaret Mitchell, *Gone With the Wind* (New York, The Macmillan Co., 1936), p. 64.

What mean ye, that ye use this proverb concerning the land of Israel, saying,
The fathers have eaten sour grapes, and the children's teeth are set on edge?

(*Ezekiel* 18:2)

In the desert
I saw a creature, naked, bestial,
Who, squatting upon the ground,
Held his heart in his hands,
And ate of it.
I said, "Is it good, friend?"
"It is bitter—bitter," he answered;
"But I like it
Because it is bitter,
And because it is my heart."

("The Heart" by Stephen Crane)

Of all smells, bread; of all tastes, salt.

(George Herbert, Outlandish Proverbs,
Selected, No. 166)

. . . to pile honey upon sugar, and sugar upon honey, to an interminable tedious sweetness.

(Charles Lamb, "Essays of Elia,"
A Chapter on Ears)

This Bouillabaisse a noble dish is—
A sort of soup or broth, or brew,
Or hotchpotch of all sorts of fishes,
That Greenwich never could outdo;
Green herbs, red peppers, mussels, saffron,
Soles, onions, garlic, roach, and dace:
All these you eat at Terré's Tavern,
In that one dish of Bouillabaisse.

("Ballad of Bouillabaisse," by William Makepeace Thackeray)

Hunger and thirst are very real senses which all have experienced. Images of these two senses are also found in literature. In *The Taming of the Shrew,* Katherine, the shrew, is being tamed partly by not being given food. Here you find the hungry Katherine saying:

> The more my wrong, the more his spite appears:
> What, did he marry me to famish me?
> Beggars, that come unto my father's door,
> Upon entreaty have a present alms;
> If not, elsewhere they meet with charity:
> But I, who never knew how to entreat,
> Nor never needed that I should entreat,
> Am starv'd for meat, giddy for lack of sleep,
> With oaths kept waking, and with brawling fed:
> And, that which spites me more than all these wants,
> He does it under name of perfect love;
> As who should say, if I should sleep or eat,
> 'T were deadly sickness or else present death.
> I prithee go and get me some repast;
> I care not what, so it be wholesome food.
>
> (*The Taming of the Shrew,* Act IV, Sc iii)

> The evening arrived; the boys took their places. The master, in his cook's uniform, stationed himself at the copper; his pauper assistants ranged themselves behind him; the gruel was served out; and a long grace was said over the short commons. The gruel disappeared; the boys whispered to each other, and winked at Oliver; while his next neighbours nudged him. Child as he was, he was desperate with hunger, and reckless with misery. He rose from the table; and advancing to the master, basin and spoon in hand, said: somewhat alarmed at his own temerity: "Please, sir, I want some more."
>
> (Dickens, *Oliver Twist,* Chap. II)

> And every tongue, through utter drought,
> Was withered at the root;

We could not speak, no more than if
We had been choked with soot.

(Coleridge, "The Rime of the
Ancient Mariner," Part II. ll. 137–138)

The thirsty earth soaks up the rain,
And drinks and gapes for drink again;
The plants suck in the earth, and are
With constant drinking fresh and fair;

(Abraham Cowley, Poems Anacreontiques,
II "Drinking")

D. *Tactile and Temperature*

The sense of touch was formerly thought to cover a range of stimuli, such as pressure, pain, and temperature, as well as touch. Now these are sometimes regarded as separate senses. All of us have experienced displeasure through the sense of touch: the rotten apple in the bottom of the barrel, fingers stuck to dry ice, the slime of polluted and stagnant ponds. We have, as well, experienced pleasure: the smoothness of satin, the softness of sand, the roughness of tree bark. There are many examples of these types of imagery in literature:

But O for the touch of a vanish'd hand,
And the sound of a voice that is still!

(Tennyson, "Break, Break, Break")

O, that I were a glove upon that hand,
That I might touch that cheek!

(*Romeo and Juliet,* Act II, Sc ii)

The night before Christmas
I cried with the cold,
I cried myself to sleep
Like a two-year-old.

(Edna St. Vincent Millay, "Ballad of
the Harp Weaver")

St. Agnes' Eve—Ah, bitter chill it was!
The owl, for all his feathers, was a-cold; . . .

(John Keats, "St. Agnes' Eve," ll. 1–2)

E. *Motion*

When you watch a dancer or a football player you respond to his movements and feel as if you yourself are dancing or running on the field. This is the sense of kinesthesis. Kinesthetic images emanate from the muscular movement of living objects—man, birds, fish and animals.

A feeling of movement may also come from inanimate objects such as the movement of automobiles, tractors, airplanes and steam shovels. In the forces of nature, too, movements can be felt such as the swaying of a tree in the wind, the waves of the sea, a turbulent stream, or a turgid river.

When you read the following passages try to experience the sense of motion involved.

Then, as a mother lays her sleeping child
Down tenderly, fearing it may awake,
He set the jug down slowly at his feet
With trembling care, knowing that most things break;

(Edwin Arlington Robinson,
"Mr. Flood's Party")

He asked water, and she gave him milk;
She brought forth butter in a lordly dish.
She put her hand to the nail, and her
right hand to the workmen's hammer; and with
the hammer she smote Sisera, she smote
off his head, when she had pierced and stricken
through his temples.
At her feet he bowed, he fell, he lay
down: at her feet he bowed, he fell: where
he bowed, there he fell down dead.

(*Judges* 5:25–27)

I'd sooner, except the penalties, kill a man than a hawk; but the great redtail
Had nothing left but unable misery
From the bone too shattered for mending, the wing that trailed under his talons when he moved.
We had fed him six weeks, I gave him freedom,
He wandered over the foreland hill and returned in the evening, asking for death,
Not like a beggar, still eyed with old
Implacable arrogance. I gave him the lead gift in the twilight.
What fell was relaxed,
Owl-downy, soft feminine feathers; but what
Soared: the fierce rush: the night-herons by the flooded river cried fear at its rising
Before it was quite unsheathed from reality.

(Robinson Jeffers, "Hurt Hawks," II)

He clasps the crag with crooked hands;
Close to the sun in lonely lands,
Ring'd with the azure world, he stands.
The wrinkled sea beneath him crawls;
He watches from his mountain walls,
And like a thunderbolt he falls.

(Alfred, Lord Tennyson, "The Eagle")

And now the raging armies rush'd
Like warring mighty seas;
The Heavens are shook with roaring war,
The dust ascends the skies!

(William Blake, "Gwin, King of Norway")

These are the hours that no one counts when time
sneaks past your chair like a cat and the reluctant foot
has not yet found the stair

has not yet made
one quiet footstep further toward the night.

(James Hearst, "After Chores")

The ambulance at top speed floating down
Past beacons and illuminated clocks
Wings in a heavy curve, dips down,
And brakes speed, entering the crowd.
The doors leap open, emptying light;
Stretchers are laid out, the mangled lifted
And stowed into the little hospital.

(Karl Shapiro, "Auto Wreck")

Lay me on an anvil, O God.
Beat me and hammer me into a crowbar.
Let me pry loose old walls;
Let me lift and loosen old foundations.
Lay me on an anvil, O God.
Beat me and hammer me into a steel spike.
Drive me into the girders that hold a skyscraper together.
Take red-hot rivets and fasten me into the central girders.
Let me be the great nail holding a skyscraper through
blue nights into white stars.

(Carl Sandburg, "Prayers of Steel")

F. *Equilibrium*

The sense of equilibrium or balance is very important to man. In literature images of equilibrium are used more than we realize because they are connected with such ordinary activities as swimming or walking.

It is portentous, and a thing of state
That here at midnight, in our little town

A mourning figure walks, and will not rest,
Near the old court-house pacing up and down, . . .

(Vachel Lindsay, "Abraham Lincoln
Walks at Midnight")

Images of balance may be more apparent to you in the following passages from Edgar Allan Poe.

For a moment she remained trembling and reeling to and fro upon the threshold—then, with a low moaning cry fell heavily inward upon the person of her brother . . .

("The Fall of the House of Usher")

But if this idea was not, even then, altogether adopted, I could at least doubt no longer, when, arising from the bed, tottering, with feeble steps, with closed eyes, and with the manner of one bewildered in a dream, the thing that was enshrouded advanced boldly and palpably into the middle of the apartment.

I trembled not—I stirred not—for a crowd of unutterable fancies connected with the air, the stature, the demeanor, of the figure, rushing hurriedly through my brain, had paralyzed—had chilled me into stone. I stirred not—but gazed upon the apparition.

("Ligeia")

II. SELECTIONS WITH A VARIETY OF IMAGES

Since a number of images may be and often are combined in a piece of literature, examples of such material are included here. As you read these over determine which kinds of imagery are involved, and when you read them aloud try to respond as completely as you can to each image.

John Evelyn, *Diary,* September 3rd, 1666

. . . [A]fter dinner I took coach with my wife and son, and went to the Bankside in Southwark, where we beheld that dismal spectacle, the whole city in dreadful flames near the water-side; all the houses from the Bridge, all Thames-street, and upwards towards Cheapside, down to the Three Cranes, were now consumed . . .

The fire having continued all this night, (if I may call that night which was as light as day for ten miles round about, after a dreadful manner), when conspiring with a fierce eastern wind in a very dry season, I went on foot to the same place, and saw the whole south part of the city burning from Cheapside to the Thames, and all along Cornhill, (for it likewise kindled back against the wind as well as forward), Tower-street, Fenchurch-street, Gracious-street, and so along to Baynard's Castle, and was now taking hold of St. Paul's Church, to which the scaffolds contributed exceedingly. The conflagration was so universal, and the people so astonished, that from the beginning, I know not by what despondency or fate, they hardly stirred to quench it; so that there was nothing heard, or seen, but crying out and lamentation, running about like distracted creatures, without at all attempting to save even their goods; such a strange consternation there was upon them, so as it burned both in breadth and length, the churches, public halls, Exchange, hospitals, monuments and ornaments; leaping after a prodigious manner from house to house, and street to street, at great distances one from the other. For the heat, with a long set of fair and warm weather, had even ignited the air, and prepared the materials to conceive the fire, which devoured, after an incredible manner, houses, furniture, and everything. Here, we saw the Thames covered with goods floating, all the barges and boats laden with what some had time and courage to save, as, on the other side, the carts, etc., carrying out to the fields, which for many miles were strewed with movables of all sorts, and tents erecting to shelter both people and what goods they could get away. Oh, the miserable and calamitous spectacle! such as haply the world had not seen the like since the foundation of it, nor be outdone till the universal conflagration thereof. All the sky was of a fiery aspect, like the top of a burning oven, and the light seen above forty miles round-about for many nights. God grant my eyes may never behold the like, who now saw above 10,000 houses all in one flame! The noise, and cracking and thunder of the impetuous flames, the shrieking of women and children, the hurry of people, the fall of towers, houses and churches, was like a hideous storm; and the air all about so hot and inflamed, that at the last one was not able to approach it, so that they were forced to stand still, and let the flames burn on, which they did, for near two miles in length and one in breadth. The clouds also of smoke were dismal, and reached, upon computation, near fifty miles in length. . . .

"The Cratchits at Dinner"

from *A Christmas Carol,* by Charles Dickens

And now two smaller Cratchits, boy and girl, came tearing in, screaming that outside the baker's they had smelt the goose, and known it for their own; and, basking in luxurious thoughts of sage and onion, these young Cratchits danced about the table, and exalted Master Peter Cratchit to the skies, while he (not proud, although his collars nearly choked him) blew the fire, until the slow potatoes, bubbling up, knocked loudly at the saucepan lid to be let out and peeled . . .

Mrs. Cratchit made the gravy (ready beforehand in a little saucepan) hissing hot; Master Peter mashed the potatoes with incredible vigor; Miss Belinda sweetened up the apple-sauce; Martha dusted the hot plates; Bob took Tiny Tim beside him in a tiny corner at the table; the two young Cratchits set chairs for everybody, not forgetting themselves, and, mounting guard upon their posts, crammed spoons into their mouths, lest they should shriek for goose before their turn came to be helped. At last the dishes were set on, and grace was said. It was succeeded by a breathless pause, as Mrs. Cratchit, looking slowly all along the carving-knife, prepared to plunge it in the breast; but when she did, and when the long-expected gush of stuffing issued forth, one murmur of delight arose all round the board, and even Tiny Tim, excited by the two young Cratchits, beat on the table with the handle of his knife, and feebly cried, "Hurrah!"

There never was such a goose. Bob said he didn't believe there ever was such a goose cooked. Its tenderness and flavor, size and cheapness, were the themes of universal admiration. Eked out by apple-sauce and mashed potatoes, it was a sufficient dinner for the whole family; indeed, as Mrs. Cratchit said with great delight (surveying one small atom of a bone upon the dish), they hadn't ate it all at last! Yet everyone had had enough, and the youngest Cratchits in particular were steeped in sage and onion to the eyebrows!

"To The Leaven'd Soil They Trod," by Walt Whitman[3]

To the leaven'd soil they trod calling I sing for the last,
(Forth from my tent emerging for good, loosing, untying the tent-ropes,)
In the freshness the forenoon air, in the far-stretching circuits and vistas again to peace restored,
To the fiery fields emanative and the endless vistas beyond, to the South and the North,
To the leaven'd soil of the general Western world to attest my songs,
To the Alleghenian hills and the tireless Mississippi,
To the rocks I calling sing, and all the trees in the woods,
To the plains of the poems of heroes, to the prairies spreading wide,
To the far off sea and the unseen winds, and the sane impalpable air;
And responding they answer all (but not in words),
The average earth, the witness of war and peace, acknowledges mutely,
The prairie draws me close, as the father to bosom broad the son,
The Northern ice and rain that began me nourish me to the end,
But the hot sun of the South is to fully ripen my songs.

"Bitter for Sweet," by Christina Rossetti

Summer is gone with all its roses,
Its sun and perfumes and sweet flowers,
Its warm air and refreshing showers:
And even Autumn closes.

Yea, Autumn's chilly self is going,
And Winter comes which is yet colder;

[3] From *The Complete Poetry and Prose of Walt Whitman* as prepared by him for the deathbed edition (New York: Pellegrini and Cudahy, 1948), p. 297. Vol. I.

Each day the hoar-frost waxes bolder,
And the last buds cease blowing.

Hippolytus, by Euripides[4]

The Second Messenger's Speech

THESEUS, MESSENGER, CHORUS.

MES. Theseus, I bring thee tidings that must claim
Sorrow from thee and from thy citizens,
Be they of Athens or of Trœzene's state.

THE. What may this be? Hath aught of sudden ill,
Alarming to these neighbouring towns, befallen?

MES. Hippolytus is dead, to speak in brief,
Or draws his last short breath of vital air.

THE. Whence this? The vengeance of some injured husband,
Whose wife he, as his father's, stain'd by force?

MES. By his own car destroy'd and thy request,
Thy imprecations to thy father made,
The monarch of the main, against thy son.

THE. O gods! Now, Neptune, thou art proved indeed
My father, rightly hast thou heard my prayers.
But say, how perish'd he? how did the mace
Of Justice crush him for his wrongs to me?

MES. We on the margin of the wave-wash'd shore
His coursers held, and comb'd their flowing manes,
Weeping; for one had come with tidings to us
That on this land Hippolytus no more
Must set his foot, by thy severe decree
A wretched exile. He too came, and brought
The same sad sentence to us on the strand:
Not unattended; for a numerous train
Of youths, his loved associates, follow'd him.
After some time, mastering his griefs, he spoke,—
"What boots it to lament? My father's bidding
Must be obey'd: my servants, quickly yoke
My coursers to the car: this is a city

[4] The Plays of Euripides—Trans. by Edward P. Coleridge (London: Geo. Bell & Sons, 1904), Vol. I, pg. 106 (line 16) to p. 109 (line 4).

For me no more." Each to his office thence
Hasten'd, and in an instant to our lord
We led his coursers harness'd: from the nave
He snatch'd the reins, and sprang into the seat,
Then to the gods stretched forth his hands, and said,—
"If ever baseness stained my heart, O Jove,
May I no longer breathe this vital air;
And let my father know how much he wrongs me,
Whether I die, or view the light of heaven."
Then lash'd his steeds: attendant on our lord,
We follow near the reins, the way to Argos
Leading and Epidaurus. When we reach'd
The tract of desert where the shore swells high
'Gainst the Saronic gulf, a roaring sound
Came o'er the earth, loud as the voice of Jove,
Horrid to hear: the coursers toss'd their heads
High, and towards heaven erect their ears: our train,
Trembling like children, marvell'd whence the noise
Proceeded: to the sea-beat shore we cast
Our eyes, and saw a wave so vast, it swell'd
Reaching the skies, that to our view were lost
The cliffs of Sciron, and the Isthmus now
No more appear'd, no more appear'd the rocks
Of Esculapius: swelling on, and round
Dashing its roaring foam, on the high tide
It reach'd the shore close to the harness'd car:
There from its rolling and tempestuous flood
Cast forth a bull, a monster wild and vast,
Whose horrid bellowings through the affrighted land
Resounded: such a hideous sight the eye
Could not endure. A dreadful terror seized
The starting horses: and their lord, much train'd
In all equestrian lore, in his strong hand
Held firm the reins: like one that at the oar
Bends backward, backward so he bent, and drew
The straiten'd reins. Champing their iron bits,
They rush impetuous on, nor guiding hand,
Nor straitened rein, nor well-compacted car

Regard: if to the level plain his wheels
He guided, there, to force him back, the bull
Appear'd before him, and the maddening steeds
Affrighted: on the rough rocks if they rush'd
With wild and frantic flight, approaching nigh,
In silence he accompanied the car;
Till, dash'd against a crag, the clashing wheel
High bounding cast him headlong from his seat.
All then was foul disorder; upward flew
The pierced nave and the axle's point infix'd.
The unhappy youth, inexplicably bound
Amid the tangling harness ('gainst the rocks
His dear head dash'd, his flesh all rent), was heard
With lamentable voice to address his steeds:—
"Stop, O my coursers, mindful that these hands
Have fed you in my stalls; destroy me not:
How dreadful is my father's imprecation!
Is no one nigh, no one to save a man
Of unstain'd innocence?" Though many wish'd,
We were left far behind, and our best speed
Was slow. He, disengaged, I know not how,
From the rent harness, falls, a little life
Yet breathing: but the steeds were seen no more,
Nor the portentous bull, I know not where
Conceal'd among the crags that rise around.
I in thy house am a poor slave, O king,
Yet never shall my breast harbour the thought,
Or be persuaded, that thy son was base;
Not though the universal race of women
Should hang themselves, and every pine of Ida
Were fill'd with letters; for I know him pure.

CHO. Alas, alas, these new calamities
Have their completion: there is no redress
From fate, no refuge from necessity.

THE. So much I hate the wretch who suffer'd this,
I had a pleasure in thy words; but now
I reverence the gods, and him, because
He was my son; I therefore from these ills

Receive no pleasure, and receive no grief.
MES. Not to offend thee, whither shall we bear
The unhappy youth, what office shall we pay him?
Yet, might my wish prevail, thou wilt not be
Ungentle, 'mid his sufferings, to thy son.
THE. Bring him before me; I would see him; now,
Since he disown'd the foul stain to my bed,
My words shall charge his baseness home upon him,
Convicted by this vengeance of the gods.

III. THE ROLE OF IMAGERY

Imagery in literature clarifies and strengthens an idea by illustrating or amplifying that idea. In *Othello* the concept of the evil influence of jealousy is strengthened when Iago calls it, metaphorically, a monster.

O beware, my lord, of jealousy!
It is the green-eyed monster, which doth mock
The meat it feeds on.

(Act III, Sc iii)

Imagery is also a means of intensifying an emotion. For example, Brutus, in *Julius Caesar* (Act III, Sc i) uses images to make the emotion more acute.

. . . Stoop, Romans, stoop,
And let us bathe our hands in Caesar's blood
Up to the elbows and besmear our swords.
Then walk we forth, even to the market place,
And waving our red weapons o'er our heads,
Let's all cry, "Peace, freedom, and liberty!"

Imagery also helps create and sustain mood, as you will see in Walter de la Mare's "Silver." It is related to figures of speech in that such figures as the simile, metaphor and personification employ imagery. And, finally, it promotes unity.

Imagery is often such an important part of an author's style that many writers can be recognized, in part at least, by their use of it. Dylan Thomas has the facility of piling image on image to convey his experience; he is, indeed, a challenge to the oral interpreter. Coleridge employs imagery in a different way, using it to bring out an idea in strong relief. Shakespeare uses dominant images in his plays; for example, in *Othello,* the main image is one of "animals in action, preying upon one another," as Spurgeon says.[5]

An image is not used merely for its own sake; it is not merely an ornament. It is connected with the theme or emotion. If you see only the image without grasping its relationship to the whole poem you will miss its significance.

A poem or novel may also be built around one major image. *Moby Dick,* by Herman Melville, is built around the image of the whale which is a symbol of evil. The poet, George Herbert, used one major image in "The Pulley" where he constructed his poem around the pulley itself, which can change the direction of a pulling force. When God made man he poured from a "glass of blessings," a secondary image, riches such as strength, beauty, wisdom, honor and pleasure. When most of these blessings had been bestowed, rest still remained in the bottom of the glass. If this gift were also given, said God, man would worship God's gifts rather than God himself and "rest in Nature, not the God of Nature," which would be a loss to both man and God. God granted the "rest," that is, the other gifts, to man, but with a discontented "restlessness"; rest itself was not to be given to man. Man was to be "rich and weary" so that if goodness would not bring him to God then at least weariness would "toss" or convey him to God's breast, hence perhaps the reason for the title of the poem. The pulley is the major image here and the rest of the poem is related to that image. The word "rest" is used in several contexts, meaning "remaining" as well as "repose." The use of the word "restlessness" provides a strong contrast. The poet speaks of the "world's riches" in contrast to the "jewel" of rest, which is singled out as of special value.

[5] Caroline F. E. Spurgeon, *Shakespeare's Imagery* (Boston: Beacon Press, 1960), p. 335.

"The Pulley," by George Herbert

When God at first made man,
Having a glasse of blessings standing by,
Let us (said he) poure on him all we can.
Let the world's riches, which dispersed lie,
Contract into a span.

So strength first made a way,
Then beautie flow'd, then wisdome, honour, pleasure.
When almost all was out, God made a stay,
Perceiving that alone of all his treasure
Rest in the bottome lay.

For if I should (said he)
Bestow this jewell also on my creature,
He would adore my gifts instead of me,
And rest in Nature, not the God of Nature.
So both should losers be.

Yet let him keep the rest,
But keep them with repining restlesnesse.
Let him be rich and wearie, that at least,
If goodnesse leade him not, yet wearinesse
May tosse him to my breast.

STUDY QUESTIONS

1. Can you discover any relation between imagery and a "natural" manner in reading aloud?
2. Which type of imagery can you recall most easily? How can you account for this?
3. Do you find that colors help create "moods" or atmosphere for you?
4. Can you associate certain images with experiences or events in your own life?
5. What is the relation of the metaphor and simile to imagery?

6. Can you find a poem in which you think the images are only ornaments and not really essential?

7. Conversely, can you think of a poem in which the image is so important that if it were omitted the poem would completely fall apart?

8. Do you consider imagery in prose fiction as important as that in poetry? Is it used in the same way in both prose and poetry?

BIBLIOGRAPHY

Aggertt, Otis, and Elbert R. Bowen, *Communicative Reading* (Second edition). New York: The Macmillan Company, 1963, pp. 101–104.

Armstrong, Chloe, and Paul D. Brandes, *The Oral Interpretation of Literature.* New York: McGraw-Hill Company, Inc., 1963, pp. 257–259.

Bliven, B., "You Can Cultivate the Mind's Eye," *Reader's Digest,* Jan., 1958, pp. 109–112.

Brown, Stephen James Meredith, *The World of Imagery.* New York: Russell & Russell, 1966.

Grimes, Wilma H., and Alethea Smith Mattingly, *Interpretation: Writer Reader Audience.* San Francisco: Wadsworth Publishing Company, Inc., pp. 41–42, 83, 98, 108.

Lee, Charlotte I., *Oral Interpretation* (Third edition). Boston: Houghton Mifflin Company, 1965, pp. 181–191.

Lowrey, Sara, and Gertrude E. Johnson, *Interpretative Reading* (Revised edition). New York: Appleton-Century Company, Inc., 1953, pp. 32–45.

McNaughton, Ruth Flanders, *The Imagery of Emily Dickinson* (M.A. Thesis). Lincoln: University of Nebraska Studies, 1949.

Chapter VI

Emphasis, Sense Units, and the Pause in Literature

Meaning is projected in a number of ways, basically, by the body and voice. It can be conveyed through subtle movements of the head, eyes, hands, torso, or the entire body. The voice projects meaning by quality, pitch, intensity, and tempo. In this chapter we shall discuss in particular certain specific ways by which one can project meaning through emphasis, sense units, and pausing.

I. MEANING THROUGH EMPHASIS

When we speak of emphasis we are inclined to think of it simply as giving significance to a word or words. This may be acceptable to a certain degree, but emphasis has more latitude than merely giving *force* to a word or an idea. It is the intellectual and emotional evaluation that the sensitive oral interpreter gives to a word, phrase, clause, or rhetorical structure that most clearly and effectively brings out the intended meaning, attitude, and feeling of the literature. We can think of it as putting ideas into the sunlight and into the shadows, and the latter can be just as effective in giving significance or prominence to an idea or feeling as the former. In fact, if you were to go to the art gallery and look at paintings, your attention would center on those artists, such as Rembrandt, Titian, and El Greco, whose pictures have both light and shadow. Some people can look at pictures or sculpture and yet not see them; so, too, can readers look at a thought and yet not realize its penetrating power.

To an oral interpreter this matter of emphasis is evaluation of thought involving decision of choice—choice of the value and relative importance of the word, phrase, or clause to be read; and vocal and physical responsiveness are the means by which the reader communicates these judgments to the listener. In making your decision as to what should be emphasized, and how, you go through much the same thought process the author went through in making his choice of word and phrase.

The purpose of this section is really twofold; first, to lay the groundwork for projecting the ideas and feelings of the literature and, second, to suggest possible means that will assist the listener in responding to those ideas and feelings.

A. *The Carrying Word or Phrase*

There are, of course, key words or phrases in an idea. These are pivotal points that a writer uses to carry forward his line of thought and around which adjectives, adverbs, and descriptive clauses revolve. As an interpreter you may bring power or significance to such a word or words by a change in pitch, intensity, quality, or duration.

In the first verses of "Mr. Flood's Party" by Edwin Arlington Robinson some of the key words which are necessary to carry the basic idea are italicized:

> *Old Eben Flood,* climbing alone one night
> Over the hill between the town below
> And the forsaken upland hermitage
> That held as much as he should ever know
> On earth again of home, *paused warily.*
> The road was his with not a native near;
> And Eben, having leisure, *said aloud,*
> For no man else in Tilbury Town to hear:
> 'Well, *Mr. Flood,* we have the harvest moon
> Again, and we may not have many more;

The bird is on the wing, the poet says,
And you and I have said it here before.
Drink to the bird.' He raised up to the light
The *jug* that he had gone so far to fill,
And answered huskily: 'Well, Mr. Flood,
Since you propose it, I believe *I will.'*

B. *The New Idea*

As you prepare to read aloud always watch for the new idea. This is one of the keys to emphasis. Read Carl Sandburg's "A Couple," and notice how he employs new ideas as well as repetitions.

He was in Cincinnati, she in Burlington.
He was in a gang of Postal Telegraph linemen.
She was a pot rassler in a boarding house.
'The crying is lonely,' she wrote him.
'The same here,' he answered.
The winter went by and he came back and they married
And he went away again where rainstorms knocked down telegraph poles and wires dropped with frozen sleet.
And again she wrote him, 'The crying is lonely.'
And again he answered, 'The same here.'
Their five children are in the public schools.
He votes the Republican ticket and is a taxpayer.
They are known among those who know them
As honest American citizens living honest lives.
Many things that bother other people never bother them.
They have their five children and they are a couple,
A pair of birds that call to each other and satisfy.
As sure as he goes away she writes him, 'The crying is lonely,'
And he flashes back the same old answer, 'The same here.'
It is a long time since he was a gang lineman at Cincinnati
And she was a pot rassler in a Burlington boarding house;
Yet they never get tired of each other; they are a couple.

In the Book of Ruth an interesting new idea becomes the fulcrum for the story and advances the plot. The oral interpreter must point up the word "kinsman," because this word is first introduced at this point and it gives support to the unfolding events.

> And Naomi had a kinsman of her husband's, a mighty man of wealth, of the family of Elimelech; and his name was Boaz. (Ruth 2:1)

In the following excerpt from Harper Lee's *To Kill a Mockingbird* the new ideas can be brought out effectively through varying degrees of emphasis.

> For reasons unfathomable to the most experienced prophets in Maycomb County, autumn turned to winter that year. We had two weeks of the coldest weather since 1885, Atticus said. Mr. Avery said that it was written on the Rosetta Stone that when children disobeyed their parents, smoked cigarettes and made war on each other, the seasons would change: Jem and I were burdened with the guilt of contributing to the aberrations of nature, thereby causing unhappiness to our neighbors and discomfort to ourselves. (Chap. 8, p. 71.)

C. *Contrasts*

When an author uses contrasts, he often wishes to draw attention to one idea by offsetting it with another, thus mutually enhancing each thought.

Contrast, a part of life, is also found in literature in such diverse elements as strength and weakness, joy and grief, good and evil. An interesting image of James A. Garfield can be presented if you allow yourself to bring out the contrast in this statement:

> One moment he stood erect, strong, confident in the years stretching peacefully out before him. The next he lay wounded, bleeding, helpless, doomed to weary weeks of torture, to silence, and the grave.[1]

[1] Spoken by James G. Blaine, Feb. 28, 1882, *Modern Eloquence,* Vol. VII, p. 135.

The opposition of ideas is well illustrated by the words which become more powerful in juxtaposition.

Contrasts can be shown through the use of a negative phrase or clause followed by a positive phrase or clause. This device is especially noticeable in the "not—but" construction. The following is illustrative.

> Forasmuch as ye are manifestly declared to be the epistle of Christ ministered by us, written not with ink, but with the Spirit of the living God; not in tables of stone, but in fleshy tables of the heart. (II Cor. 3:3.)

One way of heightening the impact of this excerpt would be to increase vocal intensity while reading the affirmative phases and to subordinate this intensity while reading the negative. The ear is quick to note ideas contrasted in this manner.

D. *Comparisons*

In comparison an author sets one thing side by side with another in order to show a resemblance or difference. This can be found in everyday speech, and in advertisements, as well as in literature. In brief, comparisons are used to illustrate, and if they were not employed, some writings might be very dull. When you read the following comparisons aloud, see if you can make them clear and vivid.

Peter Bowman, writing about a soldier's experiences, uses striking comparisons in his book, *Beach Red*. Here is one example picked at random:

> Egan and Whitney are poised motionless, like trained bird dogs, while silence stretches out like a tightly drawn rubber sheet.

Robert G. Ingersoll, with this comparison, held an audience under the spell of his eloquence:

> Like an armed warrior, like a plumed knight, James G. Blaine marched down the halls of the American Congress and threw his shining lance full and fair against the brazen foreheads of the defamers of his country and maligners of his honor!
>
> (From "On Nominating Blaine")

The oral interpreter is responsible for the clear and vivid suggestion of the comparisons found in literature.

E. *Repetition*

According to Greek mythology, Echo was a fair nymph who fell in love with Narcissus. Displeased with Echo's behavior, Hera, a goddess, turned on Echo and condemned her never to speak except to repeat what had been said to her. Repetition in literature may present problems for the interpreter, but these are problems concerned with responsiveness, not the condemnation of Echo. Repetition, or "echo," may be a single word as spoken by Patrick Henry, "Gentlemen may cry peace, peace—but there is no peace;" or, it may be several clauses that begin with the same words such as Charles Dickens uses in opening the *Tale of Two Cities.*

> It was the best of times, it was the worst of times, it was the age of wisdom, it was the age of foolishness, it was the epoch of belief, it was the epoch of incredulity, it was the season of Light, it was the season of Darkness, it was the spring of hope, it was the winter of despair, we had everything before us, we had nothing before us, we were all going direct to Heaven, we were all going direct the other way—in short, the period was so far like the present period, that some of its noisiest authorities insisted on its being received, for good or for evil, in the superlative degree of comparison only.

Echo, or repetition, which satisfies the ear as well as the mind, may be found in similar construction as well as in exact words. Notice how Archibald MacLeish has used "echo" in the poem, "Wildwest."

"Wildwest," by Archibald MacLeish

There were none of my blood in this battle:
There were Minneconjous: Sans Arcs: Brules:
Many nations of Sioux: they were few men galloping:

This would have been in the long days in June:
They were galloping well-deployed under the plum-trees:
They were driving riderless horses: themselves they were few:

Crazy Horse had done it with few numbers:
Crazy Horse was small for a Lakota:
He was riding always alone thinking of something:

He was standing alone by the picket lines by the ropes:
He was young then: he was thirty when he died:
Unless there were children to talk he took no notice:

When the soldiers came for him there on the other side
On the Greasy Grass in the villages we were shouting
'Hoka Hey! Crazy Horse will be riding!'

They fought in the water: horses and men were drowning:
They rode on the butte: dust settled in sunlight:
Hoka Hey! they lay on the bloody ground:

No one could tell of the dead which man was Custer . . .
That was the end of his luck: by that river:
The soldiers beat him at Slim Buttes once:

They beat him at Willow Creek when the snow lifted:
The last time they beat him was the Tongue:
He had only the meat he had made and of that little:

Do you ask why he should fight? It was his country:
My God should he not fight? It was his:
But after the Tongue there were no herds to be hunting:

He cut the knots of the tails and he led them in:
He cried out 'I am Crazy Horse! Do not touch me!'
There were many soldiers between and the gun glinting . . .

And a Mister Josiah Perham of Maine had much of the
land Mister Perham was building the Northern Pacific
railroad that is Mister Perham was saying at lunch that

forty say fifty millions of acres in gift and
government grant outright ought to be worth a
wide price on the Board at two-fifty and

later a Mister Cooke had relieved Mister Perham and
later a Mister Morgan relieved Mister Cooke:
Mister Morgan converted at prices current:

It was all prices to them: they never looked at it:
why should they look at the land: they were Empire Builders:
it was all in the bid and the asked and the ink on their books . . .

When Crazy Horse was there by the Black Hills
His heart would be big with love he had for that country
And all the game he had seen and the mares he had ridden

And how it went out from you wide and clean in the sunlight

Another form of "echo," or repetition, is redundancy, or *pleonasm.* In impassioned speaking it is often used because it gives a high degree of emphasis or distinction to an idea. This is evident in Winston Churchill's dramatic speech, "Dunkirk," before the House of Commons, June 4, 1940, when he said,

> I have myself full confidence that if all do their duty and if the best arrangements are made, as they are being made, we shall prove ourselves once again able to defend our island home, ride out the storms of war and outlive the menace of tyranny, if necessary, for years, if necessary, alone.

When a writer or speaker presents a number of details, to achieve emphasis, he may employ redundancy or pleonasm. It is true that certain words used might be omitted, but intellectual exactness may result in emotional sterility. Theodore Roosevelt, in speaking on the subject, "The Strenuous Life," remarked,

> The timid man, the lazy man, the man who distrusts his country, the overcivilized man, who has lost the great fighting, masterful virtues, the ignorant man and the man of dull mind, whose soul is incapable of feeling the mighty lift that thrills 'stern men with empires in their brains'—all these, of course, shrink from seeing the nation undertake its new duties; . . .

The emphasis on the summarizing phrase *"all these"* helps to focus attention on the antecedents.

Moses, in speaking parting words to the Israelites, encouraged them by saying,

> The Lord thy God, he will go over before thee, and he will destroy these nations from before thee, and thou shalt possess them: and Joshua, he shall go over before thee, as the Lord hath said. (Deut. 31:3.)

In reading aloud do not be afraid to emphasize the redundant word or words. They frequently bring dignity, power and emotional impact to the idea.

This pleonastic structure is also found in poetry. Sometimes the poet, like the speaker, gives the reader a series of details which are pulled together by a summarizing phrase. Observe how this device is used in the following excerpt from "The Great Lover," by Rupert Brooke. Emphasize the summarizing phrase.

Dear names,

And thousand others throng to me! Royal flames;
Sweet water's dimpling laugh from tap or spring;
Holes in the ground; and voices that do sing:
Voices in laughter, too; and body's pain,
Soon turned to peace; and the deep-panting train;
Firm sands; the little dulling edge of foam
That browns and dwindles as the wave goes home;
And washen stones, gay for an hour; the cold
Graveness of iron; moist black earthen mold;
Sleep; and high places; footprints in the dew;
And oaks; and brown horse-chestnuts, glossy-new;
And new-peeled sticks and shining pools on grass;—
All these have been my loves.

Synonyms are words which have the same or almost the same meaning such as joyful and happy, sad and mournful, fair and just, and they can be thought of as "echoes." The pronoun too is, in a sense, a synonym. It stands for a noun; it takes the place of something. Not all pronouns, however, should be emphasized, but there are times when it is necessary that the pronoun be stressed in order to bring out the meaning and to keep the listener's attention on the progression of the idea. Here is an example that you might find interesting. What nouns are referred to in the use of "it" and "they"?

Enter not into the path of the wicked,
and go not in the way of evil men.
Avoid it, pass not by it, turn from it, and pass away.
For they sleep not, except
they have done mischief; and
their sleep is taken away, unless
they cause some to fall.
For they eat the bread of
wickedness, and drink the wine
of violence.

(Prov. 4:14–17.)

Apposition, or putting two nouns or pronouns beside one another, can also be an effective form of "echo." For example, "John Fitzgerald Kennedy, the thirty-fifth President of the United States. . . ," or, in Matthew 1:20 it is recorded that ". . . the angel of the Lord appeared unto him in a dream, saying, Joseph, thou son of David, fear not to take unto thee Mary thy wife: for that which is conceived in her is of the Holy Ghost." The closing lines of Poe's well known "Annabel Lee" read:

And so, all the night-tide, I lie down by the side
Of my darling, my darling, my life and my bride,
In her sepulchre there by the sea—
In her tomb by the sounding sea.

In reading appositives aloud think of them as "echoes" and keep them vocally close to each other.

Perhaps the most troublesome "echo" to read aloud is the *refrain.* Poets, naturally, are apt to select something that pleases the ear and that appeals to the emotions. Sometimes a refrain appears meaningless, but it usually reinforces the emotion. This will be discussed in more detail in the chapter on Poetry.

F. *Qualifying Words*

George H. W. Rylands, in his book, *Words and Poetry,* has a chapter on "Adjectives" which he opens this way, "Adjectives are sirens; they betray all whom their music beguiles. Enslave them and you are master of the poetic art. Their talents are four: they have sound, meaning, decorative value, and emotional value." The oral interpreter can take some advice from this statement. You, in emphasizing, must enslave qualifying words in relation to their significance. Read aloud this passage from "Night and Day" by Sidney Lanier, which contains many "qualifying words," or adjectives.

> The innocent, sweet Day is dead.
> Dark Night hath slain her in her bed.
> O, Moors are as fierce to kill as to wed!
> —Put out the light, said he.
>
> A sweeter light than ever rayed
> From star of heaven or eye of maid
> Has vanished in the unknown Shade.
> —She's dead, she's dead, said he.
>
> Now, in a wild, sad after-mood
> The tawny Night sits still to brood
> Upon the dawn-time when he wooed
> —I would she lived, said he.
>
> Star-memories of happier times,
> Of loving deeds and lovers' rhymes,
> Throng forth in silvery pantomimes.
> —Come back, O Day! said he.

Now "enslave" the adjectives as you read this passage from *The Red Badge of Courage* by Stephen Crane.

> About him were the rows and groups of men that he had dimly seen the previous night. They were getting a last draught of sleep before the awakening. The gaunt, careworn features and dusty figures were made plain by this quaint light at the dawning, but it dressed the skin of the men in corpselike hues and made the tangled limbs appear pulseless and dead. The youth started up with a little cry when his eyes first swept over this motionless mass of men, thick-spread upon the ground, pallid, and in strange postures. His disordered mind interpreted the hall of the forest as a charnel place. He believed for an instant that he was in the house

of the dead, and he did not dare to move lest these corpses start up, squalling and squawking. In a second, however, he achieved his proper mind. He swore a complicated oath at himself. He saw that this somber picture was not a fact of the present, but a mere prophecy.

G. *Word Order*

Among many writers and speakers the ordering or placement of the main elements in our English sentence is quite conventional. For the most part there is the typical order—subject, verb, object or complement, but frequently we have object, verb, subject. This is known as inversion.

Inversion gives variety, suspends thought, and frequently contributes to rhyme and rhythm. Inversion may, in itself, be a form of emphasis. The following will serve to illustrate:

A damsel with a dulcimer
In a vision once I saw:

(From "Kubla Khan,"
Samuel T. Coleridge)

Still I avow my hope and faith, sure and inviolate, that in the days to come the British and American people will for their own safety and for the good of all walk together in majesty, in justice and in peace. (From *Address Before United States Congress,* Dec. 26,1941, Winston Churchill)

Into the soul of this timid, unlettered
mountain maid there swept a flood of glorious resolve.

(From "Lincoln, A Man Called of God,"
John Mellen Thurston)

Although no attempt has been made to present every modification of the normal ordinary word order, we have presented several to make you aware of their power.

II. MEANING THROUGH SENSE UNITS

You should train yourself to get ideas from the printed page and to translate them into oral and visual cues for your listener. Your listener does not have the advantage of the markings on the printed page. The sense units must be suggested by you.

When you read aloud, the sense units become shorter than when reading silently. Cicero, in *De Oratore,* gives us a practical reason for this:

> It happens likewise in all parts of language, that a certain agreeableness and grace are attendant on utility, and, I may say, on necessity; for the stoppage of the breath, and the confined play of the lungs, introduced periods and the pointing of words. This invention gives such gratification, that, if unlimited powers of breath were granted to a person, yet we could not wish him to speak without stopping; for the invention of stops is pleasing to the ears of mankind, and not only tolerable, but easy, to the lungs.
>
> (Bk. III, XLVI)

The listener tends not to grasp ideas as rapidly as does the silent reader. To facilitate understanding, spoken language must be divided into smaller sense units. In reading aloud these smaller units are separated by pauses of varying duration depending upon the depth of the thought and the emotion.

Speakers and writers sometimes use certain constructions that can be cumbersome and awkward for the oral interpreter. By breaking them down into their meaningful parts the interpreter can establish their relationship to the main members of the sentence, and the listener will have less difficulty in understanding.

Let us turn our attention to the phrasing of two common grammatical constructions that we observe in everyday conversation and writing. We will see that we employ the pause to separate one group of words related to one idea from another group in order to make each idea clear.

A. *Direct Address* (*Noun of Address*)

When we address a person or persons in speaking, reading, or writing, we use a name or descriptive term. Here are a few underlined examples of such direct address.

> I am well aware, *soldiers,* that words cannot inspire courage; and that a spiritless army cannot be rendered active, or a timid army valiant, by the speech of its commander. (Catiline's Speech to His Troops)
>
> *Lord,* who shall abide in thy tabernacle? who shall dwell in thy holy hill? (Psalm 15:1)
>
> *Brutus:* Forever, and forever, farewell, *Cassius!* (*Julius Caesar,* Act V, Sc i).
>
> And so, *fellow-gladiators,* must you, and so must I, die like dogs. (Spartacus to the Gladiators.)[2]

In position, nouns of address may be initial, internal, or terminal. In the example from Psalm 15:1, it is an initial position; in Cataline's speech it is internal; and in Brutus's speech it is terminal. Frequently, in narrative literature the noun of address begins a direct quotation and is therefore in an initial position. For example, "Then Paul stood in the midst of Mars' hill, and said, 'Ye men of Athens, I perceive that in all things ye. . . .' " (Acts 17:22.)

Grammatically, the noun of address is separated from the rest of the sentence by a comma or commas, depending on its position in the sentence or clause. As an oral interpreter you must express it as a sense unit and yet relate it to the other members of the sentence. In spontaneous speech you have heard your instructor say, "Class, today we will discuss the character of Hamlet." And later in his lecture he might add, "As you can see, Class, it was a stormy interview Hamlet had with his mother." Read those two sentences aloud in a spontaneous, conversational manner and you will observe that you probably paused. You stopped after each noun of address, but if the noun of address was in the terminal or internal position, you automatically connected it with

[2] Elijah Kellogg, "Spartacus to the Gladiators," Robert Kidd, *Vocal Culture & Elocution* (Cincinnati & New York: Wilson, Hinkle & Co., 1857), p. 325.

what preceded—as we do in normal, everyday speech—and you did not pause before it.

B. *Corresponding Connectives*

Another device used by speakers and writers is corresponding connectives in order to strengthen weighty and important ideas. For a span of thought, there must be supports; these are corresponding connectives, such as neither/nor, either/or, not/but, both/and, as/so, so/as, not only/but also, whether/or, though/yet.

In oral interpretation, these corresponding connectives have two functions: they help to retard the movement of the sentence and they support the idea as it progresses. Look at the following to see how they support and group the thought so that the speech span is meaningful to the listener;

Not that I loved Caesar less, but that I loved Rome more.
(*Julius Caesar,* Act III, Sc ii)

No man can serve two masters: for either he will hate the one, and love the other; or else he will hold to the one, and despise the other. You cannot serve God and mammon. (Matt. 6:24)

In the following passages we find a slight variation of the neither/nor and the so/as in which there is a repetition of nor and as.

Ah, love, let us be true
To one another! for the world, which seems
To lie before us like a land of dreams,
So various, so beautiful, so new,
Hath really neither joy, nor love, nor light,
Nor certitude, nor peace, nor help for pain;
And we are here as on a darkling plain
Swept with confused alarms of struggle and flight,
Where ignorant armies clash by night.

("Dover Beach," Matthew Arnold)

> So I prophesied as I was commanded: and as I prophesied, there was a noise, and behold a shaking, and the bones came together, bone to his bone. (Ezek. 37:7.)

In this section we have presented two common structural devices which writers use to help convey their ideas more forcefully to the reader and listener. They are used frequently enough so that they may be considered as helpful guides in phrasing and pausing in many instances. You, as an interpreter, must always judge whether these stylistic devices are in accord with their purpose and to what extent the use of pauses, which they suggest, reinforce the meaning of the literature.

III MEANING THROUGH THE PAUSE

A. *The Pause and Punctuation*

Carlyle in *Sartor Resartus* quotes a Swiss inscription that is worthy of attention. It is: "Speech is silvern, silence is golden."

The pause is, no doubt, one of the most valuable tools of the oral interpreter. For the writer the pause grows out of the meaning of the material. He recognizes the need for it and indicates it as well as he can through punctuation marks. In the manuscript the pause is an observable element communicated and comprehended through the eye. If the oral interpreter or speaker planned and communicated his pauses using solely punctuation marks, his reading and speaking would probably be mechanical. If the writer did not punctuate *adequately*—and the oral interpreter followed this punctuation in reading aloud, the interpreter might find himself in a serious predicament. For instance, in Nicholas Udall's play, *Ralph Roister Doister,* the hero, Ralph, in order to woo a widow, Dame Christian Custance, hired a "scribbler" to write a letter for him. Unfortunately, the man lacked skill in proper punctuation and when the letter was delivered and read by the widow, she fumed, fretted, and raged. Governed by the punctuation marks, this is what she read:

Sweet mistress, where as I love you nothing at all,
Regarding your substance and richnesse chief of all,
For your personage, beauty, demeanour and wit,
I commend me unto you never a whit.
Sorry to hear report of your good welfare.
For (as I hear say) such your conditions are,
That ye be worthy favour of no living man,
To be abhorred of every honest man.
To be taken for a woman inclined to vice.
Nothing at all to virtue giving her due price.
Wherefore, concerning marriage, ye are thought
Such a fine paragon, as ne'er honest man bought.
And now by these presents I do you advertise
That I am minded to marry you in no wise.
For your goods and substance, I could be content
To take you as ye are. If ye mind to be my wife,
Ye shall be assured for the time of my life,
I will keep you right well, from good raiment and fare,
Ye shall not be kept but in sorrow and care.
Ye shall in no wise live at your own liberty,
Do and say what ye lust, ye shall never please me,
But when ye are merry, I will be all sad;
When ye are sorry, I will be very glad.
When ye seek your heart's ease, I will be unkind,
At no time in me shall ye much gentleness find.
But all things contrary to your will and mind,
Shall be done: otherwise I will not be behind
To speak. And all for all them that would do you wrong
I will so help and maintain, ye shall not live long.
Nor any foolish dolt shall cumber you but I.
I, whoe'er say nay, will stick by you til I do,
Thus, good mistress Custance, the Lord you save and keep,
From me, Roister Doister, whether I wake or sleep.
Who favoureth you no less (ye may be bold)
Than this letter purporteth, which you have unfold.

Now try reading it aloud with punctuation and pauses that assist you in suggesting Ralph's intent. Your listener should now recognize

Dame Christian Custance's pleasure. As a love message, it now becomes acceptable.

Written punctuation marks are guides for the comprehension of ideas from the printed page. But, it is the meaning rather than the punctuation marks that the oral interpreter primarily relies upon to determine his pauses. Thoughts become intelligible through the use of pauses and give the oral interpreter and the listener time to concentrate. The importance of punctuation, however, cannot be overlooked because, as Sheridan Baker in his book, *The Practical Stylist,* says, it ". . . gives the silent page some of the breath of life."

The pause has been referred to as "the punctuation mark of speech," "silence filled with thought," "your greatest means of emphasis," "a cessation of sound," and "an aid in the interpretation of thought." All of these are acceptable and worthy of consideration.

B. *The Pause for Understanding*

Frequently, pauses are necessary to prevent a complete misunderstanding of the material. In the Bible there is a passage which is, itself, simple and clear in meaning. But frequently it becomes cloudy and even ridiculous.

> . . . the shepherds said one to another, Let us now go even unto Bethelehem, and see this thing which is come to pass, which the Lord hath made known unto us.
>
> And they came with haste, and found Mary, and Joseph, and the babe lying in a manger. (Luke 2:15–16)

What does this passage convey if it is read without the pause? In the phrase, "And they came with haste, and found Mary, and Joseph, and the babe lying in the manger" the separation of ideas through pause is of great importance. Failure to use the pause correctly in this passage implies quite absurdly that all three are lying in the manger which, of course, does not convey the meaning of this passage at all. "Mary, and Joseph, (pause) and the babe lying in the manger," conveys a much more accurate meaning and an acceptable imaginative picture for the listener.

In II Chronicles 9:21 we read, ". . . every three years once came the ships of Tarshish, bringing gold, and silver, ivory, and apes, and peacocks." The word "once," at first glance, may seem out of place, but if you realize that the ships came only one time every three years, you can discover where the pause should be.

In "The Ballad of East and West" Rudyard Kipling shows how the use of a pause can completely reverse the intended meaning:

> Oh, East is East, and West is West, and
> never the twain shall meet,
> Till Earth and Sky stand presently at God's
> great Judgment Seat;

You have probably heard the first two lines of this poem quoted frequently as if the idea ended with the word "meet." This leaves the lines out of context. The first two lines are qualified by a third and fourth which clarify the meaning. It is not saying that east and west can never meet, but that they can never meet until ". . . Earth and Sky stand presently at God's great Judgment Seat; . . ." so you must not allow the thought to stop after the word "meet"; you must carry it on into the next two lines. You may choose to do this by having a very short suspensive pause, or no pause, after "meet." This "pause of suspension" in poetry was recognized by Thomas Sheridan, and later by J. E. Frobisher. As you have seen in Part II, "Meaning Through Sense Units," correct phrasing also depends largely upon the use of the pause. Each phrase is a sense unit which gives a certain word "picture." Such word "pictures" may be actual descriptive passages or abstract concepts. An oral reader should frame these "pictures" by means of pauses which come out of the meaning of the material. The following description of Lincoln from *John Brown's Body,* by Stephen Vincent Benét, provides a number of opportunities for pausing.

> Lincoln, six feet one in his stocking feet,
> The lank man, knotty and tough as a hickory rail,
> Whose hands were always too big for white-kid gloves,
> Whose wit was a coonskin sack of dry, tall tales,
> Whose weathered face was homely as a plowed field—
> Abraham Lincoln, who padded up and down

The sacred White House in nightshirt and carpet-slippers,
And yet could strike young hero-worshipping Hay
As dignified past any neat, balanced, fine
Plutarchan sentences carved in a Latin bronze;
The low clown out of the prairies, the ape-buffoon,
The small-town lawyer, the crude small-time politician,
State-character but comparative failure at forty
In spite of ambition enough for twenty Caesars,
Honesty rare as a man without self-pity,
Kindness as large and plain as a prairie wind,
And a self-confidence like an iron bar:

In long prose sentences the meaningful pause is essential in breaking the entire idea into its component parts. Study the excerpt from *You Can't Go Home Again* by Thomas Wolfe. Be sure, however, that in pausing adequately you do not overlook the importance of presenting the total continuity of thought.

Or there again, in the East-Side Ghetto of Manhattan, two blocks away from the East River, a block away from the gas-house district and its thuggery, there in the swarming tenement, shut in his sweltering cell, breathing the sun-baked air through opened window at the fire escape, celled there away into a little semblance of privacy and solitude from all the brawling and vociferous life and argument of his family and the seething hive around him, the Jew boy sits and pores upon his book.

A pause is frequently employed in parallel structure in parts of sentences or in a series of sentences. In such instances the writer attempts to keep a unity of form by using comparable or equivalent expressions. When you are aware of parallel structure, you can help clarify the meaning by the use of pauses at the end of each unit. There are endless examples of this in literature. One of the rich sources for this is the Bible. The following well-known selection from the book of *Ruth* illustrates this:

And Ruth said, Intreat me not to leave thee, or to return from following after thee: for whither thou goest, I will go; and where thou lodgest, I will lodge: thy people shall be my people, and thy God my God. (Ruth 1: 16.)

In bringing out contrasts, the pause is also helpful. "The Rocking-Horse Winner," by D. H. Lawrence, begins with a series of contrasts. The pauses you use in reading this aloud will strengthen the contrasting elements.

> There was a woman who was beautiful, who started with all her advantages, yet she had no luck. She married for love, and the love turned to dust. She had bonny children, yet she felt they had been thrust upon her, and she could not love them.

The pause is also used to strengthen the emotional impact where there is a contrast. Sometimes this comes in the surprise ending of a poem or story.

"The Tree," by Richard M. Rothman

A tree took root in barren soil,
and flourished.

The earth shook and trembled, but the tree stood,
green leaves undaunted.

A wind moaned low from out of the East
then howled at the tree in roaring glee,
and struck it in tidal fury.

But the bolt passed, and the tree stood,
a green goddess of beauty.

A jagged white bayonet pounced from the blue,
in a terrible streak it shot to the base,
and twisted and seared and tore at the tree.

But the bolt passed, and the tree stood,
its ancient green unaltered.

Yet look you at this tree,
Its leaves are withered, its branches shrivelled
The tree has fallen, dead.

Man came.

The pause is also used to clarify the meaning by bringing into strong relief the subject of a sentence or clause. It you pause slightly after the subject, you may be giving it emphasis. Read the following poem with this in mind.

"The Downland," by John Masefield

Night is on the downland, on the lonely moorland,
On the hills where the wind goes over sheep-bitten turf,
Where the bent grass beats upon the unploughed poorland
And the pine woods roar like the surf.

Here the Roman lived on the wind-barren lonely,
Dark now and haunted by the moorland fowl;
None comes here now but the peewit only,
And moth-like death in the owl.

Beauty was here, on this beetle-droning downland;
The thought of a Caesar in the purple came
From the palace by the Tiber in the Roman townland
To this wind-swept hill with no name.

Lonely Beauty came here and was here in sadness,
Brave as a thought on the frontier of the mind,
In the camp of the wild upon the march of madness,
The bright-eyed Queen of the blind.

Now where Beauty was are the wind-withered gorses,
Moaning like old men in the hill-wind's blast;
The flying sky is dark with running horses,
And the night is full of the past.

C. *The Pause for Mood and Emotion*

Pause also strengthens mood and can be most effective in projecting feeling. Here we shall discuss some of the various aspects of the pause that are related to feeling or emotion.

The pause may be used to strengthen philosophical contemplation and musing which frequently has certain emotional overtones. When

Macbeth hears of his wife's death, his deep grief turns him to a brief but poignant observation on the nature of life.

> *Macbeth:* She should have died hereafter;
> There would have been a time for such a word.
> Tomorrow, and tomorrow, and tomorrow
> Creeps in this petty pace from day to day
> To the last syllable of recorded time;
> And all our yesterdays have lighted fools
> The way to dusty death. Out, out, brief candle!
> Life's but a walking shadow, a poor player,
> That struts and frets his hour upon the stage
> And then is heard no more. It is a tale
> Told by an idiot, full of sound and fury,
> Signifying nothing.
>
> (*Macbeth,* Act V, Sc v)

The pause also creates suspense or anticipation by making one wonder what might happen. This pause may come before the important word or statement. Likewise, as you will see in Chapter VII, it enables the reader and the listener to make a transition from one idea to another. The more profound the message, or the greater the change from one emotion to another, then the longer the pause. This pause may be before or after the important idea or both at the beginning and end. The reader, as well as the listener, needs *time* to understand and appreciate—*time* to become involved.

In "The Will," a moving story by Mary Lavin, Lally, the daughter, comes home for her mother's funeral. She was not remembered in her mother's will because she made, from her mother's viewpoint, an unfortunate marriage. After the funeral her brothers and sisters urge her to start a hotel rather than to keep roomers.

> "I'll never start an hotel," said Lally. "I won't make any change now. I'd hate to be making a lot of money and Robert gone where he couldn't profit by it. It's too late now, I'm too old now."
>
> She looked down at her thin hands, with the broken fingernails, and the fine web of lines deepened by dirt. And as she did so the others looked at her too. They all looked at her; at this sister

that was younger than all of them, and a chill descended on them as they saw their own decay in hers. They had been better preserved, that was all; hardship had hastened the disintegration of her looks, but the undeniable bending of the bone, the tightening of the skin, and the fading of the eye could not be guarded against. A chill fell on them. A grudge against her gnawed at them.

In the story of Belshazzar's Feast, you will recall that the king held a great feast. Suddenly, in the midst of it, a hand wrote on the wall. The frightened king sought an interpretation and finally Daniel was brought before him. In this passage Daniel proceeds to explain the significance of the handwriting. Here the pause can be used for the profound seriousness of the message and for dramatic emphasis.

O thou king, the most high
God gave Nebuchadnezzar thy
father a kingdom, and majesty, and
glory, and honour:
And for the majesty that he
gave him, all people, nations, and
languages, trembled and feared before him: whom he would he slew;
and whom he would he kept alive;
and whom he would he put down.
But when his heart was lifted
up, and his mind hardened in
pride, he was deposed from his
kingly throne, and they took his
glory from him:
And he was driven from the
sons of men; and his heart was
made like the beasts, and his dwelling was with the wild asses: they
fed him with grass like oxen, and
his body was wet with the dew of
heaven; till he knew that the most
high God ruled in the kingdom of
men, and that he appointeth over it

whomsoever he will.
And thou his son, O Belshazzar, hast not humbled thine heart,
though thou knewest all this;
But hast lifted up thyself
against the Lord of heaven; and
they have brought the vessels of his
house before thee, and thou, and thy
lords, thy wives, and thy concu-
bines, have drunk wine in them;
and thou hast praised the gods of
silver, and gold, of brass, iron, wood,
and stone, which see not, nor hear,
nor know: and the God in whose
hand thy breath is, and whose are
all thy ways, hast thou not glorified:
Then was the part of the hand
sent from him; and this writing
was written.
And this is the writing that
was written, MENE, MENE, TE-
KEL, UPHARSIN.
This is the interpretation of
the thing: MENE; God hath
numbered thy kingdom, and finished it.
TEKEL; Thou art weighed
in the balances, and art found
wanting.
PERES; Thy kingdom is di-
vided, and given to the Medes and
Persians.
Then commanded Belshazzar,
and they clothed Daniel with scarlet, and put a chain of gold about
his neck, and made a proclamation
concerning him, that he should be
the third ruler in the kingdom.

In that night was Belshazzar
the king of the Chaldeans slain.
And Darius the Median
took the kingdom, being about
threescore and two years old.

(Daniel 5:18–31)

In conclusion, we would like to give you this bit of advice—do not be afraid to give your audience a chance to be carried along by significant silence. The meaningful pause will always be significant.

STUDY QUESTIONS

1. Find an example in your text in which a shift of emphasis can cause a change in meaning. Does the sense of the passage become obscured because of this change?
2. Find in your Bible three examples of inversion (word order). Identify each. Does your emphasis change?
3. Mention two or three modern writers in which the oral interpreter would need to give careful consideration to sense units in his preparation for reading aloud.
4. Find examples of initial, internal, and terminal direct address (noun of address) from a speech, a short story, or a poem.
5. Is emphasis a matter of judgment?
6. What is likely to be the means of emphasis used by the inexperienced oral interpreter? How might the experienced oral interpreter convey emphasis?
7. Select a letter from *Time* or *Newsweek* or one written to the editor of your college newspaper. Reduce it to the length of a telegram message. What does this teach you about the value of words and phrasing?
8. How may a pause be helpful to a listener? When does a pause lose its effectiveness?
9. What determines the length of a pause?
10. Ought an oral interpreter to rely upon punctuation? Illustrate for your class. Sometimes you pause at commas. Why?
11. What is the danger of over-grouping?

12. What is subordination? For what purposes has it been employed by the writer? Should the oral interpreter "toss it away"? What is its relationship to the central idea?

BIBLIOGRAPHY

Aggertt, Otis J., Elbert R. Bowen, *Communicative Reading* (2nd edition), pp. 133–143, 117–132. New York: Harper & Brothers, 1960.

Armstrong, Chloe, and Paul D. Brandes, *The Oral Interpretation of Literature,* pp. 134–136. New York: McGraw-Hill Book Company, Inc., 1963.

Boardman, Gail, *Oral Communication of Literature,* pp. 201–210. New York: Prentice-Hall, Inc., 1952.

Crocker, Lionel, *Interpretative Speech,* pp. 137–140, 223–229. New York: Prentice-Hall, Inc., 1952.

Grimes, Wilma H., and Alethea Smith Mattingly, *Interpretation: Writer-Reader-Audience,* pp. 49–60, 288–289. San Francisco: Wadsworth Publishing Company, Inc., 1961.

Henneke, Ben Graf, *Reading Aloud Effectively,* pp. 87–119. New York: Rinehart & Company, Inc., 1954.

Lee, Charlotte I., *Oral Interpretation* (3rd edition), pp. 98–100, 421–422. Boston: Houghton Mifflin Company, 1965.

Lowrey, Sara, and Gertrude E. Johnson, *Interpretative Reading: Techniques and Selections* (Revised Edit.), pp. 78–90, 155–167. New York: Appleton-Century-Crofts, Inc., 1953.

Mouat, Lawrence H., *Reading Literature Aloud,* pp. 10–20. New York: Oxford University Press, 1962.

Smith, Joseph F., and James R. Linn, *Skill in Reading Aloud,* pp. 133–143, 117–132. New York: Harper & Brothers, 1960.

Chapter VII

Structure in Literature: Clues and Tools

There are certain criteria which will help you evaluate a given piece of literature. Sometimes a quick reading will suffice, but if you suspect there is value in it, it may be wise to read it over several times before making a final judgment. After reading a story, play or poem, you may be tempted to conclude that there is nothing in it but meaningless obscurity. This can mislead you, for the symbolism, figures of speech and allusions may be more meaningful than you first realized, and only after some study become apparent. For example, in T. S. Eliot's "The Hollow Men," the repeated refrain, "Here we go round the prickly pear" is at first glance but a parody on a nursery rhyme, but longer contemplation will reveal more than this. The oral interpreter can raise it beyond a nursery rhyme and suggest its deeper meaning.

In order to help you arrive at a basis for judging a piece of literature, there are certain questions you can ask yourself. Two basic questions are: what is the literature trying to achieve, and how is it achieved? The arbitrary division of these two questions will help you set criteria of value as you analyze literature.

In the first question—what is the literature trying to achieve?—we are attempting to get at the purpose or intent. What is the basic idea? Is "Dover Beach," for example, a love poem, or is it a commentary upon the loss of old values with nothing in sight to take their place? Or does it present love as something permanent in a world of changing values? After we discover the answer to this, our attention may be turned to the next question—how is this accomplished?

This second question suggests an architectonic treatment of the subject. Such an approach will reveal the structure of the literature. We might make an analogy to building a house. After you decide what style of house you want—colonial, old English or Spanish—you settle upon the details. You determine the size, shape, number of rooms, the brick, the type and location of doors and windows. Alone, none of these items will make a house to suit your basic idea, but when they are put in the right relation to each other and given unity, they can make a pleasing and functional house. So it is in the creation of literature, for there, too, the various elements must be integrated.

Just as you want a proper setting for your house, so must an author have the right background for his work. He must know where the event or idea will take place. Will it be Renaissance Italy, which Browning liked as a rich and colorful background, the Midwest of Carl Sandburg, or the New England of Robert Frost? Will it have war as a background, which Stephen Crane and Leo Tolstoi used, or family life in which Clarence Day, Jane Austen and Louisa May Alcott delighted?

The form that a writer uses may vary in several ways. This form, as Coleridge says, must come out of "the properties of the material," and must have a structure all its own.

Although we often separate form from content, they are, in the ideal state and in the finished work of distinction, actually inseparable. For, as Walter Pater says, they ". . . completely saturate each other."

While we want to understand a piece of literature as clearly as possible, we are sometimes in danger of analyzing it to such an extent that we have only a lifeless pulp left. What T. S. Eliot said of criticism can apply equally to analysis. He refers to the "lemon squeezer" school of criticism wherein the procedure is to "extract, squeeze, tease, press every drop of meaning out. . . ."

Therefore, although we shall temporarily break down the structure of literature into some of its components we must remember that, like a puzzle, no part is complete in or by itself. The meaning becomes clear only when the components fit tightly into place and become a highly integrated part of the whole.

I. CLUES TO ANALYZING LITERATURE

A. *Title*

When you attempt to analyze a piece of literature there are certain clues which will help you to get at the meaning. One of these is the title itself. You may decide to read a piece of literature because the title intrigues you; it may puzzle you, or it may give you a hint as to what to expect. That title may be of considerable help in interpreting the theme or nature of the work. It may be an obvious title such as "Home Thoughts From Abroad," or it may be the name of a character, place, event, or a quotation from literature. Many novels, stories and plays get their names from a place, such as *East Lynne,* "Kenilworth," *Barchester Towers.* Some plays and novels get their names from the main character, such as *Anna Karenina, Jane Eyre, Macbeth* and *Othello.* Other titles may be an allusion to classical mythology, such as "Ulysses," "Glorious Apollo," or "Venus Transiens." Sometimes titles come from the Bible, such as *The Little Foxes,* (Song of Solomon 2:15), *The Voice of the Turtle* (Song of Solomon 2:12), *Grapes of Wrath* (Suggested by Isaiah 63:1–6, but the phrase actually was used in "The Battle Hymn of the Republic"). Shakespeare, and other writers, have provided titles for a number of pieces of literature, such as the plays: *Both Your Houses* by Maxwell Anderson, "A plague o' both your houses!" (*Romeo and Juliet,* Act. III Sc. I); *Dear Brutus,* by James Barrie, "The fault, dear Brutus, is not in our stars, But in ourselves, that we are underlings." (*Julius Caesar,* Act I Sc. II). Keats used the phrase, "alien corn," in "Ode To A Nightingale," which was later used as a title for a play. Sometimes titles are events, such as MacLeish's "The Fall of the City," or Cowper's "The Loss of the Royal George," or Longfellow's "Paul Revere's Ride," or Byron's "The Destruction of Sennacherib."

When the oral interpreter and his audience are aware of the significance of the title and its possible implications, in terms of its origin in literature, religion, or history, it will serve as a clue and make possible a richer understanding of the material.

B. *Theme*

Sometimes a topic sentence in a story or poem may also be a clue to its meaning. It may tell you what the literature is trying to say; that is, what the theme is. The word "theme" comes from a Greek word meaning "to place, set, lay down." It is defined as a subject or topic on which one speaks or writes. In "Home Thoughts From Abroad," Browning states the main idea in the first two lines:

> Oh, to be in England
> Now that April's there,

After this, he describes the beauties he would find in England at this time. Robert Frost gives his theme in the first two lines of "Mending Wall":

> Something there is that does not love a wall,
> That sends the frozen ground-swell under it,

and from this and further musings on the topic he builds his poem. Sidney Lanier states the theme in his poem, "Opposition," in the line

> Of fret, of dark, of thorn, of chill,
> complain no more. . . .

In Wordsworth's sonnet the first line

> The world is too much with us,

presents the basic idea after which he gives examples to support his theme. In his "Character of the Happy Warrior," he gives the theme both in the title and in the first line, and begins to elaborate upon it in the third line,

> Who is the happy warrior? Who is he
> That every man in arms should wish to be?
> —It is the generous Spirit, who, when brought
> Among the tasks of real life, hath wrought
> Upon the plan that pleased his boyish thought:

Edwin Arlington Robinson develops the theme of failure through short lyrics, sonnets, and poems in blank verse. Carl Sandburg presents strength, the common man, the industrial world and prophecy in his themes. In your study of literature, you will see that each writer tends to have certain themes that interest him, and he uses them in a variety of situations.

The theme or idea usually grows out of the writer's experience. Very often the subject has a wide appeal to mankind; it has a universality. It is essential that you understand the theme of the material and its relationship to the entire literary object even though it may not be in accord with your own viewpoint. The theme alone does not make a literary work. It is not necessarily a preachment in direct terms, but evolves from the total meaning of the experience.

C. *Meanings of Words*

When we do not understand a word (symbol) we frequently go to the dictionary. But sometimes the definition found there does not give the meaning of the word as intended by its context. In *On Style,* Pater says that words achieve a meaning through an ". . . intuitive condition of mind, [and] it must be recognized by like intuition on the part of the reader, . . ."[1] He also believes that "all language involves translation from inward to outward."[2] The author has a certain meaning in mind which he tries to convey in his writing. You may have another meaning in mind when you read it aloud, and the hearer may have still another meaning in mind when he hears it. While all three—the author, the oral interpreter and the listener—have the same word, or group of letters in mind, and while the interpreter and the listener are attempting to arrive at the author's context of a word, there are some differences which exist due to the variety of experiences and associations each has had.

There are many words in literature which you do not use or hear every day. In the following from Macbeth you encounter the word "incarnadine."

> The multitudinous seas incarnadine,
> Making the green one red.

In "The Cloud" by Shelley, the word "cenotaph" is rather important to the meaning of the whole poem:

> I silently laugh at my own cenotaph,
> And out of the caverns of rain,
> Like a child from the womb, like a ghost
> From the tomb, I arise and unbuild it again.

[1] Walter Pater, Essay on Style in *Appreciations with An Essay on Style* (London: Macmillan & Co.), 1920, p. 33.

[2] *Ibid.,* p. 34.

In Robert Burns's poem, "The Cotter's Saturday Night," it will help you if you know that a "cotter" is a peasant or farmer. Scott's "Coronach" has several unusual words in three consecutive lines:

> Fleet foot on the corrie,
> Sage counsel in cumber,
> Red hand in the foray,
> How sound is thy slumber!

When you know that "corrie" means the side of a hill, "cumber" a difficulty, and "foray" a struggle or conflict, you will have a clearer picture of the person Scott is eulogizing.

Words may be assigned denotative and connotative meanings. The first, denotative, establishes the nature and meaning of the specific object. The second, connotative, colors a word and arouses emotional reactions in us.

H. S. Langfeld says that the meaning of an object is the attitude the individual has toward that object. The writer, who usually wants us to have a certain attitude toward an object or word, uses everything at his disposal to create such an attitude. The reader, whether he is reading silently or aloud, brings his own background of experiences and associations to words and that background further determines the meaning he gets. You can only get the intended meaning through a careful study of the literature, aided by your own past experiences and associations and through your vicarious experiences and associations in literature. T. S. Eliot says, ". . . what a poem means is as much what it means to others as what it means to the author; . . ."[3] The same is true of words. Words do not have meanings. People have meanings. Your task as an oral interpreter is to assist your listener in attaching to the words of literature those meanings which you believe appropriate to the intended literary experience.

The oral interpreter can easily take advice from *Through the Looking-Glass:*

> "That's a great deal to make one word mean," Alice said in a thoughtful tone.

[3] T. S. Eliot, *The Use of Poetry and the Use of Criticism,* "The Modern Mind" (Lecture given at Harvard Univ., March 17, 1933) (New York: Barnes & Noble, Inc.), 1957, p. 130.

"When I make a word do a lot of work like that," said Humpty Dumpty, "I always pay it extra."

D. *Symbolism*

Symbolism has been used for centuries to arouse responses. One of the early Christian symbols was the fish, a symbol of Jesus was the lamb, and a sacred Egyptian symbol was the scarab. Colors, too, take on symbolic meaning; red may suggest violence, blue coolness; and, of course, words themselves are symbols.

The word "symbol" comes from a Greek root meaning "to throw together." It is something which represents or takes the place of something else. The symbol and the thing symbolized are quite distinct from each other and each maintains its own individuality. Yet the symbol must suggest the connection or kinship with that which it symbolizes, and that kinship must seem plausible.

In literature you may find various treatments of symbolism. Sometimes its use is obvious, such as the use of the eagle or the Statue of Liberty as symbolic of the United States of America. A hill or mountain is frequently symbolic of a struggle. In "Parnassus," Tennyson used the word "mountain" as symbolic of the poet's struggle to achieve ageless fame. In "The Brook," he used the brook itself as symbolic of eternal life.

Sometimes symbolism is not so obvious. The interpreter will need to perceive the relationship between the intangible thing and the symbolism which the author has suggested for his particular situation. In "The Poems of Our Climate," Wallace Stevens uses pink and white carnations in a bowl of clear water to represent the uncomplicated, untortured "I." Remember that in symbolism there is a kinship between the tangible and the intangible.

E. *Allusions*

Very often an author makes allusions to places or characters to illustrate or clarify his idea. In "Adonais," Shelley writes:

> . . . where was born Urania
> When Adonais died?

Since Urania was a heavenly muse and the patroness of astronomy, Shelley is asking why the constellations were allowed to bring about the death of Adonais. In "Hermes Trismegistus," Longfellow writes:

Where are Helios and Hephaestus,
Gods of eldest eld?
Where is Hermes Trismegistus,
Who their secrets held?

Who are Helios, Hephaestus and Hermes Trismegistus? They are important to the poet's meaning, and you as a reader must understand his references to them. In "Hymn: Before Sun-Rise, in the Vale of Chamouni" Coleridge says: "The Arve and Arveiron at thy base rave ceaselessly." You need to know where Chamouni is, and what the Arve and Arveiron are.

"To Helen," often considered one of Poe's best poems, contains allusions to classical legends. The "Nicean barks" refer to the graceful ships used by Nicea long ago. What were these ships like? Why does he refer to the Naiads? Who were they, and why does he refer to their "airs"? Why does he mention the agate lamp, and Psyche?

Helen, thy beauty is to me
Like those Nicean barks of yore,
That gently, o'er a perfumed sea,
The weary, wayworn wanderer bore
To his own native shore.

On desperate seas long wont to roam,
Thy hyacinth hair, thy classic face,
Thy Naiad airs have brought me home
To the glory that was Greece
And the grandeur that was Rome.

Lo! in yon brilliant window-niche
How statue-like I see thee stand,
The agate lamp within thy hand,
Ah! Psyche, from the regions which
Are Holy Land!

Allusions sharpen meaning and often carry great emotional power.

F. *Attitude*

"The power of one mind to appreciate the attitude of another, the sympathetic instinct by which we can appreciate another's point of view must be developed," wrote S. S. Curry.[4] The oral interpreter in analyzing literature should note the attitude of the literature and of the characters involved.

When you study a piece of literature, try to discover what viewpoint or attitude the literature is attempting to establish. It may be an attitude of optimism as in Browning's "Rabbi Ben Ezra"; or an attitude of patriotic bravery as in Henry Fifth's "Once more into the breach" (*Henry V,* Act III, scene 1); an attitude of sorrow as *Richard III* (Act I, scene 2) where Lady Anne mourns over the body of the king; an attitude of hatred in Richard III himself; an attitude of indifference in the response of the women in "Four Preludes on Playthings of the Wind" by Carl Sandburg; or the attitude of tolerance on the part of the son toward his alcoholic father in Chekhov's "The Father."

The writer may reinforce an attitude through his choice of words, figures of speech, linguistic structure, rhythm, tempo and repetition. These attitudes should be communicated by the oral interpreter through vocal and physical responsiveness.

G. *Critical and Historical Investigation*

In addition to studying the text of the literature, it will help if you go beyond that to see if there are other pertinent facts you need to know. For example, it is often of value to read critical comments on the author or by the author. What do critics say about his work, and what does he say, either about his own work or about that of another writer? Further, he may, either in an essay or even a poem, give his own philosophy of writing as has been done by Edgar Allan Poe, Matthew Arnold, T. S. Eliot and Karl Shapiro. Often a knowledge of the author's life can clarify his ideas and add interest to his work.

For critical reviews of literature you may turn to *The Saturday*

[4] S. S. Curry, *Lessons in Vocal Expression* (Boston: The Expression Company, 1895), p. 195.

Review, The Kenyon Review, Current Biographies, The New York Times Book Review, The Educational Theatre Journal, Celebrity Register, Biography Index, Publications of the Modern Language Association (PMLA), and *Contemporary Authors.* Sources of criticism are almost limitless.

Frequently a knowledge of the times and society in which the writer lived will provide meaningful insights. A concept of Victorian England adds to the significance of Charles Dickens' novels just as a knowledge of Renaissance Italy adds to an understanding of Robert Browning's poems. Awareness of the period in which Euripides or Ibsen wrote provides additional perspective into the significance of their plays. Improved understanding may come from biographies, autobiographies, letters, or from the social history of a period.

II. THE TOOLS OF LITERATURE AND READING ALOUD

The writer enhances and clarifies his meaning through craftsmanship and he uses certain tools for this purpose which have particular significance for the oral interpreter.

In contrast to the more obvious suggestions for getting meanings as mentioned above, there are others which are subtler and of which you may be less aware. Some of these have their origin in the field of aesthetics. You will find in the following pages a description of some of the writer's tools which the oral interpreter can explore in his search to discover meanings. They will help give you an appreciation of what the writer is attempting to do and how he accomplishes it.

A. *Onomatopoeia*

When the sound of the word helps convey meaning it is an onomatopoetic word. Novelists and poets frequently try to convey the idea of a word through its sound as well as its assigned definitive meaning. When you read aloud, see that your tone and diction bring out the "sound" meaning. At the same time, do not allow the tone to become so dominant that it draws attention to itself.

One of the best known examples of onomatopoeia in American literature can be found in *The Bells* by Poe, wherein the poet attempts to convey through sound the various types of bells ringing, from silver bells to bronze bells. Notice how he uses sounds, such as nk, t, l, s, m and n to achieve this. He describes the silver bells as they

> . . . tinkle, tinkle, tinkle,
> In the icy air of night:
> While the stars that oversprinkle
> All the heavens, seem to twinkle
> With a crystalline delight;
> Keeping time, time, time,
> In a sort of Runic rhyme,
> To the tintinnabulation that so musically wells
> From the bells, bells, bells, bells—
> Bells, bells, bells—
> From the jingling and the tinkling of the bells.

And in contrast he uses other sounds such as cl, r, ng, l, j (as in danger and jangling), sw, tw, and s (z) to describe how the brazen bells

> . . . clang, and clash, and roar! . . .
> Yet the ear, it fully knows,
> By the twanging—
> And the clanging—
> How the danger ebbs and flows;
> Yet the ear distinctly tells—
> In the jangling
> And the wrangling
> How the danger sinks and swells,
> By the sinking or the swelling in the anger of the bells . . .

In "Meeting at Night" Browning also suggests the idea through an emphasis on sounds. You can hear the prow of the boat in the wet sand through the sh, qu (as in quench), ch, sl, and s sounds as he says:

As I gain the cove with pushing prow,
And quench its speed i' the slushy sand.

And later observe how he uses sounds, such as t, p, k, s and ch to convey

A tap at the pane, the quick sharp scratch
And blue spurt of a lighted match, . . .

Remember to respond to words in their total context. The listener's attention should be drawn to the literary experience rather than to words in isolation.

B. *Figures of Speech*

Figures of speech are unusual ways of expressing ideas in an effort to make them vivid, clear, and fresh. They are not merely ornaments; rather, their purpose is to deepen the experience for the reader.

While there are many figures of speech, we shall include only those which are most frequently used in literature; such as the metaphor, simile, personification, hyperbole, metonymy, synecdoche and irony. You should have a clear concept of the use of the figure of speech in relation to your judgment of the intent of the literature.

The *metaphor,* which comes from a Greek word meaning "to carry over" or "to transfer" is one of the most effective of all of the figures of speech. Aristotle defines it as giving something a "name that belongs to another." It changes a word from the usual meaning assigned, to that which is unusual; yet, because of some similarity, it seems appropriate. It is used in both poetry and prose and part of its appeal is in its unique quality.

There are endless numbers of metaphors in literature. In "Hymn Before Sun-Rise, in the Vale Chamouni" Coleridge refers to the eagles as "playmates of the mountain-storm" and to the lightning as "the dread arrows of the clouds." There are many metaphors in the Bible as well, such as "Judah is a lion's whelp" or "the Lord is my shepherd."

The power of the metaphor has been well described by James Russell Lowell, who said, ". . . a metaphor is no argument, though it be sometimes the gunpowder to drive one home and embed it in the memory." Metaphors are ways of strengthening and intensifying an experience which an author wishes to communicate and to which he wants you to respond. In reading aloud be aware of the basic idea which the metaphor represents. The real object and the metaphor should be vocally balanced since they are equally important.

The *simile* is akin to the metaphor. While the metaphor definitely states that an object *is* something, such as "all the world's a stage," the simile says it is *like* something. In the simile the word *like* or *as* is usually used. The comparison should strengthen the original object when you read aloud. The simile is a kind of illustration of a word or action. Therefore, it should carry vocal weight comparable to the object it illustrates. Like the metaphor, there is also vocal balance between the real object and the thing with which it is compared.

> High in front advanced,
> The brandished sword of God before them blazed,
> Fierce as a comet.
>
> (Milton, *Paradise Lost,* Bk. XII)

> . . . Thou, from whose unseen presence the leaves dead
> Are driven, like ghosts from an enchanter fleeing, . . .
>
> (Shelley, "Ode to the West Wind")

> The Assyrian came down like the wolf on the fold.
>
> (Byron, "The Destruction of Sennacherib")

In *personification* abstract ideas and inanimate objects are given human characteristics, appearance or feelings to clarify the author's idea. In "The Passions," the poet William Collins gives Melancholy the appearance of a human:

> With eyes upraised, as one inspired,
> Pale Melancholy sate retired; . . .

Personification requires you to have a distinct image, usually visual, of the object personified. This strong image should be so clear to you that it is reflected in your vocal tone. A slight pause after the subject may help strengthen the visual picture for you and the listener. In "Ode," Collins speaks of ". . . Spring, with dewy fingers cold. . . ."

In the *apostrophe* an imaginary or real person or abstraction is spoken to directly. This has been used by many poets; for example, in "Ode," William Congreve addresses "Daughter of Memory, immortal Muse, Calliope." John Keats, in "Ode to Psyche," writes

> O Goddess! hear these tuneless numbers,
> wrung
> By sweet enforcement and remembrance dear,
> And pardon that thy secrets should be sung
> Even into thine own soft-conch'd ear: . . .

And Thomas Gray, in "The Progress of Poesy," says

> Awake, Aeolian lyre, awake,
> And give to rapture all thy trembling strings . . .

In reading the apostrophe aloud the oral reader will have a concept of the real or imaginary object he is addressing.

A *hyperbole* is an exaggeration to create an effect, to emphasize, to make an impression. It is often associated with the use of numbers to impress a reader or hearer. When you read it aloud see that the hyperbole points up its exaggeration. This can be done through sustension of tone, change of pitch or a slight increase in intensity. Wordsworth, speaking of the "Daffodils," says,

> Ten thousand saw I at a glance,
> Tossing their heads in sprightly dance. . . .

In "The Deserted Village," Goldsmith writes,

> If to the city sped—What waits him there?
> To see profusion that he must not share;
> To see ten thousand baneful arts combin'd
> To pamper luxury, and thin mankind; . . .

Metonymy is used to signify an object rather than the ordinary name of the object. It is an associational substitution such as "Red, White and Blue" for the American flag, "bower" for tree, or "sceptre" for "kingdom." It implies something else, which your voice may carry by a subtle inflection or a slight pause after the metonymic word.

> Amidst thy bowers the tyrant's hand is seen,
> And desolation saddens all thy green: . . .
>
> (Goldsmith, *The Deserted Village*)

> This is my son, mine own Telemachus,
> To whom I leave the sceptre and the isle, . . .
>
> (Tennyson, "Ulysses")

Synecdoche is a figure of speech in which a more inclusive term is used for a less inclusive term or the reverse. For example, in the Lord's Prayer the phrase, "Give us this day our daily bread," implies more than merely the provision of bread alone; that is, a part is used to represent the whole, just as "faces" is used to indicate human beings.

Irony, another figure of speech, is evident when one says one thing and means just the opposite. The real meaning is not necessarily apparent. It is often associated with a mocking attitude, and Puttenham in *The Arte of English Poesie* called it the "dry mock." We may hear pleasantness only to realize a "sting of rebuke in its tail." If you are in the midst of an angry mob and someone remarks, "what a pleasant restful place," the usual meanings given these words are obviously not the meanings intended. When Swift, in "A Modest Proposal," suggests that the Irish parents sell their children to English landlords, he is using irony. Irony may also be used to blame by seeming to praise. It is in this sense that, in *Julius Caesar,* Antony repeatedly refers to Brutus as an "honorable man." Irony can be communicated very effectively by the oral interpreter since it depends largely upon the voice to convey its effect.

A *paradox* is a statement which at first glance appears to be the antithesis of what one normally expects and accepts, yet despite this it proves to be reasonable and true. It has in it an element of contradiction which may be found in a single statement or in sequential and contrasting statements. It is a means of emphasizing an idea and of implanting it forcibly upon the mind. Let us look at the following sonnet by John Donne:

> Batter my heart, three person'd God; for, you
> As yet but knocke, breathe, shine, and seeke to mend;
> That I may rise, and stand, o'erthrow mee, ' and bend
> Your force, to breake, blowe, burn and make me new.
> I, like an usurpt towne, to 'another due,
> Labour to' admit you, but oh, to no end,
> Reason your viceroy in mee, mee should defend,
> But is captiv'd and proves weake or untrue.
> Yet dearely 'I love you,' and would be loved faine,
> But am betroth'd unto your enemie:
> Divorce mee, 'untie, or breake that knot againe,
> Take mee to you, imprison mee, for I
> Except you' enthrall mee, never shall be free,
> Nor ever chast, except you ravish mee.

In this sonnet, composed largely of monosyllables and dissyllables, the poet presents a paradoxical situation in which the speaker uses parallel antithetical statements each of which seems to contradict the other. There is a pull of opposites, but these opposites are resolved into a singleness of idea. The speaker asks God to "batter" his heart since God has, so far, merely gently tried to "knock" and "mend." He asks God to help him "rise and stand," yet to accomplish this God must bend His "force to brake, blowe, burn and make me new." He cannot be persuaded to good; rather, he must be forced to it because, although he would like to admit God, his weak reason is held captive and he yields to the tempter as a town is usurped by an unwelcome invader. Although he loves God, he is betrothed to God's enemy. Unless God imprisons him he shall never be free, and unless God "ravish" him he shall never be "chast." This fusion of opposites and contradictions increases the complexity of the theme and requires stress, tension and effort to effect a resolution of the seeming conflict. The oral interpreter will bring out the meaning as he brings out the opposites, for, while they appear to be in contradiction, they actually support and reinforce the basic idea.

C. *Unity and Harmony*

Most of you have heard of the "three unities" in drama—the unities of time, place and action—which were attributed to Aristotle and rigidly followed by the French classical writers. Actually, there should be unity in any piece of literature, be it poetry, fiction or drama, so that the author's purpose can be achieved effectively.

This interest in unity is deeply rooted in man. Langfeld says that ". . . the law of unity is a fundamental one in aesthetics because it is also a fundamental law of mind." Man wants to experience a sense of unity in his environment and in his life. Goethe said that it was possible for man to be happy only when he finds himself to be a ". . . part of the whole," which gives him a feeling of harmony.

Unity can be obtained in a number of ways. Sometimes it is strengthened by using a single setting, such as in Shaw's play *Candida.* It can also be achieved by harmony of mood, such as is found in Robert Frost's "Stopping By Woods On a Snowy Evening." When you read a story with a number of characters in it, you like to see a relationship between the characters which in itself gives unity. If there are several plots, you like to see them interwoven and interrelated. If there is one plot, you like to see its essential characters and action developed clearly and in a unified manner.

Dominance or emphasis also gives unity. Certain elements may be stressed to demand more attention. In *Othello,* the characters of the Moor, Desdemona, his wife, and Iago, his ancient, have greater dominance than the other characters, for they are the center of the plot and are important throughout the play. In *Anna Karenina,* our attention is fixed on the dominant character of Anna. Sometimes unity is further strengthened through an object, such as the handkerchief in *Othello,* or the knife in John Steinbeck's "Flight" which is emphasized in the opening of the story and is the same knife that ultimately brings about Pepe's tragedy.

Good literature is generally so well unified in its thought and structure that each single part is necessary to make it complete; if one part is removed the totality is damaged and its effectiveness diminished. When you study your material, look for the unifying elements in it. See that your concept of unity is clear in relation to the theme, mood, plot, and characters, so that you can convey that unity when you read aloud.

Harmony in literature may be found in linguistic structure or satisfying arrangement of sounds, words or thoughts. Many examples of this can be found, as in "The Tiger" by William Blake, The Ten Commandments, and the poetry of Swinburne and Dylan Thomas. Harmony serves to strengthen and re-enforce unity.

D. *Repetition*

As you have seen in Chapter VI, repetition is a useful device. In prose or poetry repetition is one of the tools that gives unity, emphasizes an idea or an emotion, or creates a mood. It may do this in several ways; for example, by repeating exact words, as was often done in the old ballad refrain, when a whole line was repeated. Or the repetition of a phrase, as in the "Lady of Shalott," by Tennyson, where thirteen of the nineteen stanzas end in the words, "The Lady of Shalott," can give unity. It may be the repetition of form. For example, in "Lord Randall" there is a series of questions and answers which gives form to the ballad and tells the story at the same time. In this ballad there is also repetition in the last line of each stanza where Lord Randal says, either "For I'm weary wi' hunting, and fain wad lie down," or "For I'm sick at the heart, and I fain wad lie down." Both of these techniques give unity to this ballad.

Some kinds of repetitions may not be recognized at first. There may be a repetition of an idea instead of specific words or phrases, or sounds may be repeated that help, through their repetition, to emphasize an idea or create a mood. When sounds are used in this sense, they are referred to as alliteration, assonance, or consonance.

Alliteration, in which the first sound is repeated in several words placed near each other has long been a popular device in poetry and prose. It makes use of certain sound values which help strengthen the intended meaning and give a unity:

> Wailing, wailing, wailing, the wind over land and sea
>
> (Tennyson, "Rizpah")

Fix'd fate, free will, foreknowledge absolute . . .

(Milton, *Paradise Lost,* Bk. II)

He spoke; and Sohrab smiled on him, and took
The spear, and drew it from his side, . . .

(Arnold, "Sohrab and Rustum")

Assonance is the repetition of vowel sounds in words. The use of repeated vowel sounds near each other intensifies meaning, helps create mood, and strengthens the emotional impact. These repeated sounds may be scattered throughout the line. In the two following lines notice how the *o* sound is repeated.

Ah, broken is the golden bowl! the spirit flown forever!

(Poe, "Lenore")

*Consonance,** the repetition of consonant sounds, can also create mood and evoke emotional responses. In the following selection you will observe the repetition of various consonant sounds, such as *b, t, d, w;* note that while many of the sounds are the same, the only actual words repeated are "about," "the," and "and." Thus, it is the sound that helps unify the idea.

About, about, in reel and rout,
The death-fires danced at night;
The water, like a witch's oils,
Burnt green, and blue and white.

(Coleridge, "Rime of the Ancient
Mariner," Part II)

Another kind of repetition is found in *rhyme.* Rhyme helps give unity in that it links one line to another line by repeated sounds. It may also emphasize the rhythm and thereby heighten emotion. Observe how it does this in stanzas from "Requiescat," by Oscar Wilde.

Tread lightly, she is near
Under the snow,

* The term 'consance' was used in Edith Rickert's *New Methods for the Study of Literature,* pp. 192, 208. University of Chicago Press, 1927.

Speak gently, she can hear
 The daisies grow.
All her bright golden hair
 Tarnished with rust,
She that was young and fair
 Fallen to dust.

Meter, too, with its regular feet is a repetition of certain beats which create a rhythm. The usual meters are iambic, (u-), trochee (-u), anapest (u u -), dactyl (- u u), spondee (- -), and pyrrhic (u u). The repetition which meter affords gives literature a unity in the movement or flow of the line and it provides a sense of form, yet meter must never obscure the meaning by dominating it with too strong a mechanical beat. A more detailed discussion of meter will be found in Chapter IX, *The Oral Interpretation of Poetry.*

E. *Variety*

Variety is pleasing in literature and in the oral interpretation of literature because it holds attention, has an element of surprise, and strengthens emotional reactions.

A writer uses this tool of literature in a number of ways. He may change from description to narration; he may use sentences of different length and structure; he may use a rich vocabulary; he may use a range of moods; or he may have different kinds of characters.

There are other ways in which a writer achieves variety. He may chronicle a range of events and actions such as Anthony had in Allen's *Anthony Adverse,* or such as the Forsyte family experienced in Galsworthy's *The Forsyte Saga.* He may present a number of crises differing in degree. He may attain variety when his characters have different attitudes toward the same circumstances, as do the characters in *John Brown's Body,* by Benét, or in Browning's *The Ring and the Book.*

Variety may also be an effective tool when a writer elaborates upon a theme. For example, in the sonnet, "On First Looking Into Chapman's Homer," Keats writes:

Much have I travell'd in the realms of gold,
 And many goodly states and kingdoms seen;

Round many western islands have I been
Which bards in fealty to Apollo hold.

Keats might simply have said, "I have travelled in many lands including Greece," but instead, he elaborates on this idea in order to set the background for the rest of the poem. He gives several examples, which constitute variety, in order to hold attention and interest. Variety is important and useful when it is integrated into the fibre of the literary object. It is through your own grasp of each unit, and the relation of unit to unit, that you achieve a concept of variety throughout your material. Your task, as an interpreter, is to make rich those elements of variety which are inherent in the material.

F. *Contrast*

As you like variety for the freshness it provides, you may like contrasts, or opposites, for the shock or emotional impact they give. In addition, contrast helps you apprehend opposites more easily, for they become more clear when they are set side by side. For example, the so-called comic relief scenes in Shakespeare actually intensify the tragic effect by being placed next to the serious theme. This is evident in the drunken Porter's scene in *Macbeth,* where the horror of King Duncan's death is contrasted with the humor of the drunken porter. In the same play, the King's description of Macbeth's castle as a "pleasant seat," takes on tragic quality when you realize that this is to be the site of Duncan's murder.

Contrasts may be found in other literary forms as well. In the sonnet, "Ozymandias," Shelley gives an excellent example of contrast when he presents the once great monarch of whom the only remains are a broken statue.

And on the pedestal these words appear:
"My name is Ozymandias, King of Kings:
Look on my works, ye Mighty, and despair!"
Nothing beside remains. Round the decay
Of that colossal wreck, boundless and bare
The lone and level sands stretch far away.

In "Childe Harold," Byron provides a comparable example of contrast in the scintillating description of the gay ball which is harshly interrupted by the onslaught of battle and so heightens the grief that follows.

This effective tool of contrast can emphasize an idea so that it arouses a deeper emotional reaction. Contrasts, despite—and indeed because of—their great difference, can be brought together skillfully by an able writer and conveyed by an able interpreter through changes in pitch, tempo, intensity or vocal quality.

As Wordsworth says

> . . . there is a dark
> Inscrutable workmanship that reconciles
> Discordant elements, makes them cling
> Together in one society.
>
> (Wordsworth, "The Prelude")

G. *Balance*

Balance is a tool which enables a writer and an oral interpreter to keep the parts of a literary object in proper proportion to each other, so that one part does not overshadow another to the point of damaging the total effect.

Balance can be achieved in a number of ways. First of all, it is related to contrast and it may come from contrasting characters of equal importance. For example, in *Othello* there is a balance as well as contrast between the mistrust and jealousy of Othello and the complete faith and innocence of Desdemona. It may occur if one character is placed in opposition to a group. Such is the case in *Julius Caesar,* where a single character, the shrewd Marc Antony, balances the irrational but powerful mob in his famous oration (Act III, Sc ii). It may arise from a contrast of moods which balance each other. Or, it may grow out of a contrast in tempo as in Hilaire Belloc's "Tarantella."

Balance may also be established by parallel construction such as you will find in the Psalms, Proverbs and Ecclesiastes and in this excerpt from *You Can't Go Home Again* by Thomas Wolfe. In speaking of man and his works, he wrote:

> He needed speech to ask for bread—and he had Christ! He needed songs to sing in battle—and he had Homer! He needed words to curse his enemies—and he had Dante, he had Voltaire, he had Swift! He needed cloth to cover up his hairless, puny flesh against the seasons—and he wove the robes of Solomon, he made the garments of great kings, he made the samite for the young knights! He needed walls and a roof to shelter him—and he made Blois! He needed a temple to propitiate his God—and he made Chartres and Fountains Abbey! He was born to creep upon the earth—and he made great wheels, he sent great engines thundering down the rails, he launched great wings into the air, he put great ships upon the angry sea!

When you read aloud a passage in which you think there is balance between two ideas, have a clear concept of the elements that provide that balance. Put them on a mental scale and give to each idea the weight it requires. When this occurs, your voice should approximate the balance the literature dictates.

H. *Climax*

A helpful technique which is used in all types of literature—prose, poetry, or drama—is the climax. The word climax, which means "ladder" in Greek, consists of a series of ideas each of which is more important than the one that preceded it. Finally, it reaches the most important idea of all, and achieves the effect the writer desires. It does not jump about from one idea to another, but presents a gradual, logical increase in the importance of each idea so that a cumulative effect is achieved. Because of its movement and upward development, Puttenham, in *The Arte of English Poesie* (1589), called it the "marching" or "climbing" figure. It may be found in a sentence, a paragraph or in an entire literary work. Notice the "marching" or "climbing" effect in the following excerpts:

> To bind a Roman citizen is a crime, to flog him is an abomination, to slay him is almost an act of murder: to crucify him is—What?
>
> (The Second Speech Against Gaius Verres by Cicero.)

> I did not make a speech and leave others to move a resolution, I did not move a resolution, and leave others to go on an embassy. I did not go on an embassy, and leave others to persuade the Thebans. No. I went through with the business from the beginning to the end; I gave myself to you without reservation in the face of the perils that encompassed the city.
>
> ("On The Crown," by Demosthenes)

The climax is useful in several ways. First, as you see, it emphasizes the importance of one idea in relation to another. It also provides variety. Sometimes it establishes a kind of unity in its parallel statements and its parallel structure. Finally, it gives a sense of achievement and power.

Vocally you may convey the climax by an increasing intensity, volume, a more sustained tone, or conversely, by a staccato attack. You might also raise your pitch, as you build toward the climax but be careful to avoid a strained vocal effect which may weaken rather than strengthen the climax. It is important that you grasp the mental and emotional attitude intended. If you do this your vocal elements will respond more easily.

Homer's *Iliad* provides an example of building a climax in the description of the gifts brought to King Agamemnon:

> Swift as the word was given, the youths obey'd:
> Twice ten bright vases in the midst they laid;
> A row of six fair tripods then succeeds;
> And twice the number of high-bounding steeds;
> Seven captives next a lovely line compose;
> The eighth Briseïs, like the blooming rose,
> Closed the bright band: great Ithacus, before,
> First of the train, the golden talents bore:
> The rest in public view the chiefs dispose,
> A splendid scene![5]

In the *Song of Solomon* 2:11–13, observe how the young lover piles image on image to attract his beloved, reaching a climax in the last line:

[5] *The Iliad of Homer,* trans. by Alexander Pope (London: Ingram, Cooke, & Co., 1853), Book XIX, p. 172.

For, lo, the winter is past,
the rain is over and gone;
The flowers appear on the earth;
the time of the singing of birds is come,
and the voice of the turtle is heard in our land;
The fig tree putteth her green figs,
and the vines with the tender grape give a good smell.
Arise, my love, my fair one, and come away.

In this story of the South, *The Little Shepherd of Kingdom Come,* the author, John Fox, builds to a climax in describing a magnificent banquet:

> . . . The dining room was the biggest and sunniest room in the house; its walls covered with hunting prints, pictures of game and stag heads. The table ran the length of it. The snowy tablecloth hung almost to the floor. At the head sat Mrs. Dean, with a great tureen of calf's head soup in front of her. Before the General was the saddle of venison that was to follow, drenched in a bottle of ancient Madeira, and flanked by flakes of red-currant jelly. Before the Major rested broiled wild ducks, on which he could show his carving skill—on game as well as men. A great turkey supplanted the venison, and last to come, and before Richard Hunt, Lieutenant of the Rifles, was a Kentucky ham. That ham! Mellow, aged, boiled in champagne, baked brown, spiced deeply, rosy pink within, and of a flavor and fragrance to shatter the fast of a Pope; and without, a brown-edged white layer, so firm that the lieutenant's deft carving knife, passing through, gave no hint to the eye that it was delicious fat.

Note how a climax is built through the use of repetition in *The Rape of the Lock,* by Alexander Pope. Here the author in mock seriousness tells how a young man stole a lock of a maiden's hair. In this passage the maiden is lamenting her tragic loss.

But anxious cares the pensive nymph oppressed,
And secret passions laboured in her breast.
Not youthful kings in battle seized alive,
Not scornful virgins who their charms survive,
Not ardent lovers robbed of all their bliss,

Not ancient ladies when refused a kiss,
Not tyrants fierce that unrepenting die,
Not Cynthia when her manteau's pinned awry,
E'er felt such rage, resentment and despair,
As thou, sad virgin! For thy ravished hair.

I. *Anti-Climax*

The anti-climax, too, can be very effective in certain situations. It begins with the largest premise, or most expansive idea and gradually comes down to the smallest and least expansive. It frequently produces a humorous effect. In using it the voice will usually manifest less strength in volume, or intensity, as it progresses. Note the rise and fall in this excerpt from Pope's "The Rape of the Lock" (1. lines 155–158).

Then flash'd the living lightning from her eyes,
And screams of horror rend the affrighted skies.
Not louder shrieks to pitying heav'n are cast,
When husbands, or when lap-dogs breathe their last. . . .

J. *Transitions*

The New Student Dictionary defines a transition as "a passing from one subject to another properly in a natural and easy manner," and *The Oxford English Dictionary* defines it as "a passage in thought, speech, or writing from one subject to another."

In the literary object, the transition serves a number of purposes. It can provide effective change from one emotion or idea to another. Or, it may indicate a change in place, time or action. It may also be used to sharpen the differences in describing two or more characters.

In fiction, speeches, essays and poetry, transitions may consist of fairly long passages, stanzas, sentences, phrases, or even a single word. Frequently, if the writer wishes to make the transition as concise as possible, he will use phrases, such as *on the other hand, much later, the next day,* or he will use certain words which are called conjunctions or connectives. A mental bridge on which the reader can cross from one idea to the next has been provided. Some of these words are *but, or, yet, and, however, therefore, for, similarly, likewise, when, moreover, then,* and *nevertheless.*

In "A Deep-Sworn Vow," William Butler Yeats uses the words, *yet* and *or,* to make his transitions from one idea to another.

> Others because you did not keep
> That deep-sworn vow have been friends of mine;
> Yet always when I look death in the face,
> When I clamber to the heights of sleep,
> Or when I grow excited with wine,
> Suddenly I meet your face.

Shakespeare frequently uses these connective words in his sonnets to make transitions.

> I grant I never saw a goddess go,
> My mistress, when she walks, treads on the ground.
> And yet, by Heaven, I think my love as rare
> As any she belied with false compare.
>
> (Sonnet 130)

and

> Then can I grieve at grievances foregone,
> And heavily from woe to woe tell o'er
> The sad account of fore bemoanèd moan,
> Which I new-pay as if not paid before.
> But if the while I think on thee, dear friend,
> All losses are restored and sorrows end.
>
> (Sonnet 30)

Since these transitions are clearly a part of the writing you may wonder how they can be suggested by the oral interpreter. Basically, you can convey them through the pause, the voice, and the body which are your means of responding to an idea.

The pause is often an important part of the transition for it enables both you and your listener to make a mental and emotional adjustment to the new idea. The length of the pause may be determined by differences between two ideas or emotions. If, for example, there is a complete shift from one idea or emotion to its opposite, more time will usually be required than to change from one emotion to a similar emotion. Likewise, a change of years from one chapter of a novel to the next may require more time for adjustment than a shift of a few hours. However, we should remember that it is impossible to set forth rules for the length of the pause, for it is determined by each individual literary selection and by the sensitivity of the interpreter.

The voice may convey a transition by a change from a fuller to a lighter tone, or from a quick tempo to a slow tempo, or the reverse. It may change from a major key to a sad, melancholy key or from a staccato to a legato movement. You may indicate a transition by a slight shift of the body, a change of posture, or a movement of the head.

William March has a number of transitions in the opening of his story, "The Little Wife."[6] Some of these are indicated by the use of transitional words, but others are not.

> Joe Hinckley selected a seat on the shady side of the train and carefully stowed away his traveling bag and his heavy, black catalogue case. It was unusually hot for early June. Outside, the heat waves shimmered and danced above the hot slag roadbed, and the muddy river that ran by the station was low between its red banks. "If it's as hot as this in June, it sure will be awful in August," he thought. He looked at his watch: two twenty-eight—the train was five minutes late in getting out. If he had known the two twenty-three was going to be late he might have had time to pack his sample trunk and get it to the station, but he couldn't have anticipated that, of course. He had had so little time after getting that telegram from Mrs. Thompkins—barely time to pack his bag and check out of the hotel. Joe loosened his belt and swabbed his neck with a limp handkerchief. "It don't matter so much about the trunk," he thought. "One of the boys at the hotel can express it to me, or I can pick it up on my way back."
>
> Joe noticed that one end of his catalogue case protruded slightly. With his foot he shoved it farther under the seat. It was a battered black case, made strongly to withstand constant travel-

[6] "The Little Wife," from *A William March Omnibus,* by William March (New York: Holt, Rinehart, and Winston, 1956), pp. 155–156.

ing, and re-inforced at its corners with heavy copper cleats. One of the handles had been broken and mended with newer leather. On the front of the case there had once been stamped in gilt the firm name of "Boykin & Rosen, Wholesale Hardware, Chattanooga, Tenn.," but time had long since worn away the gold lettering.

The telegram had upset Joe: it had come so suddenly, so unexpectedly. He felt vaguely that somebody was playing a joke on him. He felt confused and helpless. It was difficult to believe that Bessie was so desperately sick. He sat for a time staring at his finger nails. Suddenly he remembered an appointment for four o'clock with the buyer for Snowdoun and Sims, and he rose quickly from his seat with some vague idea of telephoning or sending a message to explain his absence. Then he realized that the train was in motion. "I'll write him a letter when I get to Mobile," said Joe to himself; "he'll understand all right when I explain the circumstances. He won't blame me for breaking that date when I tell him about my wife being so sick." Joe sat down heavily in his seat and again looked at his hands.

Ahead of him two young girls were leaning out of the window and waving to their friends. Their eyes were shining and their cheeks were flushed and they were laughing with excitement at the prospect of going away.

Across the aisle sat a gaunt farm-woman. Her red-veined eyes protruded. Her neck was swollen with a goiter. In her arms she held a bouquet of red crêpe-myrtle which was already wilting in the heat. Beside her she had placed her straw suitcase and several bulky paper-wrapped parcels. She gazed steadily out of the window as if afraid that someone would catch her eye and try to talk to her.

It was very hot in the coach. The small electric fan at the end of the car droned and wheezed sleepily but succeeded only in stirring up the hot air.

Joe took from his pocket the telegram that he had received from his mother-in-law and read it again: "J. G. Hinckley, American Hotel, Montgomery, Ala. Come home at once. Doctor says Bessie not expected live through day. Will wire again if necessary. It was a boy. Mother."

III. PARAPHRASING

Frequently a poem or prose passage may seem so obscure and complicated that its meaning eludes the reader to such an extent that he does not understand what the text is saying. This may be true of classical poets like Milton, Shakespeare, and Browning, as well as some of our contemporary writers, such as Ezra Pound or Dylan Thomas. After you analyze a selection in all of the details discussed in this chapter, it may be helpful to write out or tell aloud as directly and simply as possible, what you think the literature is saying. Try to follow its line of thought, but express it in your own words and in your own style. Then read aloud what you have written to see if you have the idea. As the next step, read the author's words while you keep in mind the meaning that you have discovered through re-writing the ideas in your own words.

Paraphrasing does not mean that when you put the literary object into your own words you still have the same specific literary object that you are paraphrasing. It does permit you to say in your own words what you think the passage is trying to say; it enables you to communicate the idea and feeling the way it appears to you. While it is not *the* literary object, the paraphrase is a means of discovering and clarifying the meaning of the selection. The paraphrase may become a useful aid in working out obscure or difficult material.

STUDY QUESTIONS

1. Do you regard literary analysis as primarily a technical problem or as a problem in meaning?
2. Which do you think is preferable, the "lemon squeezer" method of criticism or no criticism?
3. Do you believe that poetic form must come out of the "properties of the material"? Are there any exceptions? Does this apply to all cases?
4. For an assignment, bring a passage from prose or poetry which depends on an understanding of allusions for its meaning.

5. Can you think of words that have different meanings to different people?

6. Prepare a short story to read aloud in which symbolism is important. In what way or ways is the symbolism important? Does symbolism present a special problem to the oral reader?

7. What is the attitude of the speaker in "A Servant to Servants," by Robert Frost?

8. What is the attitude of Abraham in the episode of Abraham and Isaac in the Bible?

9. Can you find any poems in which you feel that the sounds of the words alone give you the complete meaning?

10. Of the figures of speech, which do you think depends more upon oral delivery, the simile or irony? Why?

11. Which is stronger in its effect, the simile or metaphor? What difference might there be in reading these aloud?

12. Why do many hyperboles diminish an impact? Can you think of a character in a novel or play that relies too heavily on hyperboles? Does this give you a clue to the interpretation of the type of character you want to suggest?

13. Do you consider the use of paradox an easy technique for the oral reader to master? Give your reasons.

14. What problems does an oral reader encounter if a play or story lacks unity?

15. Bring a poem to read aloud in which there is repetition in some form. It may not be of words only. How can you avoid boring your hearers?

16. What are some of the problems involved in building to a climax in reading aloud?

BIBLIOGRAPHY

Aristotle, *Rhetoric.* Trans. by W. Rhys Roberts. New York: Modern Library, 1954.

Aristotle, *On the Art of Poetry.* Bywater, Ingram; with a preface by Gilbert Murray. Oxford: Clarendon Press, 1945.

Barnet, Sylvan; Morton Berman; William Burto, *A Dictionary of Literary Terms.* Boston, Toronto: Little, Brown and Company, 1960.

Blair, Hugh, *Lectures on Rhetoric and Belles Lettres.* Pittsburgh: James Kay & Bro., 1833.

Boas, George, *Wingless Pegasus: A Handbook for Critics.* Baltimore: The Johns Hopkins Press, 1950.

Bosanquet, Bernard, *Three Lectures on Aesthetics.* London: Macmillan & Co., Ltd., 1915.

Boulton, Marjorie, *Anatomy of Poetry.* London: Routledge & K. Paul, 1953.

Daiches, David, "The New Criticism: Some Qualifications" in *Literary Essays* by David Daiches. Edinburgh: Oliver and Boyd, 1956.

Eliot, T. S., *The Sacred Wood,* sixth edition. London: Methuen, 1948.

Friedman, Norman and Charles A. McLaughlin, *Poetry: An Introduction To Its Form and Art.* Rev. ed., New York, Evanston, and London: Harper and Row, Publishers, 1963.

Genung, John F., *The Practical Elements of Rhetoric.* Boston: Ginn and Company Publishers, 1893.

Langfeld, H. S., *The Aesthetic Attitude.* New York: Harcourt, Brace and Co., Inc., 1920.

Longinus, *On the Sublime.* Ed. by D. A. Russell, Oxford: Clarendon Press, 1964.

Pepper, S. C., *The Basis of Criticism in the Arts.* Cambridge, Mass.: Harvard University Press, 1949.

Puttenham, George, *The Arte of English Poesie,* Ed. by Willock, Gladys, and Alice Walker. Cambridge University Press, 1936.

Richards, I. A., *Principles of Literary Criticism.* New York: Harcourt, Brace and Co.; London: Routledge and Kegan Paul, 1948.

Part Four

Sharing Prose, Poetry, and Drama

Chapter VIII

The Oral Interpretation of Prose

Prose and poetry have usually been thought of as two separate forms of literature. However Shelley went so far as to say that "the distinction between poetry and prose writers is a vulgar error." For example, he regarded Plato and Lord Bacon as poets, yet when one reads their works he will assume that he is reading prose merely because the line runs across the page in the manner of prose. Indeed, some poetry, such as free verse, seems very much like prose when one hears it read aloud. So a distinction between the two is hard to make. In this chapter we shall attempt to clarify for the oral interpreter the nature of what we generally think of as "prose fiction" and the ways in which he can read it aloud effectively.

I. PROSE FICTION AND ITS ASPECTS

One of the most popular forms of prose is prose fiction, more specifically the novel and the short story. Both of these forms are concerned primarily with plot and human beings. Sometimes, however, the characters are animals, as in Orwell's *Animal Farm,* Grahame's *The Wind In The Willows* or Salten's *Bambi.* Such instances are usually limited to allegories, fables, satires or children's stories, so that you can say that the novel and short story are generally concerned with human beings and the actions of human beings.

The novel and short story have a great appeal to the reading public because of their very nature. They have elements of the drama in that characters speak, but in addition they have description and narration. Let us consider four aspects of prose fiction, namely, description, narration, characters, and dialogue.

A. *Description*

In a novel or story the author gives a clear description of the setting so that you not only know how a room or a countryside looks but he tells you, at least indirectly, how you are to feel about this setting. And in this way he helps create mood. This mood is related to the *effect* a writer wishes to produce. In the short story this effect must, Poe says, be brought out in the very first sentence.[1] Everything that the author writes should, directly or indirectly, contribute to this effect.

The setting may be important in several ways. It may, as we have said, establish the mood for the whole story, as do the grim and forbidding moors of *Wuthering Heights*. Or, it may provide the mood for a particular scene. It may prepare the reader for the action that is to take place. In the two following passages the authors create a mood through description. Find the imagery that helps create the mood so that you can experience the images when you read these selections aloud.

> The château, a modern building in Italian style, with two projected wings and three flights of steps, lay at the foot of an immense greensward, on which some cows were grazing among groups of large trees set out at regular intervals, while large beds of arbutus, rhododendron, syringas, and guelder roses bulged out their irregular clusters of green along the curve of the gravel path. A river flowed under a bridge; through the mist one could distinguish buildings with thatched roofs scattered over the field bordered by two gently-sloping well-timbered hillocks, and in the background amid the trees rose in two parallel lines the coach-houses and stables, all that was left of the ruined old château.
>
> (Gustave Flaubert, *Madame Bovary*)

[1] *The Complete Works of Edgar Allan Poe,* Volume IV (Literary Criticism), ed. by James A, Harrison, N.Y., Society of English and French Literature (Thomas Y. Cromwell and Co., 1902), p. 108.

Now look at the following description from Chekhov's short story, "A Father":

> The long yard ended, and Boris found himself in a dark entry. The swing door creaked, there was a smell of cooking and a smoking samovar. There was a sound of harsh voices. Passing through the passage into the kitchen Boris could see nothing but thick smoke, a line with washing on it, and the chimney of the samovar through a crack of which golden sparks were dropping.

Both of these descriptions not only create mood, but also prepare you for the kinds of people who live in these two places.

While the descriptive portions of a novel are frequently found at the beginning of the story or when there is a change of scene, they are often interwoven into the narration. When you go to the theatre the stage setting, lighting, furniture, and costumes come to your assistance to give a background in which the characters live and move, but in fiction description takes the place of these elements. This descriptive background, then, gives a point of attachment for the characters. It takes them out of nebulous space and gives them a specific place in which to live and function.

B. *Narration*

The narrative portions of a novel contain incidents and action which help carry the plot forward. The writer can tell in his own words what is happening as he leads you through various episodes. In the following passage from *Madame Bovary,* you will see how Flaubert presents the incidents preparatory to the marriage of Emma to Charles. The author apparently regards this as essential to the events which follow her marriage. He wishes to provide you with an understanding of the milieu in which Emma grew up, which helps explain her later actions.

> The next day by nine o'clock he was at the farm. Emma blushed as he entered, and gave a little forced laugh to keep herself in countenance. Old Rouault embraced his future son-in-law. The discussion of money matters was put off; moreover, there was

plenty of time before them, as the marriage could not decently take place till Charles was out of mourning, that is to say, about the spring of the next year.

The winter passed waiting for this. Mademoiselle Rouault was busy with her trousseau. Part of it was ordered at Rouen, and she made herself chemises and nightcaps after fashion-plates that she borrowed. When Charles visited the farmer, the preparations for the wedding were talked over; they wondered in what room they should have dinner; they dreamed of the number of dishes that would be wanted, and what should be the entrées.

Emma would, on the contrary, have preferred to have a midnight wedding with torches, but old Rouault could not understand such an idea. So there was a wedding at which forty-three persons were present, at which they remained sixteen hours at table, began again the next day, and to some extent on the days following.

Sometimes narration shows the inner workings of a character's mind, which his conversation with other characters does not permit him to reveal for he may not want other characters to know how he feels. But the author, on the other hand, does want you to know how a character thinks and feels so he, the author, tells you in his own words. Or, in some psychological fiction, the character himself may reveal his most personal feelings and thoughts in an inaudible, often disorganized and fragmentary monologue which Larbaud called the *"monologue intérieur."*[2] Such methods enable you to see the inside of the character's mind more completely than the character himself can reveal it if he is limited to conversation with other people. In the following passage, also from *Madame Bovary,* Flaubert tells you exactly how Emma feels. When you read this aloud try to discover her attitude. This will help you to understand her introspective feelings and emotions at this time.

The next day was a dreary one for Emma. Everything seemed to her enveloped in a black atmosphere floating confusedly over the exterior of things, and sorrow was engulfed within her soul with soft shrieks such as the winter wind makes in ruined castles. It was that reverie which we give to things that will not return, the lassitude that seizes you after everything is done; that pain, in

[2] "Preface," by Valery Larbaud, in *Les Lauriers Sont Coupés* by Edouard Dujardin (Paris: Albert Messein, 1924), p. 6.

fine, that the interruption of every wonted movement, the sudden cessation of any prolonged vibration, brings on.

There are various ways in which an author can present his tale. For one thing, he may write in first or third person. Most authors write in the third person, but some use first person, which helps establish a closer relationship between the narrator and the reader. Stories told in the first person, such as *Great Expectations* by Dickens, *The Razor's Edge* by Maugham, or *Madame Bovary* by Flaubert may show differences in the use of this technique. In *Great Expectations* the narrator, the "I," is the leading person in the novel whose fortunes and misfortunes are your major concern as a reader. Here you retain the viewpoint of this "I" and you see everything as he sees it. In *The Razor's Edge* the narrator is again "I"; he is not the hero but rather an observer on the sidelines. The "I" in *Madame Bovary* starts the story out and you know he is there for some pages, but then he draws into the background so completely that he ceases to be a person as such and becomes, as far as you can tell, the novelist himself. If the narrator is not an important character in the story you, as a reader, do not want to feature him, for the narrator's task is to bring the other characters and the plot into the foreground. Sometimes the author is an omniscient narrator and knows what all of the characters are thinking.

There are other techniques that writers may use to tell their stories. For example, they can use a certain background which they feel will contribute to their theme and plot. Some novels, such as Hemingway's *A Farewell to Arms,* and Tolstoy's *War and Peace* use war as a background and as a means of motivating their story. Some use small town life, as did Sinclair Lewis in *Main Street,* and Eudora Welty in "Lily Daw and the Three Ladies," while others turn to suburbia for their material. Family life, too, is often the framework used for fiction. This method was used by Galsworthy in *The Forsyte Saga,* by Guy McCrone in *Red Plush,* by Mazo de la Roche in her *Jalna* series, by Clemence Dane in *Broome Stages,* and by John Steinbeck in *The Grapes of Wrath.* Still others use a journey as the foundation for the plot. Such is the case in Smollett's *Humphrey Clinker,* Dickens' *Martin Chuzzlewit* and Paul Gallico's *Mrs. 'Arris Goes to Paris.* There may be, of course, a combination of any of these elements or of other elements to provide a framework for the novel. Some novels are told in the form of letters, so that each correspondent's character is revealed through the letters he writes, and through the letters written to or about him. This is brilliantly done in Smollett's *Humphrey Clinker* where you will meet a whole range of vivid characters through the medium of letters. Thornton Wilder, too, used this same technique in his *Ides of March*.

C. *Plot*

Plot is the pattern of a story which the writer has carefully worked out and in which certain changes occur brought about by or through character or outside forces. This pattern must have unity.

An effective plot should have both a sense of cause and result, with an element of plausibility or logic in it. It should create suspense and arouse curiosity as to "what will happen" and yet the thing that does happen must seem reasonable even though it may come as a kind of shock or surprise. The plot develops until it reaches a climax which is usually followed by a dénouement. The oral interpreter should study the structure of a plot so that he knows the nature of the climax and dénouement and can prepare his reading in terms of handling them effectively.

D. *Characters*

Earlier in this chapter you have read that the novel and the short story are concerned with human beings. Some regard character as the mainspring of the story. You, as an interpreter, build up the character in your mind out of certain clues that the literature gives you, such as what it says about the character, what other characters say about a character and what the character himself says. What the literature says about him may involve broad strokes, such as, "he rushed out of the house and raced down town," or subtle strokes which give you finer clues to his character—little gestures, habits, mannerisms, his way of walking, sitting, eating, his nervous movements, and the phrases he uses.

As an interpreter you should have a definite image of these movements, habits and mannerisms, of the posture, size, appearance and the way you imagine the person dresses. If the literature does not give you enough of this descriptive information you will need to think creatively and decide on these aspects in terms of what you do know about the characters. At this point of your creative process it may help you to actually assume the posture and physical attributes of the person and walk, sit and move as you believe he would do. Then, after you have a definite idea of the kind of person he is, you can reduce the literal action and put him in the frame of suggestion for interpretative reading.

There are other clues, however, that the literature may give you. The name of a character may be an important one. In modern fiction and drama names are not so obviously indicative of the nature of the character as they were in the Middle Ages when characters were given such names as Fool, Wisdom, Pride, or Good Counsel, but they still suggest something about the nature and personality of the character. The author knows that certain names will fit a particular type of character and others will not. For example, it will probably be difficult for you to imagine a vicious gangster with the name of Cedric or Reginald, just as it may be equally hard for you to accept very seriously a regal dowager named "Peaches." The title, *Tom Jones,* does not suggest a nobleman, for Fielding did not want to suggest that any more than did Mark Twain wish to suggest a college student when he named his character Huckleberry Finn.

There are also other clues which will help you understand a character. Some characters receive strength through being associated with an object. Anthony Adverse was associated with a religious figure, which he carried all of his life. Other characters may be associated with certain vocal expressions or phrases. For example, the old grandmother in *Jalna,* by Mazo de la Roche, repeatedly asks for a peppermint, while Scarlett O'Hara, in *Gone With the Wind,* uses the phrase, "I'll think of it tomorrow." In "Mama's Bank Account," the mother frequently mentions "the bank downtown" which suggested safety and security to her young family.

In suggesting characters in prose fiction it is essential that you understand the attitude of each character. This attitude constitutes the feelings or opinions indicated for a character toward life or toward a specific idea, situation or person. This gives a character a *raison d'être* and a function in the story. The attitude of each character should be indicated by the interpreter. The attitude is not necessarily static and may change in the unfolding of the plot. This attitude should be suggested clearly through your vocal and physical responsiveness. Contrasts of attitudes, often an integral part of fiction, will arise as characters think and feel differently.

Beyond the attitude of each character the interpreter should never lose sight of the over-all attitude of the literature in fiction, and he should make every attempt to parallel it.

While all of these clues should be suggested by a careful study of the text of the literature you, the oral interpreter, must go beyond the manuscript and draw from your own experience to bring a character to life. Your imagination is the crucible in which many elements are fused to create a living character.

E. *Dialogue*

As Vincent McHugh says in his *Primer of the Novel,* "The character and those about him come to life through dialogue: Dialogue is a kind of action, and action is bodily speech. Both are functional aspects of character and the chief means of representing it." Dialogue is one of the oral interpreter's major means of revealing character and developing the plot. It is a graphic and vital process which gives life and reality to a character through the voice and the body. When a character expresses his own thoughts in his own words, you, as an interpreter, should have a certain grasp of his personality which makes him come to life for you and for your listener. Remember that he will speak as only he, in his own particular sphere of life and with his own background and attitudes, can speak. His speech must seem to be the "natural" conversation of a human being.

But his speech consists of more than spoken words. Words are merely symbols. Man gives them meaning. These meanings must be expressed as a human being thinks and talks, as he hesitates in searching for the right word, as he rushes headlong in joy, as his joy turns to doubt or dismay, as his embarrassment causes him to talk more quietly or quickly. As his words and ideas change so do his bodily actions; he may move his head or his arm, he may incline toward or away from his listeners. All of these things the writer has in mind, but unfortunately the symbols for conveying these forms of speech on the printed page are not adequate. While an imaginative silent reader may supply this, a listening audience will be dependent upon the ability of the oral interpreter to suggest his judgments of the intent of the literature. All such responsiveness must be consistent with the characters and it must evolve from their way of thinking and feeling.

In reading dialogue aloud you must decide whether the characters are sharing the scene equally or whether one character is clearly the dominant figure.

When you read descriptive or narrative passages allow the listener to see you in full view. When you read the lines of the characters aloud, you should place the characters to the front in the realm of the audience. This will produce a consistency and unity in your style. Since these characters normally talk to each other and not to the audience, you will not look directly at the audience. Instead, you will place your characters in an imaginative realm, possibly just about the eye line of the audience. If more than one character speaks, you may find it better not to place his gaze to the right, another to the front and still another to the left. Rather, see if you can make the distinction in the personality of each character so clear that the listener will grasp at once who is speaking. This will enable each character to look front and to use the whole frontal range while speaking. Try to see in your imagination the character being addressed.

Since dialogue is often interwoven with narration be sure to distinguish between the characters who speak and the author who speaks through narration.

> Each of the Plato Four had his own villa in the country around Florence. They came in several times a week to lecture and work with Lorenzo in the *studiolo.* Lorenzo seemed eager that Michelangelo take advantage of these opportunities, and so he attended faithfully.
>
> The Platonists tried to interest him in Latin and Greek, working up charts to show him that the calligraphy of the two languages was a drawing similar in nature to his figure drawing. He took their manuscripts and assignments to his room, pored over them for hours . . . and learned little.
>
> "Nothing sticks!" he wailed to Bertoldo.
>
> Stopped, the men taught him to read aloud, poetry in the vulgate: Dante, Petrarch, Horace, Virgil. This he enjoyed, particularly

the discussions that followed his reading of *The Divine Comedy,* with the interpretation of its philosophy. The Platonists complimented him on his growing clarity of diction, then brought in Girolamo Benivieni, whom they described as "the most fervent partisan of poetry in the volgare," to teach Michelangelo how to write his own verse. When he demurred on the grounds that he wanted to become a sculptor, not a poet, Pico said:

"The structure of a sonnet is as rigorous a discipline as the structure of a marble relief. When Benivieni teaches you to write sonnets he trains your mind in the rules of logic and composition of thought. You simply must take advantage of his talent!"

Landino reassured him, "We will not try to weaken your carving arm by replacing hammer and chisel with pen and ink!"

Poliziana added, "You must not give up studying poetry. You must continue to read aloud. To be a complete artist it is not enough to be a painter, sculptor, or architect. One must also be a poet, if one is to attain full expression."

"I do so poorly," Michelangelo complained one night to Benivieni when he had tried to make the lines scan; "how can you bear to read my clumsy attempts?"

Benivieni, also a talented musician, clucked at Michelangelo's despair, sang a gay song of his own composition, then replied, "My early efforts were no better; worse, if anything. You will think you are a bad poet until the day comes when you have a need to express something; then you'll have the tools of poetry at hand, meter and rhyme, just as you have hammer and chisel on your workbench."[3]

(From *The Agony and the Ecstasy* by Irving Stone)

F. *Symbolism*

Symbolism, you will recall, is the use of one thing to represent something else. (See Chapter V.) There are many examples of symbolism in fiction. In Flaubert's *Madame Bovary,* there are instances in the

[3] Irving Stone, *The Agony and the Ecstasy* (Garden City: Doubleday & Company, Inc., 1961), pp. 115–116.

use of color and in the elements of nature. In *Moby Dick,* Melville uses the white whale as symbolic of evil.

Forster, in "The Other Side of The Hedge," employs the hedge itself as a symbol, as well as the "other side" of it. Katherine Anne Porter turns to symbolism to represent love and religion in her "Flowering Judas," of which the title itself is symbolic. There is symbolism in "Johnny Pye and the Fool-Killer," by Stephen Vincent Benét. Earlier, Hawthorne relied on it in stories such as "Young Goodman Brown" and "The Great Stone Face." Steinbeck, Hemingway, Greene and McCullers are among the many others who have utilized symbolism in fiction.

When you are studying a story try to determine what symbolism has been used. Not all fiction, however, is highly symbolic, so do not try to read it into every situation. In reading fiction aloud you should realize that symbolism has an underlying significance. It is necessary that you understand that which is symbolic and the thing it represents before you can suggest the power of the literary experience to your listeners.

G. *Irony*

Irony may be apparent in fiction in several ways. It may be irony in which a person says one thing and means another. (See Chapter V.) There is also a type of irony in which the outcome of an event or situation is the opposite to what might be expected. Either the reader, the character, or both may be surprised by the result. In "Piece of String," DeMaupassant tells the story of a French peasant whose frugality forces him to pick up a piece of string in the market place. Later, a wallet is missing and he is accused by the police of finding and concealing it. Although vindicated, he feels the need of telling everyone he meets that he did not steal the wallet. In attempting to clear his name of a theft he actually did not commit, his very persistence confirms in the minds of others that he did steal the wallet. The valiant attempts and attitude of the peasant as he protests his innocence can be conveyed by the reader's vocal and physical suggestions.

In Steinbeck's *Of Mice and Men,* George has protected the half-witted Lennie like a brother. Lennie committed a murder and George, to prevent a mob from killing Lennie, shoots him himself. The violent reversal of roles in which George changes from protector to killer, even though he does it to protect Lennie from his pursuers, creates an ironic situation. Here the interpreter must understand the attitude of each character involved and transmit it.

In *The Old Man and the Sea,* the central character has always hoped to catch a huge fish. Finally he is successful, but the fish is so large and the man so weak that he can not haul it into the boat. He ties it alongside and the sharks eat it, bit by bit, until there is nothing left. Even though he realized his ambition, he no sooner attained it than he lost it. The irony in this story comes through the old man's attitude as he talks to himself and to the fish.

II. CUTTING PROSE FICTION

Since a novel covers several hundred or more pages, it is necessary for you to cut it for reading aloud. This is no easy task when you consider that you want to reduce it to no more than an hour's presentation—which is frequently considered the maximum for an oral reading. This means that you must select, first of all, *the main plot* of the story, and then the particular episodes in that plot which will best convey the *impression* you believe the literature is attempting to create. Usually you will find it necessary to eliminate subplots, or to reduce them to a few comments unless they are inextricably interwoven into the main plot. Minor characters, too, can be eliminated. Choose only those episodes which most effectively reinforce the theme and which will maintain the attention of your listener.

After you have indicated that a certain character or characters are speaking, by naming them, you may cut out such explanatory items as "he said" or "she said with a laugh," and reveal by your actual interpretation who is speaking and how he speaks. By all means, include dialogue, which usually carries the plot forward. Include sufficient narration and description so that your listeners can follow the development of the plot in its proper setting.

The first chapter of *Great Expectations,* by Charles Dickens, is a good example of an opening chapter which throws you at once into the action of the story combining description, narration, characterization, and dialogue. Here is a suggested cutting. After you have made your cutting, it may help if you type your material so that when you read it orally, you do not need to jump from one part of the page to another.

> My father's family name being Pirrip, and my Christian name Philip, my infant tongue could make of both names nothing longer or more explicit than Pip. So, I called myself Pip, and came to be called Pip.
>
> I give Pirrip as my father's family name, on the authority of his tombstone and my sister—Mrs. Joe Gargery, who married the blacksmith. ~~As I never saw my father or my mother, and never saw any likeness of either of them (for their days were long before the days of photographs), my first fancies regarding what they were like, were unreasonably derived from their tombstones. The shape of the letters on my father's, gave me an odd idea that he was a square, stout, dark man, with curly black hair. From the character and turn of the inscription, "*Also Georgiana Wife of the Above,*" I drew a childish conclusion that my mother was freckled and sickly. To five little stone lozenges, each about a foot and a half long, which were arranged in a neat row beside their grave, and were sacred to the memory of five little brothers of mine—who gave up trying to get a living exceedingly early in that universal struggle—I am indebted for a belief I religiously entertained that they had all been born on their backs with their hands in their trouser-pockets, and had never taken them out in this state of existence.~~
>
> Ours was the marsh country, down by the river, within, as the river wound, twenty miles of the sea. My first most vivid and broad impression of the identity of things, seems to me to have been gained on a memorable raw afternoon towards evening. At such a time I found out for certain, that this bleak place overgrown with nettles was the churchyard; and that Philip Pirrip, late of this parish, and also Georgiana wife of the above, were dead and buried; ~~Alexander, Bartholomew, Abraham, Tobias, and Roger, infant children of the aforesaid, were also dead and buried;~~ and that the dark flat wilderness beyond the

churchyard, intersected with dykes and mounds and gates, with scattered cattle feeding on it, was the marshes; and that the low leaden line beyond was the river; and that the distant savage lair from which the wind was rushing, was the sea; and that the small bundle of shivers growing afraid of it all and beginning to cry, was Pip.

"Hold your noise!" cried a terrible voice, as a man started up from among the graves at the side of the church porch. "Keep still, you little devil, or I'll cut your throat!"

A fearful man, all in coarse grey, with a great iron on his leg. A man with no hat, and with broken shoes, and with an old rag tied round his head. A man ~~who had been soaked in water, and smothered in mud, and lamed by stones, and cut by flints, and stung by nettles, and torn by briars, who limped, and shivered, and glared and growled, and~~ whose teeth chattered in his head as he seized me by the chin.

"O! Don't cut my throat, sir," I pleaded in terror. "Pray don't do it, sir."

"Tell us your name!" ~~said the man.~~ "Quick!"

"Pip, sir."

"Once more," ~~said the man, staring at me.~~ "Give it mouth!"

"Pip, Pip, sir."

"Show us where you live," ~~said the man.~~ "Pint out the place!"

I pointed to where our village lay ~~on the flat inshore among the alder trees and pollards, a mile or more from the church.~~

The man, after looking at me for a moment, turned me upside down, and emptied my pockets. There was nothing in them but a piece of bread. When the church came to itself—for he was so sudden and strong that he made it go head over heels before me, and I saw the steeple under my feet—when the church came to itself, I say, I was seated on a high tombstone, trembling, while he ate the bread ravenously.

"You young dog," ~~said the man, licking his lips,~~ "what fat cheeks you ha' got."

I believe they were fat, though I was at that time undersized, for my years, and not strong.

"Darn me if I couldn't eat 'em," ~~said the man, with a threatening shake of his head,~~ "and if I han't half a mind to't!"

I earnestly expressed my hope that he wouldn't, and held tighter to the tombstone on which he had put me; partly, to keep myself upon it; partly, to keep myself from crying.

"Now lookee here!" ~~said the man.~~ "Where's your mother?"

"There, sir!" ~~said I~~.

He started, made a short run, and stopped and looked over his shoulder.

"There, sir!" I timidly explained. "Also Georgiana. That's my mother."

"Oh!" ~~said he, coming back.~~ "And is that your father alonger your mother?"

"Yes, sir," ~~said I,~~ "him too; late of this parish."

"Ha! ~~he muttered then, considering.~~ "Who d'ye live with—supposin' you're kindly let to live, which I han't made up my mind about?"

"My sister, sir—Mrs. Joe Gargery—wife of Joe Gargery, the blacksmith, sir."

"Blacksmith, eh?" ~~said he.~~ And (he) looked down at his leg.

After darkly looking at his leg and at me several times, he came closer to my tombstone, took me by both arms, and tilted me back as far as he could hold me; so that his eyes looked most powerfully down into mine, and mine looked most helplessly up into his.

"Now lookee here," ~~he said,~~ "the question being whether you're to be let to live. You know what a file is?"

"Yes, sir."

"And you know what wittles is?"

"Yes, sir."

After each question he tilted me over a little more, so as to give me a greater sense of helplessness and danger.

"You get me a file." He tilted me again. "And you get me wittles." He tilted me again. "You bring 'em both to me." He tilted me again. "Or I'll have your heart and liver out." He tilted me again.

~~I was dreadfully frightened, and so giddy that I clung to him with both hands, and said, "If you would kindly please to let me keep upright, sir, perhaps I shouldn't be sick, and perhaps I could attend more~~."

~~He gave me a most tremendous dip and roll, so that the church jumped over its own weather cock. Then, he held me by the arms in an upright position on the top of the stone, and went on in these fearful terms:~~

"You bring me, to-morrow morning early, that file and them wittles. You bring the lot to me, at that old Battery over yonder. You do it, and you never dare to say a word or dare to make a sign concerning your having seen such a person as me, or any person sumever, and you shall be let to live. You fail, or you go from my words in any partickler, no matter how small it is, and your heart and your liver shall be tore out, roasted and ate. Now, I ain't alone, as you may think I am. There's a young man hid with me, in comparison with which young man I am a Angel. ~~That young man hears the words I speak. That young man has a secret way pecooliar to himself, of getting at a boy, and at his heart, and at his liver. It is in wain for a boy to attempt to hide himself from that young man. A boy may lock his door, may be warm in bed, may tuck himself up, may draw the clothes over his head, may think himself comfortable and safe, but that young man will softly creep and creep his way to him and tear him open.~~ I am keeping that young man from harming of you at the present moment, with great difficulty. I find it very hard to hold that young man off of your inside. Now, what do you say?"

I said that I would get him the file, and I would get him what broken bits of food I could, and I would come to him at the Battery, early in the morning.

"Say, Lord strike you dead if you don't!"

I said so, and he took me down.

"Now," ~~he pursued,~~ "you remember what you've undertook, and you remember that young man, and you get home!"

"Goo-good night, sir," ~~I faltered.~~

"Much of that!" ~~said he, glancing about him over the cold wet flat.~~ "I wish I was a frog. Or a eel!"

At the same time, he hugged his shuddering body in both his arms—clasping himself, as if to hold himself together—and limped towards the low church wall. ~~As I saw him go, picking his way among the nettles, and among the brambles that bound the green mounds, he looked in my young eyes as if he were eluding~~

~~the hands of the dead people, stretching up cautiously out of their graves, to get a twist upon his ankle and pull him in.~~

When he came to the low church wall, he got over it, like a man whose legs were numbed and stiff, and then turned round to look for me. When I saw him turning, I set my face towards home, and made the best use of my legs. But presently I looked over my shoulder, and saw him going on again towards the river, still hugging himself in both arms, and picking his way with his sore feet among the great stones dropped into the marshes here and there, for stepping-places when the rains were heavy, or the tide was in.

The marshes were just a long black horizontal line then, as I stopped to look after him; and the river was just another horizontal line, not nearly so broad nor yet so black; and the sky was just a row of long angry red lines and dense black lines intermixed. On the edge of the river I could faintly make out the only two black things in all the prospect that seemed to be standing upright; one of these was the beacon by which the sailors steered—like an unhooped cask upon a pole—an ugly thing when you were near it; the other a gibbet, with some chains hanging to it which had once held a pirate. The man was limping on towards this latter, as if he were the pirate come to life, and come down, and going back to hook himself up again. It gave me a terrible turn when I thought so; ~~and as I saw the cattle lifting their heads to gaze after him; I wondered whether they thought so too.~~ I looked all round for the horrible young man, and could see no signs of him. But now I was frightened again, and ran home without stopping.

III. THREE SHORT STORIES

THE VETERAN, by Stephen Crane*

Out of the low window could be seen three hickory trees placed irregularly in a meadow that was resplendent in springtime green.

* McClure's Magazine, Vol. VII, No. 3, August, 1896, pp. 222–224.

Farther away, the old, dismal belfry of the village church loomed over the pines. A horse meditating in the shade of one of the hickories lazily swished his tail. The warm sunshine made an oblong of vivid yellow on the floor of the grocery.

"Could you see the whites of their eyes?" said the man who was seated on a soap-box.

"Nothing of the kind," replied old Henry warmly. "Just a lot of flitting figures, and I let go at where they 'peared to be the thickest. Bang!"

"Mr. Fleming," said the grocer—his deferential voice expressed somehow the old man's exact social weight—"Mr. Fleming, you never was frightened much in them battles, was you?"

The veteran looked down and grinned. Observing his manner, the entire group tittered. "Well, I guess I was," he answered finally. "Pretty well scared, sometimes. Why, in my first battle I thought the sky was falling down. I thought the world was coming to an end. You bet I was scared."

Every one laughed. Perhaps it seemed strange and rather wonderful to them that a man should admit the thing, and in the tone of their laughter there was probably more admiration than if old Fleming had declared that he had always been a lion. Moreover, they knew that he had ranked as an orderly sergeant, and so their opinion of his heroism was fixed. None, to be sure, knew how an orderly sergeant ranked, but then it was understood to be somewhere just shy of a major-general's stars. So when old Henry admitted that he had been frightened, there was a laugh.

"The trouble was," said the old man, "I thought they were all shooting at me. Yes, sir, I thought every man in the other army was aiming at me in particular, and only me. And it seemed so darned unreasonable, you know. I wanted to explain to 'em what an almighty good fellow I was, because I thought then they might quit all trying to hit me. But I couldn't explain, and they kept on being unreasonable—blim!—blam!—bang! So I run!"

Two little triangles of wrinkles appeared at the corners of his eyes. Evidently he appreciated some comedy in this recital. Down near his feet, however, little Jim, his grandson, was visibly horror-stricken. His hands were clasped nervously, and his eyes were wide with astonishment at this terrible scandal, his most magnificent grandfather telling such a thing.

"That was at Chancellorsville. Of course, afterward I got kind of used to it. A man does. Lots of men, though, seem to feel all right from the start. I did, as soon as I 'got on to it,' as they say now; but at first I was pretty flustered. Now, there was young Jim Conklin, old Si Conklin's son—that used to keep the tannery—you none of you recollect him—well, he went into it from the start just as if he was born to it. But with me it was different. I had to get used to it."

When little Jim walked with his grandfather he was in the habit of skipping along on the stone pavement in front of the three stores and the hotel of the town and betting that he could avoid the cracks. But upon this day he walked soberly, with his hand gripping two of his grandfather's fingers. Sometimes he kicked abstractedly at dandelions that curved over the walk. Any one could see that he was much troubled.

"There's Sickles's colt over in the medder, Jimmie," said the old man. "Don't you wish you owned one like him?"

"Um," said the boy, with a strange lack of interest. He continued his reflections. Then finally he ventured: "Grandpa—now—was that true what you was telling those men?"

"What?" asked the grandfather. "What was I telling them?"

"Oh, about your running."

"Why, yes, that was true enough, Jimmie. It was my first fight, and there was an awful lot of noise, you know."

Jimmie seemed dazed that this idol, of its own will, should so totter. His stout boyish idealism was injured.

Presently the grandfather said: "Sickles's colt is going for a drink. Don't you wish you owned Sickles's colt, Jimmie?"

The boy merely answered: "He ain't as nice as our'n." He lapsed then into another moody silence.

. . . . .

One of the hired men, a Swede, desired to drive to the county-seat for purposes of his own. The old man loaned a horse and an unwashed buggy. It appeared later that one of the purposes of the Swede was to get drunk.

After quelling some boisterous frolic of the farm-hands and boys in the garret, the old man had that night gone peacefully to sleep, when he was aroused by clamoring at the kitchen door. He grabbed his trousers, and they waved out behind as he dashed forward. He could hear the voice of the Swede, screaming and blubbering. He pushed the wooden button, and, as the door flew open, the Swede, a maniac, stumbled inward, chattering, weeping, still screaming. "De barn fire! Fire! Fire! De barn fire! Fire! Fire! Fire!"

There was a swift and indescribable change in the old man. His face ceased instantly to be a face; it became a mask, a gray thing, with horror written about the mouth and eyes. He hoarsely shouted at the foot of the little rickety stairs, and immediately, it seemed, there came down an avalanche of men. No one knew that during this time the old lady had been standing in her night-clothes at the bed-room door, yelling: "What's th' matter? What's th' matter? What's th' matter?"

When they dashed toward the barn it presented to their eyes its usual appearance, solemn, rather mystic in the black night. The Swede's lantern was overturned at a point some yards in front of the barn doors. It contained a wild little conflagration of its own, and even in their excitement some of those who ran felt a gentle secondary vibration of the thrifty part of their minds at sight of this overturned lantern. Under ordinary circumstances it would have been a calamity.

But the cattle in the barn were trampling, trampling, trampling, and above this noise could be heard a humming like the song of innumerable bees. The old man hurled aside the great doors, and a yellow flame leaped out at one corner and sped and wavered frantically up the old gray wall. It was glad, terrible, this single flame, like the wild banner of deadly and triumphant foes.

The motley crowd from the garret had come with all the pails of the farm. They flung themselves upon the well. It was a leisurely old machine, long dwelling in indolence. It was in the habit of giving out water with a sort of reluctance. The men stormed at it, cursed it; but it continued to allow the buckets to be filled only after the wheezy windlass had howled many protests at the mad-handed men.

With his opened knife in his hand old Fleming himself had gone headlong into the barn, where the stifling smoke swirled with the air-currents, and where could be heard in its fulness the terrible chorus of the flames, laden with tones of hate and death, a hymn of wonderful ferocity.

He flung a blanket over an old mare's head, cut the halter close to the manger, led the mare to the door, and fairly kicked her out to safety. He returned with the same blanket, and rescued one of the workhorses. He took five horses out, and then came out himself, with his clothes bravely on fire. He had no whiskers, and very little hair on his head. They soused five pailfuls of water on him. His eldest son made a clean miss with the sixth pailful, because the old man had turned and was running down the decline and around to the basement of the barn, where were the stanchions of the cows. Some one noticed at the time that he ran very lamely, as if one of the frenzied horses had smashed his hip.

The cows, with their heads held in the heavy stanchions, had thrown themselves, strangled themselves, tangled themselves: done everything which the ingenuity of their exuberant fear could suggest to them.

Here, as at the well, the same thing happened to every man save one. Their hands went mad. They became incapable of everything save the power to rush into dangerous situations.

The old man released the cow nearest the door, and she, blind drunk with terror, crashed into the Swede. The Swede had been running to and fro babbling. He carried an empty milk-pail, to which he clung with an unconscious, fierce enthusiasm. He shrieked like one lost as he went under the cow's hoofs, and the milk-pail, rolling across the floor, made a flash of silver in the gloom.

Old Fleming took a fork, beat off the cow, and dragged the paralyzed Swede to the open air. When they had rescued all the cows save one, which had so fastened herself that she could not be moved an inch, they returned to the front of the barn and stood sadly, breathing like men who had reached the final point of human effort.

Many people had come running. Someone had even gone to the church, and now, from the distance, rang the tocsin note of the old bell. There was a long flare of crimson on the sky, which made remote people speculate as to the whereabouts of the fire.

The long flames sang their drumming chorus in voices of the heaviest bass. The wind whirled clouds of smoke and cinders into the faces of the spectators. The form of the old barn was outlined in black amid these masses of orange-hued flames.

And then came this Swede again, crying as one who is the weapon of the sinister fates. "De colts! De colts! You have forgot de colts!"

Old Fleming staggered. It was true; they had forgotten the two colts in the box-stalls at the back of the barn. "Boys," he said, "I must try to get 'em out." They clamored about him then, afraid for him, afraid of what they should see. Then they talked wildly each to each. "Why, it's sure death!" "He would never get out!" "Why, it's suicide for a man to go in there!" Old Fleming stared absent-mindedly at the open doors. "The poor little things," he said. He rushed into the barn.

When the roof fell in, a great funnel of smoke swarmed toward the sky, as if the old man's mighty spirit, released from its body—a little bottle—had swelled like the genie of fable. The smoke was tinted rose-hue from the flames, and perhaps the unutterable midnights of the universe will have no power to daunt the color of this soul.

In this short story, plot is very important. Divided into two parts, the first is relatively placid. Here, Stephen Crane prepares us for the power and significance of the second. At the opening of the story, Mr. Fleming, a respected war veteran, admitted to his friends in the country grocery store that he ran from the enemy in the war, that he had been afraid, but that he got used to it, and lost his fear. His grandson was "horror stricken" at this confession. His idol had fallen. As they walk home the boy is silent. "Anyone could see that he was much troubled." But his grandfather only commented on the colts in a "medder"; he liked colts. When he asked the boy if he wouldn't like a colt like the one in the "medder," the boy replied, "He ain't as nice as our'n."

In the second part of the story the scene shifts to the farm where the "Swede," an un-named character, returns drunk from town. Later the old man, Fleming, is awakened by the screams of the Swede, calling that the barn is burning. The "old lady" in her nightgown adds to the excitement by yelling, three times, "What's th' matter?" From here on the story centers around the panic and horror of the fire. The Swede and the other farm hands are helpless under pressure, in contrast to the clear-thinking old man. He rescued an old mare, then five more horses; his clothes are on fire, his whiskers and hair almost burned away. Not waiting for water to be thrown on his clothes, he rescued the cows who had "strangled themselves, tangled themselves" in fear. He released one cow that, "blind and drunk with fear," had trampled on the Swede whom the old man saved. When all of the cows, except one, were rescued and the men looked sadly at the burning barn, the Swede suddenly remembered that the colts had been forgotten. The old man tried to save the colts—we remember his interest in the colts in the first part of the story as well as his grandson's remark, "They ain't as nice as our'n,"—but in the attempt he died as the roof fell in.

There are only three characters of importance in this story. Mr. Fleming ("the old man"), his grandson Jim, and the "Swede." The old man is the hero and the symbol of courage, the Swede is an element of fate who motivates the course of events, and the grandson provides the leverage for the irony. The boy faces a psychological crisis when he realizes that this great man, his grandfather, was afraid in battle. The boy lost his psychological anchor; where was he to turn for an ideal?

Crane provides for unity in setting, character and plot. For example, he mentions the "dismal belfry of the village church" in the opening of the story which seems innocently unimportant until we later hear the bell ringing to tell of the fire. Again in the first part, the old man comments on the colt in the meadow, and the boy replies "He ain't as nice as our'n." It seems to be a faint foreshadowing, when we look back on it, of the tragedy that follows, for it is the attempt to save the colts that brings about the old man's death. Unity is also achieved by the focus on the old man, the only character present throughout the story.

The major element of contrast is made between the two parts of the story, which are complete opposites in setting, action, emotion and mood. In the first part it is a bright sunny day in a country grocery store; there is a happy contented mood—that is, except for the disillusioned boy. The action is leisurely. In the second part we see essentially a barn, first in the black of night and then in the light of wild flames, "laden with tones of hate and death, a hymn of wonderful ferocity." Here the action is intense, rapid, and filled with physical movement and suspense.

Crane's figures of speech are outstanding for their vividness and force. He uses metaphor, simile and personification; he gives visual imagery an aspect of sound, such as "The long flames sang their drumming chorus in voices of the heaviest bass." He gives to flames a living human quality, such as "It was glad, terrible, this single flame, like the wild banner of deadly and triumphant foes." Even the reluctant well ". . . continued to allow the buckets to be filled only after the wheezy windlass had howled many protests at the mad-handed men." The clumsiness and excitement of the men is expressed in "Their hands went mad." Crane's use of verbs to propel his plot convey mood, tempo, and attack in themselves; he conveys urgency in action words: grabbed, dashed, yelling, hurled, leaped, sped, stormed, clung, shrieked, howled, smashed, whirled, staggered, and clamored.

He uses onomatopoeia in sentences, such as "But the cattle in the barn were trampling, trampling, trampling, and above this noise could be heard a humming like the song of innumerable bees." A frequency of aspirates in the second part of the story gives a feeling of breathlessness in phrases, such as "With his opened knife in his hand old Fleming himself had gone headlong into the barn . . ." and in "The cows, with their heads held in the heavy stanchions, . . ." He uses alliteration in phrases, such as "the stifling smoke swirled," and assonance in "strangled themselves, tangled themselves."

The transition from the first part of the story to the second is very abrupt. The writer simply doesn't provide one. He jumps from one part to the next without apology or explanation. The first line of the second part does lead us into the second episode, but it is scarcely a transition from the first. The oral reader will probably want to have a considerable pause and change of attitude as he moves from the first episode to the next.

Crane's use of color is certainly dramatic and some of it, perhaps most of it, is symbolic as well. Goethe's study on color seems to have been known to him. In the first part of his story the colors are cheerful and pleasant; in the second where they are more frequently used, they suggest and reinforce emotion. Crane uses neutral colors in contrast to strong colors to heighten the effect; sometimes he uses a sequence of several neutral or strong colors. At word of the fire the old man's face is gray "like a mask," and the barn is mystic in the black night. Then a lantern overturns and has "a wild little conflagration of its own," which prepares us for greater conflagrations. Next, "a yellow flame leaped out at one corner and sped and wavered frantically up the old gray wall." Again, a neutral color to heighten the "yellow flame." Then there is a momentary flash of silver. Now the violence is acute: "A long flare of crimson on the sky," followed by the form of the barn outlined "in black amid these masses of orange-hued flames." Color has reached its climax of intensity; it can do no more. The next image is quite different. The color is no longer violent; rather, it is tinted "rose-hue from the flames," suggesting dawn, the triumphant dawn of another world for a courageous soul.

In this story, told in the third person, the oral interpreter shares the events with his listener. He builds the plot from a state of rural tranquility to rural ferocity. Particularly in the second part, the interpreter's mood comes out of the visual, auditory and kinesthetic imagery which carry the intensity and horror of the situation. The interpreter will note that Crane says little specifically about the old man; in the first part the old man literally describes himself and reveals his own attitude and philosophy, but in contrast he does describe the attitude and reactions of the disillusioned boy. In the second part, the old man says nothing directly, until at the turning point, his humanitarian attitude and his courage bring forth, in his own words, his determination to save the colts. Here the interpreter will give significance to the old man's few, but important words, for these determine the course of the action. In the last paragraph there is a change of attitude from one of intensity to that of resolution and philosophical observation.

JOCK TAMSON'S TALE by Margaret Linton

Jock Tamson never could quite figure out how he came to run away from home and take to a seafaring life. Most of the yarns he had read about boys running away dealt with orphans who lived with hard hearted aunties or boys with heavy handed stepfathers, but Jock had none of these worries. Amateur psychologists and rejected children had not been invented when he was a boy so, as far as Jock knew, his Mother loved him about average and his old man was no worse than other folks'. Even his older brother treated him right, sometimes fighting with him and sometimes fighting for him. But Jock ran away to sea when he was 12 years old.

Being big for his age and not afraid of hard work he had no trouble in getting a job and he was soon far from his native Scotland, bound for Australia and an unexciting life of adventure—unexciting because Jock was unexcitable, but adventurous because he was unafraid of life and never sidestepped a new experience, being of the opinion that in the long run it was usually easier to face things than to run away from them. Though not by nature curious, he never shunned the unknown but ploughed stolidly on his way, secure in the knowledge that no matter what happened to him, either he'd win through or that it would be "all over for Jock." That he should try to mold his life after a certain pattern never entered his head. He never grumbled, he never dodged, he never endured anything he did not like. If something in his surroundings did not suit him, he either changed it or went away from it. In his old age (and he lived to be very old), he could say with truth, "I never was a drinkin' man, an' I never was a fightin' man frae choice but mony's the wallop I got intae. See that scar above my eye? That scar is about 50 years old. That was where a friend o' mine felled me with a bottle wan nicht I should hae left him alane and minded my own business." And then Jock would matter-of-factly relate the story of how he got the scar.

They had just reached Wapatike after a long hard voyage and the belligerent friend, one MacNiven, had been celebrating shore leave as a sailor will. He made a good try at spending his entire earnings for the trip and was still hard at this task when the ship was due to leave port. Jock went ashore in search of him and eventually found him in the lowest part of town. MacNiven, annoyed at being disturbed and being, moreover, in no mood to go back to sea, offered some resistance. Jock here explains, "I thocht it wad be easier tae carry him unconscious than tae drag him fightin' all the way, so I hit him a whack on the ear—but no' hard enough. Insteed o' fellin' him, it jist angert him an' he played skelp at me an' felled ME! There we baith lay helpless in wan o' the lowest parts in Wapatike. What a' happened tae us afore we came to, I'll never know, but I woke up in a wee dark room an' MacNiven, he says tae me, says he,

"Jock. We're in the jail."

"Oh," says I, "What for?"

"I don't rightly know," says MacNiven, "but it seems we've nae money; nane o' us. I spent the maist o' mine but I don't know whit happened to yours. After I'd knocked you down, somebody hit me over the back of the head so when we were found we were both unconscious. We were too bad hurted tae talk an' we've nae papers tae say wha we are, sae the police locked us up. But he's a dacent sort o' fellow the warder. Comes frae Stornoway so, of course, thinks naebody can navigate a ship except a MacBrayne skipper, but otherwise he's a sensible enough laddie in his way."

Further conversation was interrupted by Jock falling asleep again at this point. He was aroused later by the arrival of the "dacent fellow from Stornoway" who entered with a long face and a heavy heart.

"Ach now—an iff thiss issna the sorry bussiness. The two of yiz lockit up for disorderly conduct an' me meanin' to haf gone into the town to enjoy a guid Saturday evening before the Sabbath overtakes us again. You wouldn't haf the price of a decent fine on ye I suppose even iff I coult find his Honour for ye? No? Well, I was expectin' that. Nobody gets picked up from Waterfront Alley with any money left in their pockets. But it iss the great pitty for Saturday iss the night I like to foregather with some of the boys."

"You couldna lend us the price o' a fine till we get a job, could ye?" asked MacNiven.

Macleod, the warden, scratched his head and thought for a long minute.

"Well, I coult and I coultn't if you understand me."

"Could ye mak it a wee thing clearer maybe," prompted MacNiven.

"It's like this. If I lend you both a fine I wouldn't have enough left to make it worrth my while to go into the town and if I don't lend you the fine I'll haf to stay here and guard you and even if I lend you the fine if I can't find Jimmy Brian (that's his honour) ye can't get oot onyway. It's a sorry bussiness any way ye like tae look at it."

Sorry to have done a fellow countryman out of his Saturday night spree, Jock and MacNiven sought hard to find a way out.

"What's yer rules aboot guardin' prisoners?" queried MacNiven.

"I would haf to look it up in The Regulations," answered Macleod, and he rummaged through the table drawer in search of the same. Locating them behind the clock, he read out a long screed of lawyer's English, punctuating the reading according to his need for breath rather than according to the dots and commas and such like nonsense with which the pages were strewn, so there may be some excuse for Jock and MacNiven if they did not interpret the regulations very accurately.

"That sounds tae me like all ye have to do to guard a prisoner is tae swear somebody in as a special warden, so whit's tae hinder ye swearin' me in tae guard Jock, an' swearin' Jock in tae guard me? Then ye could go intae the town as usual."

The more Macleod thought about this solution the harder he found it to see any flaw in it. Solemnly he administered the necessary oaths and handed over the key to their room. Only then did he see the next problem. He had only one key for each room and they would need to have a key each. If he gave the key to Jock that was all right for Jock to guard MacNiven, but if Jock was also to be MacNiven's prisoner, MacNiven must also have a key. It would never do for the prisoner to have a key and the warden to have none. This called for another meeting of great minds but, as Jock was wont to remark, "There's aye a way oot. It's the findin' it that maks the man."

MacNiven was equal to the test. "If you have jist wan key for each room how about puttin' me in that wee room at the back an' leavin' Jock here?"

"Och now, that would never do at all, at all," objected Macleod. "I couldn't enjoy myself if I thought I had put you two fine boys in solitary on a Saturday night. That would make a very long evening for you all by yourselves. You would be wantin' a game of the cards, would you not?"

"Cannat very well play cairds when we've nae money. Would ye maybe have a set o' the dominoes?"

But the key question had to be settled first or the evening's entertainment would be denied to some of them, either Macleod or his prisoners.

"I think I've got it," said Jock. "Gie Mac a key tae lock me in, an' me a key tae lock Mac in, an' let us baith come oot an' play dominoes in your office till lock up time."

This was agreed upon, the keys were duly handed over and off went Macleod to the town before any more problems should turn up. Jock and MacNiven played dominoes till they were sleepy and then they got ready to perform their wardenly duties. MacNiven had actually locked Jock in before they realised their plight.

"Jock, how are ye goin' to get out now to lock me up?"

"Losh keep me!—I never thocht o' that. Let me oot till we see what's tae be done." A long thoughtful silence reigned and then came the solution.

"We'll each hae tae lock ourselves in an' then fling the key out between the bars."

There's always a way out—and having found it, they slept well. When Macleod returned, he found the two keys on the floor and his prisoners safely locked in their respective cells.

WHAT I WISH (OH, I WISH) I HAD SAID,
by Arthur Cavanaugh*

Were I a painter, as Aunt Tillybird had grandly hoped, I would use crayon to draw this portrait of her. I would use pale colors—citron, ocher, faint umber—and sketch her in quick, scrawling lines: the red hair (dyed), arranged in slight dishevelment; the tentative, wavering smile; the soft eyes that were uncertain, speculative, and something more (frightened? defeated?) that I could never quite define. I would sketch her seated—no, lighted on a chair, in that manner she had, like an anxious bird poised for flight. Tillybird. Her father gave her the nickname when she was a child, and she had been called by it ever since. Certainly, she never appeared offended by the name. She even used it herself. " 'Lo, there, Robbie," she would say when I answered the telephone. "This is Aunt Tillybird. How's the world treating you?" She never seemed to mind the name at all, but I wonder about it. Birds, after all, are fragile creatures, meant to be treated with gentleness, not cruelty. I, of all the family, have cause to reflect on that.

Aunt Tillybird was my mother's sister; her only relative, in fact, except for some third cousins in Yonkers, whom we children had never met. Not that we saw much of Aunt Tilly. A schoolteacher and unmarried, she lived, as we did, in Brooklyn, but in a section as far removed from ours as the sun from the earth. Aunt Tilly lived in the fashionable Heights section, in an apartment building that boasted not only a doorman, but a man to run the elevator. There wasn't, I think, a single doorman in our neighborhood, unless you counted the attendant who, after taking your ticket, opened the door for you at Loew's Gates. There weren't even any apartment buildings in our neighborhood. Just five-story tenement flats and houses—unbroken rows of them that stretched, it seemed to me, to the outer rim of the world. We lived in the Bushwick section of Brooklyn, on Warbisher Street, and I cannot remember a time when I didn't hate it. Aunt Tillybird must have hated it, too. When she came down the street to our house, she always walked with her eyes pinned ahead, her glance avoiding the squatting stoops and sagging porches. Perhaps it was partly why she didn't visit us more often. She came to the house for Christmas dinner each year, laden with gifts, and if there were a First Communion in the family or a confirmation or graduation, Aunt Tilly showed up then, too, casting herself adrift among my father's large, noisy clan, the Connertys. But that marked the extent of her visits. For us, she represented a shadowy figure in the family drama, confined mostly to the wings. She was our Aunt Tillybird, who wore perfume and displayed hair of a peculiar reddish shade and who had traveled to Europe twelve times to view the cathedrals and art museums. Very likely, if my mother hadn't got sick one winter, the pattern of the relationship would never have changed. Aunt Tillybird would never have become a part of our lives—or, at any rate, a part of mine.

I was eleven years old, that winter. All week, my mother had lain upstairs in bed with a cold. At night, I could hear her coughing—terrible, racking coughs—and the pad of my father's feet as he got up to give her medicine. Then, one night, she was carried down the stairs on a stretcher, wrapped in blankets, her head rolling back and forth. She was taken by ambulance to Saint Mary's Hospital, and for a week, the word "pneumonia" floated through the house; "pneumonia," and "crisis," and "holding her own." My sister Margaret stayed home from school to take care of us, and my father was absent from the dinner table at night, remaining at the hospital until visitors' hours were over at nine.

After two weeks, my mother was still in Saint Mary's, and some new, sharper worry had begun to pinch at my father's face. He sat at night in the kitchen with Vincent, my older brother, and talked about it. I stood outside the door and listened. "Taking more X rays," I heard my father say between long silences. "Calling in this specialist. . . . By Saturday—"

"What's this you're up to?" Margaret demanded, coming up to me. "Okay, Robbie. Start moving."

"By Saturday, what?" Vinny asked, in the kitchen.

"Well—we'll get the verdict, son."

"*Robbie.* Up to bed."

I dawdled up the stairs, dragging my feet over the steps. "Verdict" was a word you heard in crime movies. James Cagney was always waiting around to hear verdicts. Then, in the next scene, he'd be working in the prison machine shop. I went up the stairs, seeing a vision of my mother as if she were in prison. I saw her white hospital bed placed in a cell, behind bars. By Saturday—

On Saturday, it rained. We got up early to offer Mass and Communion for my mother. "Pray hard for her," my father admonished. After Mass, he left us on the church steps and headed for the hospital with Vinny, who, as the eldest, had the privilege of going along.

As we went into the house, the phone was ringing. It was Aunt

Tillybird. Since my mother had been taken to Saint Mary's, she had called the house regularly. "That you, Robbie? Don't suppose there's any news yet. . . . Well, I'll keep in touch. Toodle-oo."

By lunchtime, Aunt Tilly had called four times.

We sat around the living room that day—Dan, Roseanne, and me. Dan was listening to a football game on the radio. Roseanne—she was the youngest next to me—sat sulkily on the lumpy sofa and thumbed through a movie magazine. I sat in the Morris chair, knees pulled up. The house was cold—in winter, it was always cold. Upstairs, Margaret was housecleaning. There would be the roar of the vacuum cleaner, then silence, then the whooshing roar again as she plugged in the cleaner in another room. Verdict. . . .

I got up from the Morris chair, went into the dining room, and spread newspapers on the table. I got out the water-color set I'd purchased two months before with my birthday money. Against a stack of telephone directories, I propped a colored photograph of a New England landscape. I would paint a picture of the scene and send it to my mother. I would paint her a whole batch of pictures, which she could put on the walls of her hospital room, to make it look pretty. I dipped the brush in a saucer of water and moistened the disks of colors. I held the brush over the drawing paper. A blob of water trickled from the brush onto the paper. I watched the wet circle widen and seep through the paper. Verdict. Verdict. Will the prisoner please rise and— I put my head down on the table and hid my face.

Then I heard the doorbell ring.

"Eeek, look who it is!" shrilled Roseanne, peering out at the porch from the living-room window. "That's all we need today, some of that silly talk of hers."

"Aunt Tillybird!" I shouted, and ran to the front hall. There was something I'd been wanting to tell Aunt Tilly. I opened the door, and there she was.

She wore a shiny pink raincoat; in her hands she held a pink umbrella, a purse, and a wet cakebox. "Greetings, Master Robbie."

I opened my mouth to speak, but the words got twisted together, and I just stood there.

Aunt Tillybird paid no attention. Emitting little breaths of laughter, she edged into the hall, bringing with her a festive air. "How are all the lovely childees?" (She pronounced this last "*chill*-dees," in the belief, I think, that it constituted Old English.)

Margaret came down the stairs and marched toward the door, in her new capacity of hostess.

" 'Lo, Margaret." Aunt Tillybird held out the cakebox. "Here you are, some goodies from that French bakery on Henry Street. *Pâtisserie, une bonne pâtisserie.* Let's hear you say it, Marg."

It was Aunt Tilly's practice, on her visits to the house, to conduct among us a running course in French, concentrating on vocabulary and gender (of which, I learned later, she had the shakiest of acquaintances).

Margaret struggled with the pronunciation, *"Ooone bun paa-tees-ury."* The cakebox she bore away to the kitchen contained, I knew, ladyfingers, for Aunt Tilly never brought any other form of food to the house.

I took her umbrella and raincoat.

"Thank you, Robbie. Say, you're getting tall. The famous Connerty height." A vague smile on her lips, Aunt Tilly looped her purse over her arm and patted her red hair. It was as if she had arrived for a party and found no party underway. "I take it your, umm, dad's not home yet."

"No, he isn't."

It relieved her, I sensed, to learn that my father was still at the hospital, for that meant painful discussions would not need to be launched into immediately. "Well," said Aunt Tilly, and turned to survey the living room, awash with swollen, sagging furniture, uneven tables, and tilting lamps. Blocking her entrance into the room was Dan, who lay sprawled on the floor, absorbed in the football game blaring from the radio. "What ho, there, Daniel," she greeted him, in the jocular tone she assumed with all males over the age of fifteen. Dan did not answer. And since he made no attempt to rise, she proceeded to step over him. Safe on the other side of the room, Aunt Tilly lowered herself onto the sofa, as if expecting its imminent collapse. The radio blared away. "Ah, football," she declared. "The sport of kings."

"I thought that was horse racing," Dan said.

A little laugh, a bow. *"Monsieur* is correct. Horse racing it is, to be sure. Will I ever forget the splendors of Longchamps! That's a celebrated racing track outside Paris, you know. *Champs,* you see, means fields."

Dan sprang toward the radio and turned up the volume. "Quiet, Aunt Til. I want to hear this."

Aunt Tillybird made no comment. She looked down at her purse, a smile still on her face. She clicked the round gold clasp on the purse open and shut. Then she turned to Roseanne. "Well, tell us, Roseanne, what have you been doing lately that's worthwhile?"

In truth, Aunt Tilly's inquiries were not always easy to answer. Roseanne rolled her eyes and sucked at her mouth. "Uh—well, last week I got this idea I'd be a nurse someday," she offered.

"Très bien," said Aunt Tillybird, and then her eyes met mine.

I stepped clumsily toward the sofa. I had been rehearsing what I wanted to say, but again the words got twisted in my mind. I blurted out, "Aunt Tillybird, you know the birthday money you sent me? I bought a water-color set with it. A water-color set," I repeated, as the sound of the front door opening struck silence into us all.

We watched as my father appeared in the front hall. Behind him, Vinny closed the door noiselessly. Margaret materialized in the dining-room doorway, wiping her hands on a dish towel. Dan quickly turned off the radio. It was time, time now to learn the verdict. I saw Aunt Tillybird's eyes fasten on my father's white, worried face as if upon a dreaded apparition.

"Damned linoleum's coming apart," my father said, kicking at the hall flooring. "Might know the weather would be rotten, too." He nodded at Aunt Tilly, noting her presence for the first time. "Good of you to come, Tilly."

"Greetings, James."

My father nodded again, then walked heavily into the dining room.

Vinny pointed at Dan, Roseanne, and me. "No horsing around, understand? How are you, Aunt Tilly?" He went into the dining room. "Drink, Dad? Maybe you'd better." Then he ducked into the kitchen.

I saw that Aunt Tilly's hands, clicking and unclicking the gold clasp of her purse, were shaking. But she got up and went into the dining room. Once there, however, resolve deserted her. She gave a nervous laugh, turned to the china closet, and clapped her hands together as if in delighted surprise. "Why," she exclaimed, "Peg's still got that darling sugar and creamer from the tea set Papa bought Mama abroad. On their wedding trip, Papa and Mama visited *Wien*—that's German for Vienna."

Roughly, my father pulled out a chair from the dining table, cutting short the guided tour. He sat down silently. Vinny came in from the kitchen with a bottle of whisky and a shot glass. He filled the glass and handed it to my father.

My father emptied the glass. He wiped his hand across his mouth. "It's bad, Til," he said. "It's bad news, I'm afraid."

Whatever he was going to say, I didn't want to hear it. I didn't want to learn the damned verdict. My father was seated in the chair nearest the kitchen door, the chair where my mother always sat. I didn't want him sitting there. It was her chair. Since the night she had gone to Saint Mary's, we had kept it vacant, ready for when she came home. Now my father was sitting in the chair as if she weren't coming home any more. I didn't want to hear what he was going to tell us about her.

"Now, James," Aunt Tilly ventured, "whatever the news, I'm sure—"

I stepped into the dining room. "You know what I was telling Aunt Tilly about?" I said to my father. "I was telling her about the water-color set I bought with her birthday money. And you know what, Dad?"

My father regarded me in blank astonishment.

Vinny said, "For God's sake, Robbie."

But I went right ahead. "You know what I'm going to do, Dad?" I rattled on. "I'm going to paint a whole bunch of pictures for Mom, so she can decorate her hospital room. See, I've got a couple already done." I went to the china-closet drawer, where I kept my drawings. "See, Dad, I copy 'em from magazines."

"What the living hell are you talking about?" he demanded. *"Drawings?"* He reached out, grabbed the drawings, and flung them onto the carpet. "Your mother's coughing blood, and you stand there prattling about pictures. Holes in her lungs, do you understand?" he shouted. "She has to go away, but you don't care about that. Oh, no, you just want to chatter about—" He stopped and looked away from me. "I'm sorry, Robbie."

"That's okay." I picked up the drawings and put them on the table.

"It was nothing important," I said, and walked out of the dining room. I stood at the front door and looked out at the rain and the street. There was silence in the dining room, then voices again, as the discussion resumed. I put my hands over my ears, still not wanting to hear about my mother.

"How long will it be for?" I heard Margaret ask.

"A year, anyway. Depends. Maybe two."

I heard Aunt Tilly say, "The money will be managed. Somehow it will."

"My God, Tilly, do you know what a year at that kind of place costs?"

I pulled open the door and stepped out onto the rickety porch. The rain was hitting against the porch railing, loosening the cracked, peeling paint. I thought of the plans my father had made to paint the house in the spring. New paint job, new linoleum for the hall, new furnace, new water heater—yet nothing would ever improve it. The others—Vinny, Margaret, Dan, and Roseanne—didn't feel like this about the house. They were happy living there. They didn't mess around with stupid water-color sets and paintbrushes.

I heard a sound behind me. It was Aunt Tillybird. "Here he is," she said, "the artist viewing nature!" She held my drawings in her hand. "Mustn't worry about your mother, Robbie. We'll get her well again."

I hugged the porch post and contemplated Warbisher Street. "Some nature to view, isn't it?" I said.

"Yes," Aunt Tillybird murmured.

"The rest of the family doesn't seem to mind. I don't know why I do."

"It's because," she told me, "you're different." She looked down at the drawings. "I can't imagine why it took till today for me to recognize it. Poor eyesight, I guess."

I kept looking at the street, and in the slanting rain, I seemed to glimpse my mother coming along the cracked sidewalk, bundles of groceries in her arms. The kitchen. What a nice, cozy place it was, with her bustling around the stove, listening to you talk while she fixed supper. I felt tears on my face. I turned my head away, so that Aunt Tillybird wouldn't see.

Her hands made awkward movements. It wasn't her usual role to give comfort, and she didn't quite know how to proceed. "Say, now,

Robbie," she began, after a moment. "I was thinking about something. An aspiring artist needs, you know, to become acquainted with art. He needs to visit museums and study the masters. Look, how would you like to go to the city next Saturday and tour the Metropolitan? Oh, the Rembrandts there, the El Grecos! Will you be busy next Saturday?"

I got out my handkerchief and blew my nose. "I—I don't think so," I said.

"Fine! We'll make it a date, then."

And that was how my life with Aunt Tillybird began.

"Feast yourself," Aunt Tillybird proclaimed. She drew to a halt in the gallery doorway and gestured dramatically. "Drink in the beauty of it, Robbie. Velázquez, of course." She folded her arms and studied the painting that gleamed from the wall of the room ahead. We were in a gallery on the second floor of the Metropolitan. "What *is* the title? Oh, it's famous."

I ran over to the gold-framed painting, which was of a boy dressed in a red suit. "It's named Don Manuel Osario de—something or other," I called back to Aunt Tilly. "And it's by Goya."

"Well," she said, "they're both Spanish, at least."

It was more than two years since the rainy winter Saturday. Soon after that day, my mother had been taken to Greenville Sanatorium, in Saranac, New York. I had not seen her in two years. I was thirteen now. And I was going to be a painter when I grew up.

Aunt Tilly stood beside the Goya painting and regarded the red-suited boy. "Notice the fantastic texture," she advised. "Examine the skin tones. Unique!" She consulted the clutch of museum brochures in her hand. "Shall we finish the second floor or try something else, Robbie? The auditorium has a movie at two—a tour of the châteaux country. How's that sound?"

"Fine," I told her. "I'd like that."

"And, oh, a new Tintoretto's on display in the Recent Acquisitions Room. Why don't we head there first?"

I moved close to her. Here, in this radiant place suffused with light, Warbisher Street did not exist. Here, I could forget that my mother had gone far away from me. Forgetting was a trick I had trouble with at home. It was hard not to think about my mother there. Often at night, I would wake up calling for her. Or at supper I would look up, expecting to see her come through the swinging kitchen door. Then I would glance at the empty chair near the door and go back to eating, trying not to think about her. I tried not to think of school, too, or Warbisher Street, or the rows of houses that I hated. There was only one thing I wanted to think about: my Saturdays with Aunt Tilly.

Saturday had become like a flower, a gigantic, beautiful flower that bloomed out over the other days of the week, concealing them. Every Saturday, I would get up early, put on a fresh white shirt and my Sunday suit, and take the trolley to the tall, brick building where Aunt Tilly lived. The doorman already knew me there. He would greet me by name, and the elevator man would converse with me as he sped the car to the tenth floor.

"You're a regular escort for Miss Quinlan, aren't you?" he would say. "I don't believe your aunt's ever had a visitor till you started showing up. She's just been all alone, just living in that little apartment, coming and going all by herself."

The apartment Aunt Tilly lived in had surprised me. It consisted of one small room, with a single window that looked out on a back court. Against one wall was a studio couch covered with a paisley shawl; at night, Aunt Tilly took off the paisley shawl, and the couch became her bed. In an alcove in the corner was a pullman kitchen, hidden by a screen. Prints and reproductions covered nearly every inch of Aunt Tilly's walls. A steamer trunk pasted with travel labels stood near the window. Books were everywhere—dusty old books and old opera programs; old issues of *Art Annual;* guidebooks to museums and galleries; souvenir menus from trips to Paris and Rome and Madrid. The room was crowded, so that you couldn't move about in it very easily. It was small, Aunt Tilly's apartment, small and dark and cluttered; it gave you a surprise when you walked in the first time.

Now Aunt Tilly turned one way and then the other, surveying the museum rooms on each side of us. "Now, which is the quickest way to the main stairs?"

"If we go back through the rooms where we already were," I said, "we'll end up in that big blue room. And the main stairs are right beyond."

"Of course!" she cried. "*Exactly* the way." We turned and started back through the maze of rooms. "I believe you already know this place better than I, Robbie. I'm awfully eager to see the new Tintoretto. Those Venetian painters were so bold, such a command of color and form. Hungry yet?"

"No, I'm fine."

"We can always stop for lunch."

"But then we'll miss the movie."

Aunt Tilly stopped and looked at me. "You really like our Saturdays, don't you?" she said.

I stared up at her. Her eyes were a clear blue, like the blue in Giotto paintings. They were soft, pretty eyes, without meanness (but with something else—fear? defeat?) in them. I thought of my mother and the stretcher carrying her down the stairs, and of how far away she was. My mouth trembled. "Our Saturdays," I told Aunt Tilly, "are all I have."

Sometimes on a Saturday, especially at Christmastime, Aunt Tilly liked to stroll through the glittering department stores on Fifth Avenue, inspecting the wares. On her tours, she never made any purchases. She would pause at a counter, tempted by a bright silk scarf or a pair of French gloves. Her purse would click open, then shut again, and she would laugh. "Got to save my pennies." Afterward, we would go into a hotel—the Plaza, usually—and sit in the lobby, so that Aunt Tilly could rest her feet. She would watch the gold elevator doors glide open and the guests alight from the red-carpeted cars.

"One day, perhaps, you'll be a painter of prominence," she would say to me, "and you'll stay here."

"When I do," I would tell her, "I'll invite you to lunch with me every day. I'll have a one-man show at a big gallery, and the best painting will be a portrait of you, Aunt Tilly."

"Really, Robbie? My!"

Now and again on a Saturday, Aunt Tilly would propose still another activity. She would consult the shipping news, to learn what ships might be sailing that day. On sailing days, visitors were allowed on board the ships. "The *Normandie* leaves at three," Aunt Tilly would announce. "What say, Robbie? Shall we hop over to the pier?"

I think I liked, best of all, visiting the great, glistening liners tied up at the North River piers. Aunt Tilly and I would climb the visitors' gangplank and set out to tour the entire ship. We would inspect the lounges, the swimming pools, the cabins, the dining rooms, pushing our way through the crowds of visitors, through the smoke and babble of voices, the clinking glasses raised in farewell toasts.

Having traveled to Europe twelve times, Aunt Tilly knew a lot about ships. "There's nothing," she would declare, "to equal an ocean voyage. Shipboard life is such a restorative—and you meet such congenial people. Interesting people who *do* things."

At some point in her dissertations on shipboard life, the announcement "All visitors ashore, all visitors ashore" would issue from the loudspeaker. Aunt Tilly would give one last, lingering glance at a tea salon or a writing room, and then we would go back down the gangplank and stand at the end of the pier, among the crowds waving and shouting, and watch the ship depart. Aunt Tilly and I would stand there long after the crowds had gone, and watch the ship until there was nothing more to see than a curl of smoke far down the river. Often it was cold on the pier. Aunt Tilly would hug her arms to her body, pull up the collar of her coat, and look silently toward the curl of smoke.

I would stand next to her and think of the little one-room apartment, dark and cluttered, and the travel labels pasted to the steamer trunk. "You haven't been to Europe in a couple of years," I'd remind her. "You didn't go last year or the year before."

"No, I didn't."

"Are you making plans to go?" I would ask her. "I'll bet you'll go next summer."

Aunt Tilly would hug her coat collar to her face, wisps of red hair escaping from her hat. "We'll see, Robbie," she'd answer. "We'll see."

"Penny for your thoughts," said Aunt Tillybird, as we reached the bottom of the museum stairs and sat down on a bench.

I scuffed at the floor with my feet. "You know what I wish, Aunt Tillybird?" I said.

"What, Robbie?"

"I wish there didn't have to be anything except paintings and statues and—" I struggled for the right word—"I don't know." I kicked at the floor. "I wish there was only Saturday and coming to the city with you."

Aunt Tilly was silent for a moment. "I know what you mean." She looked at the gift counter and at the people clustered in front of the displays. "When I was young," she said, "I felt so deeply about art. I planned to make it my career, you know. Oh, yes. I was going to be an artist. I only started teaching school so that I could save the money to study in Paris. But when I finally got there—"

I turned and looked at her face. Her head was tilted a little to the side, and her eyes had a faraway expression. "What happened?" I asked.

She shook her head, as if in amusement at her folly. "Well, I'm not sure, exactly. I'd signed up to take a course at the Sorbonne. I was to be in Paris the whole summer. But I—I was just too timid to attend classes. I felt—well, what if it turned out that I couldn't paint after all? I was afraid, I guess, that I would fail."

"You shouldn't have been afraid, Aunt Tilly," I said. "You should have marched into those classes and painted away, and the dickens with the rest."

"Should I have?" mused Aunt Tilly, patting my arm. "Shall we have a look at the Tintoretto now?"

We got up from the bench and went to the Recent Acquisitions Room. On the wall farthest from the entranceway hung the Tintoretto, brilliant with color and power.

Aunt Tillybird gazed at the painting with soft eyes. Her voice was little and quiet. "I guess I settled for just looking," she said. "Yes, I became just one of the onlookers."

Later, when we had left the museum and were seated in a sandwich shop on Madison Avenue, Aunt Tilly told me that we would not be meeting next Saturday. She was going to Saranac to visit my mother.

"Oh," I said.

Aunt Tilly pressed a spoon against the tea bag in the cup of steaming water. She removed the tea bag and stirred the amber water slowly. "Has your father said anything yet?"

I looked up from my plate. I didn't want to know, I didn't want to—

"Perhaps he's waiting till it's definite," Aunt Tilly went on.

I felt my heart hammering. "Till *what?*" I asked.

She regarded me across the table. "If all goes well, your mother will be coming home soon, Robbie. We'll be bringing her home to you." Then she said, her hand reaching out, "It's all right, Robbie. It's all right. No one's too old to cry. . . ."

My life with Aunt Tillybird did not end when my mother came

home—that is, not right away. Our Saturdays continued. It was simply that they didn't occur as frequently.

The house on Warbisher Street became transformed. It was still—and would be forever—a derelict, squeezed-together little house in need of patching. But now it became the place where my mother was, the place she had left and had come back to, the place where she could be found laughing in the kitchen, or counting sheets and pillowcases in the upstairs hall.

And I was growing up. I was a freshman, then a sophomore, then a senior in high school. I was writing stories for the school magazine, and my name was on the masthead of the school newspaper. "Robert F. Connerty," it read, "Assistant Editor." I had decided that I didn't, after all, want to be a painter. I would be a writer, instead.

Saturdays found me busy with my own activities. There were assignments to finish for the school paper. There were parties to go to at night. There wasn't the time, I decided, to spend a Saturday trailing around New York with Aunt Tillybird. If I wanted to go to the city—why, I could go by myself now.

Aunt Tillybird was pleased when I told her of my resolve to become a writer. "A Balzac in the family," she declared on the phone one night. "A Kipling in our midst."

"In the winter issue of the *Anchor,*" I informed her, "I had three selections."

"Three selections," said Aunt Tillybird. "Imagine. I guess you're not going to turn out to be an onlooker, Robbie."

"No, sir," I told her. "Anyway, that's why I can't meet you Saturday." Aunt Tilly had phoned to invite me to a Cézanne exhibit. "I have to go to a journalism conference that day," I told her. "I've been chosen to represent the *Anchor* staff. So I'll be busy, you see. But thanks for asking me, Aunt Tilly."

There was a silence on the phone, then the little laugh. "Well, we'll try to make it another time, then. Toodle-oo for now, Robbie."

"Good-by, Aunt Tillybird," I said.

Good-by, Aunt Tillybird. . . . Good-by, Aunt Tillybird. . . .

I was twenty-seven years old the last time I saw Aunt Tillybird. I had become a writer—or, at any rate, I had published stories in magazines and been hired to work on a movie script (the studio dropped me after a month). I was living in New York and had just signed a publisher's contract for my first book. With the advance, I was planning to get married and go to Europe. It was a spring day, I remember, and John Crane, an old friend from college, had invited me to go with him to an exhibit of Piranesi drawings at the Metropolitan. The Piranesi drawings were on display in the Special Exhibits Room.

We took the elevator upstairs, started down the long corridor, and there, at the end of a corridor, was Aunt Tillybird.

I stopped, uncertain for a moment if it was she. The small figure looked even smaller; the frail shoulders were stooped; the hair was more white than red. And then I *was* sure. Of course it was Aunt Tilly.

"Aunt Tillybird," I called. The small figure continued its slow progress down the corridor. Apparently, she had not heard me. "Aunt Tillybird," I called again.

She turned slowly, and as she caught sight of me, a smile broke like sunlight across her face. "Robbie," she said. "Well, Robbie. How's the world treating you?"

I introduced John to her. How long had it been, I wondered, since I had seen her last? Not since Dan's wedding last winter—almost a year. Why hadn't I phoned her? Aunt Tilly had retired from teaching and was living on her pension. She looked old.

Birds are fragile creatures, meant to be treated with gentleness, not cruelty. Yes, I have reflected on that.

As I stood talking to Aunt Tilly in the museum corridor, I knew what I should do. John was a painter; he had just returned from Europe; he was exactly the sort of person Aunt Tilly had once treasured meeting. What I should do was invite Aunt Tilly to view the Piranesi exhibit with us, and afterward, I should take her to lunch. Instead, I said, "Well, it's been wonderful running into you, Aunt Tilly. We've got to get together soon. I wish I weren't so rushed today. I'd ask you to lunch with us, but I have to be downtown in less than an hour."

And she replied, "You'd better hurry to the Piranesi, then. You wouldn't want to miss it." Then her thin, weightless hand gripped my arm, and she raised her face for a kiss. "Good-by, Robbie dear."

"Good-by, Aunt Tillybird."

Two months later, just before I was married and left for Europe, Aunt Tilly died. The elevator man found her on the studio couch in the little one-room apartment, the paisley shawl thrown over her. She had died in her sleep without making a sound, without telling anyone.

After the funeral, I went with my mother to the apartment to sort through Aunt Tilly's keepsakes: the dusty books, the prints and reproductions, the souvenir menus and guidebooks. In the bottom drawer of her desk, I found the water-color drawings from that long-ago day on Warbisher Street.

"Poor Aunt Tilly," I said. "She used to tell me she was just one of the onlookers. How hard it must have been, always to look on, never to do anything."

"Never to do anything?" repeated my mother, angrier than I had ever seen her. *"Never to do anything?"*

Then she told me what I should, of course, have known.

"Where did you imagine the money came from?" she asked, her face stiff with anger. "How do you think I was able to stay at Greenville? She gave me back to all of you. I'd call that doing something, wouldn't you?"

This portrait of Aunt Tilly is constructed of words only. It is nothing that can be hung on a wall or viewed in a gallery. Perhaps it does not matter, for she is not here to view it. Yet it is for her I have painted it.

I have kept her things—the books, the souvenirs, the prints. I have kept, too, the bitter memory of my last meeting with her. How I wish—will always wish—that I had said, instead of good-by, what I had never told her, as I tell her now a thousand times in my prayers. How I wish I had said, *"Aunt Tillybird, I love you."*

IV. THE ORAL INTERPRETER'S RESPONSIBILITIES

After you have read each story and have been absorbed in each experience, read them again and this time regard them more objectively. Ask yourself why the author used dialogue, description, or narration in a certain place and what effect he achieved by so doing. Then notice precisely what each scene or episode contributes toward the unfolding of the theme and consider what techniques you must employ to convey this experience to your listeners. At this point if your material needs cutting, this is the next step in your preparation.

Above all, remember that in reading prose fiction aloud, the "book" is in your mind. The text of the literature reveals the story as adequately as it can; it gives you the plot, and the most suitable characters. But even at that, it cannot reveal all, for language does not have the power to convey the many nuances of thought, emotion, and character, which the voice and body can supplement. It can only convey them in part. As an oral interpreter, you must suggest the potential of the literary experience in such a way that your listener is better able to fulfill the potential in his own experience.

STUDY QUESTIONS

1. What do you think distinguishes prose from poetry?
2. How would you define a short story?
3. How would you compare a short story by Flaubert, such as "The Legend of St. Julian, The Hospitaler," and "Johnny Pye and The Fool-Killer," by Stephen Vincent Benét?
4. What similarities, and differences, do you find in "The Bride Comes to Yellow Sky" by Stephen Crane, and "The Little Wife," by William March?
5. What do "The Use of Force," by William Carlos Williams and "Surgery," by Anton Chekhov, have in common? How do they differ? What is the author's attitude in each?
6. How does a novel differ from a short story? (In number of characters, subplots, description and style?)
7. Do you think that an introduction should always be given when one reads a story aloud? Why or why not?
8. How many different characters do you think can be clearly suggested in a short story? In a novel?

BIBLIOGRAPHY

Aldridge, John W., *Critiques And Essays on Modern Fiction.* New York: Ronald Press, 1952.

Booth, Wayne C., *The Rhetoric of Fiction.* Chicago: University of Chicago Press, 1961.

Burke, Kenneth, *The Philosophy of Literary Form.* Rev. ed., 1957. New York: Vintage Books, 1957.

Curry, Samuel Silas, *Imagination and Dramatic Instinct.* Boston: School of Expression, 1896.

Eliot, George, "The Art of The Novel." Edgar, Pelham, pp. 146–152, also Eliot, George, *The Personal Edition of George Eliot's Books.* Volume XI, New York: Doubleday, Page & Co., 1901.

Forster, E. M., *Aspects of The Novel.* New York: Harcourt, Brace & World, Inc., 1954.

James, Henry, *The Art of The Novel.* New York: Charles Scribner's Sons, 1934.

Lubbock, Percy, *The Craft of Fiction.* New York: The Viking Press, 1957.

Maugham, W. Somerset, *Points of View.* London: Heinemann, 1958.

McHugh, Vincent, *Primer of The Novel.* New York: Random House, 1950.

Mirrielees, Edith Ronald, *The Story Writer.* Boston: Little, Brown & Co., 1939.

Poe, Edgar Allan, "The Philosophy of Composition" in *Golden Age of American Literature,* Ed., Miller, Perry, Braziller, 1959.

Pritchett, Victor Sawton, *The Living Novel and Later Appreciations.* Rev. & expanded ed., New York: Random House, 1964.

Thompson, David W., and Virginia Fredricks, *Oral Interpretation of Fiction: A Dramatic Approach.* Minneapolis: Burgess Publishing Co., 1964.

Warren, Robert, and John T. Purser, *An Approach to Literature.* New York: Appleton-Century-Crofts, 1952.

Watt, Ian P., *The Rise of The Novel;* Studies in Defoe, Richardson, and Fielding. Berkeley: University of California Press, 1957.

Wellek, René, and Austin Warren, *Theory of Literature.* New York: Harcourt, Brace & World, Inc., A Harvest Book, 1956.

Chapter IX

The Oral Interpretation of Poetry

Reading silently or aloud is an active creative process in which you yourself draw together all of the elements of a poem and understand their effect on each other. You emotionally and intellectually live through the total experience. In this way, the poem "happens" to you.

Walt Whitman said of his *Leaves of Grass,* "I seek less to state or display any theme or thought, and more to bring you, reader, into the atmosphere of the theme or thought—there to preserve your own flight." Whitman uses the words "image-making work" for poetry, which indicates, in part, what the reader is expected to contribute to the reading of a poem. Actually, the reader brings to life the whole complex of images, words, phrases, rhythm, rhyme, thought and feeling, and how he reacts to these is predetermined by his own life experience and by his immediate attitude at the time he reads.

"Poetry," according to Stephen Spender, "is the attempt to imagine, in terms of the transitory forms of the present in which a generation lives, the universal nature of man's being." Robert Frost gets at the significance of poetry when he says that it is ". . . a way of remembering what it would impoverish us to forget."

Coleridge, whose *Ancient Mariner* is an epic in imaginative literature, says that "The poet . . . brings the whole soul of man into activity, with the subordination of its faculties to each other according to their relative worth and dignity. He diffuses a tone and spirit of unity, that blends, and . . . *fuses,* each into each, by that synthetic and magical power, to which I would exclusively appropriate the name of imagination." He adds, "I feel strongly and I think strongly, but I seldom feel without thinking or think without feeling."

Poetry demands imaginative listening from the silent reader, the oral interpreter, and the members of an audience alike. Poets think in terms of this, and oral interpreters must realize it.

The ability of the poet to call upon his imagination and produce a vivid and meaningful impression is a mark of his genius. Your ability to stimulate imaginative listening which is in harmony with the impressions you, in turn, have suggested is a mark of your genius.

I. THE UNIQUE ELEMENTS OF POETRY

The language of the poem and the rhythm of the poem are the two additional and unique elements which you must consider when reading poetry aloud.

A. *The Language of the Poem*

The language of the poem presents your first challenge. You must always be alert to the effect produced by the words, their juxtaposition and their relationship to each other. It is the uniqueness of this relationship that gives them new value. Certain figures of speech, such as metaphors, similes, and personification, are particularly significant, as you will see in the following passages.

Effective oral reading can bring out these figures of speech, such as the rasping and rustling sound of the rats' feet in this simile.

Our dried voices, when
We whisper together
Are quiet and meaningless
As wind in dry grass
Or rats' feet over broken glass
In our dry cellar

(T. S. Eliot, "The Hollow Men")

Note the calm grandeur of this personification.

Let me not to the marriage of true minds
Admit impediments. Love is not love
Which alters when it alteration finds,
Or bends with the remover to remove.
O no! It is an ever-fixed mark
That looks on tempests and is never shaken.
It is the star to every wandering bark,
Whose worth's unknown, although his height be taken.
Love's not Time's fool, though rosy lips and cheeks
Within his bending sickle's compass come.
Love alters not with his brief hours and weeks,
But bears it out even to the edge of doom.
If this be error and upon me proved,
I never writ, nor no man ever loved.

(William Shakespeare, "True Love," Sonnet 116)

Observe the human qualities that Keats gives to autumn as he addresses that season.

Who hath not seen thee oft amid thy store?
    Sometimes whoever seeks abroad may find
Thee sitting careless on a granary floor,
    Thy hair soft-lifted by the winnowing wind;
Or on a half-reap'd furrow sound asleep,
    Drows'd with the fume of poppies, while thy hook
    Spares the next swath and all its twinèd flowers:
And sometimes like a gleaner thou dost keep
    Steady thy laden head across a brook;
Or by a cider-press, with patient look,
    Thou watchest the last oozings hours by hours.

(John Keats, "To Autumn")

Very often words not only carry their denotative and connotative meaning, but even convey a meaning by their sound. This, as you remember, is called onomatopoeia. Tennyson's "Rizpah" has an excellent example of this in the lines

Wailing, wailing, wailing, the wind over land and sea—
And Willy's voice in the wind, 'O mother come out to me.'

Through a lingering exaggeration of the "w," "n," and "ng" sounds, Tennyson brings the very sound of the wind within the range of your ear.

B. *Rhythm, Meter and Rhyme*

Rhythm in poetry cannot be regarded as the same as that in a motor where the beat goes on at exactly the same interval without variation. That is merely a mechanical repetition. Poetic rhythm grows out of the beat as it is modified by feeling, meaning, stress, tempo, pitch and quality.

Mediocre poetry emphasizes the beat of the meter so forcibly that the meaning is obscured or weakened by the meter. Therefore, when the oral reader reads a poem of little distinction, he must compensate for the deficiencies of the poem by breaking up its sing-song monotony.

The difference between a mechanical beat and rhythm is clear if we consider the lines:

Lives of great men all remind us
We can make our lives sublime
And departing leave behind us
Footprints on the sands of time.

(H. W. Longfellow, "A Psalm of Life")

Certainly the theme is admirable in this poem, but the rhythm is mechanical and the oral or silent reader must fight against its sing-song beat. Now look at this sonnet by John Milton:

Avenge O Lord, thy slaughtered saints, whose bones
Lie scatter'd on the Alpine mountains cold;
Even them who kept thy truth so pure of old,
When all our fathers worshipt stocks and stones,
Forget not: in thy book record their groans

Who were thy sheep and their ancient fold
Slain by the bloody Piemontese that rolled
Mother with infant down the rocks. Their moans
The vales redoubled to the hills, and they
To heaven. Their martyred blood and ashes sow
O'er all the Italian fields where still doth sway
The triple tyrant: that from these may grow
A hundredfold, who, having learn'd thy way,
Early may fly the Babylonian woe.

In this poem, the poet, incensed at barbaric acts, asks God to wreak vengeance and remember those "slaughtered saints whose bones lie scatter'd on the Alpine mountains cold. . . ." The moans of these go from the vales to the hills and on to heaven. He further beseeches God to sow their blood and ashes so that others, rising from their blood and ashes may escape from tyranny.

The thought, feeling and rhythm are so effectively unified that at no time is the rhythm too dominant or obtrusive. Rather, it reinforces and intensifies the emotion. There is no separation of content and form here any more than there is in spoken speech. There is no inclination to recite this in sing-song fashion when you read it.

While some rhythm is so subtle that you are scarcely aware of it, other poetry has such strong rhythm that you are conscious of it at once. Compare, for example, the excerpt from "The Wasteland" by T. S. Eliot and Hilaire Belloc's "Tarantella," or the excerpt from Lew Sarett's "Squaw Dance":

April is the cruellest month, breeding
Lilac out of the dead land, mixing
Memory and desire, stirring
Dull roots with spring rain.
Winter kept us warm, covering
Earth in forgetful snow, feeding
A little life with dried tubers.
Summer surprised us, coming over the Starnbergersee
With a shower of rain; we stopped in the colonnade,
And went on in sunlight, into the Hofgarten,
And drank coffee, and talked for an hour.

(T. S. Eliot, "The Wasteland")

When you read aloud the following selections you can exploit the rhythm because this is the factor the poet depends on for his effect.

"Tarantella," by Hilaire Belloc

Do you remember an Inn,
Miranda?
Do you remember an Inn?
And the tedding and the spreading
Of the straw for a bedding,
And the fleas that tease in the High Pyrenees,
And the wine that tasted of the tar?
And the cheers and the jeers of the young muleteers
(Under the vine of the dark verandah)?
Do you remember an Inn, Miranda,
Do you remember an Inn?
And the cheers and the jeers of the young muleteers
Who hadn't got a penny,
And who weren't paying any,
And the hammer at the doors and the Din?
And the Hip! Hop! Hap!
Of the clap
Of the hands to the twirl and the swirl
Of the girl gone chancing,
Glancing,
Dancing,
Backing and advancing,
Snapping of a clapper to the spin
Out and in—
And the Ting, Tong, Tang of the Guitar!
Do you remember an Inn,
Miranda?
Do you remember an Inn?
    Never more;
    Miranda,
    Never more.
    Only the high peaks hoar:
    And Aragon a torrent at the door.
    No sound

In the walls of the Halls where falls
The tread
Of the feet of the dead to the ground
No sound:
But the boom
Of the far Waterfall like Doom.

"The Squaw Dance," by Lew Sarett

Beat, beat, beat, beat, beat upon the tom-tom,
Beat, beat, beat, beat, beat upon the drum.
Hóy-eeeeeee-yáh; Hóy-eeeeeee-yáh!
Shuffle to the left, shuffle to the left,
Shuffle, shuffle, shuffle to the left, to the left.
Fat squaws, lean squaws, gliding in a row,
Grunting, wheezing, laughing as they go;
Bouncing up with a scuffle and a twirl,
Flouncing petticoat and hair in a whirl.
Rheumatic hags of gristle and brawn,
Rolling in like a ponderous billow:
Fair squaws lithe as the leaping fawn,
Swaying with the wind and bending with the willow;
Bouncing buttock and shriveled shank,
Scuffling to the drumbeat, rank on rank;
Stolid eye and laughing lip,
Buxom bosom and jiggling hip,
Weaving in and weaving out,
Hí! Hi! Hí! with a laugh and a shout,
To the beat, beat, beat, beat, beat upon the tom-tom,
Beat, beat, beat, beat, beat upon the drum;
Hóy-eeeeeee-yáh! Hóy-eeeeeee-yáh!
Hí! Hi! Hí! Hi! Hóy-eeeeeeeeeeeee-yáh!

Contributing to the rhythm of a poem are both the stanza, the foot and the verse. The stanza is a division of thought, within a poem. It is a standing or resting place. This division is an aid to the oral and silent reader in that it helps clarify the development of the poet's theme. When the same stanza form is maintained in a poem it helps establish rhythm and unity. When the stanza varies within a poem, the poet has done this deliberately to produce a desired effect and the change will help to make the oral reader aware that there is something different to be expressed. A stanza may range in length from two to an indefinite number of lines. Long stanzas are frequently found in odes. For example, in "The Bard," by Thomas Gray, there is a stanza of twenty lines. This creates a particular challenge to the oral reader in that he must sustain a unit of thought and feeling for a prolonged time.

Although there are many stanza forms in English, we shall discuss only those which are frequently used. The shortest, consisting of 2 lines, is the couplet. Many poets, including Chaucer, use this stanzaic form but perhaps when the couplet is mentioned, most people think of Alexander Pope. Pope used it extensively because it lends itself to the concise and pithy statements of which he was such a master. A glance at his "Essay on Criticism" will bear this out. For example:

> In Poets as true Genius is but rare,
> True Taste as seldom is the Critic's share. . . .

Its phrasing, as Pope uses it, is a particular challenge to the oral reader, because it presents the danger of monotony if the form is allowed to dominate the thought.

The tercet, a stanza consisting of 3 rhyming verses, gives a compactness and may suggest an impetuous quality as in "The Bracelet to Julia" by Robert Herrick.

"The Bracelet to Julia," by Robert Herrick

When I tye about thy wrist,
Julia, this my silken twist;
For what other reason is't,

But to show thee how in part,
Thou my pretty Captive art?
—But thy Bondslave is my heart:

'Tis but silke that bindeth thee,
Snap the thread, and thou art free:
But 'tis otherwise with me;

I am bound, and fast bound so,
That from thee I cannot go;
If I co'd, I wo'd not so.

The quatrain, one of the most frequently used stanza forms, consists of 4 verses. It is sometimes in abab pattern as in "Virtue," by

George Herbert, (1593–1633). Note that there is a progression in the first three stanzas, but with a retention of part of the rhyme scheme in each. The fourth stanza brings out the contrast in both idea and form for the oral interpreter.

Sweet day, so cool, so calm, so bright,
    The bridal of the earth and skie:
The dew shall weep thy fall tonight,
    For thou must die.

Sweet rose, whose hue, angry and brave
    Bids the rash gazer wipe his eye,
Thy root is even in its grave,
    And thou must die.

Sweet spring, full of sweet day and roses,
    A box where sweets compacted lie,
My music shows you have your closes,
    And all must die.

Only a sweet and virtuous soul,
    Like seasoned timber, never gives;
But though the whole world turn to coal,
    Then chiefly lives.

Another form of the quatrain is found in Herbert's "Discipline," where the rhyme scheme of the first and last stanzas is the same, but with progression between these.

"Discipline," by George Herbert

Throw away thy rod,
Throw away thy wrath:
    O my God,
Take the gentle path.

For my heart's desire
Unto thine is bent:
    I aspire
To a full consent.

Not a word or look
I affect to own
    But by book,
And thy book alone.

Though I fail, I weep:
Though I halt in pace,
    Yet I creep
To the throne of grace.

Then let wrath remove;
Love will do the deed:
    For with love
Stonie hearts will bleed.

Love is swift of foot;
Love's a man of warre,
    And can shoot
And can hit from farre.

Who can scape his bow?
That which wrought on thee,
    Brought thee low,
Needs must work on me.

Throw away thy rod;
Though man frailties hath,
    Thou art God:
Throw away thy wrath.

The stanza in the ballad form, which has long been recited aloud, often consists of four verses with an abcb rhyme scheme. The Spenserian stanza, which consists of nine verses, is of special interest to the oral reader, for this stanza permits a greater variety of pauses than the couplet or the alternating rhyme of the quatrain. Read the following example, paying special attention to phrasing and pausing:

A little lowly hermitage it was,
Downe in a dale, hard by a forests side,
Far from resort of people, that did pas
In traveill to and froe: a little wyde

There was an holy chappell edifyde,
Wherein the hermite dewly wont to say
His holy thinges each morne and even-tyde:
Thereby a christall streame did gently play,
Which from a sacred fountaine wellèd forth alway.

(*The Faerie Queene*—Edmund Spenser
Book I Canto I—XXXIV)

One aspect of rhythm is meter. Meter is a regular, or nearly regular, recurring beat caused by stress on syllables. A syllable may be given a heavy stress or it may be unstressed, for example in the word "water" the first syllable is stressed and the latter is unstressed. In poetry certain groupings of syllables make up a "foot." The word "foot" goes back to the days when the rhythm of a poem was accompanied by the movement of the feet.

The number of feet in a line of poetry may vary. It is possible to have a line of one foot or more. Lines are described in terms of the kind of meter and the number of feet, such as monometer (one foot), dimeter (two feet), trimeter (three), tetrameter (four), pentameter (five), hexameter (six), heptameter (seven) and octameter (eight).

Some of the commonly used feet are the iambus (U—), trochee (—U) anapest (UU—), and dactyl (—UU). The spondee (—) can be found in two successive words of one syllable such as "Hail Chief." The pyrrhic (UU) is used in two consecutive unstressed sounds such as 'on a (mountain).'

The meters which you will most frequently encounter are the iambic, trochaic, anapestic and dactylic. The meter helps give you the basic structure, but when you read aloud you should not emphasize it at the expense of losing the meaning. The iambic, regarded as nearest to ordinary conversation, consists of an unstressed (unaccented) syllable followed by a stressed (accented) syllable.

I wandered lonely as a cloud
That floats on high o'er vales and hills,
When all at once I saw a crowd,
A host, of golden daffodils;

Beside the lake, beneath the trees,
Fluttering and dancing in the breeze.

("Daffodils," by William Wordsworth)

The trochaic consists of an accented followed by an unaccented beat.

As it fell upon a day
In the merry month of May,
Sitting in a pleasant shade
Which a grove of myrtles made,
Beasts did leap and birds did sing,
Trees did grow and plants did spring;
Every thing did banish moan
Save one nightingale alone:

("The Nightingale," by Richard Barnefield)

The anapest consists of two unaccented beats followed by an accented beat.

And the sleep in the dried river-channel where bulrushes tell
That the water was wont to go warbling so softly and well.

(Robert Browning, "Saul," Section IX)

The dactyl consists of an accented and two unaccented syllables as in

"The Skylark," by James Hogg

Bird of the wilderness,
Blithesome and cumberless,
Sweet be thy matin o'er moorland and lea!
Emblem of happiness,
Blest is thy dwelling-place—
Oh, to abide in the desert with thee!

While all poetry has rhythm, it does not necessarily have rhyme. Blank verse, for example, is unrhymed iambic pentameter (five feet.) It is frequently used in longer poems which tell a story and have dramatic or philosophical elements. It is a medium which Shakespeare has used so effectively in his plays.

> Macbeth: Methought I heard a voice cry "Sleep no more!
> Macbeth doth murder sleep"—the innocent sleep,
> Sleep that knits up the raveled sleave of care,
> The death of each day's life, sore labor's bath,
> Balm of hurt minds, great nature's second course,
> Chief nourisher in life's feast.
>
> (*Macbeth,* Act II, Sc ii)

Another form of unrhymed verse, free verse, in contrast to traditional verse, has much greater freedom in its meter. Here the rhythm of ordinary speech supersedes formal meter. It is not at all new for Walt Whitman used it in the nineteenth century.

"Song of Myself," by Walt Whitman

(6)

A child said *What is the grass?* fetching it to me with full
hands;
How could I answer the child? I do not know what it is any
more than he.

I guess it must be the flag of my disposition, out of hopeful
green stuff woven.

Or I guess it is the handkerchief of the Lord,
A scented gift and remembrancer designedly dropt,
Bearing the owner's name someway in the corners, that we
may see and remark, and say *Whose?*

Or I guess the grass is itself a child, the produced babe of
the vegetation.
Or I guess it is a uniform hieroglyphic,
And it means, Sprouting alike in broad zones and narrow zones,
Growing among black folks as among white,
Kanuck, Tuckahoe, Congressman, Cuff, I give them the
same, I receive them the same.

And now it seems to me the beautiful uncut hair of graves.
Tenderly will I use you curling grass,
It may be you transpire from the breasts of young men,
It may be if I had known them I would have loved them,
It may be you are from old people, or from offspring taken soon
out of their mothers' laps,
And here you are the mothers' laps.
This grass is very dark to be from the white heads of old mothers,
Darker than the colorless beards of old men,
Dark to come from under the faint red roofs of mouths.

O I perceive after all so many uttering tongues,
And I perceive they do not come from the roofs of mouths
for nothing.
I wish I could translate the hints about the dead young men
and women,
And the hints about old men and mothers, and the offspring
taken soon out of their laps.

What do you think has become of the young and old men?
And what do you think has become of the women and children?

They are alive and well somewhere,
The smallest sprout shows there is really no death,
And if ever there was it led forward life, and does not wait
at the end to arrest it,
And ceas'd the moment life appear'd.

All goes onward and outward, nothing collapses,
And to die is different from what any one supposed, and luckier.

Much poetry, however, is in a rhyme form. Rhyme can enhance our pleasure in reading poetry aloud by accentuating the rhythm. The repetition of a rhymed sound gives us a sense of both familiarity and anticipation and it can also assist in unifying a poem. Rhymes have been classified as masculine or as feminine. In a masculine rhyme, which is frequently found in poetry, the last sound in the line is accented.

O how I long to travel back,
And tread again that ancient track!

That I might once more reach that plain
Where first I left my glorious train; . . . .

("The Retreate," by Henry Vaughan)

"Rain at Night," by Helen Hoyt

Are you awake?
Do you hear the rain?
How rushingly it strikes upon the ground
And on the roof, and the wet window pane.
Sometimes I think it is a comfortable sound,
Making us feel how soft and snug we are;
Closing us off in the dark
Away from the dark outside. . . .
The rest of the world to-night seems dim,
Mysterious and far. . . .
Oh, there is no world left! Only darkness,
Darkness stretching wide
And full of the blind rain's immeasurable fall!
How nothing must we seem unto this ancient thing!
How nothing unto the earth, and we so small.
Oh, wake, wake!
Do you not feel my hands cling?
One day it will be raining as it rains to-night,
The same wind blow—
Raining and blowing on this house wherein we lie—
But you and I,
We shall not hear, we shall not ever know.
O love, I had forgot that we must die.

Feminine rhymes have a weak or unaccented syllable at the end of a line. Feminine rhymes are sometimes referred to as double rhymes, which means that the last two syllables, in the line, the accented and the unaccented, rhyme with a corresponding line. The feminine rhyme with its lightness and freshness is often found in the verses of Ogden Nash, such as:

. . . , if called by a panther,
Don't anther.

Richard Armour, also a writer of humorous verse, likewise uses feminine endings.

"Money"

Workers earn it,
Spendthrifts burn it,
Bankers lend it,
Women spend it,
Forgers fake it,
Taxes take it,
Dying leave it,
Heirs receive it,
Thrifty save it,
Misers crave it,
Robbers seize it,
Rich increase it,
Gamblers lose it . . .
I could use it.

In a triple rhyme the last three syllables rhyme with those in a corresponding line. Sometimes these, as well as double rhymes, are used for humorous effect as they are in the following verse:

When a felon's not engaged in his employment,
Or maturing his felonious little plans,
His capacity for innocent enjoyment
Is just as great as any honest man's.
Our feelings we with difficulty smother
When constabulary duty's to be done;
Ah, take one consideration with another,
A policeman's lot is not a happy one.

(W. S. Gilbert: "The Policeman's Lot"
Pirates of Penzance, Act II)

But triple and double rhymes are by no means limited to humorous material as you will see in this excerpt from the very serious poem "The Bridge of Sighs," by Thomas Hood.

One more Unfortunate,
  Weary of breath,
Rashly importunate,
  Gone to her death!

Take her up tenderly,
  Lift her with care;
Fashioned so slenderly,
  Young, and so fair!

Look at her garments
  Clinging like cerements;
Whilst the wave constantly
  Drips from her clothing;
Take her up instantly,
  Loving, not loathing.

In addition to rhymes at the end of lines, poetry may have a rhyme within the line which is called an internal rhyme. Notice how effectively Poe uses this in "The Raven," where, for example, "dreary" rhymes with "weary" and "rapping" rhymes with "tapping." When you read these aloud, catch the rhythmic flow which the internal rhyme provides, but avoid a mechanical beat or stress on the rhyming words.

Once upon a midnight dreary, while I pondered, weak and weary,
Over many a quaint and curious volume of forgotten lore,—
While I nodded, nearly napping, suddenly there came a tapping,
As of someone gently rapping, rapping at my chamber door.
" 'Tis some visitor," I muttered, "tapping at my chamber door—
Only this and nothing more."

In "The Cloud," Shelley uses the same form of internal rhyme on alternate lines. Notice how this tends to strengthen the flow of the line.

I bring fresh showers for the thirsting flowers,
  From the seas and the streams;
I bear light shade for the leaves when laid
  In their noonday dreams.
From my wings are shaken the dews that waken

The sweet buds every one,
When rocked to rest on their mother's breast,
As she dances about the sun.
I wield the flail of the lashing hail,
And whiten the green plains under,
And then again I dissolve it in rain,
And laugh as I pass in thunder.

When you read aloud do not lapse into a sing-song effect and mechanical monotony by stressing the rhyme rather than the meaning. This may happen if you pause automatically at the end of a line even though the meaning is carried over into the next line. If you find that you are pausing too long at the end of the line, you may overcome it if you write the meaning of the poem in your own words, or if you write out the entire poem as if it were prose, thereby putting less emphasis on the rhyme.

In these lines from "Fall, Leaves, Fall," if you have a long pause, drop your voice at the end of each line, and stress the rhyme, you will draw attention to the form rather than the meaning.

"Fall, Leaves, Fall" by Emily Brontë

Fall, leaves, fall; die, flowers, away;
Lengthen night and shorten day;
Every leaf speaks bliss to me
Fluttering from the autumn tree.

I shall smile when wreaths of snow
Blossom where the rose should grow;
I shall sing when night's decay
Ushers in a drearier day.

Now read it for meaning. Do not ignore the basic rhythm of the poem, and do not ignore the fact that there are both end-stopped lines and enjambment, that is, lines that carry the meaning over into the next line. If you find that you are still stressing the rhyme at the end of every line it may help if you start with a poem in blank verse or free verse with unrhymed lines. A good poem to help overcome this fault is the portrait of Julia in Byron's *Don Juan.*

If you find that you give poetry too much of a sing-song effect so that you beat out every line with ta-ti-ta-ti-ta, you are letting the meter get in the way of the meaning. Usually the meter must not stand out so obviously or so mechanically that it calls attention to itself. It may be considered as the skeletal basic structure, but it alone does not make a poem any more than the chassis alone makes an automobile. If a poem is well written, the meter will be so deftly interwoven that it will be submerged and subordinated to the meaning; indeed, it will support the meaning.

Likewise, the structure of the stanza should not stand out too clearly, and it must not be isolated but must be an integral part of the poem. It may help if you think of the stanza in poetry as if it were a paragraph in prose.

In this part of the chapter you have been introduced to some of the ingredients of poetry. Nor must you forget to include imagery which you have encountered in Chapter V. If you are aware of the purpose and function of these, they will help you in understanding and communicating the meaning of poetry to others.

II. TEMPO AND THE PAUSE IN READING POETRY

Two aspects of reading poetry which are often difficult for the interpreter to grasp are the pause and tempo. You may have wondered when and where to pause in reading, or you may have had difficulty in determining how rapidly or how slowly a poem should be read.

In reading poetry there may be several kinds of pauses. There may be a pause at the end of a line, depending upon whether a thought unit ends there. There may also be a pause for meaning near the middle of the line. This pause, a tradition from early poetry, is called the caesura. It creates a rhythmic effect in the two parts of a line and it enabled the ancient reciter to take a breath. This pause may be very slight, or long, depending upon the idea and the emotions. Pauses may also be used in poetry to clarify the meaning, for emphasis or for suspense. See Chapter VI for a more detailed discussion of the use of the pause.

The best way to determine the tempo is to look to the meaning. If the poem suggests philosophic introspection, musing, or thoughtfulness, it may, by the very nature of the poet's attitude, profit by a slow or moderate tempo. If it is exciting, or suggests quick action, or a series of events coming quickly in succession, it may call for a more rapid tempo. It is very difficult to determine the exact tempo to be used in reading any poem, but remember that there are as many tempos that can be used in reading poetry or prose aloud as there are rates or speeds in life, for poetry is a reflection of life.

In addition to looking to the meaning and the mood to determine the tempo, the poet may give you other clues as well. If he uses continuant sounds, such as m, n, ng, f, v, s, sh, zh, he may be tacitly suggesting that certain words or phrases are to be read in a slow tempo, or sustained. Conversely, if he uses explosive sounds such as p, b, k, t, d, he may want to suggest speed. But, as simple as this appears, you cannot rely on mere sounds to give you a clue to the tempo. It is always the meaning that is the determining factor.

Another indication of tempo may be the length of the line or phrase. Short lines or short phrases may suggest a quicker tempo. Tempo may also be affected by the frequency and closeness of the rhyme. When there is internal rhyme in the line the poet may be suggesting a quicker tempo. If the rhymes at the ends of the lines are close together, as in couplets, this may also indicate a degree of speed. But here, too, meaning is the ultimate decisive factor.

Read the following poems aloud and see if you can decide, in terms of both meaning and style, the tempo that the literary experience suggests.

"Spring," by Thomas Nashe

Spring, the sweet Spring, is the year's pleasant king;
Then blooms each thing, when maids dance in a ring,
Cold doth not sting, the pretty birds do sing,
  Cuckoo, jug-jug, pu-we, to-witta-woo!

The palm and may make country houses gay,
Lambs frisk and play, the shepherds pipe all day,
And we hear aye birds tune this merry lay—
  Cuckoo, jug-jug, pu-we, to-witta-woo!

The fields breathe sweet, the daisies kiss our feet,
Young lovers meet, old wives a-sunning sit,
In every street these tunes our ears do greet—
  Cuckoo, jug-jug, pu-we, to-witta-woo!
    Spring! the sweet Spring!

"Meeting at Night," by Robert Browning

The grey sea and the long black land;
And the yellow half-moon large and low;
And the startled little waves that leap
In fiery ringlets from their sleep,
As I gain the cove with pushing prow,
And quench its speed in the slushy sand.

Then a mile of warm sea-scented beach;
Three fields to cross till a farm appears;
A tap at the pane, the quick sharp scratch
And blue spurt of a lighted match,
And a voice less loud, thro' its joy and fears,
Than the two hearts beating each to each!

III. THE SPEAKERS IN POETRY

It will help you to interpret a poem orally if you know who is speaking in it. The poet does not necessarily express his own feelings in every poem he writes. Both Aristotle and Isidore of Seville have made us aware of this. Isidore of Seville (c. 560–636) said that there are three possible types of speakers in poetry. In one of these the poet speaks for himself and expresses his own feelings, as he often does in the lyric and the sonnet. When the poet speaks for himself in his own character, he may be talking to himself or to other people. In this case the poet will probably reveal his own personal attitude.

Some poets, however, are interested in human personalities and instead of doing the speaking themselves they create characters who speak. This is the second type of speaker in poetry. Such is the case in the monologue. In Robert Frost's "A Servant to Servants" the poet himself is not speaking, but rather the lonely woman who lives on an isolated farm. The ideas she expresses are primarily hers. Likewise, in "My Last Duchess," Robert Browning does not identify himself with the duke. The duke is a completely separate personality who is not speaking for Browning at all. He is a creation of Browning, but he speaks for himself to an imaginary character, usually in a specific place. In the monologue the speaker places the listener slightly above the eyeline of the audience. There may also be several characters speaking in a poem. For example, two characters speak to each other in the following poems. You will notice that the second selection is an example of a unique use of the sonnet.

"For Anne Gregory," by William Butler Yeats

"Never shall a young man,
Thrown into despair
By those great honey-coloured
Ramparts at your ear,
Love you for yourself alone
And not your yellow hair."

"But I can get a hair-dye
And set such colour there,
Brown, or black, or carrot,
That young men in despair
May love me for myself alone
And not my yellow hair."

"I heard an old religious man
But yesternight declare
That he had found a text to prove
That only God, my dear,
Could love you for yourself alone
And not your yellow hair."

"Piazza Piece," by John Crowe Ransom

—I am a gentleman in a dustcoat trying
To make you hear. Your ears are soft and small

And listen to an old man not at all,
They want the young men's whispering and sighing.
But see the roses on your trellis dying
And hear the spectral singing of the moon;
For I must have my lovely lady soon,
I am a gentleman in a dustcoat trying.

—I am a lady in beauty waiting
Until my truelove comes, and then we kiss.
But what grey man among the vines is this
Whose words are dry and faint as in a dream?
Back from my trellis, Sir, before I scream!
I am a lady young in beauty waiting.

In the third type, which Isidore calls the "mixed" form, the poet combines these two ways of speaking so that both the *characters* and the *poet* himself speak in the same poem. This is the case, as Isidore says, in Virgil's *Aeneid.* It is also true in the epics *Beowulf, The Iliad,* and *The Odyssey,* and in some modern poetry, such as Edward Arlington Robinson's "Mr. Flood's Party." In the latter poem the poet describes the setting and the character, just as the novelist does, and gives his own impression of the place and the incident, but he has Eben speak words that are Eben's and that express Eben's personal feelings. Again, in *John Brown's Body,* Stephen Vincent Benét speaks for *himself* and gives his own impression of the situation and characters, but he also creates characters who speak for *themselves* and express their own ideas.

Read the following two poems and you will see how each poet speaks for himself and how his created characters express their own ideas.

"The Ghost," by Walter de la Mare

"Who knocks?" "I, who was beautiful,
Beyond all dreams to restore,
I, from the roots of the dark thorn am hither.
And knock on the door."

"Who speaks?" "I—once was my speech
Sweet as the birds on the air,

When echo lurks by the waters to heed;
'Tis I speak thee fair."

"Dark is the hour!" "Ay, and cold."
"Lone is my house." "Ah, but mine?"
"Sight, touch, lips, eyes yearned in vain."
"Long dead these to thine . . ."

Silence. Still faint on the porch
Brake the flames of the stars.
In gloom groped a hope-wearied hand
Over keys, bolts, and bars.

A face peered. All the grey night
In chaos of vacancy shone;
Nought but vast sorrow was there—
The sweet cheat gone.

"O Where Are You Going?" by W. H. Auden

"O where are you going?" said reader to rider,
"That valley is fatal when furnaces burn,
Yonder's the midden whose odours will madden,
That gap is the grave where the tall return."

"O do you imagine," said fearer to farer,
"That dusk will delay on your path to the pass,
Your diligent looking discover the lacking
Your footsteps feel from granite to grass?"

"O what was that bird," said horror to hearer,
"Did you see that shape in the twisted trees?
Behind you swiftly the figure comes softly,
The spot on your skin is a shocking disease?"

"Out of this house"—said rider to reader,
"Yours never will"—said farer to fearer,
"They're looking for you"—said hearer to horror,
As he left them there, as he left them there.

In "Foolish About Windows," Carl Sandburg, the poet himself, apparently, speaks and reports the dialogue of the carpenter and three neighbors. When you read this aloud, remember that a single speaker is reporting what the other characters are saying.

"Foolish About Windows," by Carl Sandburg

I was foolish about windows.
The house was an old one and the windows
were small.
I asked a carpenter to come and open the
walls and put in bigger windows.
"The bigger the window the more it costs,"
he said.
"The bigger the cheaper," I said.
So he tore off siding and plaster and laths
And put in a big window and bigger windows.
I was hungry for windows.

One neighbor said, "If you keep on you'll be
able to see everything there is."
I answered, "That'll be all right, that'll be
classy enough for me."

Another neighbor said, "Pretty soon your house
will be all windows."
And I said, "Who would the joke be on then?"
And still another, "Those who live in glass
houses gather no moss."
And I said, "Birds of a feather should not throw
stones and a soft answer turneth away rats."

Now that you have some idea of the three types of speakers in poetry, let us consider attitude. It is important for the oral reader to know the attitude of the poet and that of the characters in poetry. Attitudes involve the feelings or opinions of the poet or his characters. The poet wants his oral or silent reader to take one or more specific emotional or mental positions toward an event, a situation, idea or person.

In a poem the poet presents an attitude which is either his own or that of one of his characters. The poet will accomplish this through the use of particular words, phrases, figures of speech and sentence structure. The oral interpreter will discover the attitude through careful study. If he is concerned with both the poet's attitude and that of his characters he then has a dual purpose. Let us look at the poems that you have just read. In "Anne Gregory" do the characters have similar attitudes? In what ways are they alike or different? In "Foolish About Windows" are the reported attitudes of the neighbors, the carpenter and the narrator the same? Sometimes the attitude can change within a specific poem. Shakespeare's Sonnets XXIX and XXX are examples of this.

These attitudes, which determine the vocal tone and other vocal elements of the oral reader are one of the major keys to understanding and interpreting literature.

IV. TYPES OF POETRY

A. *The Lyric*

In ancient Greece a lyric poem was one which was sung or recited to the lyre. Gradually the lyre was abandoned, but the nature of the poem remained. It is an outpouring of intense feeling expressed in striking and melodious language. In the lyric the poet himself usually is the speaker. By its very nature it is nearly always a shorter poem, a brief passionate outburst rather than a lengthy narrative of ordered events, for such concentrated feeling cannot be long sustained.

The lyric is usually subjective. The interpretation of this type of poetry will depend largely upon the ability of the oral reader to convey its intimate and personal nature through his voice. The lyric will often express a universal feeling. Here the poet may be speaking to himself, to others, or even to an inanimate object. Try to decide whom the speaker is addressing in the following lyrics:

"Into My Heart An Air That Kills,"
by A. E. Housman

Into my heart an air that kills,
  From yon far country flows:

What are those blue remembered hills,
What spires, what farms are those?

That is the land of lost content,
I see it shining plain,
The happy highways where I went
And cannot come again.

"Music I Heard With You," by Conrad Aiken

Music I heard with you was more than music,
And bread I broke with you was more than bread;
Now that I am without you, all is desolate;
All that was once so beautiful is dead.

Your hands once touched this table and this silver,
And I have seen your fingers hold this glass.
These things do not remember you, belovèd,—
And yet your touch upon them will not pass.

For it was in my heart you moved among them,
And blessed them with your hand and with your eyes;
And in my heart they will remember always,—
They knew you once, O beautiful and wise.

"John Anderson My Jo," by Robert Burns

John Anderson my jo, John,
When we were first acquent,
Your locks were like the raven,
Your bonnie brow was brent;
But now your brow is beld, John,
Your locks are like the snaw;
But blessings on your frosty pow,
John Anderson, my jo!

John Anderson my jo, John,
We clamb the hill thegither;
And monie a cantie day, John,
We've had wi' ane anither;

Now we maun totter down, John,
But hand in hand we'll go,
And sleep thegither at the foot,
John Anderson, my jo!

"Parting," by Emily Dickinson

My life closed twice before its close;
It yet remains to see
If Immortality unveil
A third event to me,
So huge, so hopeless to conceive,
As these that twice befell.
Parting is all we know of heaven,
And all we need of hell.

B. *The Sonnet*

Poets are versatile contrivers and many are adept at using strong fetters to force their feelings into a chosen mold; such are the sonneteers. One of the forms of poetry which has been popular for a long time is the sonnet, a concentrated form of expression, consisting of fourteen lines and frequently in iambic pentameter verse. This poetic form was brought to England in the sixteenth century from Italy. Even though it keeps to its specific form it is by no means merely a *tour de force* or a matter of only technical skill. Many poets have used it successfully to express deep feelings and emotions which might not have been so well expressed in a longer poem. Because of its limitation of fourteen lines, the poet cannot waste words when he writes. Both in the writing and in the oral reading of it, every word is important. It has to give its message with conciseness and intensity. You, the oral reader, must be aware of its compact and tightly knit nature which makes it a challenge. It may be very personal, as are many well known love sonnets, or it may express deep religious feelings or the poet's philosophy. Sometimes it can tell an incident which brings it near to narrative poetry.

There are two forms in which the sonnet is written. The Italian form consists of two parts, an octave and a sestet. The octave consists of eight lines which usually rhyme abba abba. The sestet rhymes cdcdcd or cde cde, or in some variations of these schemes. The English or Shakespearean sonnet consists of three quatrains and a couplet, often rhyming abab cdcd efef gg.

The sonnet may treat a subject in a variety of ways. For example, it may present a series of questions which are later answered. Differences in intensity, as well as in building, in the several parts can help bring out the meaning.

Sonnet LXV, by William Shakespeare

Since brass, nor stone, nor earth, nor boundless sea
But sad mortality o'ersways their power,
How with this rage shall beauty hold a plea,
Whose action is no stronger than a flower?
Oh, how shall summer's honey breath hold out
Against the wreckful siege of battering days
When rocks impregnable are not so stout,
Nor gates of steel so strong, but Time decays?
O fearful meditation! Where, alack,
Shall Time's best jewel from Time's chest lie hid?
Or what strong hand can hold his swift foot back?
Or who his spoil of beauty can forbid?

Oh, none, unless this miracle have might,
That in black ink my love may still shine bright.

In the following sonnet Edna St. Vincent Millay uses a somewhat different approach. In the octave she describes the situation; in the first five lines of the sestet she asks three questions and in the final line she gives the answer.

From "Epitaph For The Race of Man"
Sonnet XVIII, by Edna St. Vincent Millay

Here lies, and none to mourn him but the sea,
That falls incessant on the empty shore,
Most various Man, cut down to spring no more;

Before his prime, even in his infancy
Cut down, and all the clamour that was he,
Silenced; and all the riveted pride he wore,
A rusted iron column whose tall core
The rains have tunnelled like an aspen tree.
Man, doughty Man, what power has brought you low,
That heaven itself in arms could not persuade
To lay aside the lever and the spade
And be as dust among the dusts that blow?
Whence, whence the broadside? whose the heavy blade? . . .
Strive not to speak, poor scattered mouth; I know.

Or, the poet may build a series of statements describing a state of affairs and then summarize them, giving a new viewpoint at the end:

Sonnet LXVI, by William Shakespeare

Tired with all these, for restful death I cry,
As, to behold desert a beggar born,
And needy nothing trimmed in jollity,
And purest faith unhappily forsworn,
And gilded honour shamefully misplaced,
And maiden virtue rudely strumpeted,
And right perfection wrongfully disgraced,
And strength by limping sway disabled,
And art made tongue-tied by authority,
And folly, doctorlike, controlling skill,
And simple truth miscalled simplicity,
And captive good attending captain ill.
  Tired with all these, from these would I be gone,
  Save that, to die I leave my love alone.

In "Maple and Sumach," C. Day Lewis describes a beautiful autumn scene and then uses it as the basis for a comparison to the life of man.

Maple and sumach down this autumn ride—
Look, in what scarlet character they speak!
For this their russet and rejoicing week

Trees spend a year of sunsets on their pride.
You leaves drenched with the lifeblood of the year—
What flamingo dawns have wavered from the east,
What eves have crimsoned to their toppling crest
To give the fame and transience that you wear!
Leaf-low he shall lie soon: but no such blaze
Briefly can cheer man's ashen, harsh decline;
His fall is short of pride, he bleeds within
And paler creeps to the dead end of his days.
O light's abandon and the fire-crest sky
Speak in me now for all who are to die!

When you read sonnets aloud you should be governed by the thought. If one part is in strong contrast to another the difference must be very clear in your mind. The greater the difference in the parts, the longer it will take you to make the transition from one emotion or attitude to another; this may mean that you will need to pause to realize fully in your own mind the change in attitude.

Not all sonnets have parts which are so easily distinguishable as are those you have just read. Some of them move from one part to the other with subtlety, as in this sonnet by Christina Rossetti:

"The First Day," by Christina Rossetti

I wish I could remember the first day,
First hour, first moment of your meeting me,
If bright or dim the season, it might be
Summer or Winter for aught I can say;
So unrecorded did it slip away,
So blind was I to see and to foresee,
So dull to mark the budding of my tree
That would not blossom yet for many a May,
If only I could recollect it, such
A day of days! I let it come and go
As traceless as a thaw of bygone snow;
It seemed to mean so little, meant so much;
If only now I could recall that touch,
First touch of hand in hand.—Did one but know!

C. *The Ode*

The ode has been considered as a form of the lyric. As E. W. Gosse says, it is "any strain of enthusiastic and exalted lyrical verse, directed to a fixed purpose, and dealing progressively with one dignified theme." It is longer than the usual lyric, more detailed and more complicated. It is elevated in style and it sometimes contains lines of varying length. Examples are "Ode for General Washington's Birthday," by Robert Burns, "Ode to Evening," by William Collins, "Ode to a Nightingale," by John Keats and "Ode for the American Dead in Korea," by Thomas McGrath. In these odes there is a definite purpose and a reflective quality. These two characteristics are usually typical of the ode. Like the lyric, the emphasis is, for the oral reader, on the inner feeling and voice rather than upon external gesture. The ode is a difficult form of poetry to read aloud.

D. *The Narrative*

Story telling in verse is indeed an ancient art. As you know, in early Greece the *Iliad* and the *Odyssey* were recited to awestruck listeners. In the Middle Ages romantic tales were told in verse in castle halls. And today people still enjoy reading and hearing poems that tell a story.

In narrative poetry you will find more diversity than in other types. There may be characters and these characters may speak to each other. There may be descriptive passages to depict the setting and mood, and there may be informative portions to present the action of the story. The narrative poem may be of any length; the epic, for example, such as *The Iliad* and *Beowulf,* is a long narrative poem, and has been compared to the novel. The short narrative poem has certain elements in common with the short story. Frost's "The Death of the Hired Man," Chaucer's *Canterbury Tales* and Burns' "Tam O'Shanter" are examples of such poems.

Some narrative poems are told in blank verse. Many poets prefer blank verse for narrative poetry and for drama because it has a freedom akin to prose. But narratives are also told in rhyme, as is the "Badger," by John Clare. In this poem the speaker is the poet himself.

"Badger," by John Clare

When midnight comes a host of dogs and men
Go out and track the badger to his den,
And put a sack within the hole, and lie
Till the old grunting, badger passes by.
He comes and hears—they let the strongest loose.
The old fox hears the noise and drops the goose.
The poacher shoots and hurries from the cry,
And the old hare half wounded buzzes by.
They get a forked stick to bear him down
And clap the dogs and take him to the town,
And bait him all day with many dogs,
And laugh and shout and fright the scampering hogs.
He runs along and bites at all he meets:
They shout and hollo down the noisy streets.
He turns about to face the loud uproar
And drives the rebels to their very door.
The frequent stone is hurled where'er they go;
When badgers fight, then everyone's a foe.
The dogs are clapt and urged to join the fray;
The badger turns and drives them all away.
Though scarcely half as big, demure and small,
He fights with dogs for hours and beats them all.
The heavy mastiff, savage in the fray,
Lies down and licks his feet and turns away.
The bulldog knows his match and waxes cold,
The badger grins and never leaves his hold.
He drives the crowd and follows at their heels
And bites them through—the drunkard swears and reels.

The frightened women take the boys away,
The blackguard laughs and hurries on the fray.
He tries to reach the woods, an awkward race,
But sticks and cudgels quickly stop the chase.
He turns agen and drives the noisy crowd

And beats the many dogs in noises loud.
He drives away and beats them every one,
And then they loose them all and set them on.
He falls as dead and kicked by boys and men,
Then starts and grins and drives the crowd again;
Till kicked and torn and beaten out he lies
And leaves his hold and cackles, groans, and dies.

You will recall that in some narrative poetry both the poet and the characters he has created speak. When you read narrative poetry aloud, you must keep your story in perspective and give your attention to the *whole* story of which each character is a part. You should take a sympathetic interest in the emotional reactions of each character. You should respond emotionally by understanding how each character feels. This will be an empathic response on your part, and you will not lose yourself in one character at the expense of the total story. Be sure that you see each character as part of a mosaic which contributes to a complete picture.

Try to decide upon the nature of the poem. Is the emphasis upon the series of events or is it upon the characters? If it is concerned with the latter, try to decide what kinds of characters they are. How do they react to the same situation? In Frost's "The Death of the Hired Man," because they have different approaches to life, the man and his wife react in completely different ways. Does the poet tell you what to think of the characters, or does he leave it up to you to draw your own conclusions? As you study the poem you will become aware of its mood, structure and development. You will decide how the story builds to its climax and you will attempt to recreate its mood.

As we have said, narrative poetry often has dialogue in which the characters speak to each other. When a character speaks, you, the interpreter, usually want to suggest something of his personal characteristics; he must be a distinct individual to you and to your listeners. In reading the lines of a character you should place him in the sphere of the audience. This means that your viewers will see your face at full range and not in profile. When two or more characters talk to each other, these characters, too, will see each other in the sphere of the audience so that both characters will be in full range of the audience and not in profile at any time. You may feel that you need to place one of these characters slightly to the left or to the right as you face the audience. Actually, even this is usually unnecessary. Give each character a freedom of frontal movement. Instead of placing one to the left and one to the right as that character speaks, concentrate upon the differences in the personality and voice of the characters to make them clear to the audience. However, when one character speaks to another you should keep the character to whom he is talking in one specific location. Usually it is best to keep the character to whom one is speaking straight in front of him.

If it should happen that your characters are very similar then you may be justified in definitely placing one of them slightly to the left and the other slightly to the right. And if you have a number of characters who speak, it may be necessary to place them. But resort to this technique only when it is absolutely essential. Always remember to keep the characters within the range of the audience and never allow them to be on the stage.

In the following narrative poems try to discover the mood, the development of the action and the nature of the characters. Be sure you distinguish between the poet as a speaker and the character he has created. Yet, remember to maintain an overall unity and do not make the character stand out as if it were an impersonation.

"Mr. Flood's Party," by Edwin Arlington Robinson

Old Eben Flood, climbing alone one night
Over the hill between the town below
And the forsaken upland hermitage
That held as much as he should ever know
On earth again of home, paused warily.
The road was his with not a native near;
And Eben, having leisure, said aloud,
For no man else in Tilbury Town to hear:

"Well, Mr. Flood, we have the harvest moon
Again, and we may not have many more;
The bird is on the wing, the poet says,
And you and I have said it here before.
Drink to the bird." He raised up to the light
The jug that he had gone so far to fill,
And answered huskily: "Well Mr. Flood,
Since you propose it, I believe I will."

Alone, as if enduring to the end
A valiant armor of scarred hopes outworn,
He stood there in the middle of the road
Like Roland's ghost winding a silent horn.
Below him, in the town among the trees,
Where friends of other days had honored him,
A phantom salutation of the dead
Rang thinly till old Eben's eyes were dim.

Then, as a mother lays her sleeping child
Down tenderly, fearing it may awake,
He set the jug down slowly at his feet
With trembling care, knowing that most things break;
And only when assured that on firm earth
It stood, as the uncertain lives of men
Assuredly did not, he paced away,
And with his hand extended paused again:

"Well, Mr. Flood, we have not met like this
In a long time; and many a change has come
To both of us, I fear, since last it was
We had a drop together. Welcome home!"
Convivially returning with himself,
Again he raised the jug up to the light;
And with an acquiescent quaver said:
"Well, Mr. Flood, if you insist, I might."

"Only a very little, Mr. Flood—
For auld lang syne. No more, sir; that will do."
So, for the time, apparently it did,
And Eben evidently thought so too;
For soon amid the silver loneliness
Of night he lifted up his voice and sang,
Secure, with only two moons listening,
Until the whole harmonious landscape rang—

"For auld lang syne." The weary throat gave out,
The last word wavered; and the song being done,
He raised again the jug regretfully
And shook his head, and was again alone.
There was not much that was ahead of him,

And there was nothing in the town below—
Where strangers would have shut the many doors
That many friends had opened long ago.

"Goliath," by Walter de la Mare

Still as a mountain with dark pines and sun
He stood between the armies, and his shout
Rolled from the empyrean above the host:
"Bid any little flea ye have come forth,
And wince at death upon my finger-nail!"
He turned his large-boned face; and all his steel
Tossed into beams the lustre of the noon;
And all the shaggy horror of his locks
Rustled like locusts in a field of corn.
The meagre pupil of his shameless eye
Moved like a cormorant over the glassy sea.
He stretched his limbs, and laughed into the air,
To feel the groaning sinews of his breast,
And the long gush of his swollen arteries pause:
And, nodding, wheeled, towering in all his height.
Then, like a wind that hushes, gazed and saw
Down, down, far down upon the untroubled green
A shepherd-boy that swung a little sling.
Goliath shut his lids to drive that mote,
Which vexed the eastern azure of his eye,
Out of his vision; and stared down again.
Yet stood the youth there, ruddy in the flare
Of his vast shield, nor spake, nor quailed, gazed up,
As one might scan a mountain to be scaled.
Then, as it were, a voice unearthly still
Cried in the cavern of his bristling ear,
"His name is Death!" . . . And, like the flush
That dyes Sahara to its lifeless verge,
His brows' bright brass flamed into sudden crimson;
And his great spear leapt upward, lightning-like,
Shaking a dreadful thunder in the air;
Span betwixt earth and sky, bright as a berg

That hoards the sunlight in a myriad spires,
Crashed: and struck echo through an army's heart.
Then paused Goliath, and stared down again.
And fleet-foot Fear from rolling orbs perceived
Steadfast, unharmed, a stooping shepherd-boy
Frowning upon the target of his face.
And wrath tossed suddenly up once more his hand;
And a deep groan grieved all his strength in him.
He breathed; and, lost in dazzling darkness, prayed—
Besought his reins, his gloating gods, his youth:
And turned to smite what he no more could see.
Then sped the singing pebble-messenger,
The chosen of the Lord from Israel's brooks,
Fleet to its mark, and hollowed a light path
Down to the appalling Babel of his brain.
And like the smoke of dreaming Soufrière
Dust rose in cloud, spread wide, slow silted down
Softly all softly on his armour's blaze.

One of the most popular types of narrative poetry is the ballad which has recently been revived through folk songs. Its strong rhythm and simple story make it easy to understand and interesting to read aloud. Originally ballads were handed down from one generation to another by endless recitings so that they were memorized swiftly by having been heard so many times. They had strong emotions such as love, anger, jealousy, revenge, fear, which were easy to grasp as they told their story. The plots, which were compressed and compact, dealt with legends or historical facts as seen from the viewpoint of unsophisticated village and rural folk. The characters were sometimes the common people and sometimes the gentry and royalty. The plots had elements of mystery, depicted treacherous acts, tragic love, and adventuresome heroes.

Description in the ballad is brief, since the local people knew their countryside and did not need to have it described for them. The same applies to the characters, who are revealed by what they say and do. Details are usually omitted. There is often dialogue which requires special consideration by you, the oral reader, for dialogue is often the chief means of telling the story and developing the plot. Thus it is up to the characters to keep the story moving through what they say to each other. In some cases an entire ballad is told in dialogue.

When you read a ballad aloud remember that you are merely telling a story and that you are not a participant. Do not attract attention to yourself; rather, focus your attention on the characters and the plot. Treat it with a certain vigor, since it is simple, direct and fresh in its style.

Transitions in the ballad, which will seem very abrupt to you at first, are left up to you to make, for the ballad does not worry about them. They are implied in the plot, but they are not usually explicitly stated; therefore, your imagination has to take care of them. A pause, a change of tempo, pitch, intensity, or vocal quality, or a slight shift of bodily position can help effect this.

The ballad has frequent repetitions of words, phrases or whole lines, which gradually grow in their emotional significance as the story rises to a climax. Some ballads have a refrain repeated after every stanza. These repetitions and refrains intensify the emotion and develop an attitude toward the course of events. Sometimes there is a series of questions and answers, as there is in "Lord Randal." You may read these in the same way throughout the ballad, but often they will add to the effectiveness of the story if you allow the emotional intensity, as the plot develops, to color your interpretation of the repeated phrase. The repetition also serves to intensify the rhythm, which is so important in the ballad, just as it helps unify the story and mood.

In "Lord Randal" you will notice how effectively the caesura, or the pause near the middle of the line, is used in the speeches of Lord Randal, in the third line of each stanza in which he speaks. Here the caesura slows down the tempo, and emphasizes the physical weakness of Lord Randal. Each part of the line carries a complete idea in itself:

"I have been to the wild wood; mother, make my bed soon,"

Variety is obtained in this ballad in the questions of the mother and in the answers of Lord Randal. The last line of each stanza is the same except for the very last line of the ballad which strengthens and helps build the climax. The first four stanzas end with

"For I'm weary wi' hunting, and fain wald lie down."

but the very last stanza by way of contrast and emphasis ends

"For I'm sick at the heart, and I fain wald lie down."

The climax begins to develop in the fourth stanza where the mother asks about the bloodhounds. In the fifth stanza it breaks forth in the mother's lines:

"Oh, I fear ye are poison'd Lord Randal, my son!"

after which the peak of the climax is reached in Lord Randal's reply.

"Lord Randal"
(Anonymous)

"O where hae ye been, Lord Randal, my son?
O where hae ye been, my handsome young man?"
"I hae been to the wild wood; mother, make my bed soon,
For I'm weary wi' hunting, and fain wald lie down."

"Where gat ye your dinner, Lord Randal, my son?
Where gat ye your dinner, my handsome young man?"
"I dined wi' my true-love; mother, make my bed soon,
For I'm weary wi' hunting, and fain wald lie down."

"What gat ye to your dinner, Lord Randal, my son?
What gat ye to your dinner, my handsome young man?"
"I gat eels boil'd in broo; mother, make my bed soon,
For I'm weary wi' hunting, and fain wald lie down."

"What became of your bloodhounds, Lord Randal, my son?
What became of your bloodhounds, my handsome young man?"
"O they swell'd and they died; mother, make my bed soon,
For I'm weary wi' hunting, and fain wald lie down."

"O I fear ye are poison'd, Lord Randal, my son!
O I fear ye are poison'd, my handsome young man!"
"O yes! I am poison'd; mother, make my bed soon,
For I'm sick at the heart, and I fain wald lie down."

In reading a narrative poem remember that you are a medium of expression for the poet and do not permit your own personality or vocal skill to be so obvious that you draw attention to yourself when your main purpose is to draw attention to the story. Long ago, Stephen Hawes advised that a story be given "with humble voice" which means that the personality and vocal skill of the reader or story teller should not interfere with and overshadow the story itself.

V. ANALYSES OF FOUR POEMS

Four poems and an analysis of each follow. Read each poem carefully and relate your judgments of it before reading the analysis. Then compare your judgments with those of the authors.

"The Express," by Stephen Spender

After the first powerful plain manifesto
The black statement of pistons, without more fuss
But gliding like a queen, she leaves the station.
Without bowing and with restrained unconcern
She passes the houses which humbly crowd outside,
The gasworks and at last the heavy page
Of death, printed by gravestones in the cemetery.
Beyond the town, there lies the open country
Where, gathering speed, she acquires mystery,
The luminous self-possession of ships on ocean.
It is now she begins to sing—at first quite low
Then loud, and at last with a jazzy madness—
The song of her whistle screaming at curves,
Of deafening tunnels, brakes, innumerable bolts.
And always light, aerial, underneath
Retreats the elate metre of her wheels.
Steaming through metal landscape on her lines,
She plunges new eras of white happiness,
Where speed throws up strange shapes, broad curves
And parallels clean like trajectories from guns.
At last, further than Edinburgh or Rome,
Beyond the crest of the world, she reaches night
Where only a low stream-line brightness
Of phosphorus on the tossing hills is light.
Ah, like a comet through flame she moves entranced,
Wrapt in her music no bird song, no, nor bough
Breaking with honey buds, shall ever equal.

A. *Spender's "The Express"—An Analysis*

In this poem the poet, Stephen Spender, uses an express train as a symbol of applied technology. He focuses on the train throughout the poem and describes it in relation to the objects it passes. In the poem there are no animate objects, a feature which gives added strength to the concept of the Express as a living being in relation to the inanimate objects around it.

At the opening of the poem the Express, after her preliminary explosive, staccato, authoritative sounds, leaves the station in great dignity, "gliding like a queen" out of the mundane and unattractive station. In regal contrast she goes by the humble houses with "restrained unconcern," then by the equally unattractive gasworks and on past the static, lifeless cemetery with its imprint of death. This part of the poem presents a contrast between the live, royal queen, reserved and dignified, and the objects nearby. Here the poet uses the simile to compare the Express to a queen.

In the next part of the poem the Express leaves the town and goes into the country. Here she moves with "speed" and although still a queen she has a mysterious quality of assured completeness that is like the composure of a ship at sea. With this new-found assurance, she dares to let herself go to the extent of singing. At first she sings quietly, but this marvel of technology with bolts and brakes goes on her own strength, sings loudly, and ultimately breaks into a "jazzy madness." She even whistles as she takes the curves and dashes through tunnels. Her wheels have a light, "elate" or exalted rhythm. One wonders, does this meaning of "elate," as Webster indicates, suggest "undue self-satisfaction"? She goes "steaming" through the landscape of metal, not nature, in which she finds a new age of happiness, the self-sufficiency of the modern industrial world, a breaking with tradition, where speed changes the aspect of things; here there are unusual shapes, great curves, and tracks, ominously, as "clean" as trajectories from guns.

Here the Express takes on a new relationship. She has gone beyond the mundane, such as Edinburgh, and the antiquity of more distant Rome, and even beyond the summit of the world into the realm of night or, possibly, chaos. Here the only light, or hope, is a line of phosphorus in the hills. Now the Express is compared to a comet, enraptured with her new universe and making a music that even surpasses that of the song of birds or the budding blossoms. But whether the Express herself believes in her musical skill, or whether this is an observation of the poet, Spender leaves up to the reader to decide.

This poem achieves its power through its constant focus on the Express, with all other images or ideas indicated in relation to the Express. In the first part of the poem the Express shows complete disinterest in the tight compression of man-made towns, but she becomes fully alive, and when she goes beyond the world into night, "like a comet," she moves in ecstasy and complete happiness, in harmony with the cosmos. This poem seems to suggest that applied technology has gone, perhaps, beyond the grasp of man.

In "The Express" the imagery and figures of speech are both consistent and yet changing. Certain similes and metaphors are used in relation to the "queen." The first of these is the force of the "plain manifesto," a public declaration or "black statement" by a sovereign, perhaps in print; the Express glides "like a queen," and she does not bow. Another cluster of images and metaphors centers around the implied printed declaration or manifesto and "the heavy page of death, printed by gravestones." As the Express progresses there is a change in the nature of her movement. At first she "glides" smoothly, then she "plunges" or thrusts into new eras, perhaps recklessly, and finally blazes "like a comet," indicating three degrees of speed and kinds of movement which the oral reader will want to convey. There are onomatopoetic effects in such lines as the staccato, explosive "p" and "t" sounds; and the sibilants suggest the starting efforts of the Express which subside into legato movements as the "queen," without bowing and with restrained unconcern is on her way. These, too, the oral reader can experience through kinesthetic, visual and auditory imagery, just as he can convey the clarity and precision of the movement in the lines "underneath/ Retreats the elate metre of her wheels." Note that the poet uses the word "speed" only twice, yet the meaning and sound of the words he uses reinforce this idea. Assonance and consonance are to be found in the passages quoted and throughout the poem.

There is within this highly unified poem a remarkable range of variety and contrast which the oral reader will want to convey in tempo, staccato or legato touch, and in intensity. The imagery and figures of speech will take on significance in relation to the reader's power of imagination.

The attitude of the poet, who is apparently the "speaker," is not didactic or critical; rather, it is one of wonder toward the power of technology.

"On the Beach at Night Alone," by Walt Whitman

On the beach at night alone,
As the old mother sways her to and fro singing her husky
  song,
As I watch the bright stars shining, I think a thought of the
  clef of the universes and of the future.

A vast similitude interlocks all,
All spheres, grown, ungrown, small, large, suns, moons,
  planets,
All distances of place however wide,
All distances of time, all inanimate forms,
All souls, all living bodies though they be ever so different,
  or in different worlds,
All gaseous, watery, vegetable, mineral processes, the fishes,
  the brutes,
All nations, colors, barbarisms, civilizations, languages,
All identities that have existed or may exist on this globe,
  or any globe,
All lives and deaths, all of the past, present, future,
This vast similitude spans them, and always has spann'd,
And shall forever span them and compactly hold and enclose
  them.

B. *Whitman's "On the Beach at Night Alone"—An Analysis*

Whitman enjoyed being on the beach where he often received inspiration. In "On the Beach at Night Alone" he seeks, and finds, the relationship of all things, living, dead, animate and inanimate, and past, present and future.

This poem, written in Whitman's usual free verse, consists of two parts. In the first part Whitman is alone on the beach, where he frequently turns for philosophical contemplation. Here, at night, he is aware of the "old mother," the ocean, as she rhythmically and huskily sings. The sea, the stars and the beach bring to his mind the "clef," or key of the "universes," and of the future. This symbolic setting, with its personification of the ocean, and its visual, motor and auditory imagery prepares us for the second part of the poem in which Whitman makes his philosophical observations.

Hearing the sea and looking at the heavens he realizes that there is an inseparable relationship, or likeness in all things. First he sees this likeness in the spheres, the suns, moons, and planets; he sees it in all relationships of space and in all "distances of time." Removing his thoughts from the heavens, he further sees this similarity in all lifeless forms. This bond exists in the tangible world as well as in the intangible world of the spirit. It exists in "all souls, all living bodies." There is something in every soul that unites all souls just as there is a similarity in all living bodies, different though they may be. He does not limit these similarities to souls and bodies of this world only, but expands his concept to cover all worlds. Further, he sees a relationship in the mineral and animal world.

Then he focuses on nations, race and color, the barbarians and the civilized, as well as on the languages of man and continues his theme of similitude. Once again he expands his concept to include similarities on his globe or "any globe." From here he turns to life and death and sees a similarity, rather than opposites, even in them. Either they occurred thousands of years ago, now, or will occur ages in the future. But regardless of what, where and when, the speaker believes that a "vast similitude" spans all things, "and shall forever span them."

In the first stanza the structure is not particularly complicated. The sea, referred to as the "fierce old mother" and the "old mother" in other poems, is here personified merely as the "old mother," as going back and forth, she huskily sings.

In the second stanza there is a philosophical statement, an observation on everything "that was or shall be," consisting of about 11 lines all in one sentence. This stanza, in contrast to the first, has strong emotive power. It is a realization of the oneness or likeness, of all things throughout time. This concept is so strong as it convinces and overwhelms the poet that he emphatically repeats the word "all" twelve times in this sentence. His idea drives him so forcibly that he ignores the possibilities of using several additional sentences, which are grammatically possible yet emotionally far less powerful. Rather, to reinforce the emotions he uses phrase after phrase, noun after noun and image after image to express his feelings.

While Whitman says specifically that he is not interested in expression for its own sake, nor in music for its own sake, he manages to obtain both in this poem. In the first stanza of "On the Beach" his s, sh, and ch sounds suggest the sounds of the sea. In the second stanza these sounds continue as if the sounds of the sea carry through his thought here as well, providing both harmony and unity. There is a variety in his observations and therefore in his sounds. The poem grows gradually from quietness to intensity of feeling in the last lines of the poem. To summarize, in this poem Whitman builds up concepts of unity which embrace all eternity and infinity.

"The Leaden Echo," by Gerard Manley Hopkins

How to kéep—is there ány any, is there none such, nowhere
known some, bow or brooch or braid or brace, láce, latch
or catch or key to keep
Back beauty, keep it, beauty, beauty, beauty, . . . from vanishing
away?
Ó is there no frowning of these wrinkles, rankèd wrinkles deep,
Dówn? no waving off of these most mournful messengers, still
messengers, sad and stealing messengers of grey?
No there's none, there's none, O no there's none,
Nor can you long be, what you now are, called fair,
Do what you may do, what, do what you may,
And wisdom is early to despair:
Be beginning; since, no, nothing can be done
To keep at bay
Age and age's evils, hoar hair,
Ruck and wrinkle, drooping, dying, death's worst, winding sheets,
tombs and worms and tumbling to decay;
So be beginning, be beginning to despair.
O there's none; no no no there's none:
Be beginning to despair, to despair,
Despair, despair, despair, despair.

"The Golden Echo," by Gerard Manley Hopkins

Spare!
There ís one, yes I have one (Hush there!);
Only not within seeing of the sun,
Not within the singeing of the strong sun,
Tall sun's tingeing, or treacherous the tainting of the earth's air,
Somewhere elsewhere there is ah well where! one,
Ońe. Yes I cán tell such a key, I dó know such a place,
Where whatever's prized and passes of us, everything that's fresh
and fast flying of us, seems to us sweet of us and swiftly away
with, done away with, undone,
Úndone, done with, soon done with, and yet dearly and
dangerously sweet
Of us, the wimpled-water-dimpled, not-by-morning-matchèd face,
The flower of beauty, fleece of beauty, too too apt to, ah! to fleet,
Never fleets móre, fastened with the tenderest truth
To its own best being and its loveliness of youth: it is an ever-
lastingness of, O it is an all youth!
Come then, your ways and airs and looks, locks, maiden gear,
gallantry and gaiety and grace,
Winning ways, airs innocent, maiden manners, sweet looks,
loose locks, long locks, lovelocks, gaygear, going gallant,
girlgrace—
Resign them, sign them, seal them, send them, motion them
with breath,
And with sighs soaring, soaring síghs deliver
Them; beauty-in-the-ghost, deliver it, early now, long before
death
Give beauty back, beauty, beauty, beauty, back to God, beauty's
self and beauty's giver.
See; not a hair is, not an eyelash, not the least lash lost; every hair
Is, hair of the head, numbered.
Nay, what we had lighthanded left in surly the mere mould
Will have waked and have waxed and have walked with the wind
what while we slept,
This side, that side hurling a heavyheaded hundredfold
What while we, while we slumbered.

O then, weary then why should we tread? O why are we so
haggard at the heart, so care-coiled, care-killed, so fagged,
so fashed, so cogged, so cumbered.
When the thing we freely fórfeit is kept with fonder a care,
Fonder a care kept than we could have kept it, kept
Far with fonder a care (and we, we should have lost it) finer,
fonder
A care kept.—Where kept? Do but tell us where kept, where.—
Yonder.—What high as that! We follow, now we follow.—Yonder,
yes yonder, yonder,
Yonder.

C. *Two Poems by Gerard Manley Hopkins—An Analysis*

Gerard Manley Hopkins writes not for the eye, but for the ear. As he said "My verse is less to be read than heard."[1] And of all of his poems perhaps that is the most true of "The Leaden Echo" and "The Golden Echo," for after he wrote it he said that he "never did anything more musical."[2] Therefore, we have evidence from the poet, as well as from the poem itself, of an outstanding quality in this poem. In fact he wrote it as a "maidens' song" in *St. Winefred's Well,* an unfinished play.[3]

At the opening of the poem, the speaker is disturbed over the fleeting nature of beauty. Obviously under stress, he asks:

"How to kéep—is there any any, is there none such, nowhere
known some, bow or brooch or braid or brace, láce, latch
or catch or key to keep
Back beauty, keep it, beauty, beauty, beauty, . . . from vanishing
away?"

Thus he establishes his theme. After this preliminary question is asked, the leaden reply comes with emphatic, repetitive and discouraging state-

[1] *The Letters of Gerard Manley Hopkins to Robert Bridges,* Claude Colleer Abbott (ed.) (London: Oxford University Press, 1935), Vol. I. Letter XXXVII, p. 46.

[2] *The Correspondence of Gerard Manley Hopkins and Richard Watson Dixon* (London: Oxford University Press, 1955), Vol. II. Letter XXXVII, p. 149.

[3] *Ibid.,* Vol. I. Letter LXIX, p. 106.

ments which become more hopeless as the echo says there is no hope for warding off age, hoar hair, death, "tombs and worms," therefore, one can only accept despair. "The Leaden Echo" gives us no solace and no solution to the original question, how to "keep back beauty." The echo seems to reply "de profundis"—There is nothing left to life.

But "The Golden Echo," in direct contrast, then picks up the refrain of "The Leaden Echo," but only the last syllable. The word "despair" changes, surprisingly to "Spare!", and in contrast, we come to focus on a new attitude—an attitude of hope, of positive assertion where the Golden Echo replies affirmatively that there is a way to "keep back beauty." It is not within the world or the reach of the sun, but there is a key to the answer. This grows from a quiet Golden Echo to certain recurring emphasis and conviction in

> "Somewhere, elsewhere there is ah well where! one,
> Óne. Yes I cán tell such a key, I dó know such a place,"

The poet asserts that although what one prizes passes away "fast flying," "done away with," there is an everlasting beauty. And the way to preserve it is to give it up, to give it back to God, who himself gives beauty. This done, beauty is not lost, not a hair or an eyelash is lost. What one flings into the furrow and there forgets, "will have come to ear meantime"[4] a hundredfold. If this is true, he rhetorically asks, why should one be discouraged, vexed, care-laden, when the thing one gives up is preserved far more fondly than man could keep it. It is preserved "yonder." The speaker asks where it is kept and the reply comes back "yonder," at which the speaker exclaims:

> "What high as that! We follow, now we follow.
> Yonder, yes, yonder, yonder,
> Yonder."

So the theme may be that he who willingly relinquishes what is cherished, not striving to keep it back or make it static, but letting it go on and on to fulfill its destiny, even to letting it go "yonder," will find it kept with "fonder a care," while man would have lost it.

This poem has the ability to carry the oral reader along with it.

[4] *Ibid.,* Vol. I, Letter XCI, p. 159.

Its irregular rhythms and rhymes give it freedom. The simple language, consisting largely of one or two syllable words with some three syllable words, gives power. There is also a balance within the line, as in "Yes I can tell such a key, I do know such a place, . . ."

Hopkins' sentence structure is completely untraditional and confusing upon first acquaintance. For example, in the following passage he has set the verb "is" early in the passage.

> "See: not a hair is, not an eyelash, not the least lash lost; every hair
> Is, hair of the head, numbered.

Or he may change the structure and plan of a line, as he does in the opening lines:

> "How to keép—is there any any, is there none such, nowhere known some, bow or brooch or braid or brace, lacé, latch or catch or key to keep
> Back beauty, keep it, beauty, beauty, beauty, . . . from vanishing away?"

This unique sentence structure is very important in his style as it provides suspense, anticipation and intensity. His long tumbling sentences, as if the words simply have to fall out and cannot be checked, give a strong feeling of impetuosity.

Hopkins achieves his musical effects in a variety of ways. First of all, he is keenly aware of rhythm which he achieves largely through repetition. Repetition takes the form of repetitions of sounds and of exact words, and phrases. In the sound repetitions, he employs alliteration in such phrases as "bow or brooch or braid or brace," "dearly and dangerously sweet," "Looks, locks, maiden gear, gallantry and gaiety and grace," and in "Will have waked and have waxed and have walked with the wind what while we slept, . . ." At the same time, in this passage he achieves tonal variety by changing the vowel sounds in "have waked and have waxed and have walked." He repeats words such as: ". . . to keep back beauty, keep it, beauty, beauty, beauty, . . ." The word "beauty," is repeated four times successively in "The Leaden Echo" and seven times in "The Golden Echo." "Despair" is repeated eight times in "The Leaden Echo" and "yonder" is repeated five times in proximity at the end of "The Golden Echo."

Phrases, too, are repeated such as "No, there's none, there's none. O no there's none . . ." and "So be beginning, be beginning to despair." Some of his repetitions are very close. Some build steadily and relentlessly to an immensity of feeling. Others are placed a number of lines apart and keep the theme pounding at the listener's ear. For example:

> "No there's none there's none, O no there's none . . ." which is followed eleven lines later by a slight variation: "O there's none; no no no there's none . . ."

A quality which he strove for in his poetry was design and pattern which would give distinction and individuality to his work. He employed "the native and natural rhythm of speech, the least forced, the most rhetorical and emphatic of all possible rhythms . . ." He also used figures of speech and imagery. His imagery, which ranges from visual, auditory and tactile to olfactory in "The Leaden Echo" fades away in the second poem, "The Golden Echo," as the emphasis shifts from the tangible to the spiritual."

Hopkins was accused of both oddity and obscurity; he admitted the former, but denied obscurity. Had his critics relied on his advice to *hear* his poetry, they might have spared him this criticism.

"Parting Without A Sequel," by John Crowe Ransom

She has finished and sealed the letter
At last, which he so richly has deserved,
With characters venomous and hatefully curved,
And nothing could be better.

But even as she gave it
Saying to the blue-capped functioner of doom,
"Into his hands," she hoped the leering groom
Might somewhere lose and leave it.

Then all the blood
Forsook the face. She was too pale for tears,
Observing the ruin of her younger years.
She went and stood

Under her father's vaunting oak
Who kept his peace in wind and sun, and glistened
Stoical in the rain; to whom she listened
If he spoke.

And now the agitation of the rain
Rasped his sere leaves, and he talked low and gentle
Reproaching the wan daughter by the lintel;
Ceasing and beginning again.

Away went the messenger's bicycle,
His serpent's track went up the hill forever,
And all the time she stood there hot as fever
And cold as any icicle.

D. *Ransom's "Parting Without A Sequel"—An Analysis*

In *The New Criticism,* John Crowe Ransom says that it is his "feeling that we have in poetry a revolutionary departure from the convention of logical discourse and that we should provide it with a bold and proportionate designation." Such a description seems to fit his poem "Parting Without A Sequel."

In this poem we do not find ordinary conversational speech. There is a careful placement of words, and a compactness not typical of daily conversation.

"Parting Without A Sequel" presents a lover's quarrel in which we see only the girl and her reactions to the situation. We do not know how the man feels or whether he expects a break in their relations.

As the poem opens, the girl is quite determined to "tell him off" as he deserves to be told off, in "characters venomous and hatefully curved." She tries to emphasize her feelings of anger and hatred, yet the last line in the first stanza—"And nothing could be better"—sounds like a forced statement—as if she needs to reinforce her resolution to break off. Kinesthetic imagery shows her actions in this stanza.

In the second stanza, a note of doubt—even regret—enters the picture. The girl has scarcely given the letter to the messenger, a "blue-capped functioner of doom"—scarcely a human being, merely an agent of miserable fate—before she has strong conflicting emotions. There is a conflict in both the body and mind of the girl. She even has a wild hope that he will lose the letter or leave it somewhere. He is so sinister that he seems, this inferior servant, to leer at her. In this stanza the action slows down to two physical acts: when the girl gives the letter to the "groom" and when he leers. Here the action is largely internal—that is, it presents the thoughts in the girl's mind. Compared to the first stanza, it is like a still photo, a movie that suddenly changes into a static picture.

In the third stanza we see the girl's reaction to what she has done. Beyond tears or feeling, she sees her life ruined. Here Ransom uses enjambment between the third and fourth stanzas, ending the third stanza with suspense in the incomplete statement "she went and stood." In the fourth stanza we find that she went to a spot that gave her security, to "her father's vaunting oak," so steady and sure that it proudly and serenely displays itself, stoic in any weather. The girl respects this image of strength and sound judgment and listens to it if it speaks. Here the strength of this tree is described in visual and auditory imagery. Whether the father is alive or dead the poet does not specifically tell us, but the oak appears to be a symbol for the father. Here the sounds are sustained and there is a slowing of pace; only the last line, "if he spoke," might imply that he does not always speak. Why not? Could it be that the girl is not always ready, or there, to listen? Does she not always need to rely on the father symbol?

The next stanza reveals that this is one of the times when he speaks, gently, but nevertheless reproachfully to the pale daughter "by the lintel." Why "by the lintel"? Does this suggest that the girl is on the threshold of life? The rain excites and disturbs, "rasps" the bare leaves of the oak, suggesting the unpleasant sound of discipline, yet intermingled with kindness. This ceases and is then repeated.

In the final stanza the "blue-capped functioner of doom," is now merely "the messenger." Why has his description so altered? Perhaps the "father's vaunting oak" has given the girl some understanding and perspective, so that this messenger is not such a dismal symbol as he had been. Yet he still has unpleasant connotations for he makes tracks like a serpent.

And here we can see a shift in the poem. In the first part of the poem the girl's acts are "venomous" and "hatefully curved," like a snake. But in the last stanza the metaphor is changed and the messenger assumes a reptilian quality as his "serpent's track" goes away. Thus the serpent-like quality shifts from the girl who wrote the letter to the messenger who bears the letter. And as he bears the letter she looks on in a confusion of contradictory emotions. The girl is so shaken that she is in a fever and chill. The poem ends with the girl in a state of shock. How she will eventually feel we can only guess. But the title tells us that there is no sequel.

You might consider this poem in several ways. Do you think it is presenting a tragic situation? Do you think the poet might be somewhat wryly amused at this "tragedy"? How old do you think the girl is?

Ransom has written this poem in quatrains with an abba pattern, in which the rhyme changes in each stanza. There are metrical variations which apparently Ransom intended, for, as he says, a poet "is capable of writing smooth meters and then roughening them on purpose." Ransom regards meter or stress as related to meaning for he says "But it is surprising how often the stress at a new place puts a new light on a given situation; or rather, looks at the situation from a new but quite possible perspective." ("The Strange Music of English Verse," Kenyon Review, Vol. 18, Summer 1956, p. 466.) And in the same article he says, "rhythm is the marriage of the meter and the language . . ."

Despite the poet's contention that sounds in themselves rarely convey meaning, there seems to be some indication to the contrary in this poem. For example, in the first stanza there is a predominance of "t," "d," and other explosive sounds in "finished," "sealed," "letter," "at last," "which," "richly," "deserved," "characters," "hatefully curved" and, "could be better." These suggest the quick, nervous, slightly explosive actions of the girl.

This poem shows evidence of alliteration, assonance and consonance. Alliteration is found throughout the poem. In the first stanza the c (k) sound gives a staccato effect in

> "With *c*haracters venomous and hatefully *c*urved,
> And nothing *c*ould be better."

and in the second stanza

> "Into *h*is hands," she *h*oped the *l*eering groom
> Might somewhere *l*ose and *l*eave it."

and further on

> "*F*orsook the *f*ace."
> "*R*asped his sere *l*eaves, and he talked *l*ow and gentle
> *R*eproaching the wan daughter by the *l*intel;

Consonance, the repetition of consonant sounds, is found in such clusters as the repetition of s and z (s) sounds in the first stanza which suggests the reptile-like attitude of the angry girl. This carries over into the second stanza where she hisses "Into his hands." The t and d sounds already noted suggest her quick nervous movements as she accomplishes her task. In the fourth stanza the explosive k is repeated in "oa*k*," "*k*ept," "stoi*c*al" and "spo*k*e." And in the last stanza the hissing s sounds are transferred to the messenger, who assumes the snake metaphor, in "messengers," "bicycle," "serpent," "stood," "as," "icicle." Assonance, too, is present in "cu*r*ved—dese*r*ved"—"f*i*nished—r*i*chly," "d*oo*m—gr*oo*m," "*o*ak—st*o*ical—sp*o*ke"; "w*e*nt—m*e*ss*e*nger—w*e*nt—for*e*ver" among others.

Mr. Ransom says that he does not know how poetry should be read. Possibly, he says, it should be read twice, "once as rhythmed verse and then as pure prose."[5] If it is to be a prose reading, he advises that a "rather bold and primitive and rhythmical reading" be tried in reading to the "general public."[6] When you read "A Parting Without A Sequel" you may experiment with it in several ways.

STUDY QUESTIONS

1. Do you agree with Stephen Spender's definition of poetry?
2. Does Robert Frost's definition of poetry hold for most of our contemporary poetry? Discuss this in terms of some of the well known poets today.

[5] "The Strange Music of English Verse," Kenyon Review, Vol. 18, p. 463, Summer, 1956.

[6] *Ibid.*

3. Do you agree with Wordsworth that "poetry is the spontaneous overflow of powerful feeling"? Can you think of any exceptions to this?

4. When you read aloud the excerpt from T. S. Eliot on page 235 do you want your voice to literally suggest the sound of "rat's feet" on broken glass? Why, or why not?

5. Do you think any "great" poetry can or should be read with a strong rhythmical beat? If so, why? Can you give an example?

6. Can you find another example of poetry which requires a range of pauses as does *The Faerie Queene* by Spenser?

7. Why do you think the terms "masculine" and "feminine" rhyme are used? How do they affect your oral reading of such poems? Which carries more "weight"?

8. How does "enjambment" affect the oral reading of a poem? Does it increase the danger of mechanical rhyming? How about end-stopped lines?

9. How would you arrive at an idea of the appropriate tempo of the two poems in this chapter, "Spring" and "Meeting at Night"?

10. Is all poetry highly charged with emotion? How do you think you can determine this? Are there different levels of emotion in poems?

11. Is there more, or less, emphasis on the "intellectual" in modern poetry?

12. Can you discover any difference in the emotional impact possible in the Italian and Shakespearean sonnet forms?

BIBLIOGRAPHY

Alden, Raymond Macdonald, *English Verse.* New York: Holt and Co., 1903.

Allen, Don Cameron, *Image and Meaning: Metaphoric Traditions in Renaissance Poetry.* Baltimore: The Johns Hopkins Press, 1960.

Aristotle, *On the Art of Poetry,* trans. by Bywater, Ingram; with a preface by Gilbert Murray. Oxford: Clarendon Press, 1945.

Blackmur, R. P., *Form and Value in Modern Poetry.* Garden City, New York: Doubleday Anchor Books, 1957.

Brewer, Robert Frederick, *Orthometry—The Art of Versification and the Technicalities of Poetry.* New & rev. ed. Grant, Edinburgh, 1918.

Brooks, Cleanth, *The Well Wrought Urn: Studies in the Structure of Poetry.* New York: Reynal and Hitchcock, 1947.

Coleridge, S. T., *Biographia Literaria.* London: J. M. Dent & Co. New York: E. P. Dutton & Co., 1906.

Coombes, H., *Literature and Criticism.* London: Chatto and Windus, 1965.

Crane, R. S., *The Languages of Criticism and The Structure of Poetry.* Toronto: University of Toronto Press, 1953.

Daniels, Earl, R. K., *The Art of Reading Poetry.* New York: Farrar and Rinehart, 1941.

Dolman, John Jr., *The Art of Reading Aloud.* New York: Harper and Bros., 1956.

Eliot, T. S., "Tradition and the Individual Talent" in *American Literary Essays,* ed. by Leary, L. R., New York: Crowell, 1960.

Empson, W. M., *Seven Types of Ambiguity.* London, 2nd edition revised and re-set. New York: New Directions, 1947.

Fogerty, Elsie, *The Speaking of English Verse.* 4th edition. London: Dent. New York: Dutton, 1937.

Horace, *On The Art of Poetry* (*In Classical Literary Criticism*). Trans. with an introduction by T. S. Dorsch. Baltimore: Penguin Books, 1965.

Lanier, Sidney, *The Science of English Verse.* New York: Chas. Scribner's Sons, 1908.

Plutarch, *How the Young Man Should Study Poetry.* Plutarchus: *Moralia,* with an English translation by Frank Cole Babbit, Vol. I. London: W. Heinemann, Ltd. New York: G. P. Putnam's Sons, 1929–65.

Pulos, C. E., *The New Critics and The Language of Poetry.* Lincoln: The University, New Series no. 19, 1958.

Ransom, John Crowe, *The New Criticism.* Norfolk, Conn.: New Directions, 1941.

———, "The Strange Music of English Verse," *Kenyon Review,* Vol. 18, p. 460. Summer, 1956.

Rice, John, *An Introduction to the Art of Reading.* London: J. & R. Tonson, 1765.

Saintsbury, George, *Historical Manual of English Prosody.* London: Macmillan & Co., Ltd., 1910.

Shelley, Percy B., *A Defense of Poetry.* Ed. by Mrs. Shelley, reprinted from the edition of MDCCCXLV. Indianapolis: The Bobbs-Merrill Co., 1904.

Wordsworth, Wm., *Preface to the Lyrical Ballads* (In *Century Readings in the English Essays,* ed. by L. Wann, p. 257).

Chapter X

The Oral Interpretation of Drama

Drama, as a branch of literature, arches over the years from Aeschylus to Edward Albee. The many playwrights have attempted to recreate man's reactions and responses to his life and his environment. Their conceived stories have been presented upon stages before an audience through living persons, dramatic dialogue, planned action, and characteristic costumes. As playwriting developed these were supplemented with setting and lighting.

In theatre the communication of a playscript has the combined efforts and support of playwright, producer, director, actor, designer, costumer and stage technician, and it is a shared responsibility. In the oral interpretation of drama it is an individual responsibility to share the communication of the playscript. The oral interpreter has before him the same script as those performing in the theatre, but he employs only his voice and suggested physical action as the medium of communication. Before the oral interpreter can recreate characters and situations—a requirement and challenge for the interpreter of drama—it is essential that he investigate how the playwright has organized his material in order that he may be sensitively aware of human responses and human situations.

The search for the nature of drama has extended over the years. It was Aristotle, Greek philosopher and teacher, who first observed the practices of playwriting; later, in 17th Century France, the Neo-classicists began to codify certain principles; and in the 19th Century it was Gustave Freytag, German novelist, playwright and critic, who attempted to demonstrate the structure of a play in terms of the "well made" play. More recently commentators have rejected many of these concepts from the past and have attempted to find other approaches. Moreover it is to be remembered that there exists today drama, such as that of the "theatre of the absurd," which does not easily fall into the traditional concepts of analysis.

Since analysis is a key to the understanding and communication of a play, or even a scene from a play, this chapter will introduce the oral interpreter to some of the basic principles of dramatic composition. It will also suggest certain techniques and skills that might assist him in stimulating a listener response which is in harmony with his judgments of the intent of the play.

I. BASIC ELEMENTS OF DRAMATIC COMPOSITION

The playwright, from early times to the present, has been concerned with projecting his thought and feeling through theatrical technique. Like a poet or novelist, a playwright should choose subject matter which interests him and, hopefully, his audience. It may be an event or situation, a character or characters, a philosophic concept, a political point of view, or a psychological interaction, but *it must be something which will lend itself to treatment in dramatic form.* Interlaced with this material will be a theme, which may be directly or indirectly communicated to an audience. The playwright tries to make his presentation of subject matter and theme both interesting, entertaining, believable, and moving; these elements must be an intrinsic part of the play's structure.

A. *Plot*

When you read a play aloud, your listeners are naturally interested in "what happens." Aristotle referred to this as the *fable* and to him it was the principal aspect of drama, and had to have a beginning, a middle, and an end. In order to understand more fully this first basic element of dramatic composition, we shall take a brief look at how the dramatist has arranged or laid out his fable, as well as the distinctive function for each part. This will, we hope, make the oral interpreter aware of his responsibility toward the communication of that particular part. The five parts for our consideration are: exposition or background, conflict, crises, climax, and dénouement. In addition we will discuss briefly two kinds of dramatic coloration related to plot: dramatic irony and symbolism.

1. *Exposition or Background.* Information about the setting, the historical background (if any), the characters, and significant past or present events in their lives is called exposition. The dramatist may adopt one or more means of suggesting or revealing to the reader and listener this information. For example, he may use a chorus, a prologue, a telephone conversation, a character's movement, or dialogue. Through whatever method he chooses, the dramatist strives to be interesting and clear; and he wants his exposition to act as a springboard for the action of the story.

You, the interpreter, will also have an informative introduction. This is obviously necessary because you do not have an atmospheric and suggestive setting that implies the mood and provides the environment. For the most part, your listener has to rely upon aural rather than visual stimulation. Your introduction should orient your listener to the literary experience and create a sense of expectancy. In brief, your introduction should convey "what is afoot" and establish rapport with the listener.

Your introduction may be entirely original, or entirely from materials written by the playwright, or a combination of these. Since the interpreter of drama does not utilize description or comments as extensively as when he is reading from a novel, your material for giving information should be carefully selected.

Consider for a moment the dramatist's contribution. J. M. Barrie superbly relates "what is afoot" in his play, *The Twelve-Pound Look.*

> If quite convenient (as they say about cheques) you are to conceive that the scene is laid in your own house, and that Harry Sims is you. Perhaps the ornamentation of the house is a trifle ostentatious, but if you cavil at that we are willing to re-decorate: you don't get out of being Harry Sims on a mere matter of plush and dados. It pleases us to make him a city man, but (rather than

lose you) he can be turned with the scrape of a pen into K. C., fashionable doctor, Secretary of State, or what you will. We conceive him of a pleasant rotundity with a thick red neck, but we shall waive that point if you know him to be thin.

It is that day in your career when everything went wrong just when everything seemed to be superlatively right.

In Harry's case it was a woman who did the mischief. She came to him in his great hour and told him she did not admire him. Of course he turned her out of the house and was soon himself again, but it spoilt the morning for him. This is the subject of the play, and quite enough too.

Harry is to receive the honour of knighthood in a few days, and we discover him in the sumptuous 'snuggery' of his home in Kensington (or is it Westminster?), rehearsing the ceremony with his wife. They have been at it all the morning, a pleasing occupation. Mrs. Sims (as we may call her for the last time, as it were, and strictly as a good-natured joke) is wearing her presentation gown, and personates the august one who is about to dub her Harry knight. She is seated regally. Her jewelled shoulders proclaim aloud her husband's generosity. She must be an extraordinarily proud and happy woman, yet she has a drawn face and shrinking ways as if there were some one near her of whom she is afraid. She claps her hands, as the signal to Harry. He enters bowing, and with graceful swerve of the leg. He is only partly in costume, the sword and the real stockings not having arrived yet. With a gliding motion that is only delayed while one leg makes up on the other, he reaches his wife, and, going on one knee, raises her hand superbly to his lips. She taps him on the shoulder with a paper-knife and says huskily, 'Rise, Sir Harry.' He rises, bows, and glides about the room, going on his knees to various articles of furniture, and rising from each a knight. It is a radiant domestic scene, and Harry is as dignified as if he knew that royalty was rehearsing it at the other end.

Those exact words of J. M. Barrie, indeed, serve as an interesting and intriguing introduction for the oral interpreter to read to his listener.

Another contribution of the dramatist, which can be utilized profitably as background information, is dialogue. In Ibsen's *A Doll's House,* the conversation between Nora and Mrs. Linden (Act I), and in Shakespeare's *Hamlet,* the dramatic speech of the Ghost (Act I, Sc v) are examples of dialogue that give exposition necessary for the understanding and and development of the plot. Such material can be incorporated *per se* or paraphrased for your introduction to the play.

You may prefer to make an original contribution, as was the case in the following example of a student's introduction.

> For my final reading, I have chosen to read from Andre Obey's *Noah,* a dramatization of Noah and the Ark. In the words of Brooks Atkinson, former theatre critic of the New York *Times,* Noah's voyage ". . . begins auspiciously enough with Noah, his wife, his three sons and neighbor's girls embarking with the animals on God's ark in the hope of a brave, new world. When at length the rain is over, the grand beauty of the great waters fills them with rejoicing and they dance with exuberance around the deck in the dawn of a golden age. But the canker of the old world has crept on board. Ham [the eldest son] is the sore spot. He doubts. He taunts his shipmates with old misgivings. He belabors his father with skeptical questions. And "Noah" becomes the story of a kindly, simple old man who grows lonely in his faith, who pilots his craft safely to shore in the midst of doubts, . . ."[1] In this final scene we see Mama old and senile and very, very tired from her long voyage. We see the children as they turn against and leave their father. And we see Noah as he struggles to understand this God who has led him on this trip. The scene opens with Mama on the Ark's deck, more or less, talking to herself.

Whether an introduction is chosen directly from the dramatist or written by you, it should set the scene in such a way that the listener will want to become involved. Your introduction should, in the process of involvement, include one or more of the following: (1) vital facts about the author and the play, (2) distinctive word pictures of the characters and the setting, (3) elements of conflict in the play either by implication or specific statement, or (4) personal experiences revealing

[1] Brooks Atkinson, "Noah's Ordeal by Water the Subject of a Fantasy From the French of Andre Obey," *The New York Times,* Thursday, Feb. 14, 1935 (Amusements), p. 25.

your association with the play. Any one of these alternatives should improve the emotional and intellectual receptivity of your listener.

2. *Conflict.* Conflict, according to Milton Marx in his book, *The Enjoyment of Drama,* is "the essence of drama." John Gassner states that ". . . it is the peculiar nature of the drama that it concentrates on those relationships that generate difficulties or oppositions and that often produce *conflicts.*"[2] And he refers to it as one of the dynamics of drama.

The problem of conflict may arise from a situation or from a clash of personalities or ideas within the play. The interpreter will note that there are forces at work in what may be termed the protagonist and the antagonist, who are the main characters. It is with the protagonist in most instances that the listeners sympathize, or identify themselves. His adversary is known as the antagonist. The interpreter should be aware of the fact, however, that the antagonist is not always a single human being. It is entirely possible for this adversary to be a force, such as nature, as in *Wheat,* by J. Clark Weaver; society, as found in *The Weavers,* by Gerhart Hauptmann; a struggle within the individual, as in *Death of a Salesman,* by Arthur Miller; environment, as in Sidney Kingsley's *Dead End,* and Elmer Rice's *Street Scene;* or fate, as in Sophocles' *Oedipus Rex.*

To assume that the protagonist is always a "good" person is unrealistic. It is possible that he or she may have some undesirable qualities while those of the antagonist may be sometimes desirable.

The oral interpreter will set the protagonist on a course of action which the dramatist has complicated by putting roadblocks in his path. The protagonist must attempt to overcome these before he can reach his objective. The antagonist attempts to thwart this by providing conflict in the drama, therefore the interpreter should make him strong enough to accomplish this.

3. *Crises.* William Archer in his book, *Play-Making,* asserts that ". . . a play consists, or ought to consist, of a great crisis, worked out through a series of minor crises."[3] These crises are situations in which a character or characters become involved to the point whereby they must

[2] John Gassner, *Producing the Play* (New York: The Dryden Press, 1941), p. 18.

[3] William Archer, *Play-Making* (Boston: Small, Maynard and Company, 1912), p. 138.

resolve their plight either by making a decision, or by taking a definite course of action. As might be expected there will be clashes of interest resulting in emotional excitement.

A carefully executed example can be found in Arthur Miller's *Death of a Salesman.* Willy Loman meets his boss, Howard Wagner, to tell him that he would like to get off the road, to secure an increase in salary, and to be a floor salesman for the company in New York. At first Howard is indifferent to Willy, for he is more interested in his wire recorder. Willy, nevertheless, continues to state his case in spite of the disinterest on the part of Howard. Finally, Howard informs Willy that he is not to represent the company any longer, and fires him. Here, indeed, is a minor crisis where the clashes of interest are strong. The result is a strong emotional response on the part of the characters as well as the listener. This episode also serves to illustrate how a minor crisis helps to complicate the plot, build suspense, and develop characterization. In your study of a drama, you will become aware that crises vary in degrees of importance and reach their full impact when they approach the point of greatest interest and intensity—usually the last serious crisis in the play.

When you prepare to read a portion of a play aloud, in which crises appear, it may be necessary to build each one to a certain high point, but when that particular crisis is solved the tension will diminish giving the interpreter and the listener a degree of emotional relaxation. For example, in *Romeo and Juliet* the nature of a single crisis can be observed when you read aloud the scene where Juliet is waiting for the nurse to bring her news of the plans for her marriage. As the scene opens, you should convey Juliet's impatience while waiting for the nurse to return with this important news. The fact that she is so slow in returning increases the tension and strengthens the crisis. When the nurse does come, she herself continues the state of crisis by not giving Juliet the desired information at once. She shifts the topic, comments on her own aches and pains, and makes references to extraneous matters, all of which sustain the suspense and strengthen the crisis. Finally, with a change of pace the nurse gives Juliet the information that she has been waiting for since the scene first opened. It culminates in a directive:

> *Nurse.* Then hie you hence to Friar Laurence' cell,
> There stays a husband to make you a wife.

Now comes the wanton blood up in your cheeks,
They'll be in scarlet straight at any news.
Hie you to church, I must another way,
To fetch a ladder by which your love
Must climb a bird's nest soon when it is dark.
I am the drudge, and toil in your delight,
But you shall bear the burden soon at night.
Go, I'll to dinner, hie you to the cell.

Juliet. Hie to high fortune! Honest Nurse, farewell.

(Act II, Sc v)

4. *Climax.* After a series of crises the dramatic composition points toward another crisis which is decisive—one in which the intensity is greater than in any of the others. Climax is that point in the play where the conflict between the protagonist and the antagonist is so acute that a final decision or solution has to be reached. Structurally, it may be termed as the turning point of the play, and figuratively speaking, it is the "last step" wherein the protagonist, in pursuit of his objective, may succeed or fail according to the plan of the dramatist.

The "ring episode" (Act III) between Essex and Elizabeth in *Elizabeth The Queen,* by Maxwell Anderson, the "confession episode" (Act IV) in the cell of the Salem jail in *The Crucible,* by Arthur Miller, the merciless examination scene of the boy in Terence Rattigan's *The Winslow Boy* (Act II), and the trial scene (VI) in *Saint Joan,* by George Bernard Shaw are examples of climax scenes.

Before attempting to read aloud the climax scene of a play, you should make a careful and thorough analysis of it and the events leading up to it. For instance, if you were to read the trial scene of *Saint Joan,* certainly you should be aware of what has already happened as well as of the four sections or divisions that are inherent in the scene itself: (1) the introduction of The Inquisitor and D'Estivet to Warwick, (2) the preparation for the trial which reveals contrasting characters, (3) the trial itself, and (4) the conclusion in which the account of the burning is reported on stage in the classical tradition.

After making your analysis, you then should think in terms of how you might best suggest the climax vocally and physically. This will depend, of course, upon your concept of each of the characters involved in the scene. It is often helpful to determine what single aspect of vocal technique can best suggest the thoughts and emotions of the characters involved. Consideration of the passage in terms of those vocal techniques (such as volume, rate, pitch, and quality) which are most appropriate in suggesting the motivations of the character, is valuable and essential. Varying degrees of muscular tension, as dictated by the character and the situation, will determine your physical responsiveness.

In the reading of a climax, try to avoid a melodramatic style. You might well take to heart Hamlet's advice to the Players:

> . . . do not saw the air too much with your hand, thus, but use all gently; for in the very torrent, tempest, and (as I may say) whirlwind of your passion, you must acquire and beget a temperance that may give it smoothness. O it offends me to the soul to hear a . . . fellow tear a passion to tatters, to very rags, . . . It out-herods Herod. Pray you avoid it.
>
> * * *
>
> Be not too tame neither; but let your own discretion be your tutor.
>
> (*Hamlet,* Act III, Sc ii)

5. *Dénouement.* Thus far the dramatist has disclosed certain extenuating circumstances to his audience through exposition, has unveiled for his listeners opposing forces at work through conflict and has unfolded suspenseful events sharply through crises. He has also reached the final solution to the conflicts involved in the climax whereby the protagonist has achieved or failed in his objective, or a compromise has been effected between him and the antagonist. But in spite of this ordered progression, the dramatist has not completed his play. He has still another task—to resolve the issues of the play and thereby hold the interest of the audience, perhaps not at the highest peak, but a bit longer, and to provide it with plausible answers to these issues. What will happen now? How will the character or characters react or adjust to the postclimactic situation? These answers are furnished through the *dénouement* or resolution. It is here that the dramatist presents the outcome of the situation and the disposition of the character or characters.

In *Oedipus Rex,* by means of the Epilogue, Sophocles divulges the manner of Jocasta's death, the self-inflicted blinding of Oedipus, and the desire of Oedipus to become an exile. These are the logical resolutions or *dénouement,* to the old shepherd's revelation that Oedipus murdered his own father and married his own mother.

In a short final scene, Rudolf Besier, in *The Barretts of Wimpole Street* (Act III, Sc ii), furnishes a satisfying reaction to the decision and departure of Elizabeth for a life of happiness with Robert Browning.

In *Julius Caesar,* Act V supplies the necessary outcome for the murder of Julius Caesar when Brutus and Cassius, the remaining conspirators, are defeated at Philippi. Here Cassius, believing that all was lost, said to Pindarus:

> . . . Here, take thou the hilts,
> And when my face is covered, as 'tis now,
> Guide thou the sword. [Pindarus stabs him.]
> Caesar, thou art revenged
> Even with the sword that killed thee.
>
> (Act V, Sc iii)

Brutus, not wanting to be taken prisoner, says to Strato, his servant:

> Hold then my sword, and turn away thy face
> While I do run upon it. Wilt Thou Strato?
> . . . .
> Farewell, good Strato. Caesar, now be still.
> I killed not thee with half so good a will.
>
> (Act V, Sc v)

The *dénouement* may be parallel with the climax, but more often it follows, and is usually short.

Unfortunately, "falling action" has been a general term associated with *dénouement.* Actually, the listener's interest in the plot must not fall but ought to be sustained; and it is from this that you should take your cue. Every effort on your part must be made to maintain the interest that the dramatist has created for the listener in terms of situation and character. To do this you should be fully aware of the significant points to be cleared up for the listener, so that he recognizes the solution of the situation as convincing. To accomplish this your concept of the characters and the situation must be reflected vocally and physically in the pointing and timing of lines.

6. *Dramatic Irony.* Although dramatic irony is projected through dialogue, it is dramatic coloration woven into the plot by the dramatist. There are a number of ways in which it may be used in a play, some of which will be mentioned here. It is used verbally when the speaker says one thing and means just the opposite. For example, as you have already seen in Chapter VII, when Mark Antony refers to Brutus as an "honorable man," he wishes to imply just the opposite. This type of irony depends particularly upon vocal and physical flexibility.

The dramatist also uses dramatic irony in the plot of his play when events turn out to be the opposite of what one might expect. We expect Macbeth to become king, as the witches foretell, but we do not expect the tragedy that follows. Further, Lady Macbeth appears to be so strong in the opening scene of the play where she drives Macbeth on to his goal that her subsequent collapse and death are an ironic turn of events which we do not expect. There is the same kind of irony in Barrie's *The Admirable Crichton,* where the whole family is marooned on an island and the butler actually becomes the head of the family. This irony is further intensified when, upon returning to civilization, the butler immediately assumes his traditional role as if the island episode had never happened.

There is also irony when the spectators know more about a character or a situation than some of the other characters know. Such is the case when Othello repeatedly speaks of "Honest Iago," whom the audience knows is not honest. In *Hamlet,* the king and queen come to the play which Hamlet has chosen to test the king's guilt. Hamlet tells us he is going to have a play presented to "catch the conscience of the king!" He and the audience know of this plot but the king and queen are innocent of this scheme. In *Cyrano de Bergerac,* the audience knows that Cyrano writes Christian's love letters to Roxane and that Cyrano is secretly in love with her, but Roxane does not learn this until Cyrano is dying.

Your knowledge of what constitutes the ironic situation depends on your understanding of the meaning of the play, and its characters and its plot. Watch for the reversal from the expected to the unexpected, and be aware of the way the dramatist tells the listener more about the plot and characters than some of the characters themselves know.

To project irony it is imperative that you comprehend the attitude and feelings of the character or characters, point lines carefully, and look for the double-edged words or phrases. The suggestion of irony requires considerable vocal and physical skill.

7. *Symbolism.* Symbolism has been defined as the representation of one thing by another. Often in drama a tangible object is used as symbolic of the intangible. In the Greek theatre masks and colors were used symbolically so each character type wore a specific style of mask. Royalty wore purple and those in mourning wore dark colors, but in the Roman theatre young men wore purple and the old men white. The name of a character may be symbolic of the trait or quality inherent in the person, such as Discretion, Good-Deeds, and The Intruder. An incident or plot may also have symbolic overtones as in Synge's *Riders to the Sea* or Ibsen's *The Master Builder.*

Perhaps it may well be that Synge in his play, *Riders to the Sea,* was not primarily interested in attempting to be a symbolist, but rather more interested in developing a "slice of life" of the people he knew so well. Thus he wrote a picturesque story of an old woman who had lost her husband and her six sons to the destructive sea. Nevertheless, out of this drama of poetic language, tragedy and sorrow, there is subjective symbolism. Take, for example, the sea. Could it not represent the inexorable fate that engulfs Maurya's family and herself? A fate that brings death as well as a resigned peace to Maurya. Synge observed, "The maternal feeling is so powerful in these islands that it gives a life of torment to the women," and ". . . the women live only for their children."[4] Synge successfully communicates this idea and through it Maurya "becomes a universal symbol of maternal grief."[5]

Henrik Ibsen was noted for his use of both realism and symbolism. In his *The Master Builder,* a young man represents the spirit of youth, while the master builder represents the older generation. He even climbs the church tower, a symbol of his achievement.

[4] Francis Bickley, *J. M. Synge and the Irish Dramatic Movement* (Boston & New York: Houghton Mifflin Company, 1912), p. 35.

[5] Elizabeth Coxhead, *J. M. Synge and Lady Gregory* (published for the British Council and the National Book League by Longmans, Green & Co., 1962), p. 15.

Symbolism can be found in many plays in the nineteenth and twentieth centuries. The vine leaves in *Hedda Gabler* typify drunkenness. In *A Dream Play,* by August Strindberg, a bud surmounts a castle and blossoms into a huge chrysanthemum denoting eternity. Anton Chekhov in *The Cherry Orchard* gives the orchard symbolic meaning—a happiness of former days, a past now gone. Numerous examples can be found in the plays of Gerhart Hauptmann, Maurice Maeterlinck, and Georg Kaiser. In the 20th Century the symbolistic technique has become a favorite dramatic device. The typewriter and the diagram of the keyboard, the jonquils, and the glass animals took on a significance of reality, girlhood, and an imaginative kingdom in Tennessee William's *The Glass Menagerie.* Garcia Lorca in his *Blood Wedding* used the horse to indicate virility, and wheat to symbolize regeneration and life itself.

The symbolic meaning of an object, character or incident may indeed vary from interpreter to interpreter, and individuals may not always be in agreement. Millett and Bentley, in commenting on symbolism, have said:

> "At its best and at its worst, it stimulates the mind and the imagination by encouraging the quest for values that do not lie casually on the surface of the work of art. Such a quest is justified if it does not go too boldly beyond the meanings that the poet or dramatist has indubitably indicated or suggested."[6]

Your introduction may include a discussion of the play's symbolism. In addition to the play itself, costuming, hand properties, settings and lighting may have symbolic importance, which need to be explained to the listener.

B. *Character and Characterization*

If a dramatic experience is to emerge from a play, there must be the element of character as well as plot. Each in reality complements the other. A well-drawn character, the life-blood of the play, is a recognizable person who lives within the plot and who reveals it through his dialogue, his action, and his relationship with situations and other per-

[6] Fred B. Millett and Gerald Eades Bentley, *The Art of the Drama* (New York: D. Appleton-Century Company, 1935), p. 162.

sons in the drama. In your analysis of a character or characters, you will discover that the dramatist has stamped him with certain predominant traits and motives which distinguish him from another character. This individual impression is known as characterization. Actors and interpreters should seek out those touches of characterization which the dramatist has sensitized in various ways.

1. *Social Discourse.* The dramatist may write a lengthy description, as George Bernard Shaw often did, or he may introduce the character to the listener by having others describe him or talk about him. This we call social discourse. In reading Eugene O'Neill's, *Ah Wilderness!,* a brief but enlightening discussion by the Miller family gives the listener an idea of what seventeen-year-old Richard is like.

MRS. MILLER (*suddenly-startledly*): But where's Richard? We're forgetting all about him. Why, where is that boy? I thought he came in with us from breakfast.

MILDRED: I'll bet he's off somewhere writing a poem to Muriel McComber, the silly! Or pretending to write one. I think he just copies—

ARTHUR (*looking back toward the dining-room*): He's still in the dining-room, reading a book. (*Turning back—scornfully*) Gosh, he's always reading now. It's not my idea of having a good time in vacation.

MILLER (*caustically*): He read his school books, too, strange as that may seem to you. That's why he came out top of his class. I'm hoping before you leave New Haven they'll find time to teach you reading is a good habit.

MRS. MILLER (*sharply*): That reminds me, Nat. I've been meaning to speak to you about those awful books Richard is reading. You've got to give him a good talking to—(*She gets up from her chair*). I'll go up and get them right now. I found them where he'd hid them on the shelf of his wardrobe. You just wait till you see what—(*She bustles off, rear right, through the front parlor.*)

MILLER (*plainly not relishing whatever is coming—to Sid, grumblingly*): Seems to me she might wait until the Fourth is over before bringing up—(*Then with a grin*) I know there's nothing to it, anyway. When I think of the books I used to sneak off and read when I was a kid.

SID: Me, too. I suppose Dick is deep in Nick Carter or Old Cap Collier.

MILLER: No, he passed that period long ago. Poetry's his red meat nowadays, I think—love poetry—and socialism, too, I suspect, from some dire declarations he's made. (*Then briskly*) Well, might as well get him on the carpet. (*He calls*) Richard. (*No answer—louder*) Richard. (*No answer—then in a bellow*) Richard!

2. *Bearing and Action.* Insight into a character's personality can also be communicated by physical bearing and action. What a character does on the stage usually reveals this. For example, in *As You Like It,* Touchstone, the court fool, has to remind Audrey, his country sweetheart ". . . Bear your body more seeming, Audrey . . ." (Act V, Sc iv). When you read the lines of Audrey and Touchstone, you may find it helpful to suggest their bearing in order to convey the differences in their background and personalities. A physical act may also reveal personality. As you may recall, in *The Taming of the Shrew,* Katherine strikes her suitor, Petruchio, which helps confirm her description as a shrew. In this play, the actor will use overt and literal action while speaking these lines. That is, Katherine will actually strike Petruchio, whereas the oral interpreter will merely describe this act or will suggest such actions by a slight movement of the body or hand, but he will not use the same literal action that an actor will use in this situation.

3. *Psychic Dimension.* The dramatist will provide a psychic dimension for each of his characters. To measure that dimension an actor or interpreter needs to discover what the character is thinking and feeling about himself and others, his attitude, his hopes and fears, and his conflict with others or within himself. In truth, the mental and emotional activity of a character is fascinating not only to the audience, but to an actor or interpreter. Although the dramatist has provided this information in the development of his plot, he uses two reliable sources, the soliloquy and motivation, to reveal a character's psychic dimension.

The soliloquy, a particular type of speech which discloses the character's thoughts and gives insight into his personality, needs special attension. When you read a soliloquy aloud, you should realize that it is a very subjective form of speech in which the character is speaking to himself. The character does not address a listener directly but is overheard by him and, consequently, he does not attempt to have direct eye contact with a listener. He is thinking aloud and will lose any artificiality that he may ordinarily have when talking to other people. Therefore, when you read a soliloquy aloud it is important to remember that it is an inner revelation of a character's thoughts which requires a reflective quality of expression.

In *Julius Caesar,* Brutus gives you and your listener insight into his own character as well as his impression of Caesar in the following soliloquy. Although Brutus loves Caesar he indicates the possible dangers of Caesar's growing power and seeks a means to avert disaster.

It must be by his death and for my part
I know no personal cause to spurn at him,
But for the general. He would be crowned.
How that might change his nature, there's the question.
It is the bright day that brings forth the adder,
And that craves wary walking. Crown him?—That—
And then, I grant, we put a sting in him,
That at his will he may do danger with.
The abuse of greatness is when it disjoins
Remorse from power; and to speak truth of Caesar,
I have not known when his affections swayed
More than his reason. But 'tis a common proof
That lowliness is young ambition's ladder,
Whereto the climber—upwards turns his face.
But when he once attains the upmost round,
He then unto the ladder turns his back,
Looks in the clouds, scorning the base degrees
By which he did ascend. So Caesar may.
Then, lest he may, prevent. . . .

(*Julius Caesar,* Act II, Sc i)

Although insight into a personality can be gained through social discourse, bearing and action, and the soliloquy, the interpreter should seek out those cues of motivation which will help him to determine the character's involvement in the total drama. What induces or motivates a character to act as he does? What causes him to speak and respond as he does? Finding the answers to these questions does much toward discovering the character's "raison d'etre." A searching of the text will provide you with a character's degree of involvement. Macbeth was motivated by ambition, Mio in *Winterset* by a sense of revenge and conviction, Dr. Stockmann in *An Enemy of the People* by a cause. Each involvement affected the character's relationship with and attitude toward the other characters in the play. Motivation or inner urge to reach a goal is a means of evaluating and revealing a character.

C. *Dialogue*

Dialogue is so closely related to action and character that it is difficult to separate them, however, a few observations on its functions and problems in reading it aloud may be helpful to you.

1. *Functions.* One of the major functions of dialogue is *exposition.* If one were to give a label to this, it might be tagged as the "informative language" of the characters. Dialogue can introduce the characters of the play, give one a hint as to the condition or situation in which they find themselves and sometimes indicate time and place. Notice this carefully executed conversation which mentions the locale, names and describes the characters, and indicates the situation in which they are involved.

Bassanio. In Belmont is a lady richly left,
And she is fair and, fairer than that word,
Of wondrous virtues. Sometimes from her eyes
I did receive fair speechless messages.
Her name is Portia, nothing undervalued
To Cato's daughter, Brutus' Portia.
Nor is the wide world ignorant of her worth,
For the four winds blow in from every coast
Renownèd suitors. And her sunny locks
Hang on her temples like a golden fleece,
Which make her seat of Belmont Colchos' strand,

And many Jasons come in quest of her.
O my Antonio, had I but the means
To hold a rival place with one of them,
I have a mind presages me such thrift,
That I should questionless be fortunate!

Antonio. Thou know'st that all my fortunes are at sea,
Neither have I money nor commodity
To raise a present sum. . . .

(*The Merchant of Venice,* Act I, Sc i)

It was Carlyle who once said, "The kind of speech in a man betokens the kind of action you will get from him." This then, is the second function of dialogue—to *develop action.* Notice, in the following dialogue how the action is moved forward in the words of Lady Macbeth when she greets Macbeth.

Lady Macbeth. Great Glamis! Worthy Cawdor!
Greater than both, by the all-hail hereafter!
Thy letters have transported me beyond
This ignorant present, and I feel now
The future in the instant.

Macbeth. My dearest love,
Duncan comes here tonight.

Lady Macbeth. And when goes hence?

Macbeth. Tomorrow, as he purposes.

Lady Macbeth. Oh, never
Shall sun that morrow see!
Your face, my Thane, is as a book where men
May read strange matters. To beguile the time,
Look like the time, bear welcome in your eye,
Your hand, your tongue. Look like the innocent flower
But be the serpent under 't. He that's coming
Must be provided for. And you shall put
This night's great business into my dispatch,
Which shall to all our nights and days to come
Give solely sovereign sway and masterdom.

Macbeth. We will speak further.
Lady Macbeth. Only look up clear.
To alter favor ever is to fear.
Leave all the rest to me.

(*Macbeth,* Act I, Sc v)

Likewise, the significant dialogue between Friar Laurence and Romeo literally points the direction that the plot of *Romeo and Juliet* will take.

Friar. Be plain, good son, and homely in thy drift.
Riddling confession finds but riddling shrift.
Romeo. Then plainly know my heart's dear love is set
On the fair daughter of rich Capulet.
As mine on hers, so hers is set on mine,
And all combin'd, save what thou must combine
By holy marriage. When, and where, and how,
We met, we wooed and made exchange of vow,
I'll tell thee as we pass; but this I pray,
That thou consent to marry us today.
Friar. Holy Saint Francis, what a change is here!
Is Rosaline, that thou didst love so dear,
So soon forsaken? . . .
Romeo. Thou chid'st me oft for loving Rosaline.
Friar. For doting, not for loving, pupil mine.
Romeo. And bad'st me bury love.
Friar. Not in a grave
To lay one in, another out to have.
Romeo. I pray thee, chide not. She whom I love now
Doth grace for grace and love for love allow.
The other did not so.
Friar. Oh, she knew well
Thy love did read by rote and could not spell.
But come, young waverer, come, go with me,
In one respect I'll thy assistant be;
For this alliance may so happy prove,
To turn your household's rancor to pure love.

Romeo. Oh, let us hence. I stand on sudden haste.
Friar. Wisely and slow. They stumble that run fast.

(Act II, Sc iii)

Ben Jonson said, "Language most shows a man: speak that I may see thee." Language is the playwright's means of giving *dimension to his characters* and it should be unique to each. This harmony or unity between the character and his language is necessary if the character is to be plausible and believable. The dramatist must "hear" his own characters when he writes, and he must make every attempt to provide each with a language that makes him intelligible and convincing as a person. He assigns their speech so that they may be seen. To do this he gives careful consideration to choice of words, idioms, and verbal devices that help to develop and sustain a personality. In turn, the oral interpreter can profit by bearing them in mind as he studies the play.

There is every reason to believe that Richard Brinsley Sheridan "heard" Mrs. Malaprop as he penned her lines for *The Rivals*. Note how the language harmonizes with and unifies her personality. Her affected use and misuse of the language give indications of her personality.

MRS. MALAPROP: Observe me, Sir Anthony. I would by no means wish a daughter of mine to be a progeny of learning; I don't think so much learning becomes a young woman; for instance, I would never let her meddle with Greek, or Hebrew, or algebra, or simony, or fluxions, or paradoxes, or such inflammatory branches of learning—neither would it be necessary for her to handle any of your mathematical, astronomical, diabolical instruments.—But, Sir Anthony, I would send her, at nine years old to a boarding-school, in order to learn a little ingenuity and artifice. Then, sir, she should have a supercilious knowledge in account;—and as she grew up, I would have her instructed in geometry, that she might know something of the contagious countries;—but above all, Sir Anthony, she should be mistress of orthodoxy, that she might not misspell and mispronounce words so shamefully as girls usually do; and likewise that she might reprehend the true meaning of what she is saying. This, Sir Anthony, is what I would have a woman know;—and I don't think there is a superstitious article in it.

J. M. Synge brings his characters, in *Riders to the Sea,* to life partly through colorful dialect and the rhythm of their speech. As you read Maurya's speech listen to its poetic quality. Maurya has just sprinkled the Holy Water over Bartley.

MAURYA. It isn't that I haven't prayed for you, Bartley, to the Almighty God. It isn't that I haven't said prayers in the dark night till you wouldn't know what I'd be saying; but it's a great rest I'll have now, and it's time surely. It's a great rest I'll have now, and great sleeping in the long nights after Samhain, if it's only a bit of wet flour we do have to eat, and maybe a fish that would be stinking.

The short, terse staccato lines of Macbeth and Lady Macbeth reveal their tension and suspense when they are under stress. We "see" them through this sharp and curt dialogue.

Macbeth. I have done the deed. Dids't thou not hear a noise?
Lady Macbeth. I heard the owl scream and the crickets cry. Did not you speak?
Macbeth. When?
Lady Macbeth. Now.
Macbeth. As I descended?
Lady Macbeth. Ay.
Macbeth. Hark! Who lies i' the second chamber?
Lady Macbeth. Donalbain.

(*Macbeth,* Act II, Sc ii)

In *Richard II,* Shakespeare's imagery, through metaphorical language, helps to characterize the patriotic Gaunt. As he waits for King Richard II, feeling compulsion to speak of his beloved native country, he says:

This royal throne of kings, this scepter'd isle,
This earth of majesty, this seat of Mars,
This other Eden, demi-Paradise,
This fortress built by Nature for herself

Against infection and the hand of war,
This happy breed of men, this little world,
This precious stone set in the silver sea,
Which serves it in the office of a wall
Or as a moat defensive to a house,
Against the envy of less happier lands—
This blessed plot, this earth, this realm, this England,
This nurse, this teeming womb of royal kings,
Feared by their breed and famous by their birth,
Renowned for their deeds as far from home,
For Christian service and true chivalry,
As in the sepulchre in stubborn Jewry
Of the world's ransom, blessed Mary's Son—
This land of such dear souls, this dear dear land,
Dear for her reputation through the world,
Is not leased out, I die pronouncing it,
Like to a tenement or pelting farm.
England, bound in with the triumphant sea,
Whose rocky shore beats back the envious siege
Of watery Neptune, is now bound in with shame,
With inky blots and rotten parchment bonds.
That England, that was wont to conquer others,
Hath made a shameful conquest of itself.
Ah, would the scandal vanish with my life,
How happy then were my ensuing death!

(*Richard II,* Act II, Sc i)

A classic example of verbal imagery is given to us by Edmond Rostand in his *Cyrano de Bergerac.* Cyrano's eloquent description of his own nose is truly in character, for it reveals a "touch of the poet" that springs from the emotion of a sensitive individual.

Ah no! young blade! That was a trifle short!
You might have said at least a hundred things
By varying the tone, . . . like this, suppose, . . .
Aggressive: "Sir, if I had such a nose
I'd amputate it!" Friendly: "When you sup

It must annoy you, dipping in your cup;
You need a drinking-bowl of special shape!"
Descriptive: " 'Tis a rock! . . . a peak! . . . a cape!
A cape, forsooth! 'Tis a peninsular!"
Curious: "How serves that oblong capsular?
For scissor-sheath? or pot to hold your ink?"
Gracious: "You love the little birds, I think?
To find their tiny claws a roomy perch!"
Truculent: "When you smoke your pipe . . . suppose
That the tobacco-smoke spouts from your nose,—
Do not the neighbors, as the fumes rise higher,
Cry terror-struck: The chimney is afire!?"
Considerate: "Take care, . . . your head bowed low
By such a weight . . . lest head o'er heels you go!"
Tender: "Pray get a small umbrella made,
Lest its bright color in the sun should fade!"

(Act I, Sc iv)

Having gained some insight into a few literary devices that dramatists have used to "verbally paint" a character's portrait at a particular moment in the play, now turn to the "Requiem" of *Death of a Salesman* and the last twenty speeches of Scene V in *Saint Joan*. There you will find typical dialogue that reveals each character. How the dramatists, Arthur Miller and George Bernard Shaw, have achieved this is for you to discover. And if one or more of their devices make such an impact on you that you "see" the character, sense the atmosphere, and catch the attitude, then "play them up," but remember that in actual performance the devices are synthesized and should not be obviously apparent. They are provided by the dramatist to "show the man" through his language.

2. *Problems in Reading.* The dramatist uses dialogue as his chief vehicle to convey an experience. Your task, as an interpreter, is to activate the dialogue through vocal and physical suggestion. There are, however, certain problems in reading dialogue aloud.

The first of these is how much physical action you may use in suggesting a character. It is suggested that you start out with more and broader action than is needed, for this will give you the range and possibilities for interpreting the character. If you are too restrained or inhibited, this practice in the preliminary use of broad action may help you to respond physically as well as to stimulate your imagination. Restraint should not be exercised until your potential range of responsiveness has been explored. After you have a kinesthetic response to the character, and know how he moves, sits, stands and handles objects, then allow the realistic details to be refined to the point of significant *suggestion* and use suggestion rather than literal action.

The interpreter does not act out the role of each character when actually presenting the play. But this is not to say that you will have no bodily response. The actor is free to use his entire body in such a way as to represent Julius Caesar, Willy Loman, Amanda Wingfield, or Nora Helmer. But you as an interpreter, cannot move around so extensively or so literally. Your responsiveness should *suggest* rather than represent. While you read the words of Caesar, Willy, Amanda, or Nora, your attitude, projected through stance and suggested action, can reveal a strong empathic response to the characters.

A second problem is where you, the interpreter, should "place" your characters. An actor becomes the character and locates himself within the environment of the literary experience. This experience is usually on-stage. As a result the actor's focus is on-stage, in front of the listeners. The interpreter does not become the character and, consequently, does not locate himself within the environment of the literary experience. In oral interpretation, the environment of the literary experience is located in the realm of the audience—in the imagination of the listener. As a result, the interpreter's focus is off-stage into the realm of the audience. When you read you do not have another visible person to whom you direct your remarks; rather, you talk to an imaginary character somewhere in the realm of the audience. You contact him in your imagination; you *imagine* that you see him. Through eye contact you indicate where this character is located. Such an imaginative process helps your audience visualize a character's position.

When several characters speak you do not necessarily place one of them to the right side of the audience and one to the left. This may be done if it is essential to listener understanding. But when you feel that your listener has clearly differentiated between the characters in the literary experience, your focus may become more general. Basically it is not the placement of the characters, but rather your *understanding* of them as reflected in your vocal and physical responsiveness that makes each a distinct personality.

Another problem is to determine who is speaking and to whom the speech is directed. You should make each character so distinct that he cannot be confused with others. It may be of help to your listener if, early in the dialogue, you insert the name of the person to whom a speech is addressed particularly when the character makes his entrance. Often the dramatist does this for you such as in these lines:

> *Lane.* Lady Bracknell and Miss Fairfax. [Algernon *goes forward to meet them. Enter* Lady Bracknell *and* Gwendolen.]
>
> *Lady Bracknell.* Good afternoon, dear Algernon. I hope you are behaving very well.
>
> *Algernon.* I'm feeling very well, Aunt Augusta.
>
> *Lady Bracknell.* That's not quite the same thing. In fact the two things rarely go together. [*Sees* Jack *and bows to him with icy coldness.*]
>
> *Algernon.* [*To* Gwendolen]. Dear me, you are smart!
>
> *Jack.* You're quite perfect, Miss Fairfax.
>
> *Gwendolen.* Oh! I hope I am not that. It would leave no room for developments, and I intend to develop in many directions. [Gwendolen *and* Jack *sit down together in the corner.*]
>
> *Lady Bracknell.* I'm sorry if we are a little late, Algernon, but I was obliged to call on dear Lady Harbury. I hadn't been there since her poor husband's death. I never saw a woman so altered; she looks quite twenty years younger. And now I'll have a cup of tea, and one of those nice cucumber sandwiches you promised me.
>
> *Algernon.* Certainly, Aunt Augusta.
>
> (Oscar Wilde, *The Importance of Being Earnest,* Act I.)

3. *Dramatist's Directives for Line Reading.* One of the means by which the dramatist sometimes helps you in interpreting dialogue is to implant within the dialogue itself a directive for speaking a line. Here is an example from Ibsen's *Hedda Gabler:*

Tesman: Oh, I almost think I understand you, Hedda! Great Heavens! Do you really mean it! Eh?
Hedda: Don't shout so. The servant might hear.

(*Hedda Gabler,* Act IV.)

This line of Hedda's indicates how Tesman has spoken and is a directive for interpreting the line. Oh the other hand, the dramatist may merely imply or subtly suggest a way to read a line. Shakespeare hints at this in the context of this passage:

Hamlet: Why, right! You are in the right!
And so, without more circumstance at all,
I hold it fit that we shake hands and part;
You, as your business and desires shall point you,
For every man hath business and desire,
Such as it is; and for my own poor part,
Look you, I'll go pray.
Horatio: These are but wild and whirling words, my lord.
Hamlet: I am sorry they offend you, heartily; Yes, faith, heartily.
Horatio: There's no offense, my lord.

(*Hamlet,* Act I, Sc v)

Robert Sherwood, in his play *Abe Lincoln in Illinois,* has Mentor Graham, a teacher, tell Abe how he erroneously read a speech of Webster's and then how he should read the lines.

Mentor [*reaching for a newspaper in mess on table*]: I want you to read this—it's a speech delivered by Mr. Webster before the United States Senate. A fine document, and a perfect usage of the Imperative Mood in its hortatory sense. Here it is. Read this—down here. [*He leans back to listen.*]
Abe [*takes paper, leans forward into the light and reads*]: "Sir," the Senator continued, in the rich deep tones of the historic church bells of his native Boston, "Sir—I have not allowed myself to look beyond the Union, to see what might be hidden in the dark recess behind. While the Union lasts . . ." [Abe *has been reading in a montone, without inflection.*]

> *Mentor* (*testily*): Don't read it off as if it were an inventory of Denton Offut's groceries. Imagine that *you're* making the speech before the Senate, with the fate of your country at stake. Put your own life into it!
>
> *Abe:* I couldn't use words as long as Dan'l Webster.
>
> *Mentor:* That's what you're here for—to learn! Go ahead.
>
> (Act I, Sc i)

In this illustration Robert Sherwood not only openly tells the interpreter, through the speeches of Graham, how to speak the lines, but he further provides the interpreter with a suggestion of how he, Sherwood, through his bracketed reading guide, wants the young Lincoln to read the lines.

In considering carefully the dramatist's directives for reading or delivering lines, you should avoid the Plutarchian criticism, "You speak the things you should speak but you speak them not in the manner they should be spoken." You must allow nothing to interfere with the intent of the literature in your primary function of inciting the listener to create image after image in his own mind.

D. *Spectacle*

The dramatist is usually aware of the type of stage and style of scenery he wants as well as the colors he envisions and the emotional quality that these can express. Henry Irving, the actor, in an address to the students of Harvard University, cautioned the managers of theatres to be discreet in the use of materials:

> Music, painting, architecture, the endless variations of costume, have all to be employed with a strict regard to production of an artistic whole, in which no element shall be unduly obtrusive.

There is little else to say except that the visual side does add its part to the projection of the meaning. In reading drama you, of course, do not have at your command the actual materials of the stage that Irving mentioned. You will not dress as a certain character, nor will you use stage properties. These materials need to be *imagined* by the interpreter and his listener. You may, however, find it meaningful to describe dress, properties, and setting in your introduction to the act or episode you are to read.

II. ANALYSIS OF A SCENE

In analyzing a scene from a play for reading aloud, the oral interpreter should seek out those dramatic elements of structure that will help him to understand more fully the play and the playwright, as well as those elements that normally elicit a response from a listener. With these as rational bases let us examine Scene II of Tennessee Williams' the *Glass Menagerie,* the Rubicam Business College episode (such a title is appropriate because the play itself is episodic in nature). This analysis is intended to be indicative but not definitive.

The situation is as follows. Amanda is seen returning to the apartment in the late afternoon, as Laura polishes her collection of glass, a symbol of her unrealistic and private world. Laura quickly puts away her ornaments when she hears her mother's footsteps. Amanda enters and after uttering her insinuating words, "Deception? Deception?", which set the tone for much of the episode, she removes from the wall and tears up the diagram of a typewriter keyboard, as well as a chart of the Gregg Alphabet, symbols of a realistic world. There follows the startling disclosure as to why Laura has not been attending her classes at Rubicam's Business College. Laura has spent her days walking, going to the movies, and visiting places, such as the art museum and the zoo. Amanda, desperately aware that she has been deceived by Laura, now shows her anxious concern over Laura's impending future as an unmarried woman. Amanda brings up the subject of a boy, any boy, that Laura might have liked. Amanda earnestly hopes that this might lead to a possible suitor and eventually to marriage. The scene ends with Amanda glossing over the fact that Laura is a cripple and urges her to develop charm in spite of her slight handicap.

In this episode we have not only external conflict of personal objectives, but conflict within the characters themselves. Amanda wants security for her children in a realistic world, and Laura wants to be left alone in her private world. As an interpreter of drama, you should never underestimate the instinctive interest that conflict has for a listener, for through his imagination he becomes an actual participant and attentive spectator.

As a scene this presents only one crisis in a series of crises within the play. The characters' involvement over Laura's attending business college, and her future life of possible dependency, momentarily, is resolved by Amanda's climactic idea that, "Girls that aren't cut out for business careers usually wind up married to some nice man. Sister, that's what you'll do." A statement which in itself reflects the lack of realism in Amanda's own thinking.

Symbolism within this episode has been previously referred to, and as for irony, it is apparent. We first sense it when Amanda talks about her inability to find strength to continue, yet throughout her dialogue she gives no indication of this loss of strength. In fact, you are more convinced of her vitality and strength. In the context of the entire play there is irony in Amanda's solution to Laura's situation. In spite of Amanda's suggestion (in this scene) that Laura must have vivacity and charm, Laura's attempt at charming the "gentleman caller" comes to nothing.

As you read the scene and think about it, you are cognizant, no doubt, of the realistic language blended with the poetic. One might call it poetic-realism. Concisely stated, it is writing wherein the characters are sharply portrayed, framed in an episode of family life, highlighted by emotional frustration, and placed within the poetic environment apart from the main stream of life in St. Louis.

The realistic dialogue in the scene is evident in Amanda's unsympathizing, voluble, and pointed discourse contrasted with Laura's amiable, informative and direct dialogue. Words and phrases, such as "deception," "bewildered," "shy," "pretending," "disappointed," "painful," "crippled," "sick at the stomach," and "grudging patronage," fill the imaginative mind of the listener and help to figuratively sketch a portrait of the characters.

Through carefully woven and well integrated dialogue and revealing stage directions, as well as the strained and precarious situation that Williams brings to view, there emerges a frustrated, pathetic, domineering, tender, Southern lady-like Amanda and a shy, frightened, apologetic, sensitive, world-removed Laura.

It is interesting to note that the dialogue in this episode is biographical in respect to Laura's character. This is presented in a sequence of short and long speeches. The long speeches for the most part are in touching narrative style which provide the interpreter with an added challenge of interpretation. They are not monotonic nor monorhythmic speeches, but rather challenge the reader to recreate the numerous changes of tempo and attitude during Amanda's speeches.

The technical mechanics in the scene, such as the screen device, the use of music, and the symbolism might well be presented and discussed in the interpreter's introduction.

The analysis of such a scene as this is not only a key to understanding, but it provides a basis for the interpreter for making his judgments, as well as reinforcing his interpretation.

III. THE CHALLENGE OF SCENE SELECTION AND CUTTING

A. *Obligations*

The oral interpreter of drama has fundamental obligations to the dramatist and to himself, which cannot be ignored. A brief review of these obligations will point up the challenge that the reading aloud of drama has for the interpreter.

A contractual obligation is assumed between the playwright and the interpreter when the latter chooses to read drama. Contractual in the sense that the former has provided the property, and the latter has obligated himself to transmit it to the advantage of both parties involved. The playwright's property is his play which is representative of how he sees life, which has been molded into a certain literary form, which has been carefully structured, and which has an aesthetic mode. To fulfill his contractual obligation the interpreter should not violate the intent of that property, should make a careful study and analysis of the play, and for reading aloud should make every effort in his cutting of it and not forfeit the values of the play. All of which challenge his understanding and interpretative ability as an artist.

A personal obligation is placed on the interpreter when he assumes the responsibility for the exercise of high moral and intellectual standards both in the choice of his play, or a scene from it, and in its interpretation. The interpreter should never cheapen his art, his audience, or himself by imposing shoddy reading matter or performance. The individual member of the audience may read privately whatever his personal tastes dictate but when he becomes a part of an audience, the responsibility for the selection of the play, or a scene from it, becomes that of the interpreter. Likewise, the interpreter as an individual may read for himself whatever his personal tastes dictate, but when he takes on the responsibility of an audience, he must become objective in his approach to his public reading.

Because the interpreter as an artist properly thrives on favorable audience reaction and enjoys the spotlight of unusual accomplishment, he should make every effort to select a play which reveals his best self and to which the audience can respond with propriety. In order to meet this challenge, he would be wise to weigh the personal and situational factors which face the interpreter and his concern for his audience.

B. *Factors of Selection*

The matter of taste is a significant factor in choosing a play or scene. Your choice reflects your taste, and therefore it is essential to be as discriminating as possible. Although today we are inclined to be more candid and less reticent toward licentiousness, the interpreter needs to bear in mind that he usually has a captive and critical audience and may find himself being criticized by his fellow classmates and his listeners for using questionable material. A suppression or the open expression of such depends upon your moral and artistic tastes as well as those of the audience. The interpreter at all times needs the respect of his audience and he is obliged to maintain at least as high a standard as his listeners. If he violates his own accepted standards or those of his audience, he should reevaluate his choice. Neither the interpreter nor his audience wish to be labeled as "prudish," but the strict adherence to the accepted standards of good taste should be a positive formula to be used.

A determining factor in selecting a play or scene is whether it is worth the reader's time and effort. The well prepared interpreter will spend a substantial amount of time in studying the play both silently and orally before presenting it to his listening audience. His decision is reached not after a quick and superficial reading, but after a substantial number of readings. It is possible that a scene that he does not like at all on a first or successive reading might become a highly favored one. On the other hand, if the scene is assigned by the instructor, the interpreter may study it thoroughly, and in the inductive process, he may learn to like it and recognize its potential for effective communication. Indeed, it may be assigned to him by his instructor as a direct and provocative challenge which he needs.

An interpreter's vocal characteristics, abilities and skills are fundamental factors in making his selection. A girl with a toneless, flute-like, or seraphic voice might find great difficulty in reading the wedge-shaped and biting dialogue of Lillian Hellman, the rhythmic prose of Tennessee Williams, or the conversational quality of Anton Chekhov. And a young man with a blatant, discordant, or metallic voice might discover that the lyrical and visionary words of William Shakespeare, Henrik Ibsen or Dylan Thomas might prove equally difficult.

As a reader develops vocal range and insight he has greater latitude in his choices. However, if the necessary emotional quality for the scene is projected in an artificial or excessive manner, the latitude will be diminished. Should the emotional attainment of the scene be beyond the interpreter's experience his choice may be restricted, but he should accept the challenge to grow.

An unquestioned factor in selecting a scene is how well you identify with the character's thought, or situation. The identification factor in selecting a scene emerges more strongly if you are attracted or repelled by the "personal magnetism" of the character, if the playwright has given you a unique and concrete verbalization of the character's imaginative or realistic mind, and if he and his character have stirred within you an association of ideas and feelings.

A situational factor to consider in making a choice is the length of the scene. Is it too long or too short to meet the time limit requirement furnished by the instructor or by the members of the class? If it is too long, can the selection be cut effectively without destroying the essence of the meaning? In planning to read before a civic organization certainly the time element is important to your listeners because of the official commitments they have made and must meet.

Another important matter is the number of characters in the scene. Practical wisdom warns against getting involved with too many characters. Three might be sufficient, in fact, even two might be quite enough to handle. It will be helpful if the playwright has characters, within the scene, who are somewhat in contrast to each other in age, background, personality traits, or speech.

A final factor for the interpreter to take into account is whether or not the scene that he presents has an instinctive sense of completeness which gives a feeling of unity to the listener. An episode, incident, or action which is complete in itself, and which leaves, at best, a vivid impression, and which, at least, creates an earnest desire in the listener to read the complete play deserves respectful consideration.

C. *Cutting*

In cutting a scene one should keep in mind the obligations and factors previously mentioned. They are, in fact, the broad guide lines for cutting. There are, however, specific directives that are helpful. They are: (1) Cut from your script the playwright's acting and reading suggestions, the descriptions of the setting and costumes, and the expositions of the staging. But use these omissions that you make as a means of analyzing and understanding the scene. And if certain ones seem necessary for the communication of the scene, rephrase the playwright's ideas and express them informally. (2) Characters that do not contribute to the forward movement of the scene, nor have a strong impact upon the characters within the scene, nor on the audience, can be cut. If the "butcher, baker, and candlestick maker" seem essential, it is possible that they may be incorporated into the dialogue of the major characters who carry the scene in order to make the progression of the ideas comprehensible to the audience. (3) If the scene begins by referring to or is a restatement of what has previously happened, it is strongly advisable to cut this information and include it in your personal introduction to the scene. Perhaps the motivation for this, on the part of the interpreter, is to get into the dialogue quickly so that it engrosses the listener in the dramatic situation. (4) Cut those parts that depend strongly upon extensive stage business for effectiveness.

Here is a final word to the interpreter regarding the cutting of a scene. Although the broad guide lines and specific directives are representative of observations made in the classroom and have proved to be helpful, the greatest guide line to cutting is *experience*. The more you practice it and test it the easier it is to do and the more competent and effective you become.

Fifty Suggested Episodes or Segments

PLAY	*AUTHOR*	*CHARACTER*	*IDENTIFICATION*
Admirable Crichton, The	Barrie, J. M.	Crichton, Lady Mary	Declaration of Love
Ah, Wilderness!	O'Neill, Eugene	Muriel, Richard	The Beach Scene
All My Sons	Miller, Arthur	Kate, Joe	Consequence of the faulty material repercussion
Anastasia	Bolton, Guy	Anna, Empress	The Interview
Arsenic & Old Lace	Kesselring, Joseph	Mortimer, Abby, Martha	Mortimer discovers their secret
Bad Seed, The	Anderson, Maxwell	Rhoda, Christine	Christine's discovery
Barretts of Wimpole Street, The	Besier, Rudolf	Bella, Bevan, Eliz, Henrietta, Octavius	Bella's visit
Billy Budd	Coxe, Louis, and Chapman, Robert	Billy, Claggart	Topside Conversation
Browning Version, The	Rattigan, Terence	Taplow, Frank	Meeting & discussion of "remove"
Corn is Green, The	Williams, Emlyn	The Squire, Miss Moffat	Miss Moffat seeks the squire's advice
Corn is Green, The	Williams, Emlyn	Morgan, Miss Moffat	The Morgan Essay
Crucible, The	Miller, Arthur	Danforth, Proctor, Hale, Elizabeth	The Confession
Death of a Salesman	Miller, Arthur	Willy, Howard	Seeking home office job but fired

Death of a Salesman	Miller, Arthur	Linda, Willy	Opening scene
Death of a Salesman	Miller, Arthur	Charley, Biff, Linda, Happy	The Requiem
Desire Under the Elms	O'Neill, Eugene	Abbie, Ephraim	Their son and the future
Diary of Anne Frank, The	Goodrich, Frances and Hackett, Albert	Anne, Peter	Peter's admiration and gratitude
Ethan Frome	Davis, Owen & Davis, Donald	Zeena, Ethan, Mattie	Morning after the church sociable
Ethan Frome	Davis, Owen & Davis, Donald	Mattie, Ethan	On crest of the hill
Glass Menagerie, The	Williams, Tennessee	Amanda, Laura	Rubicam's Business College
Glass Menagerie, The	Williams, Tennessee	Jim, Laura	Gentleman caller
Glass Menagerie, The	Williams, Tennessee	Tom, Amanda	Argument scene
Green Pastures	Connelly, Marc	God, Noah, Noah's wife	Lord visits Noah
Harvey	Chase, Mary Coyle	Veta, Dr. Sanderson	Committing Elwood
Inherit the Wind	Lawrence, Jerome and Lee, Robert E.	Brady, Drummond, Judge	Brady testifies and is questioned
I Remember Mama	van Druten, John	Mama, Katrin	A special treat—an ice cream soda
I Remember Mama	van Druten, John	Mama, Miss Moorhead	Unpublished ms and recipes
J. B.	MacLeish, Archibald	Zuss, Nickles	Casting the roles

Fifty Suggested Episodes or Segments (*Continued*)

PLAY	*AUTHOR*	*CHARACTER*	*IDENTIFICATION*
Lady's Not For Burning, The	Fry, Christopher	Mayor Tyson, Thomas, Jennet	Jennet accused
Lady's Not For Burning, The	Fry, Christopher	Girl, Soldier	Discussion of life and people
Life with Father	Lindsay, Howard and Crouse, Russel	Father, Vinnie	Vinnie's accounts
Long Day's Journey Into Night	O'Neill, Eugene	James, Edmond	Confrontation scene
Mary of Scotland	Anderson, Maxwell	Mary, Elizabeth	Carlisle Castle meeting of Mary and Elizabeth
Member of the Wedding, The	McCullers, Carson	Berenice & Frankie	Frankie's obsession and her knife throwing
Miracle Worker, The	Gibson, William	Annie, Kate, Keller, James, Helen	Homecoming party
Miss Julie	Strindberg, August	Jean, Julie	The meeting of two worlds
Mourning Becomes Electra	O'Neill, Eugene	Christine, Adam Brant	Christine's power over Brant
Mr. Roberts	Heggen, Thomas & Logan, Joshua	Roberts, Captain	Confrontation scene
My Fair Lady	Lerner, Alan J. and Frederick Lowe (Based on Pygmalion by G. B. Shaw)	Higgins, Eliza, Mrs. Pierce, Pickering	The interview
No Time for Sergeants	Levin, Ira	Will, Psychiatrist	The psychiatrist's test

Old Lady Shows Her Medals, The	Barrie, J. M.	Mrs. Dowey, Kenneth Dowey	The "son" visits
Our Town	Wilder, Thornton	Emily, George, Stage Manager	At the drugstore
Peter Pan	Barrie, J. M.	Peter, Wendy	Wendy meets a stranger
Playboy of the Western World	Synge, John Millington	Christy, Pegeen, Widow	"The curiosity man"
Prologue to Glory	Conkle, E. P.	Ann, Abe	Proposal
Romeo and Juliet	Shakespeare, William	Juliet, Nurse	Juliet tries to get the news
Summer and Smoke	Williams, Tennessee	Alma, John	Youthful flirtation
Teahouse of the August Moon	Patrick, John	Sakini, Colonel Purdy	Laundry survey
Touch of the Poet, A	O'Neill, Eugene	Nora, Sara	Comfort & Anxiety
Winslow Boy, The	Rattigan, Terence	Sir Robert Morton, Ronnie	Sir Robert interrogates Ronnie

IV. SUGGESTED EXCERPTS

These suggested excerpts from plays lend themselves to reading aloud. They vary from two to eight minutes in length so that several may be read during the class hour and still give the instructor and class members time for constructive criticism. The list, it is hoped, will save you time in your search for material, but is by no means a substitute for studying and reading the entire play. Only in a few cases is there any need for a cutting of the suggested episode. In compiling this list the major objective has been to provide the student with a dramatic motivated unit of thought for oral communication.

STUDY QUESTIONS

1. How did Leland Powers' method of presenting a play to an audience differ from the method advocated by the authors of your text?
2. Look at the opening or introduction of a play by James Barrie, George B. Shaw, or Tennessee Williams. How can this be an aid to the oral interpreter?
3. What is "personation?" "Impersonation?" What can the oral interpreter learn from these methods of portrayal that will help him in his characterization?
4. Should an oral interpreter lose his own identity in creating a character of a scene?
5. How does an oral interpreter gain insight into a character?
6. As an interpreter how would you project a sense impression to an audience, such as the odor of burned meat, a vivid sky, the turn of a key in the door, accepting a thorny rose, tasting a lemon?
7. How does an oral interpreter communicate to an audience an aside, a soliloquy, or stream-of-consciousness line?
8. Distinguish between timing and tempo in drama. What is meant by rhythm in a drama?
9. How did King Lear, Romeo, Uncle Vanya, or Tom Wingfield

create atmosphere within the framework of a scene? How does the oral interpreter recreate this atmosphere?

10. Does there need to be a more controlled sense of performance in the interpretation of drama than in other literary forms? Why?

11. What obligations does an oral interpreter have toward the playwright, the audience and himself?

12. What do you consider to be the two most important factors for you in cutting a scene for reading aloud?

BIBLIOGRAPHY

Albright, H. D., William P. Halstead, Lee Mitchell, *Principles of Theatre Art* (Chap. 5. "Language.") Boston: Houghton Mifflin Company, 1955.

Brustein, Robert, *The Theatre of Revolt.* Boston: Little, Brown and Company, 1964. (Modern drama from Ibsen to Genet is treated by the author as an expression of revolt.)

Canfield, Curtis, *The Craft of Play Directing.* New York: Holt, Rinehart and Winston, Inc., 1963. (Chap. 9. "Cutting, Casting, First Reading.") (Section on cutting helpful to oral interpreter.)

Dietrich, John E., *Play Directing.* Englewood Cliffs: Prentice-Hall, Inc., 1953. (Chapter 2. "Drama and Human Conflict.")

Gagey, Edmond M., *Revolution in American Drama.* New York: Columbia University Press, 1947. (Chap. 4. "Poetry and Imagination.")

Lawson, John Howard, *Theory and Technique of Playwriting.* New York: G. P. Putnam's Sons, 1936. (Part I. History of Dramatic Thought.)

Marx, Milton, *The Enjoyment of Drama* (2nd edit.). New York: Appleton-Century-Crofts, Inc., 1961.

Millett, Fred and Gerald Eades Bentley, *The Art of Drama.* New York: D. Appleton-Century Company, Inc., 1935. (Part II. Dramatic Modes and Values.)

Rowe, Kenneth T., *A Theatre in Your Head.* New York: Funk and Wagnalls Company, 1960. (Chap. 6. "The Meaning of a Play.")

Steffenson, James L. Jr., editor, *Great Scenes from the World Theatre.* New York: Avon Books, a Division of The Hearst Corporation, 1965. (Approximately 70 scenes with introduction.—In the words of the editor it is "a workbook, a compendium—a carefully selected grab bag, if you like—of projects for students and instructors. . . .")

Strickland, F. Cowles, *The Technique of Acting*. New York: McGraw-Hill Book Company, Inc., 1956. (Chap. 1. "The Nature of Technique.")

Willis, Edgar E., *Writing Television and Radio Programs*. New York: Holt, Rinehart and Winston, 1967. (Scripts: "The Fugitive" and "The Dick VanDyke Show.")

Wright, Edward A., *Understanding Today's Theatre*. Englewood Cliffs: Prentice-Hall, Inc. A Spectrum Book, 1959. (Chap. 6. "The Audience and Dramatic Criticism.")

Chapter XI

The Oral Interpretation of Humor— The Comic Spirit

The oral interpreter, through humor, can help man to see his own faults and those of the world around him. Humor is frequently a means of individual and social evaluation. The word *humor* has several meanings. If you are disgruntled, you say that you are in a "bad humor"; if you are happy, you are in a "good humor." It comes from the Greek word *hygros,* meaning "moist": in this chapter you will learn something about "humorous" or "moist" literature; in other words, literature that is not dry, from the viewpoint of the interpreter.

In this chapter two aspects of humor are discussed; namely, the bodily and vocal aspects of reading it aloud, and the types of humor found in literature.

Comedy is brought to life through your suggestions and the responsiveness of the listener, so it will help if you have someone listen to you after you have worked on your material. This will give you an idea as to how well you are suggesting the humor.

I. PHYSICAL RESPONSIVENESS

Physical responsiveness helps the reader grasp the humor and, of course, it helps the listener. In reading, as we know, this bodily action will be suggestive rather than literal. The extent and degree to which physical responsiveness is used depends upon the amount or degree of suggestion dictated by the literature. If it is farcical, such as *The Importance of Being Earnest,* it will demand broader bodily response; if it is sophisticated comedy only slight bodily action may be required.

Certain techniques will help you in the oral interpretation of humorous material, such as holding a position when an audience reacts to a humorous line. You may think of holding a position as a "visual pause." This visual pause, this process of temporarily freezing, will reinforce the humor and give the listener an opportunity to enjoy it without being rushed on to a new idea.

Another visual device of help to you is "pointing" a line. In the theatre this is done by the actor looking in the direction of the audience when delivering a line. In reading, of course, you are already looking in the direction of the audience, but you may point by an extra emphasis in bodily action such as possibly raising the eyebrows, shifting the eyes, a lift of the head or a gesture.

Contrast and emphasis in physical responsiveness will also heighten the humor. Sudden relaxation after tension or suspense may strengthen humor as in "The Milksop," where the exuberant and conceited secretary is deflated. The bodily stance and response alter as the emotion or attitude changes. For example, vigorous and aggressive movements suggest strength and conviction, while withdrawing movements suggest weakness and defeat. Contradictions in movement may also suggest humor. If you reverse these and have the frightened and withdrawing character fling a challenge as he retreats, the effect is humorous.

Comedy generally has a faster pace than tragedy. In this respect it exaggerates reality. The reader of comedy must have a basic sense of ease, as opposed to tension, even though he may want to suggest tension in a certain situation.

II. VOCAL RESPONSIVENESS

Humorous effects are obtained vocally through contrasts in the use of pitch, volume, intensity, quality, tempo and diction. When these elements are used in certain proportions in a given situation, they can be comical. Sometimes a specific dominant vocal characteristic in a character will be a source of humor. In *A Midsummer Night's Dream,* each of the craftsmen (Act I, Sc ii) who meet to rehearse the play for the duke can have a distinctively unique voice which in itself is amusing.

Mrs. Malaprop, in *The Rivals,* is an affected woman who wishes to appear very learned and much of this affectation can be conveyed in her extreme ranges of *pitch.* Falstaff, too, depends upon vocal exaggerations, as do Touchstone in *As You Like It,* Madame Arcati, the clairvoyant in *Blithe Spirit,* and the young ladies in Moliere's *Les Precieuses Ridicules.* Perhaps nothing can illustrate the exaggerated use of *volume* in humor better than those inimitable episodes in *Life With Father,* by Clarence Day, for Father, especially when he is excited, always talks in loud tones, which is Mother's signal to close the doors.

A change from one vocal *quality* to another may strengthen the elements of surprise and humor. For example, when the actress, in the play *Personal Appearance* by Lawrence Riley, speaks to her "public," she uses a sweet oral tone, but when she is not on stage her voice is metallic and unpleasant. Likewise a change from a quiet subdued tone to a loud tone and a more rapid tempo reinforces the humor in "The Secret Life of Walter Mitty."

Tempo and rhythm, too, do much to convey humor, just as they help to convey tragedy. Tempo and rhythm are important in the creation of a character like Mad Margaret in Gilbert and Sullivan's *Ruddigore.* Notice the staccotto, broken terse rhythm in these lines:

Enter Mad Margaret. She is wildly dressed in picturesque tatters, and is an obvious caricature of theatrical madness.

SCENA—MARGARET

Cheerily carols the lark
Over the cot.
Merrily whistles the clerk
Scratching a blot.
But the lark,
And the clerk,
I remark,
Comfort me not!

Over the ripening peach
Buzzes the bee.
Splash on the billowy beach
Tumbles the sea.
But the peach
And the beach
They are each
Nothing to me!
And why?
Who am I?
Daft Madge! Crazy Meg!
Mad Margaret! Poor Peg!
He! he! he! he! he!

Mad, I?
Yes, very!
But why?
Mystery!
Don't call!
Whisht! whisht!
No crime—
'Tis only
That I'm
Love-lonely!
That's all!

(*Ruddigore,* Act I)

Just as there is "pointing" of humor in relation to action, there is pointing in relation to voice. In humor this process of pointing is one of several means of emphasizing a word or a line in order to give it special attention. In its broadest use, it may be a strong contrast of vocal quality, pitch, tempo, intensity or volume. If you expect a character to use strong, bombastic tone and he uses instead a weak, quiet tone, the unexpected contrast will point the humor. In Dylan Thomas's "A Child's Christmas in Wales," in the scene where the house has been on fire, the aunt comes into the room and says to the firemen with the grace of a hostess, "Would you like anything to read?" Here the change of tempo that comes with the anti-climax brings the laughter that arises from the unexpected and points the humor.

One of the most important vocal devices for conveying humor is the use of the *pause.* A pause emphasizes the element of surprise so often inherent in humor. Frequently this pause comes before the word or statement that contains the humor. In an essay by Kay Nelson in *Look Magazine,* a fifth grade child wrote of his mother:

> My mother is a very good Mother because she is a good cook and she doesn't blow her stack very often and also she is not mushy, like some Mothers. She does not go around all the time kissing and hugging me or my father or even my little brother. Or anybody else probably.

A pause after "hugging me" and another after "my little brother" and again after "else" will strengthen the humor.

The circumflex inflection, or the dual bending of pitch on a sound, is also used to point humor. This may be used in puns to accentuate the play on the words that sound the same yet imply a different meaning. In *Julius Caesar* (Act I, Sc i), the cobbler uses the pun in the words "soles," "awl," and "recover," giving a double meaning to these words. These words need to be pointed by either the circumflex inflection, a change of pitch, quality, volume, tempo or pause or by a combination of these. In the following scene from *Julius Caesar,* experiment with these techniques to see which will convey the humor most effectively.

Scene i. Rome. A street.
Enter Flavius, Marullus, and certain commoners.
Flavius: Hence! Home, you idle creatures, get you home.
Is this a holiday? What! Know you not,
Being mechanical, you ought not walk
Upon a laboring day without the sign
of your profession? Speak, what trade art thou?
1st Commoner: Why, sir, a carpenter.
Marullus: Where is thy leather apron and thy rule?
What dost thou with thy best apparel on?
You, sir, what trade are you?
2nd Commoner: Truly, sir, in respect of a fine workman, I am but,
as you would say, a cobbler.

Marullus: But what trade art thou? Answer me directly.
2nd Commoner: A trade, sir, that I hope I may use with a safe conscience, which is indeed, sir, a mender of bad soles.
Marullus: What trade, thou knave? Thou
naughty knave, what trade?
2nd Commoner: Nay, I beseech you, sir, be not out with me.
Yet if you be out, sir, I can mend you.
Marullus: What mean'st thou by that? Mend me, thou saucy fellow!
2nd Commoner: Why, sir, cobble you.
Flavius: Thou art a cobbler, art thou?
2nd Commoner: Truly sir, all that I live by is with the
awl. I meddle with no tradesman's matters nor women's matters,
but with all. I am indeed, sir, a surgeon to old
shoes. When they are in great danger, I re-cover
them. As proper men as ever trod upon neat's leather
have gone upon my handiwork.

(*Julius Caesar,* Act I, Sc i)

Often lines are so constructed that the humor comes at or near the end of a speech. In this case the reader may build gradually and steadily and give the humorous phrase more volume or intensity than the preceding part, creating a cumulative effect. In *The Importance of Being Earnest,* by Oscar Wilde, Lady Bracknell interviews Algernon, a suitor for her daughter's hand. At this point she is very clearly informing him that he is no longer in the running.

". . . You can hardly imagine that I and Lord Bracknell would dream of allowing our only daughter—a girl brought up with the utmost care—to marry into a cloakroom, and form an alliance with a parcel. Good morning, Mr. Worthing!" (Act I)

III. ATTITUDE IN READING HUMOR

Usually in reading humor, the situation will seem serious to the characters who find themselves in a distressing plight. In such a case the oral interpreter will not laugh. In the narrative portions of a humorous story, however, which are the link between the literature and the listener, the author often shows his own appreciation of the humor. Such is the case in *The Pickwick Papers,* by Charles Dickens.

When Mr. Pickwick is found by his friends with his arms around Mrs. Bardell, the situation is not at all funny to him, but both Dickens and you, the oral interpreter, view the situation humorously. So, too, in some of the narrative portions of *Tom Sawyer* the author and the oral interpreter are aware of the humor, yet for Tom, Huck, Aunt Polly, and Becky Thatcher the situation is serious. This is frequently true in James Thurber's stories. The author, the interpreter, and the listener are seeing the characters and their problems in a different light than the characters see themselves. You must convey the differences in attitude to clarify the overall viewpoint of the author and the somewhat limited viewpoint of his characters. Yet sometimes we can enjoy the humor with the character as we do in some of the nurse's speeches in *Romeo and Juliet,* in the puns of the shoemaker in *Julius Caesar,* and when George Bernard Shaw says "I often quote myself. It adds spice to my conversation."

IV. THE SOURCES OF HUMOR

A. *The Ridiculous*

Humor, whether in a play, a story, or a poem, often has an element of the ridiculous. Comedy, as Aristotle said, is an imitation of men worse than the average, whose outstanding fault seems ridiculous. This trait is not of the kind that will bring injury, "pain or harm" to other people, but it does bring out that one quality which seems ridiculous. For example, in *The Miser,* Moliere focuses his attention on Harpagon, whose dominant trait is his miserly nature which Moliere presents as ridiculous. In "My Financial Career," Stephen Leacock depicts the shy man who comes to open a bank account, but whose excessive shyness makes him appear ridiculous.

In "The Milksop," Chekhov builds his story around an insecure newspaper clerk, whose vanity and weak character the author ridicules.

And in *The Rivals,* Richard Brinsley Sheridan creates a ridiculous character in the person of Mrs. Malaprop, whose humorous trait is her abuse of the English language, of which, ironically, she prides herself on being an authority, as you have noted in her speech in Chapter X.

When animals are used as characters in literature and speak, dress, and act like human beings, they sometimes appear ridiculous. For example, in *The Wind in the Willows* by Kenneth Grahame, Mr. Toad finds himself in numerous predicaments which from a human standpoint are impossible, and this fact makes them amusing. Yet there is often a basic element of truth underlying the humor.

You may suggest the dominating feature of such characters through *your* attitude toward the character and the foible which makes him ridiculous. All of his lines which reveal the keynote of the ridiculous must be brought into strong focus in your suggestion of the character. If you read *The Miser,* his basic trait, his miserliness, must always permeate his outlook.

The way in which a character dresses may also accentuate the ridiculous. Shakespeare was aware of this when he had Petruchio, in *The Taming of the Shrew,* dress preposterously for his wedding, and again when he had Malvolio "cross-gartered." This, of course, can only come out through the narration or dialogue in reading aloud. Likewise, when a character assumes the role of the opposite sex and tries to speak and act appropriately, one is both amused and in suspense lest the disguise be discovered. Such is your feeling in observing Huck Finn dressed as a girl, Lord Fancourt Babbersly dressed as Charley's Aunt in the Brandon-Thomas play of that title, and Mr. Toad dressed as the old washerwoman.

Vocal quality and *pitch* help bring out the ridiculous in Kenneth Grahame's *The Wind in the Willows.* Mr. Toad uses a thin feeble oral quality to convince people that he is a sick old washerwoman. But, when he reveals his own identity, he completely changes his character, his vocal quality, and the pitch of his voice.

> The terrible motor-car drew slowly nearer and nearer, till at last he heard it stop just short of him. Two gentlemen got out and walked round the trembling heap of crumpled misery lying in the road, and one of them said, 'O dear! this is very sad! Here is a poor old thing—a washerwoman apparently—who has fainted in the

road! Perhaps she is overcome by the heat, poor creature; or possibly she has not had any food to-day. Let us lift her into the car and take her to the nearest village, where doubtless she has friends.'

They tenderly lifted Toad into the motor-car and propped him up with soft cushions, and proceeded on their way.

When Toad heard them talk in so kind and sympathetic a way, and knew that he was not recognized, his courage began to revive, and he cautiously opened first one eye and then the other.

'Look!' said one of the gentlemen, 'she is better already. The fresh air is doing her good. How do you feel now, ma'am?'

'Thank you kindly, Sir,' said Toad in a feeble voice, 'I'm feeling a great deal better!'

'That's right,' said the gentleman. 'Now keep quite still, and, above all, don't try to talk.'

'I won't,' said Toad. 'I was only thinking, if I might sit on the front seat there, beside the driver, where I could get the fresh air full in my face, I should soon be all right again.'

'What a very sensible woman!' said the gentleman. 'Of course you shall.' So they carefully helped Toad into the front seat beside the driver, and on they went again.

Toad was almost himself again by now. He sat up, looked about him, and tried to beat down the tremors, the yearnings, the old cravings that rose up and beset him and took possession of him entirely.

'It is fate!' he said to himself. 'Why strive? Why struggle?' and he turned to the driver at his side.

'Please, Sir,' he said, 'I wish you would kindly let me try and drive the car for a little. I've been watching you carefully, and it looks so easy and so interesting, and I should like to be able to tell my friends that once I had driven a motor-car!'

The driver laughed at the proposal, so heartily that the gentleman inquired what the matter was. When he heard, he said, to Toad's delight, 'Bravo, ma'am! I like your spirit. Let her have a try, and look after her. She won't do any harm.'

Toad eagerly scrambled into the seat vacated by the driver, took the steering-wheel in his hands, listened with affected humility to the instructions given him, and set the car in motion, but very slowly and carefully at first, for he was determined to be prudent.

The gentlemen behind clapped their hands and applauded, and Toad heard them saying, 'How well she does it! Fancy a washerwoman driving a car as well as that, the first time!'

Toad went a little faster; then faster still, and faster.

He heard the gentlemen call out warningly, 'Be careful, washerwoman!' And this annoyed him, and he began to lose his head.

The driver tried to interfere, but he pinned him down in his seat with one elbow, and put on full speed. The rush of air in his face, the hum of the engines and the light jump of the car beneath him intoxicated his weak brain. 'Washerwoman, indeed!' he shouted recklessly. 'Ho! Ho! I am the Toad, the motor-car snatcher, the prison-breaker, the Toad who always escapes! Sit still, and you shall know what driving really is, for you are in the hands of the famous, the skillful, the entirely fearless Toad!'

Another character who approaches the ridiculous in some of her methods is Carlotta, in "The Schartz-Metterklume Method," by H. H. Munro (Saki). Carlotta, an adventuresome young English girl, is mistaken for a governess and decides to play the part rather than correct the error.

The humor arises from her broad statements, and startling educational methods which are so inappropriate to the character she has assumed that they shock her employers. Usually we have a sympathetic attitude toward these humorous characters.

Sometimes writers satirize a literary style by exaggerating it so much that it appears ridiculous. This has been done by such writers as Henry Fielding, Robert Benchley, and Terry Siegel. Fielding ridicules the sentimental novel in *Joseph Andrews,* while Benchley, in his "Family Life in America," satirizes realism in literature. In this essay he describes the Twillys' house and its occupants in such a way as to make both the setting and the characters appear absurd. Here you will convey the satirical attitude of Benchley as he ridicules realistic literature, presenting an exaggerated concept of this style of writing.

The living room in the Twillys' house was so damp that thick, soppy moss grew all over the walls. It dripped on the picture of Grandfather Twilly that hung over the melodeon, making streaks down the dirty glass like sweat on the old man's face. It was a mean face. Grandfather Twilly had been a mean man and had little spots of soup on the lapel of his coat. All his children were mean and had soup spots on their clothes.

Grandma Twilly sat in the rocker over by the window, and as she rocked the chair snapped. It sounded like Grandma Twilly's knees snapping as they did whenever she stooped over to pull the wings off a fly. She was a mean old thing. Her knuckles were grimy and she chewed crumbs that she found in the bottom of her reticule. You would have hated her. She hated herself. But most of all she hated Grandfather Twilly.

Terry Siegel achieves the ridiculous by parodying the story of Hamlet in the manner of an elementary reader.

When the serious, or solemn is changed into the informal or familiar, we have, as Bergson says, parody. When you read this aloud you will support the aspect of the ridiculous if you read it in the stilted manner young children use in reading, thus treating a serious subject in a ridiculous manner.

"Fun With Hamlet and His Friends," by William Shakespeare

See the man. What a funny man. His name is Hamlet.
He is a prince.
He is sad. Why are you sad, Hamlet?
"I am sad, for my father has died," says Hamlet. "My father was the king."
"Where are you going, Hamlet?"
"I am going to the castle," says Hamlet.
On the way he meets a ghost. "Where are you going?" asks the ghost.
"I am going to the castle," says Hamlet.
"Boo hoo," says the ghost.
"What is your name, you silly ghost?" asks Hamlet, clapping his hands.
"I am your father," says the ghost. "I was a good king. Uncle Claudius is a bad king. He gave me poison. Would you like poison?"

"Oh, no," says Hamlet. "I will avenge you. What fun it will be to avenge you."

On the way he meets a girl. "Where are you going?" asks the girl.

"I am going to the castle," says Hamlet.

"Ha, ha," says the girl.

"Why are you laughing?" asks Hamlet. "You are a silly goose."

"I laugh because you are so funny," says Ophelia. "I laugh because you are schizophrenic. Are you not schizophrenic?"

"I am not schizophrenic," says Hamlet, laughing and clapping his hands. "I pretend I am schizophrenic. I pretend, for I want to fool my uncle. What fun it is to pretend I am schizophrenic."

See Hamlet run. Run, Hamlet, run. He is going to his mother's room.

"I have something to tell you, Mother," says Hamlet.

"Uncle Claudius is bad. He gave my father poison. Poison is not good. I do not like poison. Do you like poison?"

"Oh, no indeed," says his mother. "I do not like poison."

"Oh, there is Uncle Claudius," says Hamlet. "He is hiding behind the curtain. Why is he hiding behind the curtain? I shall stab him. What fun it will be to stab him through the curtain."

See Hamlet draw his sword. See Hamlet stab. Stab, Hamlet, stab.

See Uncle Claudius' blood. See Uncle Claudius' blood gush.

Gush, blood, gush.

See Uncle Claudius fall. How funny he looks, stabbed. Ha, ha, ha.

But it is not Uncle Claudius.

It is Polonius. Polonius is Ophelia's father.

What fun Hamlet is having.

"You are naughty, Hamlet," says Hamlet's mother. "You have stabbed Polonius." But Hamlet's mother is not cross. She loves Hamlet. He is a good boy.

And Hamlet loves his mother. She is a good mother. Hamlet loves his mother very much. Hamlet loves his mother very, very much.

Does Hamlet love his mother a little too much?

Perhaps.

See Hamlet run. Run, Hamlet, run. Where are you going, Hamlet?

"I am going to find Uncle Claudius," says Hamlet.

On the way he passes a brook. In the brook he sees Ophelia.

Ophelia is drowning. "Where are you going?" asks Ophelia.
"I am going to find Uncle Claudius," says Hamlet.
"Glub, glub," says Ophelia.
On the way he meets a man. "Where are you going?" asks the man.
"I am going to find Uncle Claudius," says Hamlet.
"Oh ho. I am Laertes," says the man. "Let us draw our swords. Let us duel."
"I do not think I am going to find Uncle Claudius," says Hamlet.
See Hamlet and Laertes duel.
See Laertes stab Hamlet.
See Hamlet stab Laertes.
See Hamlet's mother drink poison.
See Hamlet stab King Claudius.
See everybody wounded and bleeding and dying and dead.
What fun they are having!
Would you not like to play like that?

Sometimes humor arises when something that is normally considered as relatively simple is described in very complicated terms. This can be done by going into excessive detail so that the result is confusing and ridiculous to the uninitiated and amusing to those initiated. In "New Math Doesn't Add Up," Art Buchwald succeeds in doing this. Moreover, there is also a reversal of the situation, for, instead of the narrator helping his daughter, she instructs her father, and he is further enlightened—or confused—by the girl's teacher. The oral interpreter will probably handle this material in a very serious manner. When the narrator is first confronted by his daughter he has self-assurance in believing that he can solve the problem, but as the story develops he becomes increasingly confused and the situation is reversed so that he is the pupil and the teacher instructs him.

There has been a great deal of discussion about American education in the last 10 years and everyone has come up with his theory as to why Johnny can't add. I know why Johnny can't add. It's because his parents can't do his homework.

In the old days before N.M. (New Math) a kid could bring home his homework and his parents would go over it with him, making corrections or suggestions, and giving encouragement when the going got rough. But today the parent is in the soup because the homework is so complicated that neither the kid nor his parent knows what is going on.

For example, the other day my daughter brought home a homework assignment.

"I have to subtract 179 from 202," she said.

"It's quite simple," I said, "you put the 202 over the 179."

"But what do I do with the 10?"

"What 10?"

"The 10 that goes next to the 202."

"I don't know what 10 goes next to the 202. Let's subtract 179 from 202. Nine from two is three, and you carry one. Eight from zero is two. The answer is 23."

"We can't do it that way. We have to use a 10."

"Why 10?"

"Ten is a unit."

"I see. Well, the answer is still 23," I said.

"How do you know?"

"Because I took nine from two and eight from zero."

"That's not the way to do it."

"Oh, yeah? Well, that's the way I did it."

"My teacher says you can't take nine from two."

"Why not?"

"Because you can't borrow from something you don't give back."

"Well, I'm going to call your teacher and see how SHE subtracts 179 from 202."

The teacher was very nice on the phone. "It's really quite simple," she said. "The two on the right hand column is considered units of one. The zero in the center counts for zero tens. The two in the left hand column counts for hundreds. Therefore, you have two hundreds, zero tens, and two ones."

"You're putting me on," I said.

"Now to subtract," she said. "Go to the hundreds column and start regrouping. Two hundred will become 100. Therefore, 10 tens equal 100. Therefore, bring this 10 to the tens column. Now you have 10 tens, but you still can't subtract in the units column. Therefore regroup again. Now you only have nine tens. Take 12 from the 10 and now bring it over to the ones column because 10 ones equal one. Now you have 12 ones. Do you understand?"

"What's there to understand?" I said. "Can I ask you a very, very personal question?"

"Yes, of course."

"Is the answer 23?"

"In this case it is, but it isn't necessarily 23. If you were working in units other than 10, it could be something else."

I hung up and started swallowing a whole bottle of aspirin, but my wife caught me in time. "How many aspirins did you take?" she asked.

"I took seven and then I took five, but don't ask me what it adds up to."

A "way of life" can also be satirized. Pope, writing in heroic couplets, ridiculed it in "The Rape of the Lock," and Fielding caught the elements of the ridiculous in *Tom Jones.*

B. *Exaggeration*

When a highly exaggerated picture is presented of a place, personality, or a situation, there can also be an element of humor. Exaggeration has always been a popular form of humor in America. Such is the keynote of Frank Sullivan's "An Innocent in Texas," in which a New Yorker visits the "Lone Star State" and greatly magnifies the opulence of the land.

In reading "An Innocent in Texas," you handle it seriously, but you need not exaggerate vocally or physically to get the humor over, for the lines themselves will do that. Simply report the marvels of Texas as Sullivan found them. You will see that Sullivan relies on the absurd as well as upon exaggeration—"Two glorious suns were shining, the regular one and the special Texas sun"; "Steak is the state flower of Texas"; "Texas has the richest millionaires." He also piles exaggeration on exaggeration in describing the population of Texas.

I had heard so much about Texas that I was consumed with curiosity about our great sister republic to the south. Was it true for instance that all Texans are seven feet tall except the football players at Texas Christian and Southern Methodist, who are eight? Was it true that Rhode Island would fit 220 times into Texas, as Texas friends had so often assured me? Was it true that in the early years of the war there were so many Texans in the Royal Canadian Air Force that Canadians were often tempted to call it the Royal Texan Air Force? Did Oveta Culp Hobby . . .

I wanted to learn the answers. I wanted to see Texas in action. There was only one way to do so. Throwing a few things into my bag I took off for Houston. I travelled light—a spare ten-gallon hat, two pairs of chaps, one for business and one for formal evening wear, a lariat, a few other necessaries, and Rhode Island, which I brought along because, in the interest of accuracy, I was eager to check on that 220 story.

On a typical sparkling Texas morning I debarked at Houston. Two glorious suns were shining, the regular one and the special Texas sun. Above the hum of the city's traffic rose the pleasant susurrus of Texas voices exchanging matutinal howdies in their melodious Confederate drawl.

From the distance came the agreeable gurgle of gushers gushing in the gusheries scattered about the city, with occasionally the triumphant yodel of an oil millionaire who had just discovered a new gusher. Anon, the crack of rifle fire and the sight of a fleeing cattle rustler with a posse at his heels told me plainer than words that Texas could still dispense frontier justice.

"Yippee!" I cried, for I speak Texan fluently, and, drawing two or three six-shooters from my belt, I fired a volley of twenty-one guns in salute to Pecos Bill, John Nance Garner, General Santa Anna, Stephen F. Austin, Maury Maverick, and the Alamo.

I made Houston my first port of call because it is the metropolis and chief city of the Texan republic, although I add instantly that Dallas, San Antonio, Galveston, Waco, Wichita Falls, Fort Worth, Austin, Abilene and El Paso are also the chief cities of Texas. Other chief cities may have sprung up since I left. If so, I beg their pardon for not mentioning them.

Houston has a population of 600,000 and, Houstonians informed me, is growing at the rate of 10,000 inhabitants a day, 5,000 of them oil millionaires. Texas grows the largest and most luscious grapefruit in the world and the richest millionaires. Jesse Jones of Houston is the richest Jones in recorded history. At its present rate of growth Houston will outstrip London and New York in a decade. Perhaps sooner, since Texans are twice as big as Londoners or New Yorkers.

My day in Houston was packed with excitement. No sooner was I settled in my suite at one of the city's finer hotels than they struck oil in the cellar and immediately started tearing down the twenty-eight-story hotel to make way for the more profitable gusher. The hospitable Chamber of Commerce quickly found me agreeable quarters in a twenty-nine-story hotel and after washing up I still had time before lunch to measure Rhode Island into Houston. It goes seven times.

I shall not soon forget that lunch. We had steak. Steak is the state flower of Texas. Texas has the finest steaks and the best department stores in the country. I had heard of the Gargantuan meals to which the lusty Texans are accustomed, but after all I come from New York, the home of the late Diamond Jim Brady, who thought nothing of consuming, at one sitting, twelve dozen oysters, eight quarts of orange juice, four adult lobsters, two planked steaks and Lillian Russell, so I set to work with a will and in no time at all was pridefully chasing the last shred of tenderloin around my plate with a piece of bun.

"Yippee!" I remarked. "Here's one dam-yank that can tie on the old feedbag with any varmint in Houston."

Just then a waiter put a steak in front of me twice as big as the steak I had just eaten. The waiter was twice as big as a New York waiter.

"What's that thar, pardner?" says I.

"That thar's yore steak, pardner," says he.

"What was that thar I just et?" says I.

"That thar was jest yore hors d'oeuvre," says he.

"Yippee!" says I, but in a more chastened tone, you may be sure, and that was the last time I bragged about my appetite in Texas.

Broad and exaggerated humor can easily be noted in the following celebrated speech of Davy Crockett before Congress "On The State

Finances, State Officers, And State Affairs In General," in the panic year of 1837. Here the speaker is very earnest and serious, but the humor that arises from his exaggeration is undeniable, so the interpreter will suggest this earnestness. The dialect strengthens the humor.

Mr. Speaker:

The broken fenced state o' the nation, the broken banks, broken hearts, and broken pledges o' my brother Congressmen here around me, has riz the boiler o' my indignation, clar up to the high pressure pinte, an' therefore I have riz to let off the steam of my hull hog patriotism, without round-about-ation, and without the trimmins. The truth wants no trimmins, for in her clar naked state o' natur she's as graceful as a suckin' colt in the sunshine. Mr. Speaker! What in the name o' kill-sheep-dog rascality is the country a-comin' to? Whar's all the honor? no whar! an thar it'll stick! Whar's the state revenue? every whar but whar it ought to be!

Why, Mr. Speaker, don't squint with horror, when I tell you that last Saturday morning Uncle Sam hadn't the first fip to give to the barber! the banks suspend payment, and the starving people suspend themselves by ropes! old Currency is flat on his back, the bankers have sunk all funds in the saft arth o' speculation, and some o' these chaps grinnin' around me are as deep in the mud as a heifer in a horse-pond!

Whar's the political honesty o' my feller congressmen? why, in bank bills and five acre speeches! Whar's all thar patriotism? in slantendicular slurs, challenges, and hair trigger pistols! Whar's all thar promises? every whar! Whar's all thar performances on 'em? no whar, and the poor people bellering arter 'em everywhere like a drove o' buffaloes arter their lazy keepers, that, like the officers here, care for no one's stomach, but their own etarnal internals!

What in the nation have you done this year? why, wasted paper enough to calculate all your political sins upon, and that would take a sheet for each one o' you as long as the Mississippi, and as broad as all Kentucky. You've gone ahead in doin' nothin' backwards, till the hull nation's done up. You've spouted out a Mount Etny o' gas, chawed a hull Alleghany o' tobacco, spit a Niagary o' juice, told a hail storm o' lies, drunk a Lake Superior o' liquor, and all, as you say, for the good o' the nation; but I say, I swar, for her etarnal bankruptification.

Tharfore, I move that the only way to save the country is for the hull nest o' your political weasels to cut stick home instanterly, and leave me to work Uncle Sam's farm, till I restore it to its natural state o' cultivation, and shake off these state caterpillars o' corruption. Let black Dan Webster sittin' there at the tother end o' the desk turn Methodist preacher; let Jack Calhoun settin right afore him with his hair brushed back in front like a huckleberry bush in a hurrycane, after old Hickory's topknot, turn horse-jockey. Let Harry Clay sittin thar in the corner with his arms folded about his middle, like grape vines around a black oak, go back to our old Kentuck an' improve the breed o' lawyers an' other black sheep. Let old Daddy Quincy Adams sittin' right behind him thar, go home to Massachusetts, an' write political primers for the suckin' politicians; let Jim Buchanan go home to Pennsylvania, an' smoke long nine, with the Dutchmen. Let Tom Benton, bent like a hickory saplin with hall rolling, take a roll home an' make candy "mint drops" for the babies:—for they've worked Uncle Sam's farm with the all-scratching harrow o' rascality, 'til it's as gray as a stone fence, as barren as barked clay, and as poor as a turkey fed on gravel stones!

And, to conclude, Mr. Speaker, the nation can no more go ahead under such a state o' things, than a fried eel can swim upon the steam o' a tea kettle; if it can, then take these yar legs for yar hall pillars.[1]

Another example of the use of exaggeration can be found in this excerpt from *Ether and Me,* by Will Rogers.

This is a day of specializing, especially with the doctors. Say, for instance, there is something the matter with your right eye. You go to a doctor and he tells you, "I am sorry, but I am a left-eye doctor; I make a specialty of left eyes." A doctor that doctors on the upper part of your throat he doesn't even know where the lower part goes to. And the highest priced one of all of them is another bird that just tells you which doctor to go to. He can't cure even corns or open a boil himself. He is a Diagnostician, but he's nothing but a traffic cop, to direct ailing people.

[1] From: *Davy Crockett, American Comic Legend,* Sel. and Edit. by Richard M. Dorson. Printed at Spiral Press for Rockland Editions, N.Y., 1939, pp. 150–151.

> The old fashioned doctor didn't pick out a big toe or a left ear to make a life's living on. He picked the whole human frame. No matter what end of you was wrong he had to try to cure you single-handed. Personally, I have always felt that the best doctor in the world is the Veterinarian. He can't ask his patient what is the matter—he's got to just know.

Humor can also come out of exaggerated rhyme. W. S. Gilbert uses this in writing the librettos for the Gilbert and Sullivan operettas. Gilbert writes in triple rhymes which, as we have indicated in Chapter IX, are often used for a humorous effect:

> Here's a first-rate opportunity
> To get married with impunity,
> And indulge in the felicity
> Of unbounded domesticity.
> You shall quickly be parsonified,
> Conjugally matrimonified
> By a doctor of divinity,
> Who is located in this vicinity.
>
> (W. S. Gilbert,
> *The Pirates of Penzance,* Act I)

Humor also arises from coining new words or changing nouns to verbs as Gilbert does in the above selection from *The Pirates of Penzance.*

Sometimes particular events are satirized. "The Christmas Spectacle," by Robert Benchley is amusing in its satire on the typical, yet exaggerated, Christmas program with which many of you can identify experiences in your own lives.

Frequently humor arises from the exaggerated action and speech of a character. We compare the way *we* would speak or act, says Freud, with what the character says and does, and if the character goes beyond what we consider is necessary and fitting, then we regard him as exaggerated or affected.

While you do not exaggerate vocally or physically in "An Innocent in Texas," you do exaggerate in suggesting the character of Madame Arcati, the spiritualist, in Noel Coward's *Blithe Spirit,* a comedy-farce, in the character of Lady Bracknell in *The Importance of Being Earnest,* and in Mrs. Malaprop in *The Rivals,* in both action and voice. These exaggerations may be in speech melody, pitch range, extremes in diction and in bodily mannerisms.

Intoxication may also be a source of humor, and while it can be done effectively through exaggeration it may be even more effective if it is under-played. When reading such a scene perhaps an attempt at a little too much dignity will reveal the humor with a touch of muscular unsteadiness, more than an exaggerated swaying of the body. For example, "A Hundred Collars," by Robert Frost, may be more effective with just a touch of a wavering tone; too much might take away the subtlety of the character.

C. *The Sense of Superiority*

Another theory of humor holds that you laugh when you observe the misfortunes or limitations of another person. This gives you a sense of superiority for you have a certain joy in not finding yourself in a similar plight. At the same time, you can appreciate the misfortunes of the person, but you are far enough away to see the situation objectively and therefore you can realize the humor in it. In "The Jailer Jailed," by Chekhov, an unhappy husband tries to escape from his wife, but is always unsuccessful. His attitude and his various attempts to run away arouse sympathy yet amuse you because you feel superior to him. And, of course, Eliza Doolittle, in Shaw's *Pygmalion,* who is changing her speech and her social status, makes you feel both sympathetic and superior. The simplicity of a character may also make you feel superior. Such is the peasant in "A Culprit," by Chekhov, Tony Lumpkin in *She Stoops to Conquer* by Goldsmith, Walter Mitty in "The Secret Life of Walter Mitty," by Thurber, and Audrey in *As You Like It.*

The problems of young children also provide us with a sense of superiority when they reveal their juvenile traits. Robert Fontaine in *The Happy Time,* Clarence Day in *Life With Father,* and Virginia Cary Hudson in *O Ye Jigs and Juleps,* all endear their youthful characters to you because, as an adult, you look benignly upon them and are amused.

Dialect or foreign accent often add humor, for you feel superior to a character's strange word usage, sentence structure, inflection or gesture. The characters that Milt Gross has created in his *Nize Bebe,* and those in *Anything Can Happen,* by George and Helen Papashvily, the story of a Georgian family that comes to America, use a version of English that evokes a certain sympathetic humor.

In an episode from *The Education of Hyman Kaplan,* by Leonard Q. Ross, the instructor, Mr. Parkhill, is teaching the use of the comparative forms in English. This incident, which depends for its humor on the misuse of words and on foreign dialect, evokes kindly laughter. In reading dialect, you want to suggest the intonation, inflection, and rhythm of the speech as well as some key aspects of its articulation. The outstanding and most apparent differences of articulation will help create the effect of the dialect rather than every detail, with particular attention to the inflection and rhythm. This will convey the idea of the dialect and yet be completely understandable to your audience, while a dialect or accent that is too pronounced may not be understood.

Mr. K*A*P*L*A*N, The Comparative, and The Superlative

. . . "Now, class," said Mr. Parkhill, "I want to spend a few minutes explaining something about adjectives . . . we don't say 'good, gooder, goodest,' do we?"

"No, sir!" cried Mr. Kaplan impetuously. " 'Good, gooder, good*est?* Ha. It's to leff!"

"We say that X, for example, is good. Y, however, is —?" Mr. Parkhill arched an eyebrow interrogatively.

"Batter!" said Mr. Kaplan.

"Right! and Z is —?"

"High-cless!"

Mr. Parkhill's eyebrow dropped. "No," he said sadly.

"*Not* high-cless?" asked Mr. Kaplan increduously. For him there was no word more superlative.

"No, Mr. Kaplan, the word is *'best.'* And the word 'bad,' of which you tried to use the superlative form . . . It isn't *'bad, badder, baddest'*. It's 'bad' . . . and what's the comparative? Anyone?"

"Worse," volunteered Mr. Bloom.

"Correct! And the superlative? Z is the —?"

" 'Worse' also?" asked Mr. Bloom hesitantly. It was evident he had never distinguished the fine difference in sound between the comparative and superlative forms of "bad. '

"No, Mr. Bloom. It's not the *same* word, although it—er—sounds a good deal like it. Anyone? Come, come. It isn't hard. X is *bad,* Y is *worse,* and Z is the —?"

An embarrassed silence fell upon the class, which, apparently, had been using "worse" for both the comparative and superlative all along. . . .

"Aha!" cried Mr. Kaplan suddenly. When Mr. Kaplan cried "Aha!" it signified that a great light had fallen on him. "I know! De exect void! So easy! *Ach!* I should know dat ven I was wridink! *Bad—voise—*"

"Yes, Mr. Kaplan!" Mr. Parkhill was definitely excited.

"Rotten!"

D. *Surprise*

Humor also arises out of surprise as it does in the story of Hyman Kaplan. For example, if you expect to hear or see one thing and you see or hear something quite different, the contrast between the expected and the actual may be amusing.

In reading material which depends on surprise for its humor, the element of surprise must usually be set off from the rest of the literature in order for the unexpected to have strong impact. This may be done in a number of ways. In "Transfixed," you may suggest an unexpected change in attitude which affects quality, rhythm, and volume, and thereby the humor. The last three lines must be a strong contrast to the lyrical description of the preceding lines. In Corey Ford's "Your Wife Is Like That," the speaker appears to be a model of orderliness and precision. But two lines from the conclusion, when the unfinished sentence suddenly ends with the word "which," the interpreter comes to a dead stop, and a pause and change of time and attitude from the self-assurance of the speaker to the impersonal attitude of the editor may help strengthen the unexpected conclusion.

In "A Nincompoop," by Chekhov, the governess is called by her master to receive her salary. But, as the master proceeds to reckon up the account, he gradually takes off one sum after another that he claims should be deducted, until the girl has nothing. Then, at the end, he tells her it is all a joke and that she will receive her full salary. Here there is relief at the surprise ending, as well as a sting.

In Thurber's "The Unicorn in the Garden," the humor arises at the end of the story where there is a reversal, and you are surprised when the wife, rather than the husband, becomes the victim.

In the following selections you will find examples in which the humor arises from surprise. Decide how the surprise can be handled most effectively. Sometimes the surprise rests in a change in attitude, which, in turn, may affect tempo or intensity.

"Your Wife Is Like That," by Corey Ford

Fellow on the train last night was saying that his wife keeps string. "I'll bet my wife has over a hundred miles of string," this fellow said. "I'll bet she never threw away a piece of string in her life. She saves little pieces and ties them together. Every time she opens a package she'll spend an hour undoing each knot, and then she'll wind the string around and around her fingers into a neat ball, and tuck the loose end inside the loop, and put it away in a bureau drawer to keep. And when I ask her why she keeps it, she says you never can tell when you'll need a piece of string."

"A lot of women are like that," a fellow across the aisle said. "My wife keeps boxes. Candy boxes, jewelry boxes, hatboxes, cigar boxes—all kinds of boxes. She even keeps big boxes to keep the little boxes in. She says she can't bear to get rid of a perfectly good box because you never know when you might want a box."

"My wife keeps the paper that things are wrapped up in," said the conductor, a fellow named Smeed or Sneed. "She takes it off very carefully so she won't tear it, and flattens it to smooth out the wrinkles, and folds it once lengthwise and once across, and puts it where she'll know where it is." He picked up a pin from the aisle and stuck it absently in his lapel. "She says you never can tell when you'll have to wrap up something else."

"Tell me, Sneem," I asked him, "why are you sticking that pin in your lapel?"

"You never can tell when you'll need a pin," said Smee.

The trouble with all these fellows, I told them frankly, is that they are married to thing-keepers. Every woman is a thing-keeper at heart. Men are thing-keepers, too, but they keep only sensible things like last year's license plates, or burned-out fuses, or the hands of an old clock, or the key that used to fit the garage door before the lock was changed. The difference is that men keep things in their pockets, whereas a woman keeps things in the top of the closet. Statistics reveal that if all the things a woman keeps in a closet were taken out one by one and placed in the center of the floor there'd be enough room in the closet for all the other things she'd like to keep if she had any place to put them.

As far as I can tell, the reason women keep things is that they hate to throw them away. My wife has a collection of things she keeps in the icebox. . . . The last time I looked, there was a plate with seven string beans on it, one spoonful of mashed potato wrapped up in waxed paper, the salad I didn't eat the other night, and some giblet gravy left over from two weeks ago Sunday. She also has a pretty good collection of things she keeps in the medicine cabinet, consisting of several empty tubes (we might want to renew them sometime), a jar without a label (isn't that the poison ivy ointment that Doctor Gurry gave you last summer?), . . . and an assortment of small bottles with brown stuff caked in the bottom. On the other hand, she can never understand the things I keep, such as my fishing hat.

"I can't understand why you keep that filthy hat, George. It's a disgrace, the lining's gone, and there's a hole in the brim, and the band is all frayed where you've stuck trout flies in it, and it smells of fish."

"I keep the fish in my hat," I told her.

"And this old pair of boots with the soles gone, and this checkered shirt you've had for a thousand years, and all these pipes with the stems broken, they just clutter up the attic, George, and besides I need the space, the new washing machine came today."

"Are you going to keep the washing machine in the attic?"

"I'm saving the crate," my wife explained, "in case I ever have to send it back."

I have just taken a complete inventory of our house from top to bottom, which is the only way I can get into it these days and I have made a list of the things that people keep. They may be grouped roughly as follows:

1. *Things that go on things,* like the tops of jelly glasses, covers of peanut-butter jars, caps of bottles, lids of pots, and

saucers to put upside down over other saucers with things in them.

2. *Things that come off things,* such as buttons, buckles, suitcase straps, hinges, a bolt from Junior's bicycle, the nozzle of the garden hose, some screws that fell out of the vacuum cleaner, dear, and this nut I found lying under the car when I tried to start it this morning.

3. *Things that other things came in,* such as paper bags, egg cartons, wicker baskets, round tin boxes that contained preserved fruits—no real thing-keeper can ever resist a round tin box—and any kind of empty jar at all.

4. *Things that seem a shame to throw away,* such as a deck of playing cards with only three or four missing, the top of a pair of silk pajamas that could be used for cleaning rags or something, this vest that's still as good as ever even if the suit is all gone, and a left-hand fur mitten if we could ever find the right-hand one.

5. *Things in the cellar,* such as between thirty and forty flower pots which I knock over every time I go downstairs, the handle of an ice-cream freezer, a stack of tomato flats from last spring with the dirt still in them, and several empty barrels in case we ever have to move again.

6. *Things to keep things from going in and out,* such as old vacuum-bottle corks to plug up mouse holes, some short pieces of felt weather stripping, and a triangular section of wire mesh left over from the new porch screens which might come in handy to patch them sometime if they ever wear out.

7. *Things that have a certain sentimental value,* like the snapshots of that summer in the Adirondacks, wedding announcements, high school diplomas, that derby hat you wore in college, and all last year's Christmas cards.

8. *Things that are too nice to use,* such as the crocheted bedspread that Great-Aunt Effie made with her own two hands, that set of hand-painted demi-tasse cups that were a wedding present from the Alvords, and a bottle of Napoleon brandy we've been saving for ten years for some special occasion.

Thing-keepers have their own devices for storing the things they keep. The system of classification employed by wives in arranging the contents of shelves and bureau drawers has been baffling their husbands for years, and there is no sense in my trying to explain it here. When a man misses something his wife may ask him, "Where did you lose it?" But when a woman misses something, her husband asks her, "Where did you put it?" (If he is smart, that is.) I have been looking into the matter very carefully, and I have yet to discover a woman who doesn't know right where everything is, if she could only find it. . . .

When it comes to putting things away in closets, women follow a plan which is a cross between a squirrel storing nuts for the winter, the binomial theorem, a street map of Boston, and canasta. Objects which are used only once a year, such as Christmas-tree ornaments, are kept on the bottom shelf, right in front; whereas an item that is used every day, like the vacuum cleaner, is invariably located at the rear of the top shelf behind some hatboxes, where the wife can reach it only by means of a tall stepladder surmounted by her husband. All woolen articles are wrapped up carefully in newspapers, on which are written abbreviations like "Thwg." or "Fkl., 9/17/51." A woman can always solve the meaning of these code words by poking a hole in the paper and seeing what's inside.

The favorite storage place for a woman's things is her husband's closet. The reason for this, according to his wife, is that she never has enough closet space. . . . As a result, the top of my closet contains a complete collection of my wife's wardrobe, skillfully arranged with the larger items balanced on top of the smaller items, so that whenever the closet door is opened the entire contents cascade out onto the floor, where they may be picked up readily as soon as I regain consciousness.

It is in the kitchen, however, that the art of thing-keeping reaches its height. We got to talking about it last night on the train, and the conductor, Sneep, said that last year his wife went to visit his mother-in-law for a few days and he decided to do his own cooking while she was gone. "She told me I could find everything I needed in the kitchen," he remarked with a bitter smile. That night, when he started dinner, he reached for the tin marked "Salt," and discovered it was full of sugar. The "Sugar" tin contained coffee, and the "Coffee" tin had eggs in it. Moreover, the flour bin held potatoes, the potato bin was full of floor wax, and the breadbox was crammed to the lid with old recipes. After several hours, he said, he put on his hat and went out to a restaurant and had dinner, and when he came home he rolled up his sleeves and spent the rest of the evening re-arranging the kitchen. He put the sugar in the tin marked "Sugar." He put coffee in "Coffee." He filled the potato bin with potatoes and the flour bin with flour. He even took the pans off the stove and hung them up on hooks where they belonged, and arranged the icebox. Well, it seems his wife came home a couple of days later, and she took one look around the kitchen and smiled patiently.

"You men are all alike," she sighed. "Now it'll take me a week to get this mess straightened out again."

We all agree that men are not like that, of course. Their method of storing things is a model of precision. Everything is put right in its place, and there is never any problem of finding anything. For example, I have my own system, which

Editors' Note: The last page of Mr. Ford's manuscript is missing. Unfortunately he can't remember where he put it.

"Transfixed," by wende devlin, also has a surprise ending.

"Transfixed," by wende devlin

From Beat Poems of a Beat Mother

She speaks
to an ebony god.
And slow
the sun spans
half a sky.
It turns
to a liquid gold,
and lies aspill
on the earth's line.
One cloud
of orange
surrenders
to the night.
Spellbound

and wired to this icon,
her voice
is endless.
Translation:
Hey, Linda, will you
please get off that phone!

As you have been reading the humorous literature in this chapter you have observed that the various elements that contribute to humor are not necessarily limited so that you will find only one element such as surprise or the ridiculous in a single piece of literature. Frequently a number of these elements of humor may be found in a single selection. As you read "The Culprit," attempt to determine the sources of humor Chekhov has relied on.

First, the difference in the seemingly simple peasant's attitude is incongruous with your way of thinking and there is an element of the ridiculous in his arguments with the magistrate. Secondly, this peasant makes you feel superior because of his apparent stupidity. Moreover, you are surprised and amused at his shrewdness, for, although not ultimately successful, he actually defends himself better than you expect. How can you suggest his simplicity, his apparent stupidity and yet his cunning? What is his appearance? His posture? His diction?

"The Culprit," by Anton Pavlovich Chekhov

A puny little peasant, exceedingly skinny, wearing patched trousers and a shirt made of ticking, stands before the investigating magistrate. His hairy, pockmarked face, and his eyes, scarcely visible under thick, overhanging brows, have an expression of grim sullenness. The mop of tangled hair that has not known the touch of a comb for a long time gives him a spiderish air that makes him look even grimmer. He is barefoot.

"Denis Grigoryev!" the magistrate begins. "Step nearer and answer my questions. On the morning of the seventh of this present month of July, the railway watchman, Ivan Semyonovich Akinfov, making his rounds, found you, near the hundred-and-forty-first milepost, unscrewing the nut of one of the bolts by which the rails are fastened to the sleepers. Here is the nut! . . . With the said nut he detained you. Is this true?"

"Wot?"

"Did all this happen as stated by Akinfov?"

"It did, sure."

"Very well; now, for what purpose were you unscrewing the nut?"

"Wot?"

"Stop saying 'wot' and answer the question: for what purpose were you unscrewing the nut?"

"If I didn't need it, I wouldn't've unscrewed it," croaks Denis, with a sidelong glance at the ceiling.

"What did you want that nut for?"

"The nut? We make sinkers of these nuts."

"Who are 'we'?"

"We, folks. . . . The Klimovo peasants, that is."

"Listen, brother; don't play the fool with me, but talk sense. There's no use lying to me about sinkers."

"I never lied in my life, and here I'm lying . . ." mutters Denis, blinking. "But can you do without a sinker, Your Honor? If you put live bait or worms on a hook, would it go to the bottom without a sinker? . . . So I'm lying," sneers Denis. "What the devil is the good of live bait if it floats on the surface? The perch and the pike and the eel-pout will bite only if your line touches bottom, and if your bait floats on the surface, it's only a bullhead will take it, and that only sometimes, and there ain't no bullhead in our river. . . . That fish likes plenty of room."

"What are you telling me about bullhead for?"

"Wot? Why, you asked me yourself! Up our way the gentry catch fish that way, too. Even a little kid wouldn't try to catch fish without a sinker. Of course, somebody with no sense might go fishing without a sinker. No rules for fools."

"So you say you unscrewed this nut to make a sinker of it?"

"What else for? Not to play knucklebones with!"

"But you might have taken a bit of lead or a bullet for a sinker . . . a nail . . ."

"You don't pick up lead on the road, you have to pay for it, and a nail's no good. You can't find nothing better than a nut . . . It's heavy, and it's got a hole."

"He keeps playing the fool! As though he'd been born yesterday or dropped out of the sky! Don't you understand, you blockhead, what this unscrewing leads to? If the watchman hadn't been on the lookout, the train might have been derailed, people would have been killed—*YOU* would have killed people."

"God forbid, Your Honor! Kill people? Are we unbaptized, or criminals? Glory be to God, sir, we've lived our lives without dreaming of such a thing, much less killing anybody . . . Save us, Queen of Heaven, have mercy on us! What are you saying, sir?"

"And how do you suppose train wrecks happen? Unscrew two or three nuts, and you have a wreck!"

Denis sneers and screws up his eyes at the magistrate incredulously.

"Well! How many years have all of us here in the village been unscrewing nuts, and the Lord's protected us; and here you talk about wrecks, killing people. If I'd carried off a rail or put a log in the way, then maybe the train might've gone off the track, but . . . ppfff! a nut!"

"But try to get it into your head that the nut holds the rail fast to the sleepers!"

"We understand that . . . We don't unscrew all of 'em. . . . We leave some. . . . We don't do things without using our heads . . . We understand."

Denis yawns and makes the sign of the cross over his mouth. "Last year a train was derailed here," says the magistrate. "Now it's plain why!"

"Beg pardon?"

"I say that it's plain why the train was derailed last year . . . Now I understand!"

"That's what you're educated for, our protectors, to understand. The Lord knew to whom to give understanding . . . Here you've figured out how and what, but the watchman, a peasant like us, with no brains at all, he gets you by the collar and pulls you in. You should figure it out first and then pull people in. But it's known, a peasant has the brains of a peasant . . . Write down, too, Your Honor, that he hit me twice on the jaw, and on the chest, too."

"When your house was searched they found another nut. . . . At what spot did you unscrew that, and when?"

"You mean the nut under the little red chest?"

"I don't know where you kept it, but it was found. When did you unscrew it?"

"I didn't unscrew it; Ignashka, one-eyed Semyon's son, he gave it to me. I mean the one that was under the chest, but the one that was in the sledge in the yard, that one Mitrofan and I unscrewed together."

"Which Mitrofan?"

"Mitrofan Petrov . . . Didn't you hear of him? He makes nets and sells them to the gentry. He needs a lot of those nuts. Reckon a matter of ten for every net."

"Listen. According to Article 1081 of the Penal Code, deliberate damage to a railroad, calculated to jeopardize the trains, provided the perpetrator of the damage knew that it might cause an accident—you understand? Knew! And you couldn't help knowing what this unscrewing might lead to—is punishable by hard labor."

"Of course, you know best . . . We're ignorant folk . . . What do we understand?"

"You understand all about it! You are lying, faking!"

"Why should I lie? Ask in the village if you don't believe me. Only bleak is caught without a sinker. And a gudgeon's no kind of fish, but even gudgeon won't bite without a sinker."

"Tell me about bullhead, now," says the magistrate with a smile.

"There ain't no bullhead in our parts . . . If we cast our lines without a sinker, with a butterfly for bait, we can maybe catch a chub that way, but even that not often."

"Now, be quiet."

There is silence. Denis shifts from one foot to the other, stares at the table covered with green cloth, and blinks violently as though he were looking not at cloth but at the sun. The magistrate writes rapidly.

"Can I go?" asks Denis, after a silence.

"No. I must put you in custody and send you to prison."

Denis stops blinking and, raising his thick eyebrows, looks inquiringly at the official.

"What do you mean, prison? Your Honor! I haven't the time: I must go to the fair; I must get three rubles from Yegor for lard!"

"Be quiet; don't disturb me."

"Prison . . . If I'd done something, I'd go; but to go just for nothing! What for? I didn't steal anything, so far as I know, I wasn't fighting . . . If there's any question about the arrears, Your Honor, don't believe the elder . . . Ask the permanent member of the Board . . . the elder, he's no Christian."

"Be quiet."

"I'm quiet as it is," mutters Denis; "as for the elder, he's lied about the assessment, I'll take my oath on it . . . We're three brothers: Kuzma Grigoryev, then Yegor Grigoryev, and me, Denis Grigoryev."

"You're disturbing me . . . Hey, Semyon," cries the magistrate, "take him out."

"We're three brothers," mutters Denis, as two husky soldiers seize him and lead him out of the chamber. "A brother don't have to answer for a brother. Kuzma don't pay, so you, Denis, have to answer for it . . . Judges! Our late master the general is dead—the Kingdom of Heaven be his!—or he'd have shown you judges what's what . . . You must have the know-how when you judge, not do it any which way . . . All right, flog a man, but justly, when it's coming to him."[2]

George Meredith sums up the nature of humor as follows[3]:

"One excellent test of the civilization of a country, as I have said, I take to be the flourishing of the comic idea and comedy; and the test of true comedy is that it shall awaken thoughtful laughter.

If you believe that our civilization is founded in common-sense (and it is the first condition of sanity to believe it), you will, when contemplating men, discern a Spirit overhead; . . . and

[2] Anton Chekhov, "The Culprit," from *The Portable Chekhov,* ed. by Avrahm Yarmolinsky, The Viking Press, Inc., pp. 103–108.

[3] George Meredith, *An Essay on Comedy and the Uses of the Comic Spirit* (Westminster: A. Constable, 1897), pp. 89–90.

whenever . . . (men) wax out of proportion, overblown, affected pretentious, bombastical, hypocritical, pedantic, fantastically delicate; whenever it sees them self-deceived or hoodwinked, given to run riot in idolatries, drifting into vanities, congregating in absurdities, planning short-sightedly, plotting dementedly; whenever they are at variance with their professions, and violate the unwritten but perceptible laws binding them in consideration one to another; whenever they offend sound reason, fair justice; are false in humility or mined with conceit, individually, or in the bulk—the Spirit overhead will look humanely malign and cast an oblique light on them, followed by volleys of silvery laughter. That is the Comic Spirit."

STUDY QUESTIONS

1. Find a humorous poem or essay which you think points out some of man's faults. How can you best convey these faults in reading aloud?

2. Can you think of bodily techniques for bringing out humor in addition to those discussed in this chapter? Compare the comic technique of an easy-going rural type and that of a busybody. Can you do this and avoid the usual stereotype of such characters?

3. Does comedy always have a faster pace than tragedy? Can you think of some exceptions?

4. Will the techniques of comedy be more, or less, exaggerated in reading farce aloud? You might experiment with *Charley's Aunt* by Brandon Thomas, and a comedy such as Sheridan's *School for Scandal.*

5. Can you think of examples of rhythm in literature which is used to bring out comedy?

6. How would you classify *The Frogs,* by Aristophanes, in terms of its humor? Shakespeare's *Comedy of Errors?*

7. Why do we laugh if a dignified character slips in a mud puddle?

8. Does farce always make good material to read aloud?

9. What problems might you encounter in reading aloud humorous material with dialects?

10. Does humor with a "sting" depend on exaggeration? Why, or why not?

11. Which of the means of achieving humor do you think is most effective from the standpoint of the oral reader? Why?

BIBLIOGRAPHY

Bergson, Henri Louis, *Laughter: An Essay on the Meaning of the Comic.* New York: The Macmillan Company, 1911.

Bruère, Martha S. and Mary Ritter Beard, *Laughing Their Way: Women's Humor in America.* New York: The Macmillan Company, 1934.

Eastman, Max, *The Enjoyment of Laughter.* New York: Simon and Schuster, Inc., 1936.

Freud, Sigmund, *Wit and Its Relations to The Unconscious.* Authorized English ed, with Introduction by A. A. Brill. New York: Moffat, Yard & Co., 1916.

Leacock, Stephen Butler, *Humor and Humanity.* New York: H. Holt and Company, 1938.

Meredith, George, *An Essay on Comedy and the Uses of the Comic Spirit.* Westminster: A. Constable, 1897.

Tandy, Jennette Reid, *Crackerbox Philosophers in American Humor and Satire.* Columbia University Press, 1925.

Thorp, Willard, *American Humorists.* Minneapolis: University of Minnesota Press, 1964.

Time Essay, *American Humor: Hardly A Laughing Matter. Time,* March 4, 1966, pp. 46–47.

Whiting, Percy H., *How to Speak and Write with Humor.* New York: McGraw-Hill Book Company, Inc., 1959.

Part Five

Specialized Formats

Chapter XII

The Oral Book Review

When you hold a book in your hand you are free to seek the innermost minds of men of the past and present, to observe the life and character of a person or persons, to hear through print the thoughts of a great orator or speaker, to walk on the path of adventure and experience, to reflect on the glimmering ideas of the great and the good, to breathe excitedly as a writer weaves his golden threads of human interest, and to join a poet as he muses on the hillside.

I. THE WRITTEN BOOK REVIEW

Because of the great number of new books being published and because readers need some guidance in selecting their books, book reviewing has become popular.

A. *Definition*

The book review has been defined by Brander Matthews as "the art of informing readers just what the latest volume is, in kind, in character, and in quality." Generally the book reviewer works with contemporary literature, but he need not necessarily be limited to that. He gives his listeners a taste of what the book is about, and submits an appraisal of it.

B. *Types of Book Reviews*

In your experience you have probably been exposed to three types of book-reviews: book notices, the factual reviews, and the critical reviews.[1] It is not difficult to find one or all of these in newspapers or magazines. The *book notices* are usually short and newspaper men speak of them as "blurbs." Book publishers often use the book jacket "blurb," which is usually complimentary, to attract attention and stimulate the readers' interest. The *factual review* is often longer than the "blurb" and combines the elements of a news story and an editorial. Here the reviewer offers an appraisal of the book for the reader. In the *critical review* you may find elements of the factual review, but more emphasis is put on the book's strengths and weaknesses, its importance, its place in the realm of literature, its historical perspective, and its style. The reviewer here sits in the seat of judgment rather than in the seat of the observer. Most written reviews that appear in newspapers and magazines will fall into one of these three categories, depending upon the policy and purpose of the publication.

II. THE ORAL BOOK REVIEW

Thus far we have talked about the written book review. But what about the oral book review? (1) Why is oral book reviewing important today? (2) What are the qualifications of an oral book reviewer? (3) Does it follow the same format in presentation as does the written book review?

A. *Purpose of the Oral Book Review*

Talking about books can be, and probably is, one of the most arresting and well-attended programs that is featured by a study or social

[1] Florin L. McDonald, *Book Reviewing in the American Newspaper,* Published Ph.D. Dissertation, The University of Missouri, 1936.

group. Even the book review on radio has its share of listeners. And certainly one of the most interesting class-room programs for an oral interpreter, for both the reader and listener, can be the oral book review. The purposes of book reviewers may vary. Some reviewers believe that they (1) should stimulate the audience to read the book, others believe that they (2) should tell the story or plot, while others contend that they (3) must critically appraise the book at hand. Unfortunately, many critics in this third group attack a book in a manner reminiscent of Macbeth's words, when he said belligerently, ". . . Lay on, MacDuff and damn'd be he that first cries 'Hold, enough!' " (Macbeth, Act V, Sc viii)

B. *Qualifications of the Oral Book Reviewer*

Whatever your purpose may be, four basic qualifications are necessary as you prepare to give an oral book review. First, you must be a good speaker. This implies that you should be able (a) to analyze your audience, (b) organize your material in the light of your audience, and (c) be able to communicate it effectively. The second qualification is to be able to read well. This involves reading silently as well as orally. While reading silently your mind senses the flavor and content of the book, and with pencil in hand you mark passages or make notes that will help support what you plan to say about the book. The third qualification of an oral book reviewer can be expressed in the words of Francis Bacon. In "Of Studies," he wrote, "Read not to contradict and confute; nor to believe and take for granted; nor to find talk and discourse; but to weigh and consider."[2]

To weigh and consider—that is your responsibility as a book reviewer. You will do this by reading the book itself a number of times. The first time you read it, you will read for enjoyment; your second and third reading will be more critical of content, attitude, and style. After you have formed your own opinions, it will be of help to you to see what other critics have said in sources such as *The New York Times, Christian Science Monitor, Saturday Review, Library Journal, Time, Newsweek,*

[2] Francis Bacon, "Of Studies," *Great Essays,* Edited by Houston Peterson (New York: Pocket Books, Inc., Cardinal Edition, 1954), p. 34.

and *Book Review Digest.* In reading any book review weigh and consider what is written. Ultimately, you should make your own judgment.

Martial, a Latin author of the first century A.D., once commented, "It is not given to everyone to have a nose (i.e. skill in investigating matters)."[3] If you are to meet with some success as an oral book reviewer, you must, to some degree, qualify as a researcher or investigator—your fourth basic qualification. Under no condition should you attempt to review a book without first finding out something about the author—his background, his education, his experience, his family ties, his style, his purpose in writing the book and his philosophy. To secure this information, although you may not use all of it, is not difficult. Such information can often be found on the book jacket, even though it may be a "thumbnail sketch" of the author's life. But this information is not enough; you should go to the library and become acquainted with the author from sources such as the encyclopedia, *Current Biography, Twentieth Century Authors,* and *Who's Who In America.* Virgil, the Latin poet, says in the *Aeneid,* ". . . nor is one look enough; it delights them to linger on, to pace by his side and learn wherefore he is come."[4]

C. *Choosing the Book to Review*

Selecting the book to review is indeed not an easy task. The dominant issues in your decision will be the *suitability,* the *readability* and the *timelessness* of the book for you, your listener and the occasion.

Suitability. The book you are going to review should have the element of suitability. Remember, the backgrounds and interests of groups are different, and you should be aware that a book that may interest one group of listeners may not interest another. Naturally, you will take into consideration, insofar as possible, the group's likes and dislikes, be it biography, fiction, autobiography, or a discussion about current affairs and politics. Make your choice with these questions in mind: What kind of listeners will I have? Is it a heterogeneous or homogeneous audience? Is it a study group, a group of college students, or an audience that has

[3] (Martial, *Epigrams,* Book I, XLII.)

[4] *The Aeneid of Virgil,* trans. by J. W. Mackail (London: Macmillan and Co., Ltd., 1931), Bk. 6, p. 133.

come from Main Street to spend a quiet hour relaxing at the library? Try to find a book that you think will be suitable for the particular listeners you will have. For example, if your audience is of varied background and interests, choose a book that is not too highly specialized. If your audience is specialized, you might find it wise to select a study of some scholar on a subject of special interest to it. Max Lerner's *The Age of Overkill: A Preface to World Politics,* is an example of this type which might be better adapted to this kind of group. In any case, try to determine the interests of the particular audience that has invited you to review a book for them. For groups having general interests, select a book that has a universal appeal, such as John P. Marquand's *The Late George Apley,* Elizabeth Goudge's *The Scent of Water,* or John F. Kennedy's *Profiles in Courage.*

In selecting a book to review you must also determine whether or not the author will challenge the listeners. The silent reader can abandon the book when he loses interest, or when the story becomes vague, but the listener is caught. At the very outset his interest and his thinking must be challenged. You cannot always expect to catch the enthusiastic interest of every listener, but your aim should be to select a book that will appeal and that will challenge most people through the author's subject matter or his treatment of the subject. Is the subject matter suitable? Is the treatment too sophisticated or, on the other hand, too immature? Whether your listeners are highly educated or not, they welcome a challenge, but in any case, they do not like to be talked "down" to.

Suitability, however, should not just be centered toward the *listeners* you will have; the book should be appropriate for *you* to review. It should challenge your interest sufficiently to make you wish to share it with others.

Readability. It was Anthony Trollope, a nineteenth century English novelist, who in his autobiography wrote, "Of all the needs a book has, the chief need is that it be readable."[5] Without readability, the line of contact between author-reader-oral book reviewer-listener is lost.

Here is a word of caution that may help you as a reviewer. Avoid particularly a novel with a complicated plot or too many plots running

[5] *An Autobiography of Anthony Trollope* (New York: Dodd, Mead & Company, 1922), Chapter XIX, Sec. on Australia, p. 302.

so closely parallel that they can easily become confused. The span of attention of the listener does not tolerate the strain of carrying many plots through only the avenue of listening and seeing. The silent reader can easily turn back pages to review what may have slipped his mind in the interval between plots, but the listener cannot do this. Therefore you should be very clear in explaining the plots and in omitting unnecessary details.

Many reviewers read aloud certain passages that illustrate or support a point they wish to make. If the book has a good oral style, that is, one that lends itself to reading aloud, you will usually gain by reading such passages to your listeners. If, however, it has certain qualities, such as the extremely long and complicated sentences of Carlyle, you may find it advisable to rely more on your own words rather than the author's to describe the work.

Buffon in his *Discourse on Style* believed that a style is "the order and movement one gives to one's thoughts."[6]

The magical quality of style can transform words into a moment's monument. Abraham Lincoln did this in his Gettysburg Address; Robert Ingersoll when he spoke at his brother's grave; and John F. Kennedy as he delivered his Inaugural Address on that blustery January 20, 1961. Readability will be facilitated if there is clarity of style.

Timelessness. We live in the present, and people frequently seek books in which they can find some practical usefulness, in which they can identify themselves. Robert Louis Stevenson, after reading Meredith's *The Egoist,* which he regarded very highly, remarked,

> "Here is a book to send the blood into men's faces. It is a satire of a singular quality. It is yourself that is hunted down; these are your own faults that are dragged into the day and numbered, with lingering relish, with cruel cunning and precision. A young friend of Meredith's came to him in agony. 'This is too bad of you,' he cried. 'Willoughby is me!' 'No, my dear fellow,' said the author, 'he is all of us.' "
>
> "I have read 'The Egoist' five or six times myself, and I mean to read it again," said Stevenson, "for I am like the young friend of

[6] Buffon, "Discours sur le Style, 1753," Lane Cooper, *The Art of the Writer* (Ithaca, New York: Cornell University Press, 1952), p. 148.

the anecdote,—I think Willoughby unmanly, but a serviceable exposure of myself."[7]

The timelessness of a book has nothing to do with the date of its publication; rather, it is concerned with the pertinence of the events and their impact on character and society in terms of the present regardless of the era in which it was written. This timelessness exists whenever readers or listeners recognize that what the author has to say survives time and becomes timely for all periods.

In conclusion, the book selected for review must be worth the time of the listeners and the effort of the reviewer. It must have (1) suitability, (2) readability, and (3) timelessness.

D. *A Suggested Blueprint for Book-Reviewing*

Just as an architect or engineer consults a blueprint to do his work so, too, you might consider these recommended lines in structuring your review.

1. *Provide a get-acquainted period with the listeners and the author, but not in the stilted manner of saying when an author was born and when he died.* Introduce the author to the listener in an unusual way. To do this you might tell a story about him and the circumstances under which he wrote the book. You might even read aloud a part of the preface, foreword, or introduction. Often in one of these the author reveals his purpose and gives the listeners a taste of what the book is about. You might even read a well chosen incident from the book itself, particularly one which evokes a sensation or creates a feeling of comradeship. This may serve as an invisible handclasp and establish a bond of fellowship between the author and the listener. Two illustrations will give you an idea of what is suggested. The first is taken from the foreword of Catherine Marshall's *Beyond Our Selves.*

> For the third person whom I want to mention in connection with the writing of *Beyond Our Selves* is, of course, Leonard LeSourd, whom I married in 1959, almost eleven years after Peter's death.

[7] Theodore W. Koch, "On the Art of Reading," *Reading: A Vice Or a Virtue* (Dayton: University of Dayton, 1929), p. 48.

> I find that having an editor in the family has many compensations, along with a few drawbacks. As the editor of *Guideposts* and a writer himself, Len understands the hours that every writer must keep, the needed isolation. He is patient with me when I fall into a black mood because ideas are not flowing, sentences are wooden, and what I am turning out is just plain terrible. Always he gives me unstintingly of his fine editorial judgment.
>
> There are times, however, when I want to slam the office door on my manuscript and not think or speak of it until the next day.

As you can see, in that passage, you have learned something about the author through her intimate and brief personal introduction.

In the following you will discover how Jack Fishman not only got the idea for his book, but how he reveals his purpose in the Preface of *My Darling Clementine.*

> Winston Churchill is the Statesman the whole world recognizes. Clementine Churchill is the diplomat few know.
>
> This book—this tribute to her—began on a bomb-site in the East End of London, during the Blitz days of 1940, when I was a newspaper reporter covering the tour by the Prime Minister and his wife, of bombed areas.
>
> People who had lived through the night were cheering this man to whom they looked for leadership and hope. But it was the woman beside him—or at least, one pace behind him—who held my attention. What kind of a woman could share his life, could be his wife? The question remained unanswered for a long time. I watched her on many occasions seated in the Distinguished Strangers' Gallery of the House of Commons when her husband held the floor of the Chamber below; I covered part of her Blitz tour with Mrs. Eleanor Roosevelt.
>
> Through the years I constantly added notes and anecdotes to a file I kept at home marked "Clementine." I gathered stories and facts from people she met; people with whom she worked, and who worked for her; Ministers and their wives; Members of Parliament; relatives, friends—literally hundreds of people—known and unknown, whose paths had crossed hers. I went to many who had already written of Winston Churchill and asked

> them to view various events again from a different aspect—his wife's.
>
> To persuade her to write her own story, or to write a book about her, has been an ambition of mine since those early war days. Her husband is the most written about man of our times, but largely because she has avoided the limelight, this is the first book ever to be written about her, and her place in the Winston Churchill legend.
>
> It does not pretend to be her life story, and is in no sense a full biography, for to tell her story would occupy almost as many volumes as those written by her husband on his own incredible life.

In this Preface your listeners will not only meet Mr. Fishman, but become acquainted with the subject of his book.

2. *Decide on a line of thinking regarding the book and follow it if you want to leave your listeners with a single impression.* It is advisable for you early in the review to let your listener know what line of thinking you are taking regarding the book and to center upon it. This may vary, depending upon your own original and inventive thinking, the type of book you are reviewing, and your listeners. For example, it might be the style in Thomas Wolfe's *Of Time and the River,* the structure of John Steinbeck's *Of Mice and Men,* a character such as Atticus in Harper Lee's *To Kill A Mockingbird,* or the symbolism in Ernest Hemingway's *The Old Man and the Sea.*

After you have decided on your line of thinking, then marshal all the passages and evidence in the book that you can to support your plan. And, as an oral interpreter, do not hesitate to read them aloud for, as Frank B. Sanborn believes, ". . . copious quotations from a book give it the best kind of review."[8] Edmond Lester Pearson, in one of his lectures to a group of librarians, said, ". . . quotations, if well chosen, will tell . . . more than any amount of criticism, no matter how clever the criticism."[9] And just to assure yourself that you are in good company when employing this technique, remember that Edgar Allan Poe, as a literary critic, quoted frequently and generously from the books he read

[8] Edmond Lester Pearson, *Book Reviews* (N.Y.: The New York Public Library, 1917), p. 38.

[9] *Ibid.*

and reviewed. It is hoped that your comments will not be as severe as Mr. Poe's.

According to F. O. Matthiessen, you can best suggest the quality of a piece of literature by concentrating upon a few significant episodes in your exposition, and allow your listeners to feel for themselves its quality ". . . through the force of a few deftly foreshortened examples woven into your exposition. And if that weaving has been really skillful you won't be faced with the necessity of a heavy-handed summary for your evaluation. You will have pointed it out lightly, by analytical insights, as you went along."[10]

To illustrate how written book reviews have included quotations from the book to support a point, two brief excerpts are included here. In the first, taken from a review of *The Adventures of Davy Crockett,* illustrated by John W. Thomason, Jr., original authorship unknown, the reviewer, William Rose Benet, uses an excerpt from the book to show the richness of the language.

> . . . His colloquial language is a treat. The Texas adventures are written in the first person and in his manner. They end with Crockett's last fight in defense of the Alamo. Toward the end there is a prime example of the racy style of the narrative. It occurs in a conversation with a hunter accompanying a fifty-mule caravan passing by Bexar and bound for Santa Fe:
>
> 'I jocosely asked the ragged hunter, who was a smart, active young fellow, of the steamboat and alligator breed, whether he was a rhinoceros or a hyena, as he was so eager for a fight with the invaders. "Neither the one, no t' others, Colonel," says he, "but a whole menagerie in myself. I'm shaggy as a bear, wolfish about the head, active as a cougar, and can grin like a hyena, until the bark will curl off a gum log. There's a sprinkling of all sorts in me, from the lion down to the skunk; and before the war is over you'll pronounce me an entire zoological institute, or I miss a figure in my calculation. I promise to swallow Santa Anna without gagging, if you will only skewer back his ears, and grease his head a little." '
>
> (*Saturday Review,* Feb. 24, 1934)

[10] F. O. Matthiessen, "The Winter Critic," *Atlantic Monthly,* October 1952, p. 88.

In the *Saturday Review,* February 18, 1961, "Magic and Mystery in the Sky," Quentin Reynolds reviewed Ernest Gann's *Fate Is the Hunter.* To illustrate how Gann could be moved by nature, Reynolds has incorporated a sample of the author's description:

> But, like Saint-Exupéry and the two Lindberghs before him, he [Gann] could appreciate the magic of a clear night and, although he knew that fate was forever after him, he could become as exhilarated as they with the beauty that Nature occasionally spread above him.
>
> Venus rose to signal me from the eastern horizon and it was brilliant and inconsistent in color, changing at once from yellow to green to purple and then reversing the show, that I thought for a time it was another aircraft equipped with special lighting devices. But Venus steadied in time, proving its identity. Tagging along behind it like an errant child, a small star arose, and I watched it being chased upward by the dawn.

3. *Include, occasionally, a few well integrated "book commercials" in your review.* All of you are aware of the radio-TV commercial—the advertising spot announcement. Although you may not always appreciate it, you must recognize that it is a form of salesmanship designed to create and sustain attention, as well as to arouse a desire for the product being sold, and to motivate the listener to buy. Certainly a parallel to this can often be used in your book-reviewing. A book worth your time and that of your listeners should be worth selling. You want attention from your listeners, you want to create a desire for the book you are reviewing, and you hope to motivate these listeners to buy or borrow the book. These objectives can, in part, be accomplished through your "commercial."

There are numerous ways in which you can advertise your book such as placing the book in the world of literature, or giving a critic's opinion (don't forget your own, too). You might describe its vivid writing, indicate its significance, its strength of characterization and its ideas. Or you might recommend it for a pleasant evening's reading. Your "commercial" should be a "soft sell." Your comments should be well incorporated into your review, and they should be distinctive, convincing, and honest. Consider the variety of commercials quoted below.

> . . . *The Power of Black* is a remarkable novel, Dickensian in the variety of its characters, the vigor of its 'big scenes,' the skillful interweaving of the elements of fact and fiction, the cunning juxtaposition of drama and melodrama, and the adroit use of exaggeration, caricature, and robust humor.
>
> (From a review of Mr. B. Longman's *The Power of Black* by William Peden. *Sat. Review,* March 25, 1961, "Hunt Without Quarry.")
>
> . . . His book of recollections, *In Retrospect: The History of a Historian,* . . . is warm, quizzical, forthright, and puckish, the qualities which have endeared him to teachers and students regardless of age.
>
> (From a review of *In Retrospect: The History of a Historian,* by Arthur M. Schlesinger and reviewed by Edward Weeks. *Atlantic,* April, 1964.)
>
> But, exceptionally slow and long-drawn-out though the editing has been, the result is in most ways very satisfactory. The three volumes are superbly printed and well bound. The annotation is masterly: far fuller than might reasonably have been expected, and beautifully laid out. As scholarly tools, these books will be in demand for many generations.
>
> (From a review of *The Letters of David Garrick,* Edited by David M. Little and George M. Kahrl. *The Spectator,* Feb. 28, 1964.)

4. *Provide good transitions.* How you as a reviewer get from one idea, one example, one illustration to another, the listeners do not always have to know. They do, no doubt, recognize how smoothly the review flows, but they may not realize what it is that carries their thoughts along and gives continuity to the review. Good transitions are the connecting links between thoughts, and they help to establish a sequence. Good transitions hold the attention and prepare the listener for a new idea. They are excellent devices for getting your listeners from "here" to "there."

Transitions, which enable the reviewer to move from one idea to another, may be made by a paragraph, a sentence, a phrase, or even a single word. (A more complete discussion of transitions has been given in Chapter VI, Analyzing Literature.)

5. *Call your characters by their names.* When you structure your review, be concrete, particularly with dialogue and characters. No character can ever come to life if you refer to him as "this man," "he," or "her brother." They all have names and must be called by their names. This will do two things—it will make the situation graphic and it will avoid confusion in the mind of the listener. Characters must become real persons for the reviewer before he can make them come alive in the mind of the listener. It will help, too, if you suggest vocal differences in your characters. In dialogue, after you have once established a character, you should be able to maintain his vocal characteristics. (For further discussion of this see Chapter VIII, The Oral Interpretation of Prose, and Chapter X, The Oral Interpretation of Drama.) Often the author will give you a clue by telling you what the characters say about each other. Do not forget the help that descriptive labels provide in determining how a thought is expressed, and do not be afraid to insert the name of the character when addressing or directing a comment to another.

6. *Plan a good conclusion, use it, and stop.* There are a number of possible impressions you can leave with your listener. You may, in your summary, mention a number of points which you want your listener to carry away. You may want (a) to repeat the name of the author and the title of the book, (b) to restate the author's point of view, (c) to give your own evaluation of the author and his book, (d) to encourage your listeners to read this book or others written by the same author, (e) to show where the book fits into the great library of mankind, and finally you may want (f) to emphasize the central idea of the book. Note these brief summaries and try to decide what point the reviewer was making.

> . . . He concludes this brilliant and important volume with a section of translations from the Norse sagas dealing with the Atlantic voyages. They are accomplished translations and read as well as the rest of the book, which is saying a great deal.
>
> (From a review of *The Norse Atlantic Saga* by Gwyn Jones, and reviewed by Dom Moraes in the *Spectator,* March 6, 1964.)
>
> Like many Irish novels, *The Remainderman* is rich in eccentrics, and Mr. White has the literary taste to describe their antics with scarcely a flicker of surprise. This novel is a slight but graceful achievement.
>
> (From a review of *The Remainderman* by Terrance De Vere

White and reviewed briefly by David Lodge in the *Spectator,* Aug. 16, 1963.)

As yet no complete biography of Colette exists; nor does the present study purport to be one. Indicative of its contents, however, are the carefully chosen and startlingly appropriate titles of each of the brief chapters: 'Games of Love,' 'Parables of Experience,' and 'Sorcery and Sagacity,' to name but three. This perceptive book will persuade readers who do not know Colette to turn to her writings with interest. Those already familiar with her published work will, by the same token, gain from the present volume both profit and enjoyment.

("Colette" by Elaine Marks. Reviewed by Otis Fellows, in the *Saturday Review,* Sept. 3, 1960, "Counterpoint to the Tune of Love.")

Or, you may approach the conclusion somewhat differently so that you bring into strong focus in your last statement exactly what the book is about and/or what the listener can look for when he reads the book. Robert Daley, in reviewing *All But My Life* by Stirling Moss with Ken W. Purdy, gives this précis:

This book is about victory and defeat, suffering and near death, about fear and about love, about a man who could never be still, who demanded perfection of everyone, most of all from himself. It is a deep look inside another man's world and soul.

(*The New York Times Book Review,* Nov. 17, 1963.)

STUDY QUESTIONS

1. What are the qualifications of an effective oral book reviewer?
2. What are the advantages of using and reading aloud direct quotations from the book in a review?
3. What responsibilities does an oral book reviewer have that a public speaker does not have?
4. Study the transitions used by a book reviewer in your college or local paper. Why were they effective or not effective?
5. What does an audience expect from you as an oral book reviewer?

6. A good oral book reviewer assumes a number of roles: he is a public speaker, an oral interpreter, a judicator, and a salesman. Explain this statement.

7. Recall a recent book you read. Would it serve the oral interpreter as a suitable book for reviewing?

8. What aspects of propriety should an oral interpreter keep in mind when choosing a book to review for a particular audience?

9. Why should an oral interpreter pay particular attention to "point of view" or intent of the author in reviewing a book?

BIBLIOGRAPHY

Carter, Mary Duncan and Wallace John Bonk, "The Selector and His Tools," *Building Library Collections,* pp. 68–70. New York: Scarecrow Press Inc., 1964.

Grimshaw, Ivan Gerould, "Doing the Book Review," Chap. VII, *How To Prepare A Speech.* New York: Woman's Press, 1952.

Haverland, Stella E., *Oral Book Reviewing.* Boston: Meador Publishing Company, 1938.

Hicks, Granville, "The Journalism of Book Reviewing," *Saturday Review,* 42 (Dec. 12, 1959), 16.

Marable, M. H., "Oral Book Reviews: pastime or pitfall?" *Oklahoma Librarian,* 2 (Summer, 1952), 6–7.

McCanse, Ralph Alan, *The Art of the Book Review.* Madison: University of Wisconsin, University Extension Division, 1963.

McDonald, Florin Lee, "Book Reviewing in the American Newspaper." Ph.D. Thesis, University of Missouri, 1936.

Oppenheimer, Evelyn, *Book Reviewing for An Audience: A Practical Guide in Technique for Lecture and Broadcast.* Philadelphia: Chilton Co., Book Division, 1962.

Robb, Mary Margaret, "Oral Interpretation and the Book Review," *The Speech Teacher,* V, No. 4 (1956), 285–289.

Smith, S. Stephenson, *The Craft of the Critic,* pp. 45–62. New York: Thomas Y. Crowell Company, 1938.

Walters, Raymond, Jr., "How to Review a Book," *The Wonderful World of Books,* ed. Alfred Stefferud, pp. 184–187. New York: A Mentor Book, The New American Library, 1953.

Woolf, Virginia, *Reviewing.* London: The Hogarth Press, 1939.

Chapter XIII

Readers' Theatre

A student drama critic, after viewing a Readers' Theatre production of Dylan Thomas' *Under Milk Wood,* wrote the following in the campus newspaper:

> It seems logical that seated actors holding scripts and using only an occasional gesture would be unable to communicate with an audience. However, such was not the case in last night's performance of *Under Milk Wood.*
>
> Using only voices and facial expressions, eight actors projected a great deal of warmth and humor across the footlights of Derby Hall Theatre to an appreciative audience. Very little scenery was in evidence but no more was necessary. No theatrical costumes were worn, but these, too, would have been superfluous.
>
> It would not require a veteran theatre-goer to recognize the unusual art form which this type of Readers' Theatre represents. Several characters were suggested by each actor with two narrators functioning as a link between the audience and the play. The technique is quite effective when handled by capable actors as it was last night.[1]

The student critic had attended the production not knowing what to expect. She was surprised, pleasantly surprised. Imagine projecting "a great deal of warmth and humor" to "an appreciative audience" while reading from scripts *and,* unthinkable as it seemed, without benefit of sets, costumes or stage movement! Although the critic confused "actors" with "oral interpreters," the point was clearly made favoring the format called Readers' Theatre.

[1] Barbara Hill, "Experiment '60 Play Is Odd, But Pleases Audience," *Ohio State Lantern,* February 18, 1960.

Many, not unlike the student critic, have been skeptical *until* that first experience with Readers' Theatre well done. Then, in a burst of creative enthusiasm, the questioning and searching and doing have begun.

I. THE CONTEMPORARY IMPETUS

No appreciable opportunity for the interpreter in terms of a professional public reading platform arose until Readers' Theatre gained critical acclaim in the New York theatre. The impetus for an acceptance of this communicative art form undoubtedly started with Paul Gregory's production of *Don Juan in Hell* with Charles Laughton, Charles Boyer, Sir Cedric Hardwicke, and Agnes Moorehead. This production played in New York's Carnegie Hall in October of 1951. Among the subsequent productions were *John Brown's Body* with Tyrone Power, Raymond Massey, and Judith Anderson; *The World of Carl Sandburg* with Leif Erickson and Bette Davis; *Brecht on Brecht* with Dane Clark, Anne Jackson, Lotte Lenya, Viveca Lindfors and George Voskovec; and *Dear Liar* with Katherine Cornell and Brian Aherne. Since that auspicious start in 1951, the New York theatre has offered at least one Readers' Theatre production each year. In addition, listings in current issues of the *Educational Theatre Journal, The Quarterly Journal of Speech,* and *The Speech Teacher* provide ample testimony to the increasing emphasis being placed on this art form on campuses from coast to coast. The Interpretation Interest Group of the Speech Association of America has evidenced its strong interest through the sponsorship of the Readers' Theatre Bibliography Committee which publishes an annual listing of appropriate materials. It cannot be denied that the medium of Readers' Theatre has been professionally and educationally successful (financially and critically). Each of the New York productions has received a consensus of critical acclaim and over half of them have had national tours. College audiences have responded enthusiastically to the medium and where, ten years ago, courses in Readers' Theatre did not exist, they can now be found in an increasing number of institutions.

II. CONFLICTS IN PHILOSOPHY

The principles, techniques, forms, and formats utilized in Readers' Theatre productions (educational and professional) continue to vary. The result, understandably, has been vagueness and inconsistency of treatment. Nevertheless, a number of similarities have emerged from the New York productions. The first characteristic was the claim of most of the adaptors and/or interpreters that their productions were programs of readings and not plays. Also, in most cases the printed text was present as a symbol of both the source and the approach. Whether it was actually read, and if so to what extent, is quite another thing. The most that can be said of some of the interpreters with regard to these texts is that they pretended to read them—at least part of the time. Whether memorization had been their intent or the result of their thorough preparation is unimportant. The fact remains that the text was present as symbolic of the source of the literary experience, if not as a stimulus aid of the moment. Also, in most of the productions, the readers did without many of the physical accoutrements of the theatre and denied lateral movement on the stage in favor of locating themselves on a stool behind a lectern. These factors formed the minimal requirements for a majority of the productions.

On the one hand, there have been productions wherein the readers are actors who speak from memory (although attending to their scripts from time to time), movement is much as it would be in a theatrical production, and the literary experience is located on-stage. On the other hand, productions are seen in which the readers are more dependent on their scripts but familiar enough with the literature to allow for frequent and sustained contact with the realm of the audience, lateral movement is denied, all responsiveness is suggestive in nature, and the literary experience is projected into the realm of the audience. We endorse this philosophy. Productions which have combined elements of both are neither Readers' Theatre nor Actors' Theatre.

The professional philosophy appears to be "if something is found to work, if it elicits the desired response, it justifies itself." The educational concern appears to be "if Readers' Theatre is an art form in itself and consequently worthy of attention, how should it be defined and differentiated from other art forms?" We embrace the educational concern and endorse the effectiveness of the professional product.

III. READERS' THEATRE DEFINED

Readers' Theatre can be, and has been, defined in a number of ways. None of the definitions appear to be contradictory, but each tends to focus on a particular emphasis. If we were to ask the New York critics to define this format, they would probably say, "Readers' Theatre is the combining of expert readers and minimal staging with great literature in a manner that is theatrically stimulating." The definition is valid. We, however, would prefer to say that *Readers' Theatre is a group activity in which a piece of literature is communicated from manuscript to an audience through the oral interpretation approach of vocal and physical suggestion.* The major implication of this definition is in the term "suggestion." You are already aware of the significance of this word in oral interpretation. Its significance is equally applicable to Readers' Theatre. The readers involved are obligated to provide vocal and physical cues, individually and at times collectively, which will stimulate and enable a listener to fulfill the potential of the literary experience in his own mind. The literary experience is not seen, as is the case with the traditional theatrical production. It is imagined. It exists within the mind of the listener, not in front of him on-stage.

IV. YOU AND YOUR LISTENER

This matter of listener involvement and participation suggests two additional guidelines for the reader. (1) The reader does not physically locate himself within the setting of the literary experience. If he did, he would be usurping the function of the listener by providing the setting for him rather than allowing him to create it in his own mind. (2) The readers do not laterally interact with each other as they would in the acting situation. If they did, the listener's attention would be directed to the stage for a representation of the action rather than visualizing and sensing the action in his own mind. The setting, the situation, the characters, the interaction, are all psychologically projected to and located in *the realm of the audience.* This does not mean that the readers are not involved in the literary experience or that they do not respond physically to the experience. It means that their involvement and responsiveness is focused *forward* and never confined *within* the area in which they are located.

You have long ago concluded that there are differences in function and behavior between the oral interpreter as communicator and the actor as communicator. These differences are also true in Readers' Theatre with the communicator playing the role of oral interpreter. There is, however, one difference which is a matter of degree. The oral interpreter reading alone is obligated to share two things with his listener. He is obligated to share the intent of the literature and he is obligated to share his personal, individualized reactions to the intent (the individual personality of the reader is not minimized). In Readers' Theatre the reader tends to subordinate this second obligation of the solo reader. He tends not to project his own individuality. You will find that the literary experience projected by the group has greater impact when your listeners are less aware of the individual personalities of the readers and more aware of the personalities of the characters being suggested. In one sense this presents a dilemma. We have said that the oral interpreter as a solo reader maintains his own identity but that the oral interpreter in the group situation (Readers' Theatre) minimizes his own identity for the sake of group impact. There is a fine line between minimizing your identity and tending to become another person. It is a distinction that you will need to experiment with and observe in your class projects. Perhaps the following excerpts from three critical reviews will be helpful. In March of 1961, Michael MacLiammoir opened his one-man show in New York called *The Importance of Being Oscar.* Although the purist might argue that this production was not Readers' Theatre, the New York critics so labeled it. Robert Coleman, writing in the *New York Daily Mirror,* reported:

> If you want to enjoy acting in the grand manner, we recommend Michael MacLiammoir in *The Importance of Being Oscar.* It is in no sense a conventional reading, but rather a full-blooded, witty and moving stage performance.[2]

Coleman's "acting in the grand manner" was given the following context by critics Richard Watts, Jr. and Howard Taubman, reporting in the *New York Post* and the *New York Times,* respectively:

> He wisely makes no attempt to pretend he is acting the role of Oscar Wilde. He is Michael MacLiammoir commenting sagely, sympathetically and wittily on Wilde's life and works.[3]

> But even as he performs, Mr. MacLiammoir preserves a strong measure of his own identity. Unlike other one-man shows devoted to recalling the person and creative world of a renowned writer, Mr. MacLiammoir does not attempt to assume his subject's appearance. The Irish actor impersonates Wilde and other figures in the story but he also stands aside and comments. He is elucidator as well as protagonist, generous critic as well as versatile actor.[4]

As you see, even the professional critic can be confused. Was Mr. MacLiammoir playing the role of actor or was he playing the role of oral interpreter? Or was he playing both roles? Perhaps the problem rests with the perception of the critic. This was the case in the reviews of *Dear Liar* which played in New York in March of 1960. Richard Watts, Jr., writing for the *New York Post,* reported:

> Miss Cornell and Mr. Aherne make no direct effort to impersonate Mrs. Pat and Shaw . . . But so effective are their performances that it isn't long before they do seem to merge into the half affectionate, half infuriated pair whose intimacy was chiefly through their letters.[5]

[2] Robert Coleman, "Oscar' Grand Performance," *New York Daily Mirror,* March 15, 1961.

[3] Richard Watts, Jr., "A Brilliant Actor on Oscar Wilde," *New York Post,* March 15, 1961.

[4] Howard Taubman, "Theatre: MacLiammoir Presents Vivid One-Man Show," *New York Times,* March 15, 1961.

[5] Richard Watts, Jr., "The Playwright & The Actors," *New York Post,* March 18, 1960.

Frank Aston, reporting on the same production for the *New York World-Telegram,* wrote:

> Mr. Kilty implies his two are not impersonating Mrs. Campbell and Shaw. One wonders. In the beginning they bloom with vigor. At the end she has faded and he totters. Through the years he remains volatile, voluble, amusingly petulant. Until she is close to death she is a hard-headed spitfire, proud, pliant, rebellious, sentimental—a bundle of contradictions that, from triumph to despair, wealth to poverty, health to weakness, remains primarily a desirable woman. If this isn't impersonation it is marvelous suggestion.[6]

"Marvelous suggestion," indeed. One can but wonder how frequently it has been "marvelous suggestion" that has so stimulated the listener (including the critic) as to prompt him to conclude that he had *witnessed* the presence of a character rather than having re-created it in his own mind.

Your listener, of course, is free to conclude what he wishes. As a performer, however, you must choose the role you will play and then be consistent. To combine the roles of the oral interpreter and the actor is to take the chance that your listener will be confused. Is the predominant function of your listener that of witnessing or is it that of participating by re-creating in his own mind? What an audience is *led to believe* (through suggestion) may develop into something quite different from what he is *shown to believe* (through representation). As that which is represented (acted) is not similar to that which is suggested (interpreted), so will audience confusion exist.

It is important for you to remember that an audience is capable of fulfilling the potential of a literary experience when given appropriate and vivid cues. To be shown everything, or almost everything, is *not* a prerequisite to involvement.

V. ADDITIONAL CUES

The cues in Readers' Theatre do not, however, have to be limited to vocal and physical suggestions by the readers. Other audio and visual

[6] Frank Aston, "Cornell, Aherne Exchange Notes in Kilty's 'Dear Liar,'" *New York World-Telegram & Sun,* March 18, 1960.

cues (sound effects, music, dress, etc.) may be used so long as they are suggestive in nature—symbolic and non-illusionistic. The reader, as you know, serves as an interpreter whose objective is sharing, while the actor attempts to create the illusion of reality. A non-illusionistic or symbolic environment created by the use of additional properties will not, in itself, pull the action on-stage and can, therefore, be consistent with the Readers' Theatre format.

It is quite possible that the reader's attire could aid the listener in his participation in re-creating the desired mood. Or a particular "prop" in the right location might serve as a meaningful cue, as did the throne-like chair placed center stage in *The World of Carl Sandburg*. Sound, particularly music, has the capacity to enhance a mood and an idea, although caution needs to be exercised to avoid selecting the overly familiar tune. A fluid lighting can be used on readers about the stage, dimming on one and accentuating another to give emphasis and focus to the content of the literature. Color, whether used through lighting or costuming, should be used for its own psychological impact and must always be analogous to the sense and mood of the ideas expressed.

If you decide to use these additional cues, be sure that you are highly sensitive to the sometimes subtle differences between the abstract and the literal *and* be careful not to unbalance your production on the side of staging it. The only justification for using additional cues, or for any kind of staging, is the possibility that they may heighten or clarify your listener's involvement in the literary experience. It would, however, be a mistake to conclude that these aids are necessary prerequisites to effective Readers' Theatre. The use of lighting effects *may* help to suggest a mood or a character. The use of background music *may* heighten the emotional impact. The presence of a symbolic figure *may* focus attention on the major concern. Any such inclusion *may* make a significant contribution to the impact of the experience, but after all is said and done, nothing need be substituted or added to that Readers' Theatre experience resulting from superb oral interpretation of the manuscript.

When *Don Juan in Hell* was first presented in New York it set a note of scenic austerity and simplicity which has been emulated not only by the other offerings on the New York stage but by Readers' Theatre productions throughout the country. The basic pattern has consisted of a high stool and lectern for each of the readers, set against a neutral background. More often than not, readers have worn formal or semiformal attire. The New York critics lauded the fact that scenery was rendered unnecessary by the other elements of production. Walter Kerr, writing in the *New York Herald Tribune,* happily announced in 1951 that "the Drama Quartette has turned the tables, thrown out what was both expensive and unnecessary, and filled the vacuum with fire, intelligence and emotional power."[7] Robert Coleman, in reviewing *The Importance of Being Oscar* for the *New York Daily Mirror,* said, "It just goes to show that you don't need a lot of expensive scenery to display an actor of sensitivity at his best."[8] Walter Kerr's comment about *John Brown's Body* was: "A looting member of Sherman's army, shouting his way through the echoing halls of a deserted mansion, is far more vividly realized than he might have been had the scenic warehouses been ransacked for literal props."[9] Frances Herridge, in her *New York Post* review of O'Casey's *I Knock at the Door,* wrote, "A mere six people, on a stage bare of everything but stools and lecterns, manage to project one episode after another . . . with more vivid detail than a realistic stage version could have conveyed."[10]

VI. ARRANGEMENT OF READERS

Readers may sit or stand and their manuscripts, which serve as a stimulus aid and are symbolic of the source of the literary experience, may be held or placed on lecterns. If the arrangement of the readers varies from the traditional straight line or semi-circle, it does so to point up psychological distance between and among the characters or ideas being suggested. In this case readers could be located on different levels or at varying distances from each other. These locations might suggest to the audience degrees of conflict or harmony. Note that the function of such arrangements is to suggest psychological distance rather than a

[7] Walter Kerr, "John Brown's Body," *New York Herald Tribune,* March 15, 1961.

[8] Robert Coleman, "Oscar' Grand Performance," *New York Daily Mirror,* March 15, 1961.

[9] Walter Kerr, *op. cit.,* February 16, 1953.

[10] Frances Herridge, "O'Casey's Youth Recreated on Stage," *New York Post,* September 30, 1957.

literal location. Whatever is done must be kept in the realm of suggestion. The arrangement of the readers must not bring the action on-stage.

If, for example, your group decided to read "I Looked Down Into My Open Grave," from *Profiles in Courage,* by John F. Kennedy, the placement of the lecterns in a straight line might suggest the stateliness and solemnity of the situation that Edmund G. Ross found himself in. Another piece of literature might dictate an oblique arrangement, creating a sense of motion or action. There is also a sense of "pull" in this alignment which helps to focus attention on the reader near the center of the stage. Paul Gallico's *Love of Seven Dolls* is an excellent selection for Readers' Theatre. The reader suggesting the central character, Moche, might be placed in the center with the other readers suggesting each of the puppets placed in a semi-circle behind her.

Since the narrator is the middle man between the readers and the audience, it is usually effective to place him at one side of the group, preferably nearest the audience.

VII. TECHNIQUES FOR ENTRANCES AND EXITS

The matter of entrances and exits within the literature offers the director and reader a certain challenge. In the first place, whatever the reader does should be in keeping with the mood of the situation and the personality of the character. If you are to "move in" to a scene or episode, you may do it by simply leaning forward and placing your hand or hands upon the lectern. This gives a sense of "presence." To exit you may relax and withdraw slightly from the lectern, putting your hands in your lap. If you are standing, merely a suggestion of a step forward or backward is enough to make the entrance or exit apparent. Or you may rise from your chair when you are to appear in the scene, and when you leave, you may sit down. An entrance or exit may also be accomplished simply by lowering or lifting the head, or by slightly turning your body away from the other readers if you are located on either side of the group. One class found that an effective means of indicating an entrance or exit in the court scene of *Saint Joan* by G. B. Shaw was attained by having the readers sit on the stools with their backs to the audience. As the characters entered the scene, they merely turned around and faced the class. When they stepped out of the scene, they turned their backs on the audience. If they were "in the court room" and not a part of the conversation, but listeners, they sat in profile to the class. Perhaps one of the most unobtrusive and effective guideposts to stepping into or out of the picture is simply that of opening and closing the manuscript on the lectern. This movement in itself suggests to the audience that the character or reader has become a part of the activity, or that he has withdrawn from it.

VIII. SELECTION OF LITERATURE

A wide variety of literature has been successfully used in Readers' Theatre, including prose, poetry and drama. Usually material emphasizing conflict through ideas and characters has been most rewarding. Although all literary forms can be used, it should be remembered that one of the *unique* contributions of Readers' Theatre is the sharing of literature not usually treated by actors on stage. As a matter of fact, Readers' Theatre can do for non-dramatic literature what the theatre has done for dramatic literature: provide an opportunity for *experiencing* literature through visual and aural involvement in the dynamics of literature. This is not to suggest that drama should be avoided but, rather, that drama should not be your only source of materials. The tendency of academic programs to mainly concentrate on adaptations of drama for Readers' Theatre programs has been unfortunate. The New York theatre would not tolerate this tendency. If the critics are to see a play, they want the full treatment. For example, Howard Taubman, writing in the *New York Times* in January of 1962, said, "until we have Brecht's plays on Broadway, *Brecht on Brecht* will do." Although the critics expect the offerings to be theatrically stimulating, they do not attempt to apply the canons of dramatic literature to the Readers' Theatre offerings. Indeed, they welcome the change and, in so doing, expect a difference. Neither they nor we should accept what might appear to be a polished rehearsal of a play with scripts in hand.

With the notable exceptions of *Don Juan in Hell* (which is really too static to be accepted as a play) and John Gielgud's *Ages of Man* (which was made up of cuttings from many plays), the forte of Readers' Theatre in New York has been the presentation of works from non-dramatic genres. The source of *John Brown's Body* was an epic poem; *The Importance of Being Oscar* was drawn from Wilde's plays, novel, and various letters; *Dear Liar* was concocted by Jerome Kilty from the correspondence between George Bernard Shaw and Mrs. Patrick Campbell and from two short excerpts from his plays; *The World of Carl Sandburg* included writings from Sandburg's poems, songbook, and prose, including his biography of Lincoln; sayings, poems, songs, fragments of letters, essays and plays formed the basis of the *Brecht on Brecht* program. The various fragments of most of the programs were bridged by expositional passages supplied by the person responsible for the adaptation.

The critics responded enthusiastically to the literature of these authors as interpreted by the readers. In so doing they qualified these programs as succeeding in the most important and basic goal of oral interpretation: listener involvement in the literary experience suggested by the readers. According to the critics the author's ideas and spirit were always dominant. For example, William Hawkins reviewed *Don Juan in Hell* for the *New York World-Telegram & Sun,* October 23, 1951, and said, "It is both brilliant and generous. Brilliant because it conveys so expertly a glittering argument that is allowed to progress entirely on its own terms. Nothing interferes with the words." When he reviewed *John Brown's Body* in February of 1953, he wrote, "The work is staged so nothing interferes with the poet's phrases, in their primary function of inciting you, the listener, to create image after image of your own." Howard Taubman's review of *Brecht on Brecht* for the *New York Times* in January of 1961 included this comment: "This living anthology which began a run last night at the Theatre de Lys, is merely a glimpse into the heart and workshop of the poet and playwright. Yet it illuminates the richness of Brecht's sympathies, the edge of his humor, the acuteness of his mind, his disarming gift of self-depreciation, and, above all, his cool and flaming command of the theatre."[11]

[11] Howard Taubman, Theatre: " 'Brecht on Brecht' Opens Run," *New York Times,* January 4, 1962.

IX. THE MAJOR GUIDEPOSTS

There are at least three major guideposts to Readers' Theatre which should be kept in mind. (1) You should not lose your own identity to the extent that you "become" a character or locate the character on-stage; vivid and accurate suggestion (oral and visual cues) remain your predominant function. (2) The function of your listener is to fulfill the suggested potential of the literary experience in his own mind: *participating* in the re-creative experience rather than witnessing it. (3) Your director *may* heighten or clarify readers' suggestions (if the literature or the readers need such help) through other visual and auditory aids, so long as these aids are kept in the realm of suggestion and do *not* interfere with the function of the listener.

While it is true that the performance must not exist for its own sake alone, it is equally true that the literature simply cannot stand by itself. It is also clear that no matter how successful the brilliant reader is in drawing attention to the material rather than to himself, sensitive people will not fail to respond to him as a reader as well as to the literature. The only conclusion to be reached is that a Readers' Theatre venture is a partnership of literature and oral interpreter and listener.

STUDY QUESTIONS

1. On the basis of your reading from the books and articles listed in the bibliography for this chapter, list the several definitions of Readers' Theatre which you encountered. In what respects do they differ?

2. When would it be more appropriate to call a production Impersonators' Theatre rather than Readers' Theatre? When would it be more appropriate to call a production Actors' Theatre? Is the word *Readers'* the critical term which clarifies one of the major differences between formats?

3. How might the effectiveness of a Readers' Theatre production be determined? Would the semantic differential technique for the measurement of meaning be useful?

4. Adapt a short story for a Readers' Theatre production. If cutting is required, what principles will guide you? If staging is needed, what principles will guide you?

5. When would you prefer to communicate a short story through a single reader rather than by a group of readers?

BIBLIOGRAPHY

Armstrong, Chloe and Paul D. Brandes, *The Oral Interpretation of Literature.* New York: McGraw-Hill Book Company, Inc., pp. 289–293.

Bacon, Wallace, *The Art of Interpretation.* New York: Holt, Rinehart and Winston, Inc., pp. 306–346.

Baker, Virgil, "Reading in Action Productions of New Plays," *Players Magazine,* Vol. 35, no. 5 (Feb. 1959), 102–103.

Brooks, Keith, "Readers' Theatre: Some Questions and Answers," *Dramatics,* Vol. XXXIV, no. 3 (Dec. 1962), 14, 27.

Brooks, Keith, Robert C. Henderhan, and Alan Billings, "A Philosophy on Readers' Theatre," *The Speech Teacher,* Vol. XII, no. 3 (Sept. 1963), 229–232.

Brooks, Keith and John E. Bielenberg, "Readers' Theatre as Defined by New York Critics," *Southern Speech Journal,* Summer, 1964, pp. 288–302.

Coger, Leslie, "Interpreters Theatre: Theatre of the Mind," *Quarterly Journal of Speech,* Vol. XLIX, no. 2 (April 1963), 157–164.

Coger, Leslie, "Let's Have a Reader's Theatre," The National Thespian Society, *Dramatics,* Vol. XXIX, 25–27.

Grimes, Wilma H. and Alethea Smith Mattingly. *Interpretation: Writer, Reader, Audience.* San Francisco: Wadsworth Publishing Company, Inc., p. 331–336, 1961.

Lee, Charlotte I., *Oral Interpretation* (Third Edition). Boston: Houghton Mifflin Company, pp. 218–220, 333–335, 1965.

McCoard, William B., "Report On the Reading of Hiroshima," *Quarterly Journal of Speech.* Vol. 34, no. 2 (April 1948), 174–176.

Robertson, Roderick, "Producing Playreadings," *Educational Theatre Journal.* Vol. XII, (March, 1960), 20–23.

Sandoe, James, "A Note or Two About Playreadings," *Western Speech,* Vol. XVII, no. 4 (Oct. 1953), 225–229.

Susan, Sister Mary, "Chamber Theatre," *Catholic Theatre,* Vol. XVIII, no. 8 (May 1960), 3–4.

Part Six

Evaluation and Research

Chapter XIV

Evaluating the Communicative Act

Evaluation of your achievement as an oral interpreter by you, your peers, and your faculty is a significant part of your education. Likewise, your ability to evaluate others and the literature they read is critical to your educational growth. No art form can flourish which harbors an immunity to inspection and introspection. The challenge is to improve on what you *are* and what you *have* through the ongoing process of evaluation and re-evaluation.

Gandhi reportedly preached, "It is easy to be generous, but one must always be just." The idealism of the statement has merit. The pragmatic intent and fulfillment of the statement is complex. The question remains, "What can we do to make our evaluations more just?"

As previously stated, in oral interpretation we are concerned with the literature, the oral interpreter and the listener. Each is dependent on the other, and the goal, during the communicative act, is a union of the three. Any breakdown in arriving at our goal may be traced to the literature, or to the oral interpreter, or to the listener, or to any combination of these parts. When a breakdown occurs it is necessary to re-evaluate any one or more of these parts in an attempt to fit the part into an organic whole. Evaluation, then, involves the continuing process of analysis and synthesis of all of the related parts until we arrive at that kind of fusion which results in an effective communicative act.

When a listener becomes involved in a literary experience as the reader intended him to become involved, the communicative act has been effective. The implication here is that the *effect* is more important than the *method.* There is merit in this implication, but it needs to be qualified. The qualification is that the communicator must be playing the role of the oral interpreter. So long as the communicator functions in the role of the oral interpreter (as previously discussed), a favorable listener response is the appropriate criterion for effectiveness rather than the techniques used by the interpreter. In other words, the communicator in oral interpretation should function in the role of oral interpreter rather than in the role of actor, or impersonator, or public speaker, *and* so long as he does this we are concerned first with the effectiveness of the act (in terms of the listener response) and later, if necessary, with the method (in terms of the interpreter's techniques) and with the literature (in terms of its intent). When the listener's response has been favorable to the interpreter's judgments of the intent of the literature, the need for dissecting the parts has been minimized except as such dissection provides a model for peer approval and learning. We remind you that *during the communicative act* of oral interpretation, the interpreter's judgments of the intent of the literature *are* the predominant stimuli for the listener response. The listener is obligated to involve himself in the interpreter's judgments, which must be the result of careful analysis and synthesis of the manuscript. Listeners know that these judgments are not absolute and that there is no single right way of understanding any piece of literature. Differences of opinion, which may be revealed in a post-discussion of the intent of the literature, should not result in the conclusion that the interpreter's judgments were necessarily poorly communicated.

There are many ways of evaluating the communicative act of oral interpretation. Oral and written critiques by your peers and by your instructor are among the most popular methods. Oral discussions have particular value in that standards are exposed for the benefit of the entire class. You must, however, remember that in giving an oral critique your function is to *assist* the interpreter and your colleagues, as well as to help clarify your own thinking. The intent of your critique must never be to embarrass others or to attempt to express your own sense of superiority. Your critique should be a learning and a sharing experience intended to help others as well as yourself. The same is true of the written critique. You will find that it has particular value as a permanent record of reactions and recommendations. In writing critiques take care to be as specific and as helpful as possible. In receiving written critiques, consider each comment carefully even though divergent points of view will be in evidence. You should not expect that all listeners will be in agreement. This rarely happens. Although you may find that the reaction of the majority has the greatest impact, do not dismiss the minority response. Any group of people is composed of many audiences and each audience is a part of your concern. Written and oral critiques may be supplemented by scales, check-lists, tests for comprehension, and a host of other evaluative methodologies. These evaluations may focus attention on the understanding and appreciation of the literary experience communicated (the effect criterion), or on the appropriateness of the methods used (the technique criterion).

I. THE EFFECT CRITERION

Although your instructor is a highly specialized listener capable of providing expert responses to the effectiveness of the communicative act, he (or she) is but a single listener and cannot speak for the total listener response. You must become class oriented, rather than instructor oriented. Your function is to share with the group rather than a single individual. Certainly you will be more dependent on your instructor for guidelines and standards during the first few weeks than on your fellow students, but as you and your peers become more knowledgeable so will the group evaluation of your work become more reliable. Because your function is to stimulate a favorable response from your listeners, the test of effectiveness is determined by gauging the response of that group.

In summary, a consensus of listener response can be determined through a class discussion following the reading, through written reports revealing the listener's grasp of the meanings and emotions suggested, or through checklists and scales developed for the purpose of reflecting understanding and appreciation of a piece of literature. The degree of group understanding and/or appreciation of the literature read would indicate the degree of success of that particular communicative act of oral interpretation.

It is possible, of course, that the lack of a favorable listener response may be due to ineffective listening rather than to ineffective interpretation. When this appears to be the problem, emphasis needs to be placed on listening skills. The effect criterion happens to be such an emphasis.

When a listener *knows* that he may be called upon for a response, oral or written, he tends to become a better listener. Therefore, as the effect criterion is utilized, so should listening effectiveness improve. Or, the lack of a favorable listener response may be due to the literature selected. The literature may have been inappropriate to the medium of oral interpretation (some literature may be too complex for listener understanding and appreciation, and should be left for silent study and discussion), or the literature may have been inappropriate to the educational level of the particular audience.

If you are interested in gauging the general reaction of your listeners to your oral interpretation of a piece of literature, you might use the *General Effectiveness Scale.* Your rater, in using this scale, can check a continuum from "exceptional" to "lacking," which indicates his degree of involvement in the literary experience which you have suggested. Spaces are available for responses to five readers. The most reliable index of effectiveness for a particular interpreter will be revealed by determining which category on the continuum is the average response for the entire class *plus* the category checked by your instructor. The response of your instructor should be heavily weighted (perhaps 50%), at least during the first few weeks of your term.

GENERAL EFFECTIVENESS SCALE

	Oral Interpreters				
Degree of Listener Involvement	(1) ______	(2) ______	(3) ______	(4) ______	(5) ______
Exceptional					
Very Good					
Average					
Lacking					

Listener: ______________

If you prefer to get a general response to several criteria (each of which is an important part of your total communicative act), use the *Oral Interpretation Performance Scale.* This scale allows your listeners to evaluate your introduction, the appropriateness of your vocal responsiveness, the appropriateness of your physical responsiveness, the appropriateness of your selection, and your over-all effectiveness. Each criterion is scored on the basis of 1 to 5. Columns are provided for the scoring of five interpreters. It is important that your listener respond to each of the criteria *in terms of the literature being read,* keeping in mind that what is appropriate to one piece of literature is not necessarily appropriate to another selection. Your listener must always be mindful of the help given him in focusing on the literature rather than on you, the interpreter.

ORAL INTERPRETATION PERFORMANCE SCALE

(1–Weak) (3–Average) (5–Strong)

Criteria	Oral Interpreters				
	(1) (1–5)	(2) (1–5)	(3) (1–5)	(4) (1–5)	(5) (1–5)
Introduction					
Appropriateness of Vocal Responsiveness					
Appropriateness of Physical Responsiveness					
Appropiateness of Selection					
General Effectiveness					
Sum of Scores					
Rank Order					

Listener: ____________________

If you wish, the oral interpreters for the day may be ranked by totaling their individual scores and assigning their rank order in terms of the sum of their scores. Although competition per se may not be a laudable objective, the motivation stimulus of ranking has merit from time to time.

Another interesting and worthy measure of your success in communicating what you believe to be the intent of the literature is the comparison of your pre-reading judgments with the composite post-reading judgments of your listeners. A comparison of the profile of those judgments which you *intended* to communicate with the composite listener profile revealing what they *received* will reveal discrepancies (if any) and provide an excellent basis for evaluation and for class discussion.

For example, let us assume that you are reading from *Portrait of the Artist as a Young Man,* by James Joyce. It may be that you intend to select excerpts which you feel suggest three major ideas. (1) There is an intermingling of the world of reality and the world of a young man's fantasy dominated by the irreverence of youth as he confronts the approach-avoidance duality of the flesh and the spirit. (2) Stephen Dedalus' world is warm yet lonely and a place where beauty is the eventual rare truth, but ugliness is ever present. (3) The ties with the church were dominant features of the life of young Dedalus, but he was never able to completely embrace his religion.

Having made your judgments of the intent of the literature, you could now prepare a list of polar opposites appropriate to aspects of each of your three major contentions. Your series of continua might be represented as shown in the *Profile for Portrait of the Artist as a Young Man.*

This particular form was prepared by a student and used in the classroom. The second copy of his form shows his check marks, revealing his pre-judgments of the intent of the literature. The third copy of the form shows the composite audience profile, revealing the collective judgment of the group response after the reading.

The composite audience profile was very similar to the interpreter's pre-reading profile with the exception of the third category. In other words, the interpreter received the response he sought in terms of the first two categories, but he was not successful in communicating his judgments concerning the relationship between Stephen Dedalus and the church. Why? Were the interpreter's judgments about the intent of the literature in error? Were his judgments on content acceptable, but his

PROFILE FOR

Portrait of the Artist as a Young Man

GENERAL REACTIONS TO THE CONTENT

reality ____:____:____:____:____:____:____ fantasy
reverence ____:____:____:____:____:____:____ irreverence
loss ____:____:____:____:____:____:____ discovery
flesh ____:____:____:____:____:____:____ spirit
resistance ____:____:____:____:____:____:____ passiveness

GENERAL REACTIONS TO THE CHARACTER OF STEPHEN DEDALUS

inner ____:____:____:____:____:____:____ outer
warm ____:____:____:____:____:____:____ cold
beauty ____:____:____:____:____:____:____ ugliness
alone ____:____:____:____:____:____:____ together
submission ____:____:____:____:____:____:____ resistance

GENERAL REACTIONS TO THE RELATIONSHIP BETWEEN STEPHEN DEDALUS AND THE CHURCH

attachment ____:____:____:____:____:____:____ detachment
acceptance ____:____:____:____:____:____:____ rejection
guilt ____:____:____:____:____:____:____ innocence
injustice ____:____:____:____:____:____:____ justice

Name: ____________

judgments on delivery in error? Did the interpreter's cutting distort the appropriate context for the listener? Or was there another reason for this discrepancy?

The value of this technique should now be obvious to you. It pin-points areas of effective and ineffective communication in terms of listener response and, in so doing, improves the focus of class discussion. Also, it provides a highly reliable index of effectiveness. The technique is efficient and each student can construct continua appropriate to his literature prior to the class period.

PROFILE FOR

Portrait of the Artist as a Young Man

GENERAL REACTIONS TO THE CONTENT

reality _____:_____:_____:_____:_____:_____:_____ fantasy
reverence _____:_____:_____:_____:_____:_____:_____ irreverence
loss _____:_____:_____:_____:_____:_____:_____ discovery
flesh _____:_____:_____:_____:_____:_____:_____ spirit
resistance _____:_____:_____:_____:_____:_____:_____ passiveness

GENERAL REACTIONS TO THE CHARACTER OF STEPHEN DEDALUS

inner _____:_____:_____:_____:_____:_____:_____ outer
warm _____:_____:_____:_____:_____:_____:_____ cold
beauty _____:_____:_____:_____:_____:_____:_____ ugliness
alone _____:_____:_____:_____:_____:_____:_____ together
submission _____:_____:_____:_____:_____:_____:_____ resistance

GENERAL REACTIONS TO THE RELATIONSHIP BETWEEN STEPHEN DEDALUS AND THE CHURCH

attachment _____:_____:_____:_____:_____:_____:_____ detachment
acceptance _____:_____:_____:_____:_____:_____:_____ rejection
guilt _____:_____:_____:_____:_____:_____:_____ innocence
injustice _____:_____:_____:_____:_____:_____:_____ justice

Name: Craig William

Interpreter's Pre-Reading Profile

PROFILE FOR

Portrait of the Artist as a Young Man

GENERAL REACTIONS TO THE CONTENT

reality	____	____	____	____	____	____	____	fantasy
reverence	____	____	____	____	____	____	____	irreverence
loss	____	____	____	____	____	____	____	discovery
flesh	____	____	____	____	____	____	____	spirit
resistance	____	____	____	____	____	____	____	passiveness

GENERAL REACTIONS TO THE CHARACTER OF STEPHEN DEDALUS

inner	____	____	____	____	____	____	____	outer
warm	____	____	____	____	____	____	____	cold
beauty	____	____	____	____	____	____	____	ugliness
alone	____	____	____	____	____	____	____	together
submission	____	____	____	____	____	____	____	resistance

GENERAL REACTIONS TO THE RELATIONSHIP BETWEEN STEPHEN DEDALUS AND THE CHURCH

attachment	____	____	____	____	____	____	____	detachment
acceptance	____	____	____	____	____	____	____	rejection
guilt	____	____	____	____	____	____	____	innocence
injustice	____	____	____	____	____	____	____	justice

Name: 221 Class

Composite Audience Profile

II. THE TECHNIQUE CRITERION

Among the reasons listed in Chapter II for failure of the communicative act was *ineffective and/or insufficient cues from the reader.* If it has been determined that the communicative act was *not* effective, in terms of the effect criterion, attention needs to be given to the communicative process itself. It may be that the fault rests with the cues (the suggestions) communicated by the interpreter. These cues fall into two categories—vocal and physical. In both cases, the *appropriateness* of the cue to the literature being read is the major concern.

A discussion of the vocal cues might include such questions as these. Were the vocal intensities appropriate to the intent of the literature? Were the tempos communicated appropriate to the intent of the literature? Were the sounds appropriately audible and intelligible and meaningful? Were the vocal qualities appropriate to the intent of the literature?

A discussion of the physical cues might include such questions as these. Were the degrees of directness appropriate to the intent of the literature? Were the suggestions of muscle tonicity appropriate to the intent of the literature? Were the gestures suggested appropriate to the intent of the literature? Was there a totality of physical responsiveness and, if so, was it kept within the realm of suggestion?

It is entirely possible that a major clue rests with the question, "Did the cues, vocal and physical, complement each other?" If so, was the complement appropriate to the intent of the literature? In total, there is considerable merit to the idea of letting the literature dictate the response.

The technique criterion is frequently used prior to any consideration of the effect criterion. The assumption, in these instances, is that techniques need to be improved in order to gain the desired effect. There is nothing wrong with the assumption, so long as it is recognized that techniques are a means to an end.

The *Classroom Interpretation Check-List* may assist you in evaluating your techniques. It, of course, is also a form which may be used by your peers and your instructor in providing a profile of opinion.

CLASSROOM INTERPRETATION CHECK-LIST

INTERPRETER ______ DATE ______ASSIGNMENT ______

INTRODUCTION

Delivery: Effective __, Ineffective __, Inconsistent __
Content: Stimulating __, Not stimulating __, Inconsistent __

Comments: ____

APPROPRIATENESS OF VOCAL RESPONSIVENESS

Sounds: Meaningful __, Not meaningful __, Inconsistent __
Quality: Appropriate __, Inappropriate __, Inconsistent __
Volume: Appropriate __, Inappropriate __, Inconsistent __
Tempo: Appropriate __, Inappropriate __, Inconsistent __
Intensity: Appropriate __, Inappropriate __, Inconsistent __
Intelligibility: Good __, Not good __, Inconsistent __
Pitch: Appropriate __, Inappropriate __, Inconsistent __
Phrasing: Appropriate __, Inappropriate __, Inconsistent __
Motivation: Good __, Not good __, Inconsistent __

Mispronounced and Misarticulated words: ____________________
____

Comments: ____

APPROPRIATENESS OF PHYSICAL RESPONSIVENESS

Totality: Consistent __, Inconsistent __
Realm of suggestion __, Literal __, Inconsistent __
Focus: Appropriate __, Inappropriate __, Appropriateness inconsistent __
Individuality: Appropriately committed __, Inappropriately committed __, Not apparent __
Motivation: Good __, Not good __, Inconsistent __

Comments: ____

GENERAL EFFECTIVENESS

Attitude: Helpful __, Not helpful __
Preparedness: Sufficient __, Insufficient__

Comments: ____

LISTENER: ______________

Regardless of the scale or check-list employed, it must be usable within the time limits of your class period. Certainly there are many more categories and specifics which could be included, but to evolve a form which covers several pages would interfere with its usefulness in the classroom in terms of time and would tend to reduce critical focus. The problem, then, is to select those categories which would best assist you in evaluating others and in developing evaluative standards. Leave the rest to oral and written critiques. Also, it is important that the categories be limited to *observable* traits: those characteristics which can be seen or heard. In selecting the traits to be listed in your checklist, be sure that the vocabulary is understood by everyone. The intent is to be as objective as possible.

STUDY QUESTIONS

1. What are the difficulties in becoming group oriented rather than instructor oriented? How can these difficulties be overcome?
2. What are the pros and cons of objectivity in evaluating the communicative act of oral interpretation? Do you support the argument that objectivity has no place in the realm of aesthetics?
3. What categories would you include in a check-list which were not included in the discussion of this chapter? Why?
4. In what respects is the PROFILE scale of this chapter related to Osgood's semantic differential technique? How could it be adjusted to include his major factors?
5. Discuss outside reading sources concerned with tests and measurements in speech. Relate these sources to oral interpretation.

BIBLIOGRAPHY

Bakan, Paul, "Some Reflections on Listening Behavior," *Journal of Communication,* VI, Autumn 1956, pp. 108–112.

Beardsley, P. W., "Listening Versus Listening and Reading: A Study of the Appreciation of Poetry," M.A. Thesis, State University of Oklahoma, 1950.

Brooks, Keith, "Some Basic Considerations in Rating Scale Development: A Descriptive Bibliography," *Central States Speech Journal,* IX, 1, Fall 1959, pp. 27–31.

———, and Sr. I. Marie Wulftange, "Listener Response To Oral Interpretation," *Speech Monographs,* XXXI, March 1964, 1, pp. 73–79.

Dow, Clyde W., "A Literary Interpretation Analysis Blank," *Quarterly Journal of Speech,* XXV, April 1939, pp. 285–288.

Duncan, Melba Hurd, "Localizing Individual Problems in Oral Interpretation," *Quarterly Journal of Speech,* XXXII, April 1946, 213–216.

Fotheringham, Wallace C., "Measuring Speech Effectiveness," *Speech Monographs,* XXIII, March 1956, pp. 31–37.

Gompertz, Kenneth. "The Relation of Empathy to Effective Communication," *Journalism Quarterly,* XXXVII, Autumn 1960, pp. 533–546.

Hastorf, A. H., and I. E. Bender, "A Caution Respecting the Measurement of Empathic Ability," *Journal of Abnormal and Social Psychology,* XL, July 1952, pp. 574–576.

Heinberg, Paul, "Factors Related to an Individual's Ability to Perceive Implications of Dialogues," *Speech Monographs,* XXVIII, November 1961, pp. 274–281.

Osgood, Charles E., George J. Suci, and Percy H. Tannenbaum, *The Measurement of Meaning,* Urbana, 1957.

Chapter XV

Enrichment Through Research

Research in oral interpretation, as in all other fields, is exciting and demanding. Although you may have been attracted to the field of speech because of your performance abilities, you will find additional motivation and reward in your undergraduate career as you develop interests and abilities in research. In one sense, this development can not be escaped by the student of oral interpretation, for literary research is prerequisite to and a continuing part of every communicative act in which you participate. Your achievement as an oral interpreter of literature is, in large part, dependent on your preliminary research of the literature. As your research of the manuscript is exacting and thorough, so have you improved the probability of success in the communicative act itself. Also, your interest in evaluating the achievements of your peers has started you on the road to objectivity through observation. Not only does this activity relate to your critical insights, it introduces you to notions of quantifying listener responses.

Your emphasis on literature, the oral interpreter, and the listener has assisted you in developing and understanding standards of artistic excellence. Likewise, this emphasis has exposed you to the dynamics of the communicative act. These considerations are basic to your interests in scholarly research.

As a researcher in the area of oral interpretation you may function as a literary critic, as a historian, as an experimentalist, as an artist, as a theorist. Topics for research are abundant—limited only by your understanding of the area, your understanding of research methodology, and your creative potential.

I. CONTENT OF RESEARCH

If you will reread the bibliography at the end of Chapter I, you will quickly note the research which has focused on the literature itself, or on the reader, or on the listener. If you have read many of these articles, the significance of each to the total communicative act is apparent. In addition, it is interesting to note the scope of research activity accomplished by former graduate students in oral interpretation. The titles of their theses and dissertations, as published in the August issues of *Speech Monographs,* may broaden your insights into the field of oral interpretation and, hopefully, may stimulate your interest in graduate study in this field. As a representative sample, titles have been listed of projects completed from 1960 through 1965.

1960

(1) "An Interpretation of the Book of Job." Joseph Fielding Catmull, Ph.D., University of Utah.
(2) "Robinson Jeffers' *Roan Stallion:* An Analysis and Appraisal for the Oral Interpreter." M. Leon Dodez, M.A., Ohio State University.
(3) "A Study of the Oral Interpretation of a Play as Exemplified by a Group Play Reading of *The Relapse,* by Sir John Vanbrugh." Robert C. Heise, M.S., University of Wisconsin.
(4) "The Construction and Evaluation of Objective Test Items in Oral Interpretation." Allan Neely Schramm, M.A., Ohio State University.
(5) "A Historical Study of the Oral Interpretation Activities of the Circuit Chautauqua, 1904–1932." Nydia Joan Reynolds, Ph.D., University of Southern California.
(6) "Public Address, Theatre, and Interpretation at the Epworth League Assembly in Lincoln, Nebraska." Loren Dickinson, M.A., University of Nebraska.

(7) "A Reading Theatre Adaptation of David Copperfield for High School Students." James Franklin Bradley, Jr., M.A., Michigan State University.

(8) "A Comparative Study of Six Textbooks in Oral Interpretation." William A. Baker, M.A., Bowling Green State University.

1961

(9) "Children's Literature on Television: A Production Study." Saundra Manburg, M.A., Ohio State University.

(10) "A Dramatic Recital of Ibsen's *A Doll's House.*" Clairenell Cowan, M.A., Pennsylvania State University.

(11) "Anna Morgan: Reader, Teacher, and Director." Joyce Chalcraft Sozen, Ph. D., University of Illinois.

(12) "Theories and Methods of Representative Contemporary Poets as Readers of Their Own Poetry." Judith Edworthy Wray, Ph.D., University of Wisconsin.

(13) "Prosodic Patterns in the Poetry of Dylan Thomas." Katherine Taylor Loesch, Ph.D., Northwestern University.

(14) "William Faulkner's Humor in Selected Stories: Its Significance to the Oral Interpreter." Annette Paula Emerick, M.A., University of Arizona.

(15) "A Study of Interpretative Speech in England, 1860–1940." Evelyn Sivier, Ph.D., Wayne State University.

(16) "Preparing Plays for Oral Interpretation." Clark Strang Marlor, Ph.D., New York University.

(17) "Original Arrangements of Biblical Literature for Reader's Theatre." Anneke-Jan Boden, Ph.D., University of Denver.

(18) "An Approach to the Teaching of Oral Interpretation in Terms of Dramatic Action." Virginia Fredricks, Ph.D., University of Minnesota.

1962

(19) "An Experimental Study of Audience Response to the Oral Interpretation of Literature as Perceived Through Different Media." Sister Ignatius Marie Wulftange, Ph.D., Ohio State University.

(20) "John Ciardi: Poet-Critic on Oral Reading." Beverly Whitaker, M.A., Louisiana State University.
(21) "The Teaching of Oral Interpretation at the College Level." Audrey Ebell Christensen, D.Ed., Pennsylvania State University.
(22) "A Scale for the Measurement of Empathic Effect in Terms of Emotional Impact." Edward E. Swingle, M.A., Ohio State University.
(23) "A Study of the Oral Interpretation of the Philosophical Novel *The Fall* by Albert Camus." Jerry Dee Reynolds, M.A., Baylor University.
(24) "An Investigation of Poetry Which Captures the Interest of High School Students." Arlan Lantz Ropp, M.A., State University of Iowa.
(25) "A Reader's Theatre Presentation of Roman Catholic Playwrights —Phillip Barry, Graham Greene, and Federico Garcia Lorca." Larry Johnson, M.F.A., University of Portland.
(26) "Mark Twain's *The Mysterious Stranger:* A Study in the Adaptation of Narrative Prose Material to Reader's Theatre." William David Bonham, M.A., Southern Illinois University.
(27) "An Analytical-historical Study of the Factors Contributing to the Success of Mark Twain as an Oral Interpreter." Robert Dawson Wallace, Ph.D., University of Southern California.
(28) "An Experimental Reading Production, *The World We Live In.*" Joyce Tally, M.A., Mississippi Southern College.
(29) "A Study of Voice Control in the Nineteenth Century with Rules and Principles Applied to Literary Selections of the Period." William Earl Hanks, M.A., Miami University (Ohio).

1963

(30) "The Contributions of Hiram Corson to the Field of Oral Interpretation." Nancy Hartung, M.A., Wayne State University.
(31) "An Interpretation Study of Three Roles." James Francis Dunlavy, M.A., State University of Iowa.
(32) "Characterization, *Old Mortality,* and the Oral Interpreter." Edythe Annette Loewer, M.A., University of Oklahoma.

(33) "The Development of an Interpretative Program from the Poems and Letters of Emily Dickinson." Kristin Barry, M.A., University of Washington.

(34) "The Relationship of the Figures of Sound to the Rhythm in Certain Poems of Gerard Manley Hopkins." Ruth M. Lukanitsch, Ph.D., Northwestern University.

(35) "An Interpretative Analysis of the Fiction of Ernest Hemingway." Jo Ann Cannon, M.A., Baylor University.

(36) "An Analysis of Selected Poems of Gerard Manley Hopkins for Oral Interpretation and a Study of His Poetic Theories." Ted Donald Colson, Ph.D., University of Oklahoma.

(37) "The Use of Indigenous Material in Readers Theatre Production, with Specific Emphasis on the History of Southern Illinois." Julie Brady, M.S., Southern Illinois University.

(38) "Concepts of Imagery in the New Criticism and Implications for the Oral Interpreter of Poetry." Judith C. Espinola, M.A., University of Oklahoma.

(39) "The Group Reading of Drama: Its Essence and Aesthetic Principles." Elizabeth Annette Monroe, Ph.D., University of Wisconsin.

(40) "The Relationship of Rhetorical Discourse and Poetry, a Critical Analysis." George A. Matter, M.A., University of Pittsburgh.

(41) "An Investigation of Sex Differences in Oral Reading Adaptation to Delayed Sidetone as Measured by Fluency and Duration." Joan Dubofsky, M.A., Northern Illinois University.

(42) "An Examination of the Theories and Methodologies of John Walker (1732–1807) with Emphasis upon Gesturing." M. Leon Dodez, Ph.D., Ohio State University.

(43) "The Impact of Rhetorical Theory and Practice upon the Poetry of Walt Whitman." Gerald Paul Mohrmann, Ph.D., University of Florida.

1964

(44) "A Study of an Oral Approach to the Appreciation of Poetry." Donald Salper, Ph.D., University of Minnesota.

(45) "Interpretation of Twentieth Century Poetic Drama." Rhode Ellen Kittelson, M.A., Miami University (Ohio).

(46) "The Construction and Testing of a Forced Choice Scale for Measuring Achievement in Oral Interpretation." Agnes Louise Porter, Ph.D., Ohio State University.

(47) "Readers Theatre Production: *A Portrait of the Artist as a Young Man.*" Robert Gray Jones, M.A., Ohio State University.

(48) "A Comparative Analysis of Audience Response to Realistic and Antirealistic Drama When Perceived Through Acting, Readers Theatre, and Silent Reading." Daniel M. Witt, Ph.D., University of Denver.

(49) "A Readers Theatre Presentation of an Adaptation of Stephen Vincent Benét's *Western Star.*" Vickie Sue White, M.A., Kansas State Teachers College.

(50) "A Critical Analysis of Readers Theatre." Edgar C. Grimm, M.A., University of Maryland.

(51) "An Interpreter's Analysis of Selected Stories by Kay Boyle." Judy L. Edwards, M.A., University of Arizona.

(52) "The Literary Theories of Kenneth Burke and the Discovery of Meanings in Oral Interpretation." Saleem Macksond, Ph.D., University of California at Los Angeles.

(53) "A Comparison of the Oral Interpretation Techniques of Charles Dickens, Mark Twain, and Robert Frost." Grace Ann Henderson, M.A., Bowling Green State University.

(54) "A Structural Analysis of Selected Sonnets of Gerard Manley Hopkins." Charles Eugene Haas, Ph.D., University of Denver.

(55) "An Analysis of the Status and Value of Humorous Literature as a Vehicle for Study and Performance in the Oral Interpretation Area of Speech Education." Dorothy Bailey, M.A., Kent State University.

(56) "Archibald MacLeish: A Study of His Prosody for the Oral Interpreter." Richard Hale Carrington, Ph.D., University of Wisconsin.

(57) "The Elocutionary Theory and Practice of James Edward Murdoch." Audrey S. Kirkland, Ph.D., Wayne State University.

(58) "The Influence of the Traditional Schools of Interpretation on the Contemporary Eclectic Philosophy of Reading Aloud." Aileen L. Sundstrom, Ph.D., Wayne State University.

(59) "An Investigation of the Readers Theatre Production Style." Winnifred A. Larson, M.A., University of North Dakota.

(60) "A Historical Study of Oral Interpretation as a Form of Professional Theatre in London, 1951–1962." R. L. James Linn, Ph.D., University of Southern California.

(61) "Effects of Directive and Nondirective Criticism on Changes in Semantic Compatibility During the Preparation of a Readers Theatre Production." James R. Rockey, M.S., Southern Illinois University.

(62) "An Analysis of Current Trends Concerning Certain Basic Aspects of Oral Interpretation as Evidenced in Selected Writings in the Field, 1960–63, with Implications for Speech Education." J. Paul Albert Marcoux, Ph.D., Northwestern University.

(63) "John Walker: Elocutionist and Student of the English Language." John Hall Lamb, Ph.D., State University of Iowa.

1965

(64) "A Study of the Relationship of Point of View to the Structure of *The Alexandria Quartet* by Lawrence Durrell." Joanna L. Hawkins, Ph.D., Northwestern University.

(65) "An Investigation of Audience Response to Prose Literature When Perceived through Silent Reading, Oral Interpretation, and Readers' Theatre." Judy Lee Svore, M.A., University of Montana.

(66) "Robert Browning: An Interpreter's Analysis of Selected Monologues." Ralph H. Salgado, Jr., M.A., University of Arizona.

(67) "The Roles of Imagined Speaker and Listener in Selected Poems of E. E. Cummings." Diane McCleary Payne, M.A., University of Miami.

(68) "Poetry of Emily Dickinson: Analysis for Oral Interpretation." Diane Ruth Hahn, M.A., Ohio State University.

(69) "A Reader's Theatre Production of Sophocles' *Electra.*" Vera Loie Simpson, M.A., Texas Technological College.

(70) "A Study of Empathy and Its Relation to Aesthetic Experience and Oral Interpretation." Joyce Faye Horton, M.A., Auburn University.

(71) "Historical Backgrounds and Development of Chorus Speaking in Germany, 1918–1964." Edwina H. Snyder, Ph.D., Northwestern University.

(72) "The Development of Imagery as an Integral Element in Interpretative Reading, 1900–1960." Henry Jerry Jisha, Ph.D., Wayne State University.

(73) "Selection of Literature for Use in Oral Interpretation in Phillipine Junior College English and Speech Classes." Cesar Pascua DeGracis, M.A., University of Washington.

(74) "The Oral Interpretation of the Horror Stories of H. P. Lovecraft." Robert Stevens Fish, M.A., University of Oklahoma.

(75) "An Experimental Analysis of Narrative Poetry to be Used for Oral Interpretation." Nellie Marie Tinsley, M.A., State University of Iowa.

(76) "Public Readings in New York City from 1865 to 1870." Sara Kay Lockard, M.A., Louisiana State University.

(77) "A Study of Point of View in Three Novels by Henry James: *The Spoils of Poynton, The Wings of the Dove, The Golden Bowl.*" Lilla A. Heston, M.A., Northwestern University.

(78) "An Adaptation for Reader's Theatre of Francois Mauriac's *Woman of the Pharisees.*" Sister M. Owen Paul Monaghan, M.F.A., Catholic University of America.

(79) "The Selection, Adaptation and Presentation of Three Local-Color Short Stories for a Reader's Theatre Program." Margaret Blanche Barton, M.A., University of Houston.

(80) "The Significance to the Oral Interpreter of the Pause in the Published Stage Plays of Harold Pinter." William Keith Henning, M.A., University of Arizona.

(81) "The Sound of Poetry: Two Parallels." Jane Elizabeth Cole, M.A., Louisiana State University.

(82) "Poetry for Choral Reading Categorized by School, Grade Level, Difficulty of Reading." Jane Ellen Turek, M.A., Miami University (Ohio).

(83) "Semantic Compatibility among Interpreters during the Production of an Original Play." James C. Carver, M.A., Michigan State University.

(84) "An Interpretative Analysis of the Writing of Tennessee Williams." Elizabeth Tirey Reid, M.A., Baylor University.

(85) "*Permit Me Voyage:* A Study of A Dramatic Adaptation of the Works of James Agee." Joseph James Garry, Jr., M.A., Ohio State University.

Two conclusions are immediately apparent: (1) Graduate study in oral interpretation is being pursued in universities from coast to coast and (2) graduate work in oral interpretation was completed by an increased number of students each year during the five-year period reported. If *all* institutions had reported the titles of theses and dissertations completed, the list by years would probably have reflected even greater growth.

In terms of the titles listed, it is interesting to note the wide variety of interests. Most of the titles suggest that the researcher was following the methods of the literary critic. Some placed dominant emphasis on the literature itself (titles 1, 2, 13, 14, 23, 31, 32, 34, 35, 45, 51, 54, 56, 64, 66, 67, 68, 74, 75, 77, 81, 84), others focused on the oral interpreter (titles 12, 27, 29, 38, 41, 53, 61, 80, 83) and some concentrated on the listener (titles 9, 19, 22, 48, 65, 70). Several demonstrated an interest in reconstructing significant periods of the past (titles 5, 6, 15, 60, 71, 72, 76), while others were specifically interested in individuals of historical significance (titles 11, 30, 42, 57, 63). In addition, pedagogy was frequently treated (titles 4, 8, 18, 21, 24, 44, 46, 55, 58, 62, 73, 82). Poetic and rhetorical theory was the predominant focus in four studies: 36, 40, 43, 52. The emergence and popularity of Readers' Theatre and other specialized formats of oral interpretation is reflected in the large number of production-theses and descriptive studies reported (titles 3, 7, 10, 16, 17, 25, 26, 28, 33, 37, 39, 47, 49, 50, 59, 69, 78, 79, 85).

II. METHODS OF RESEARCH

The predominant methods of research in oral interpretation are critical, historical and experimental. Your choice of method depends on the appropriateness of the methodology to the topic selected, and on what you wish to accomplish. The following discussion deals briefly with each of these methods and is meant to give you only a brief overview.

A. *The Critical Method*

You have already been involved in the critical method through the requirement of determining the dynamics of each piece of literature which you chose to interpret in the classroom. As a literary critic in oral interpretation, your research is experience-listener oriented: experience oriented in that you have been concerned with the action of the literature in terms of *who* does or says *what* to *whom, when, where, why,* and *how;* listener oriented in that you are concerned with sharing, through re-creating, the action of the literature. The fruition of your research as a literary critic rests with your attempt to *synthesize* by vocally and physically suggesting your judgments concerning the intent of the literature. This is your unique position among literary critics. It is unique because, unlike other literary critics, you present an organic whole by answering the questions of your research simultaneously. Your action-oriented analysis is a means to an end: experiential synthesis. *The artistic sharing of this synthesis should be supplemented by a written and scholarly report of your research.*

Your research as a literary critic is dynamic—ongoing and unending because your personal involvement is motivated by the experiences of the literature and because each experience is personalized and shared. There is no research activity more rewarding than that which is motivated by personal involvement and personal reward, and there is no research activity more rewarding than that which relates to the needs of the field. When your research lacks this motivation and becomes an intellectual exercise only, it becomes a sterile and wanton activity.

It would, of course, be a gross error to conclude that the needs of the field negate the scope of the literary critic in oral interpretation to a study of the manuscript only. Experience-listener oriented research could not be so confined, for it embraces all parts of the communicative act: the literature, the reader, and the listener. Your unique function as a literary critic involves not only discovery of the action of the literature but also discovery for activating the literature in the minds of your listener. Each is related to the other. Although you may concentrate on one part at a time, you are always mindful of the inter-relationship of all parts.

The critical method is concerned with the establishment of artistic standards for appreciating the communicative act and for judging the literature involved. This method focuses attention on the textual analysis of the work being criticized so that both the oral interpreter and the listener can share in their understanding and appreciation of it. If the critic also studies the writer and his other writings, the conditions under which the material was written, the intended audience, and reviews by other critics, he does so as a contribution to his textual analysis.

The list of theses and dissertations completed between 1960 and 1965 includes a large number of studies which used the critical method. If any of these are available to you, read them. Also, you will find abstracts of many of them in the August issues of *Speech Monographs.* Among the titles of those studies which utilized this method are the following: 1, 2, 13, 14, 32, 34, 35, 45, 51, 56, 64, 66, 67, 68, 74, 77, and 84.

B. *The Historical Method*

If you have an interest in history and have enjoyed your work in history courses you may be motivated to pursue the historical method. You will be preparing yourself for scholarship in this methodology by adding a history minor to your undergraduate program, by developing a proficiency in languages appropriate to your historical interests, by improving and refining your writing style, and by gaining a historical perspective of the field of oral interpretation through reading available monographs, histories, biographies and autobiographies. *A History of Speech Education in America,* edited by Karl R. Wallace, is one source that should not be missed. Not only does this volume represent the historical method, it contains several chapters which will contribute to your perspective of this area of study. Among these are Chapter 5, "English Sources of American Elocution," by Frederick W. Haberman; Chapter 7, "Rhetorical and Elocutionary Training in Nineteenth-Century Colleges," by Marie Hochmuth (Nichols) and Richard Murphy; Chapter 8, "The Elocutionary Movement and its Chief Figures," by Mary Margaret Robb; Chapter 9, "Steele MacKaye and the Delsartian Tradition," by Claude L. Shaver; Chapter 10, "Dr. James Rush," by Lester L. Hale; Chapter 14, "Five Private Schools of Speech," by Edyth Renshaw;

and Chapter 19, "Some Teachers and the Transition to Twentieth-Century Speech Education," by Giles Wilkinson Gray. Chapter I of this book provides you with an excellent overview of the history of oral interpretation and, of course, it represents the historical method of research. If you found it particularly interesting, you already have a favorable bias for pursuing this method of inquiry.

The historian is interested in reconstructing the past. This valid purpose carries with it an obligation for accuracy. As an historian you must observe and evaluate facts and inferences, and place each in its proper perspective. At all times you are concerned with the probability of events and must sift through all available sources. In the search for historical proof you attend to both primary and secondary sources, continually testing the authenticity of those sources. In addition, you must explore the environment from which the sources came so that you can gain an understanding of the circumstances which motivated, clarified, or biased a particular document or event. The historian is a detective whose function is to reconstruct the past by putting the parts together without bias.

Among the titles of theses and dissertations which reflect the historical method are the following: 5, 6, 15, 42, 60, 63, 71, and 76.

C. *The Experimental Method*

The experimentalist in oral interpretation is usually concerned with the dynamics of a process. Having formulated hypotheses from his present knowledge of this process, he designs a controlled situation in which they may be tested. Generally, he observes behavior, measures it in the sense of quantifying his observations, and subsequently analyzes these data by means of statistical procedures and tests. These phases of the experimental method—design, measurement, and statistical analysis—are carried out in accordance with highly structured procedures which have been developed and specified in order that the experiment may meet the requirements for valid conclusions. These procedures permit the researcher to report his findings in terms of probability statements: i.e., the degree of confidence that is justified in concluding that a finding is something other than a purely chance or random effect.

This method was demonstrated, with varying degrees of experimental sophistication, in nine of the theses and dissertations previously listed: titles 4, 19, 22, 41, 46, 48, 65, 75, and 83. In addition, you will note a number of experimental studies listed in the bibliography of Chapter I. The variety of events treated in these studies suggests the potential for continued research. Unfortunately, this potential has not been seriously considered by most scholars of oral interpretation. The number of existing experimental studies does not compare favorably with the number of studies utilizing the critical and historical method. Oral interpretation scholars have tended to concentrate on the *source* of the literary experience (literature) rather than on the *event* of oral interpretation (the communicative act). The critical method has been more appropriate to this concentration. Only recently has this focus centered on the *action* of the source: the experience-listener orientation. As a result, the need for the experimental method is now becoming more widely apparent.

Considerable work needs to be done in the construction and testing of judgment measures. A valid and reliable Forced Choice Scale for measuring effectiveness in oral interpretation would be a distinct contribution. This type of scale provides for descriptions of behavior, rather than evaluations, and minimizes the bias of the rater as he is forced to select that trait which most or least describes the behavior of the interpreter without knowing which trait is most significant in terms of success or failure. Also, it should be possible to develop measures of literary appreciation and measures of empathic response. We believe that one's ability to empathize with the literature one is reading is prerequisite to successful communication of that literature, yet we have done very little in terms of measuring this empathic response.

An unlimited number of hypotheses related to processes and theories of oral interpretation need to be tested. For example, frequency and duration of eye-to-eye contact are not factors significant to listener comprehension of material read aloud; number and type of reading experiences provided in a basic course during a term are not factors significant to achievement in oral interpretation; the personality traits of oral interpreters are not significantly different from the personality traits of public speakers (or actors, or interpretive dancers, etc.); the attitude of listeners toward controversial issues can not be significantly altered by effective oral interpretation; the oral approach to the study of literature is not significantly different from the traditional literary approach in terms of literary appreciation.

Whether or not the experimental method appeals to your research bias, it is increasingly important that you acquire at least a general orientation to this method during your undergraduate career. To neglect it is to exclude a significant body of literature from your frame of reference—a body of literature which can not easily be understood or evaluated without a knowledge of its methodology. The student motivated by curiosity and dedicated to scholarly inquiry will include in his undergraduate program introductory courses in research, tests and measurements, and statistics.

The opportunities for research in oral interpretation are plentiful. The rewards will be significant, both in terms of personal growth and academic recognition. If you are interested in making a scholarly contribution, start now by (1) gaining a thorough understanding of the communicative act of oral interpretation, (2) developing a sound literary background, (3) scheduling courses exposing you to a variety of research methodologies, (4) reviewing articles, including theses and dissertations, representing variety in content and method, and (5) engaging in pilot studies under the direction of members of your faculty.

STUDY QUESTIONS

1. Review six research articles from the bibliography of Chapter I. Indicate the method utilized and detail the procedures followed. How might the findings be related to your needs?

2. Select six abstracts of theses and dissertations from the August issues of *Speech Monographs,* representing the three methods discussed in this chapter. Discuss each in terms of method, design, and findings.

3. List six topics or questions which you feel should be researched. What method or methods would probably be most profitable? Have these topics or questions been considered in this book? Have they been treated by other individuals listed in any of the bibliographies?

4. Select any two chapters from this book and identify statements which could be phrased as hypotheses for experimental testing.

5. Suggest ways in which historical, critical, and experimental research complement each other.

BIBLIOGRAPHY

Auer, J. Jeffrey, *An Introduction to Research in Speech.* New York: Harper and Brothers, 1959.

Bahn, Eugene, "Epochs in the History of Oral Interpretation," Chapter 18, *The Communicative Arts and Sciences of Speech,* Keith Brooks, editor, Columbus: Merrill Books, Inc., 1967.

Borman, Ernest G., *Theory and Research in the Communicative Arts.* New York: Holt, Rinehart and Winston, Inc., 1965.

Chase, Stuart, *The Tyranny of Words.* New York: Harcourt, Brace and Company, 1938.

Cobin, Martin, "Oral Interpretation Research: Methods, Trends, Ideas," Chapter 21, *The Communicative Arts and Sciences of Speech.* Keith Brooks, editor. Columbus, Ohio: Merrill Books, Inc., 1967.

Dow, Clyde, Editor, *An Introduction to Graduate Study in Speech and Theatre.* East Lansing, Michigan: Michigan University Press, 1961.

Frye, Northrop, *The Well-Tempered Critic.* Bloomington: Indiana University Press, 1963.

Harris, Chester W., Editor, *Encyclopedia of Educational Research.* New York: The Macmillan Company, 1960.

Kaplan, Abraham, *The Conduct of Inquiry.* San Francisco: Chandler Publishing Company, 1964.

McGrath, G. D., James J. Jelinck, and Raymond Wochner, *Educational Research Methods.* New York: Ronald Press Company, 1963.

Wallace, Karl R., Editor, *History of Speech Education in America.* New York: Appleton-Century-Croft, 1954.

INDEX

A

B

C

D

E

F

INDEX

INDEX

INDEX

I

J

K

L

INDEX

INDEX

INDEX